The
REFORMED LORD'S SUPPER FORM

The
REFORMED LORD'S SUPPER FORM

A COMMENTARY
B. Wielenga

Translated by H. David Schuringa
Edited by David J. Engelsma

REFORMED
FREE PUBLISHING
ASSOCIATION
Jenison, Michigan

Original title: *Ons Avondmaalsformulier*, published in Kampen (Netherlands) by J. H. Kok, 1913.

Scripture cited is taken from the King James (Authorized) Version. Italics in Scripture quotations reflect the author's emphasis.

The Genevan Psalter numbers 22, 36, 43, 122, and 133 are from *Book of Praise: Anglo-Genevan Psalter*, copyright © 1984, and used by permission of the Standing Committee for the Publication of the *Book of Praise*. All rights reserved.

Genevan Psalter number 51 at page 122 translated by David Koyziz (https://genevanpsalter.com/files/psalm-51/genps051_koyzis).

Cover design by Jeff Steenholdt
Interior design by Katherine Lloyd, the DESK

Reformed Free Publishing Association
1894 Georgetown Center Drive
Jenison, Michigan 49428
616-457-5970
mail@rfpa.org
www.rfpa.org

ISBN 978-1-936054-57-2
Ebook ISBN 978-1-936054-59-6
LCCN 2022951217

CONTENTS

PREFACE

TO THE TRANSLATION OF WIELENGA'S COMMENTARY ON THE LORD'S SUPPER FORM

With this volume, the Reformed Free Publishing Association (RFPA) presents to English-speaking Christians in all the world Dr. Bastiaan Wielenga's commentary on the Form for the Administration of the Lord's Supper—the only genuine and thorough commentary on this priceless Reformed liturgical form.

The form itself was adopted by the Synod of Dordt (1618–19) as the authoritative form for the administration and celebration of the sacrament of the Supper by both the Reformed churches in the Netherlands and by Dutch-speaking churches in the tradition of Dordt elsewhere in the world. Over the years the form has been adopted, translated, and used by most—if not all—Reformed churches that stand in the tradition of Dordt.

The main author of the form was Caspar Olevianus, the author also, with Zacharias Ursinus, of the Heidelberg Catechism. But Olevianus drew heavily from the form for the supper that John Calvin composed and used in Geneva. Therefore, Wielenga can say that "more than in any other component of our liturgy, Calvin's influence is noteworthy in the form for the Lord's supper" (14).

The Lord's supper form, therefore, expresses the faith of orthodox, Reformed Christianity concerning the supper and all the rich implications of the supper for doctrine and life.

Ultimately, the importance of the form inheres in the sacrament of the supper itself, of which the form is the explanatory and applicatory word. So important is the form to those Reformed churches where it is read at every celebration of the sacrament, it is honored, with the baptism form, as a "secondary creed." Dr. Wielenga wrote extensive commentaries on both of these two secondary creeds. Of the two, Wielenga judges that "the form for holy communion is [the] most precious."

The form enables Reformed believers to partake of the supper with understanding. It also instructs the Reformed churches in the sound doctrine of the supper. Although the form deliberately shuns polemics, it does distinguish the Reformed doctrine of the supper from other, erroneous doctrines of the supper. To this feature of the form, Wielenga does justice.

Rightly, Wielenga judges that his commentary on the Lord's supper form "open[s] the treasure chest of the form itself" (vii). And until now, another lock on this treasure chest—the Dutch language in which the commentary was written—has kept the chest tightly shut to English-speaking churches and believers. With this translation of the commentary, the treasure chest has finally been opened to the English-speaking ecclesiastical world.

Dr. Wielenga, a noted Dutch theologian, wrote this commentary in the early twentieth century. He was a contemporary and colleague of Abraham Kuyper and Herman Bavinck. His time was in many respects the most glorious regarding the development of the Reformed faith in the Netherlands. Wielenga represented the very best of Dutch Reformed theology. He was sound in the doctrine of Dordt. As his commentary abundantly evidences, he was remarkably learned. Above all, he had the heart of a pastor. He spoke the truth of the supper to the faith and life of the Dutch farmers.

A translator of this significant commentary must be one in spirit with the author of the commentary and competent in both Dutch and English. Happily, God has provided just the man in Dr. H. David Schuringa, a sound and learned Reformed theologian in his own right. At the same time, Dr. Schuringa possesses the warm spirituality that is required for translating an exposition of the reality of eating and drinking Jesus Christ from one language into another.

A preface to this commentary on the Lord's supper form would be remiss were it to overlook the zeal for the Reformed faith and life held by its publisher, the RFPA. In 2016 the RFPA translated and published in English Wielenga's commentary on the Reformed baptism form. With the publication of this volume on the Lord's supper form, the set of commentaries on the two sacraments is complete. They are a valuable gift to every Reformed Christian, especially to be given by parents to their children. The treasure chest of sound, insightful explanation of both sacraments is now fully opened, not only to Reformed churches, but also to Christian churches worldwide.

—Prof. David J. Engelsma, editor

FOREWORD

With gratitude to God, in this exposition of the Lord's supper form, I have completed the series of commentaries on our liturgical documents that I began ten years ago.

First appeared *The Reformed Baptism Form* in 1906,[1] followed by *Ons Huwelijksformulier*[2] in 1909. Now appears *The Reformed Lord's Supper Form*.

Certainly, other rich, liturgical forms deserve exegetical analysis and historical illumination. But these three are without question the most influential and most central in significance. They constitute an unmistakable trilogy on our liturgical landscape.

Here and there, this commentary (like my previous expositions) takes on a lecturish character in bringing to light the historical debates surrounding the Lord's supper. Nevertheless, the commentary retains its main purpose: to open the treasure chest of the form itself. A complete reproduction of every detail of the Lord's supper debate would indeed have taken me too far afield from my subject.

My sincere intention with this exposition is not to dig up unnecessary and therefore unhelpful material. While a scholarly discussion of the Lord's supper form would be immensely rich, a purely academic analysis has to date not yet been provided.

Now and then, this book mentions the exposition of Jacobus van Houte, which bears a rather genial and homiletical character. Other publications, like the priceless paperback of Dr. Gunning, "*Waarom*

---

1   Bastiaan Wielenga, *The Reformed Baptism Form: A Commentary*, trans. Annemie Godbehere, ed. David J. Engelsma (Jenison: Reformed Free Publishing Association, 2016).

2   Bastiaan Wielenga, *Ons Huwelijksformulier* [*Our Marriage Formulary*] (Kampen: J. H. Kok, 1913).

niet toegetreden?"[3] and the well-written articles of Rev. Elzenga in the *Kamper Kerkbode,* were not intended for exposition but to provide concise, practical applications. Furthermore, references I came across in Ens, Biesterveld, Barger, Mensinga, Gooszen, Kuyper, *et al,* tended to be either small fragments or not fleshed out.

May the God of the Lord's supper sanctify the reading of this book with increased understanding and devout knowledge of this form that Prof. Biesterveld rightly calls the "pearl of our liturgical texts."

—Bastiaan Wielenga
Amsterdam, July 1913

---

3 J. H. Gunning, *Waarmon niet toegetreden: het avondmaalsformulier onzer Gereformeerde Kerk voor bekommerde Christenen toegelicht* [*Why Not Approach: The Lord's Supper Form of Our Reformed Church Explained for Troubled Christians*] (Nijkerk: Uitgeverij Callenbach, 1913).

Chapter One

INTRODUCTION

1. THE LORD'S SUPPER: A SPIRITUAL HIGH POINT

The Lord's supper is where the Lord's church on earth celebrates a spiritual high point. By giving this sacrament to his people, God crowns the benefits of the covenant of grace. Here he causes religion to bloom in its mysterious beauty. Here he bestows upon his covenantal family a superb ripeness of the fruit she bears.

The Lord's supper is where heaven and earth approach each other most nearly.

The past, present, and future of redemptive history meet and join hands.

The *past,* because the supper is a meal of remembrance. It directs the soul to the central salvation event: the death of Christ. The servant humbles himself at the table to proclaim the death of the Lord. The supper is for him a remembrance, a monument to the great wonder of salvation by which God and man are reconciled. The symbolism of the supper brings to mind that unspeakable death and presents to his spirit the awful and yet glorious cross, so that he sees that cross and believes in the Son of God.

That is why the Lord's supper is the feast of faith.

But the holy sacrament also has a testimony for *today.* After all, it is a *covenantal meal* where God and man meet together: *man* to demonstrate his faithfulness to his God of the covenant, and *God* to pour out gracious, covenantal benefits upon his people. In this gathering at the same table, the covenant is confirmed, sustained, and deepened. The pilgrims rest awhile in the cool shade of the palms of

Elim and drink deeply of the fresh waters from the fountain of salvation. The inheritance is strengthened when they have become weary and discouraged. Here is what is meant in the psalms:

Of Thy great mercy heaven sings
For in the shadow of Thy wings
No son of man shall perish
Thou shalt them to Thy feasts invite,
They drink from streams of Thy delight,
Thy precious love they cherish.[1]

That is why the Lord's supper is the feast of *love*.

But it is also meaningful for the *future*. The call is for the servant to proclaim the Lord's death *till he come*, which encourages him to go forth with an eye for that great day when Jesus shall come—as king, as judge, as the bridegroom.

As the bridegroom!

Yes, because the loving fellowship tasted in the Lord's supper is a love feast not only between God and his covenantal people, but also Christ and his precious church on earth. And that church is betrothed to Christ as a bride to her bridegroom. Therefore, the supper, where Christ sits with his bride at an engagement dinner, soon will break forth into the eternal wedding banquet of the Lamb.

Christ's crucifixion in the past exists in our present love relationship with him, but already in the present is the blessing of what is coming. The Lord's supper is a prophetic guarantee of eternal life with God. It is a foreshadowing and symbol of the eternal marriage banquet with the glorified Son of Man. For the exhausted pilgrim, it opens the way for a future of endless joy that no eye has seen, no ear has heard, nor has entered into the heart of man (see 1 Cor. 2:9). Looking back to the deepest of humiliation and hellish sneering perpetrated against the Son of God, the Lord's supper points to

---

1   Tr. *Genevan Psalter* 36, trans. W. van der Kamp.

the unimaginable triumph with which Christ shall come again, to the glorification that he and his people will share. The supper binds death with life, night with morning, the cross with the crown.

That is why it is also a meal of hope.

What a marvelous symmetry!

Looking to the past, the Lord's supper is a *meal of remembrance* and therefore strengthens your *faith*. For today, it is a *covenant meal*, and so strengthens your *love*. And, as you head into the future, a *prophetic meal* that multiplies your *hope*.

2. THE MYSTICAL BEAUTY OF THE FORM

The immense spiritual value of sacramental richness offered in the form for celebration of the Lord's supper has already received significant attention. So the work of an assiduous exposition such as this may require some justification.

The forms for baptism, marriage, and the Lord's supper constitute a triad, a beautiful trilogy, that is dear to the hearts of our people. It is certainly no overstatement that of these three forms, the form for holy communion is most precious. A glory cloud of mystical devoutness hovers over this form. It holds an intimate attraction that awakens in you a feeling as if you have entered a temple where the tender souls of the highest choir lift your heart to adoration. And the gentle twilight that filters through the tall windows consecrates your soul in quiet attentiveness. Here you feel something extraordinary, that you are in touch with the heavenly, the holy. When you think of the Lord's supper, "holy" comes to mind even more quickly than when you hear the word "baptism." For here is: "put off thy shoes from off thy feet, for the place wherein thou standest is holy ground" (Exod. 3:5).

Maybe the thought occurs to you, but is it really necessary? Does a formulary that itself already so thoroughly and clearly explains the mystery of the holy communion still need yet another explanation added on top of it? Is this not bringing owls to Athens?

And we agree with you, that a special commentary on this form doesn't appear as necessary as in the case of the form for baptism or marriage. The baptismal form concerns itself with challenging issues that still, in a measure, raise serious questions for our people. Also, the form for marriage in more ways than one raises questions, such as whether an ecclesiastical benediction may be pronounced at so-called civil marriage ceremonies. But with the Lord's supper, the theological battle seems to have established its borders. Here there are no pressing questions to be moderated in the territory of ecclesiastical discussion and debate. The mighty turbulence that accompanied the supper at the time of the Reformation has been as good as put to rest. The enormous antithesis between the Lord's supper of the Reformed and the papal mass still exists but is no longer so deeply felt. The issue is not as alive as it was in former centuries. Similarly, the important doctrinal differences between Luther and Zwingli, which in the old days would set hearts on fire to take up the pen and even weapons, seem to be almost completely forgotten by our people. The war has de-escalated. The Lord's supper has lost its controversial character.

Clearly, this changing of the times, and with it a corresponding modification of emotions, cannot be denied. If we are expecting interest in the theological controversies of the form's explanation, we would show how out of step we are with the heartbeat of the church today. But we are not looking for such interest, at least not at first. Our people's faith has not only an intellectual bent, but also a more mystical side. We are not as theoretical as it sometimes appears. There is a predisposition toward *piety*. And where that piety seeks nourishment for the mind in the persistent and extensive examination of the truth, there sometimes the religious life degenerates into intellectualism. However, on the other hand, that life is deepened and strengthened precisely by the acquisition of knowledge.

If we take as a given that, of all our formularies, there is none in which the tone of pure mystique sounds so lovely and sincerely as the form for the celebration of the Lord's supper, then it should come as no surprise that the souls of the people, time and again, respond from the deepest recesses of their hearts whenever the ancient—in a good sense—language of this *uplifting* form is heard. It is that mystical experience of our people we are taking into account first of all when vying for attention to a more extensive explanation of the form.

But this is not the only reason we have to justify a special study of the formulary.

Although it appears that the language of the form, in and of itself, is simple and clear, we may never forget that it goes back for centuries so that many of its expressions can only be understood within the historical context of those earlier times. In a proper sense of the word, the form is a product of its times and therefore bears the stamp of those times. The war, the current state of spirituality, and ecclesiastical life in those days are reflected in the form.

Missing the original situation prevents one from ever getting through to the true meaning of the form. I name just one example, in the section of the form where the congregation is awakened to self-examination. By not taking into account ecclesiastical practice of communion celebrations in the days of the Reformation, there carries with it the chance that we will misunderstand the intention of our forefathers. In those days, missing the supper was rare and viewed not as a minor infraction of God's holy commandment (namely the command of the Lord, "This do in remembrance of me").

But the formulary for some now has become *dis*couragement rather than *en*couragement. The phenomenon we often see in our day of deep anxiety and spiritual heaviness, especially with a view to the supper, was not experienced so much at the time of the Reformation. At any rate, the dangerous character of this ecclesiastical staph infection, which has withered the spiritual lives of so many, had not yet been detected. Without a doubt, if the form for the Lord's supper were crafted today, the self-examination section would require a different tone that takes into account the spiritual level at which we live.

Therefore, as long as our church uses this historic form, it is important that this liturgical inheritance from the fathers be perceived in its historical light and, where necessary, to shed this historical light; by exegesis, to elucidate the language in the consciousness of our people; and further, according to our ability, to interpret the holy mysticism of the form for the heart of the congregation is the purpose that we have put before ourselves with this explanation of the form of the Lord's supper.

3. THE LITURGICAL BEAUTY OF THE FORM

Our form also holds a worthy place among ecclesiastical documents because it is dressed in liturgical beauty. It provides in a pure form of language a certain, comforting development of rich thoughts. By nature, it is pleasant and edifying, but at the same time, instructive and candid. Without dryness, it sets forth the *doctrine* of the supper in an ideal system for the soul and binds the truth that makes up the core of the Protestant theology to the heart of the congregation. The Lord's supper form does not fly as high as the baptism form, which in a brief trip offers an entire Christian worldview, but significant territory is covered along with digging deeply in the gold mine of divine revelation.

Yes, that is a distinguishing feature also of this Reformed symbol: it is *scriptural* through and through. It distinguishes itself from the other forms in that it begins with a lengthy quotation from Scripture itself, 1 Corinthians 11. This gives the congregation the sense that the language we are speaking is that of the eternal word of God. A little later in the prayer, it echoes the unique tone of Scripture in the Lord's prayer. The thanksgiving resounds with Psalm 103 in mighty accord.

And not only does the form quote the Bible, it also *interprets* Scripture according to its deepest thoughts. It lays open the utter splendor of the salvation mystery of Jesus' surety. Displayed is the righteousness that through faith is our righteousness. It unveils the mystery of the atonement through Christ's blood, and thereby reveals the heart of revelation, the gospel of the gospel.

For these reasons, the form has historical significance for the church of the Reformation that cannot be lightly dismissed. Because it purely resonates with utter clarity the doctrine of free grace, it has in no small measure contributed to the fact that our people have remained preserved to the core by the ancient truth that was the motto of the Reformation: the just shall live by faith.

Though not in the strictest sense a confession, nevertheless for centuries our church has professed this formulary as its deepest conviction of that which can save the sinner and glorify God. There radiates from this form, even in days of weakness and decay, persevering and fortifying strength. Though often even the sermon may paint a dark picture, here the old gold continues to shine in soul-enchanting radiance. The same precious fruit of the Reformation has in turn worked reformation into our daily lives to do its work in such a way that the old banner of the cross is still in full view.

But regarding its profound scriptural character, the form is not only ecclesiastically Reformed, but is also, for our people, spiritually foundational with incalculable influence. For it is precisely its scriptural depth that touches the heart with wave after wave, doing it in such a way that strikes there a deep chord.

How hard-hitting and detailed the form is where it lists the most grievous sins that people commit, and that as long as one continues in those sins, he must refrain from the table of the Lord, so that his judgment and condemnation be not all the heavier. Truly, here evil is called what it is and is put on notice. Our fathers demonstrate that we must take heed not only to doctrine but also to precision in living; not only theology but also ethics gives the clear and certain sound of the Reformation trumpet.

But after that strong language of warning, how heartwarming the gospel flute plays in order to console the heavy-laden and prostrate heart of believers. How lovely sounds the comforting melody to those who grieve for their sin. How encouraging and inviting is the form to those hesitating from a distance. We noted previously that the form is not directed to the anxious and the doubters but to believers, in so far bearing the stamp of its times, when men dared to believe. However, from such passages we see that the form very really takes into account such believers and instructs these with fatherly tenderness.

The form breathes the language of him whose hand reaches out to the little ones, those whom he is eager to gather in his arms. Time and again you hear the gospel calling and its urgency, so that also the faint-hearted are lifted up with a liberating spirit. The cross of Christ in all its precious endearment is pictured for the congregation to see. Christ in all his glory and complete sufficiency is brought near to the humble of heart. The basic tone of the teaching is constantly no more unbelief, only belief. It is press on, take courage, your heart shall experience deep joy. And who shall say that for such hearts seeking so much, though in the darkness they roam, in this formula dawns the light of salvation for as many as are eternally blessed. While not itself the fountain of living waters, nevertheless for thousands the form has served as a cup of the living water for the abundant refreshment of thirsty souls.

And that cup itself may be viewed with a careful eye. It is elegant in form and smooth to the touch. Here is evidence that our fathers also in this sense desired to be biblical, that they worked to transmit to us the beauty of Scripture. From the perspective of language and form, the assessment is that the Lord's supper form stands head and shoulders above any other liturgical documents.

Not by mesmerizing word choice or high-brow rhetoric does it distinguish itself. There is no deliberate attempt to make it pretty. But precisely in its simplicity, in its restraint, is its beauty and eloquence. However, if a characteristic of eloquence is a desire to have an effect upon the heart of the listeners, then the form is indeed eloquent, because it grips the soul and tightly hangs on to her to the end.

Sometimes the language flies a bit higher than the ordinary and approaches the sublime, especially when it portrays the intricate features of Christ's suffering and identifies the purpose and benefits of that suffering with every step on the way to the cross. In general, one of the most beautiful passages in our liturgy is that part that begins with the words, "especially, when the weight of our sins and of the wrath of God pressed out of him the bloody sweat;" and then concludes with the incomparable, "and humbled himself unto the deepest reproach and anguish of hell, both in body and soul, on the tree of the cross, when he cried out with a loud voice, 'My God, my God, why hast thou forsaken me?' that we might be accepted of God and nevermore be forsaken of Him."

When such a passage in the form, and especially in this section, is presented with singular warmth (that in beauty is comparable only with the prayer of thanksgiving after the supper), it cannot help but purely move and appropriately prepare the congregation for the holy ordinance that is about to happen. The form ushers the hearts, under the blessing of the Spirit, precisely into that experiential frame of mind and luminous vision of faith that is so necessary for the proper celebration of communion.

Truly, we may be grateful to our fathers and our God within them, by whom all things are directed in accordance with his eternal council and providence, for this priceless liturgical portion, and with heartfelt appreciation and serious attention demonstrate this thankfulness.

A virtue of the form that also may be mentioned is the complete absence of polemics. The formulary does not quarrel or reprimand, but calmly and solemnly unfolds the Reformed doctrine of the Lord's supper as if no dogmatic opposition even existed. This must amaze us all the more because otherwise our fathers did not lightly let an opportunity go by vigorously and plainly to expose difference of opinions, and in the time of the Reformation, the doctrine of the Lord's supper was especially the point of difference. The Lord's supper instruction would be the perfect time to bring it up. Our catechism, for example, which came from the same Palatinate where the Lord's supper form originated, does not hesitate to call the papal mass a condemnable idolatry.

That makes it all the more significant that the form refrains from polemics. The framers reveal good sense here, because especially when the soul is preparing itself to meet God in such a holy place, it serves well to minimize enflaming a combative spirit that could distract attention from God to man. At this meal, the entire mood should be one of peace and quiet. For here God draws near to his people in the gentleness of a quiet breeze. And the heart that truly desires to exercise fellowship with God must in *stillness* and faith seek his strength.

So now we can see, all the more clearly, our Lord's supper form as a model of liturgical beauty.[1]

4. THE FORM AS A CHILD OF ITS TIMES

Naturally, such high esteem need not exclude fair critique. Even in the admiration of ancient beauty, it is appropriate that we remain objective. In our opinion, a review of our liturgies for reworking and reforming, including the Lord's supper form (though perhaps the least), deserves comment. The summary of the grievous sins that require people to refrain from the supper, as well the recounting of the Lord's suffering, could be suitably abbreviated. The form sometimes seems too long. For many, it is too difficult to follow the whole thing without getting weary. And the minister, who is required to read the form, can only seldom do it justice. So making it a little more concise would undoubtedly strengthen it.

In addition to this, as we have already noted, the form reflects the spirituality of the century in which it was born. The same thing that goes for liturgical documents also applies to confessions. They

---

1 Cf. H. H. Barger, *Ons Kerkbook* [*Our Churchbook*] (Groningen: J. B. Wolters, 1900), 215. Barger's appraisal: "If the baptism form may be considered the most well-known, undoubtedly the Lord's supper ranks the most beautiful of our liturgical documents."

are the fruit of a particular phase in the history of the church. By nature, they are *historical* products. And though the congregation throughout the ages remains faithful to the essential content, it does not mean that with growth in spirituality the confessions do not grow as well. As to the liturgy, Luther, the most conservative of all the reformers with respect to the worship services, was convinced: "One cannot develop formularies, church orders, and liturgies that will be strong enough to last forever, or even for a long time. That is why there must be adjustment, omissions, and revisions corresponding to the changing and unique events of the times. When they no longer serve to strengthen and nourish the faith, they should be handled like worn-out shoes—thrown away and replaced."

While one might find that last comment too drastic and would not be convinced that the confessions could ever become so outdated to have to throw them away for being old and unusable, Luther is, nevertheless, correct in principle. We have always believed that in the life of the church, despite temporary setbacks and deformation, there is always progression from strength to strength and transformation from glory to glory. As the world becomes older, the antitheses deepen themselves. Sin becomes bolder and branches off into new aberrations, increasingly taking on more rebellious and more grotesque forms.

But also, the church is unfolding into greater beauty and increasing spiritual power. She is stretching her wings out further and planting her banner wherever Christ reigns. She sees the controversies (points of dispute) multiply and esteems it her calling to place confession of the truth against every new denial. But a stance requiring that expressions of the confession be delivered unchanged from generation to generation would turn the living church of God into a *petrifact* (stone wall) that denies the progress and development of God's work.

Of itself, the changing of the times is reflected the least in a symbol like the communion form. We are reminded that precisely the absence of polemics is considered a great virtue of the form. Also, in recent years, the Lord's supper is contested considerably less than baptism. The battle over the Lord's supper seems to have completely cooled off, and the struggle for the faith has gone down an entirely different avenue. Nevertheless, through it all, the form remains by its nature a *confession*. In accordance with her convictions, the Lord's congregation speaks forth what God has revealed regarding this high and holy sacrament and thereby preserves the pledge God has entrusted to her.

Also, in the preparation instruction of the form, the congregation charts the course that leads a participant to the supper. So it can't help but take into account *particular* tender spots in ecclesiastical life. There needs to be a warning against the sins of the times. The form must address the heart and life of God's people according to the days in which they live. So, in a form that was drawn up for the congregation of this time, the list of grievous sins that are listed for self-examination would be viewed somewhat differently than the series that appears in the old form.

And perhaps the self-examination section that so many "troubled" souls today have run up against should be stated differently. To be sure, the congregation should value nothing more than the scriptural requirement that we must partake of the supper in *faith*, but so many misunderstand, and it results in holding back and just staying away. It would direct a soft admonition to those who out of false "piety" disobey God's command. The situation, as is heard today in the churches, that it is a special indicator of godliness and a sign of spiritual precision when one does *not* partake of the supper, was something as good as nonexistent at the time of the Reformation. For them, it was not so much a question of the need (with such great emphasis on the self), as it was a question of God's command that took precedence. The life of the church was evident in *obedience*. And that's why life there blossomed.

A form written for our day would certainly also bring to light the sin of disobedience out of *indifference*. There can be any number of reasons that a Christian might neglect his calling to come to communion. It might be out of "anxiety" or weakness of faith. It might be because a person feels that the supper is too often desecrated by inappropriate participation and so doesn't participate as a form of protest. Nevertheless, the saddest reason is certainly when there is just no *inclination* or rather, it is felt that an unconverted life is not in harmony with the Lord's supper, and that is why they stay away.

Also, there still seems to be the situation in a number of congregations where the youth are putting off the profession of their faith, lacking even a shred of desire for the supper to proclaim the Lord's death. Indeed, they have made a premeditated decision not to come to the covenantal meal, something that in the days of the Reformation would have been extremely rare. And if it did indeed occur, it was earnestly combated, if need be, with disciplinary action. Indeed, when it comes to the celebration of communion, the churches of our day are really hurting, which is the cause of the withering of spiritual life. And it would not be excessive if this spiritual deficiency were to be contested earnestly and strongly in the Lord's supper form, because the minister of the word has the right (and the responsibility) in his preaching to instruct, even to warn, the congregation in this matter, that she must exercise more energy in her worship. Alas, there are ministers who themselves need a warning because they just go along with the errors.

So, may reflection on the Lord's supper form bring us somewhat closer to the ideal: *a born-again liturgy for the church in our day!*

5. THE ORIGIN OF THE FORM

Even more so than the form for baptism, the Lord's supper form comes straight from the liturgy of the Palatinate. In the baptism form, Datheen took over the section from the prayer to the thanksgiving almost word for word. With the Lord's supper form, you can say that he adopted it literally and completely.[2]

Under the authority of Frederick III, the Palatinate form was drawn up by Olevianus, one of the spiritual fathers of our Heidelberg Catechism.[3] When Olevianus was commissioned for this enterprise, he did so in close connection with Calvin, using his form (The Genevan Form) as building material for his work. That's why, more than in any other component of our liturgy, Calvin's influence is noteworthy in the form for the Lord's supper.

So that the reader can judge for himself to what extent our form is dependent on Calvin's, I will share a few sections from his, italicizing places that were taken over by Olevianus. Calvin would begin by offering a formulary prayer immediately following the prayer after his sermon that would lead into the Lord's supper celebration. It went like this:[4]

And since Jesus Christ not only offered his body and his blood of the cross once only for the forgiveness of our sins, but he also gives us the same as food and drink unto eternal life, help us, O God by thy grace, that we might partake of such a great benefit, a precious gift, with a sincere desire, and due diligence. That is, through assured faith may we wholly

---

2 A few small modifications were introduced only for clarification. In place of the words: "As if he himself in his own person, etc." Datheen has, "yes, so completely." In the summary of the egregious sins, Datheen fuses "brawlers" and "the cantankerous" to "quarrelsome persons." In the second half of the form he adds "in the Old Testament" to "forefathers," also for clarification. But this is all.

3 Barger, *Ons Kerkboek*, 216. In the introduction to the *Church Order*, released on Nov. 15, 1563, Frederick III says the church order that he compiled and supervised through to its printing came from the most prominent theologians, administrators, and ministers, as well as other godly professors, without naming Olevianus as the composer of the Lord's supper form. However, Südhoff explicitly describes Olevianus as the one who produced the form. Cf. Karl Südhoff, *C. Olevianus und Z. Ursinus: Leben und ausgewählte Schriften* [*C. Olevianus and Z. Ursinus: Life and Selected Writings*] (Elberfeld: Verlag von R. L Friderichs, 1857).

4 J. A. M. Mensinga, *Over de Liturgische Schriften* [*On the Liturgical Writings*] (The Hague: Theirry en Mensing, 1851), 218ff.

enjoy *his body and his blood, yea, him, our Savior himself, true God and man, the only true heavenly bread—so that we may no longer live according to our wicked, sinful nature, but he might live in us.* Work in us holy, blessed, and eternal life so that we might so *truly be partakers of the new and everlasting testament, the covenant of grace, being sure and certain that thou wilt forever be our gracious Father, nevermore imputing our sins to us, and providing us with all things for body and soul, as thy dear children and heirs.* We ask this so that we might always love thee, thank thee, and glorify thy holy name in our deeds and in our words. O heavenly Father, grant to us that we today may commemorate and celebrate this marvelous and blessed remembrance of thy dear Son, so that we might be built up in this, and proclaim the benefit of his death so that through faith in thee we might increase, be strengthened, and be all the more encouraged to call upon thee as our God and Father and to be called by thy name. Amen.

Then, after reading the Apostles' Creed, the minister continues:

Attend to the words of the institution of the holy supper of our Lord Jesus Christ, as they were delivered by the holy apostle Paul in the 11th chapter of the First Letter to the Corinthians.

For I received, he says, from the Lord, etc.

Here we have heard, beloved brothers, how the Lord held the supper with his disciples in order *thereby* to instruct us that those who are outside the fellowship of believers may not be admitted. That is why we follow this rule. And so, in the name, and upon the command, of our Lord Jesus Christ I hereby exclude from Christ's congregation *all idolaters, misusers of God's name, despisers of God, heretics, and all sectarians and degenerates* that tear down the unity of the Christian church; *those who serve false gods, those who are*

disobedient to their parents and superiors; the rebellious, muti-
neers, brawlers, quarrelsome persons, adulterers, fornicators,
thieves, misers (usurers), robbers, drunkards, gluttons, and all
those who lead offensive lives. I declare to them, that *they must
abstain from this holy table because this is holy nourishment
that Jesus provides only for believers,* members of his household, and not for those who are defiled and unsanctified.

That is why each one, according to the warning of the
holy apostle, *must examine his conscience* and search himself,
whether he experiences within a true sorrow for sin, so that
he has a right and earnest desire *henceforth to live in accordance with God's will.* And above all else, whether he places
his trust in the *mercy of God, seeking his salvation in no other
place than in Jesus Christ alone;* also *if he is laying aside all
enmity and hatred, and earnestly resolves to live in unity and
brotherly love with his neighbor.*

*If we have this testimony before God within our hearts, let
us not at all doubt that God certainly receives us as his children*
and that the Lord Jesus calls us through his word to his table,
giving us this sacrament that he shared with his disciples.

*Although we find many shortcomings and miseries within
us, as namely, that we have not perfect faith,* but we are yet
prone to unbelief and unfaithfulness toward God, *that we
do not give ourselves to serve God with that zeal as we are
bound, but have to strive daily against the weakness of our
faith and the evil lusts of our flesh, yet, since the Lord displays to us his grace in that we have this holy gospel written
in our heart by which we fight against all unbelief and doubt,
and since we are by his Holy Spirit heartily sorry for these
shortcomings and miseries and desirous to fight against our
unbelief and to live according to all the commandments of
God, therefore we rest assured that no sin or infirmity which
still remains in us against our will can hinder us from being*

received of God in grace and from being made worthy par-
ticipants of this heavenly food and drink where we seek our
life in Jesus Christ acknowledging that we lie in the midst of
death. We understand, then, that this supper is a medicine
for the impoverished conscience that is spiritually sick, and
that any value the Lord places in us is in the context of our
great displeasure with our sin and the focus of our joy, our
delight, and our satisfaction in him alone.

Also, the *Sursum Corda* that precedes the actual communion is
similar. Calvin's goes like this:

To this end, let us lift up our spirits and our hearts on high in
heaven, where Jesus Christ is, in the glory of his Father, and
from where we await him for our salvation. *And let us not*
cling with our hearts to these earthly and perishable *elements*
that we see with the eye and touch with the hand, to seek
him as if he were contained there in the bread and the wine.
Then our souls will first be rightly directed as Christ provides himself for life-giving nourishment and lasting food
as we through true faith are lifted above all earthly things to
heaven and to God, in his kingdom and dwelling. Let us be
fully satisfied then that we have the bread and the wine as
signs and seals while we seek spiritual food of which we are
assured, there, where God promises that we shall find it.

These examples sufficiently indicate that we have the Genevan
reformer to thank for more than one strikingly beautiful passage, but
at the same time, Olevianus did not completely adopt Calvin's word
for word. The Heidelberg professor made independent and judicious
use of Calvin's liturgy. Calvin's material was borrowed by him to produce a *new* and *unique* form.

The same goes for use he made of other forms in addition to
the Genevan. Olevianus had also borrowed ideas from the London

Liturgy (by á Lasco and Micron), though in lesser measure than was the case with Calvin's.[5]

And finally, there was a liturgical document from the Lutheran liturgy that served as a model. Noticeable here and there is clear influence from the Württemberg form (coming from the Württemberg Church Book of 1561).[6] The mention (or we might say the *repetition* because in the beginning of the form there is a similar mention) of the institution of the supper, which begins with the words, "And that we might firmly believe that we belong to this covenant of grace, *the Lord Jesus...*" etc. followed the example of the Lutheran form. In addition, the noteworthy exhortation to unity at the end of the instructional portion was borrowed nearly word for word from this form.[7]

---

5 Cf. Johannes Ens, *Kort Historisch Berigt van de Publieke Schriften: Rakende de Leer En Dienst Der Nederduitsche Kerken Van de Vereenigd Nederlanden* [*A Brief Historical Notice Regarding the Public Writings: Concerning the Doctrine and Worship of the Reformed Churches in The Netherlands*] (Kampen: S. Van Velzen, Jr., 1861), 224. Ens appears to see it differently. He says: "In drawing up the formulary, the Palatinate theologians took a few things from the Genevan, but by far, most of it came from M. Micron." To the contrary, Mensinga's verdict is that "when we further research the origin, we discover a small portion of overlap with Micron, but the greatest part, especially the first section on the self-examination, was borrowed from Calvin's formulary, of which the Londoners had also made use." Ibid., 214–15.

    That last observation that the Londoners had also drawn from Calvin's form explains Prof. Ens' assertion. Taken as a whole, the likeness with the London form is the greatest.

6 The form used by the Lutherans here in Holland overlaps in great measure with the Württemberg formulary.

7 Compare this pericope: "Besides, by this same Spirit we are also united as members of one body in true brotherly love, as the holy apostle says: *Seeing that we, who are many, are one bread. one body: for we all partake of the one bread. For out of many grains* etc.—then follows the words from the Würtemberger form [as per Ger. text]: *one meal is ground and one bread baked, and out of many berries, pressed together, one wine flows and is mixed together, so shall we all who by true faith are incorporated into Christ be all together one body, through brother love, for Christ our dear Savior's sake, who before has so exceedingly loved us. And show this towards one another, as John teaches, not only in words but also in deeds. May the almighty, merciful God and Father of our dear Lord Jesus Christ help us in this, through his Holy Spirit. Amen.*

So we have examples of Olevianus' work of drawing from no less than three forms of rich diversity. And from the above comparisons, the reader can verify for himself that in these instances the author borrowed significant passages. However, those who would then contend that Olevianus didn't provide any original work do not give him his due. In fact, many of the most distinctive moments in our form owe their existence entirely to him. Take, for example, the abundantly moving description of the purpose and rich benefits of Jesus' death.

First of all, let us be fully persuaded in our hearts that our Lord Jesus Christ, according to the promises made to the forefathers in the Old Testament, was sent of the Father into this world; that he assumed our flesh and blood; that he bore for us the wrath of God under which we should have perished everlastingly, from the beginning of his incarnation to the end of his life upon earth, and has fulfilled for us all obedience and righteousness of the divine law, especially when the weight of our sins and of the wrath of God pressed out of him the bloody sweat in the garden, where he was bound that we might be loosed from our sins; that afterwards he suffered innumerable reproaches that we might never be confounded; that he was innocently condemned to death that we might be acquitted at the judgment seat of God; yea, that he suffered his blessed body to be nailed to the cross that he might fasten to it the handwriting of our sins; and so has taken the curse due us upon himself that he might fill us with his blessing; and has humbled himself unto the very deepest reproach and anguish of hell, in body and soul, on the tree of the cross, when he cried out with a loud voice, *My God, my God, why hast thou forsaken me?* that we might be accepted of God, and nevermore be forsaken of him; and finally has confirmed with his death and shedding of his blood the new and eternal testament, the covenant of grace and of reconciliation, when he said, *It is finished.*

Also, to note is his heartfelt exposition and application of Paul's words of the institution:

That is, as often as ye eat of this bread and drink of this cup, you shall thereby, as by a sure remembrance and pledge, be admonished and assured of this my hearty love and faithfulness towards you; that, whereas otherwise you should have suffered eternal death, I give my body in death on the tree of the cross and shed my blood for you, and nourish and refresh your hungry and thirsty souls with my crucified body and shed blood to everlasting life, as certainly as this bread is broken before your eyes and this cup is given to you, and you eat and drink with your mouth in remembrance of me.

And finally, the particularly weighty portion of our form where the meaning, symbolism, and effectual working of the supper is set forth:

From this institution of the holy supper of our Lord Jesus Christ we see that he directs our faith and trust to his perfect sacrifice, once offered on the cross, as to the only ground and foundation of our salvation, whereby he is become to our hungry and thirsty souls the true food and drink of life eternal. For by his death he has taken away the cause of our eternal death and misery, namely sin, and obtained for us the life-giving Spirit, that we by that Spirit, who dwells in Christ as in the head and in us as his members, should have true communion with him and be made partakers of all his riches, of life eternal, righteousness, and glory.[8]

---

8   Ibid., 324, *et al.* Regarding such pericopes, Mensinga explains: "I have not been able to discover whether this section was borrowed from another liturgy, or from one with which I'm not familiar. Apparently, this is original work of the Palatinate author."

By the independent insertion of these passages, the author gives evidence of exceptional liturgical acumen. The liturgies of Calvin and à Lasco are certainly deficient in so far that so little is said regarding the benefits of Jesus suffering and the sacramental efficacy of the supper. Because Olevianus has followed the virtues of the liturgy that served him as an example, and has improved the deficiencies, our Lord's supper form is a model that can safely stand comparison with all related forms.

6. HISTORY OF THE FORMULARY

We can be brief with the remaining history of our Lord's supper form.

Already noted was that Datheen's translation made only a few minor changes from the German publication. To this day, our form has remained nearly unaltered from what Datheen prepared for our churches.[9]

From the very beginning, there was universal accord among Reformed churches in the use of Datheen's liturgy, particularly when it came to the communion form. So various synods declared that the churches should faithfully use the liturgy as once adopted.

The 1568 Assembly of Wesel had decided the following: "We deem the published text of the Lord's supper to be permanently regarded as most consistent with Christ's institution, his explicit command, and with the Pauline exposition" (Sec. VI, Art. 13).

The 1586 Synod of The Hague declared in even more detail:

Each church shall administer the Lord's supper in a manner they judge to be most suitable. Nevertheless, it is to be understood that the external ceremonies as prescribed in God's word remain unchanged, that all superstitions should be avoided, and that after the conclusion of the sermon and the general prayer from the pulpit, the form for the Lord's

---

9   This is all the more noteworthy when you consider that, over time, the Palatinate form itself underwent significant revision.

supper, including the offering of its prayer, shall be read at the table (Art. 55).

The 1618–1619 Synod of Dordt adopted this stipulation word for word.

Modifications were introduced only at the 1574 Synod of Dordt. Synod approved the following recommendation in article 79: "A brief preface to the prayer of thanksgiving after the Lord's supper shall be offered, in which we are exhorted regarding Christ's immense love and our debt of gratitude."

This proposal, apparently, can be attributed to a transmission error. Before the prayer of thanksgiving in the form is already an encouragement to gratitude. Immediately following the administration of the supper, the minister says, "Beloved in the Lord, since the Lord has now nourished our souls at his table, let us jointly praise his holy name with thanksgiving; and let each one say in his heart"; and following this are the references to Psalm 103 and Romans 5. The Palatinate liturgy then concludes with the words, "Therefore shall my mouth and heart show forth the praise of the Lord, from this time forth for evermore. Amen"; which were certainly intended as a prayer of thanks. However, immediately follows "or thus." And then comes the thanksgiving that we have always used, "*O merciful God and Father, we thank thee with all our heart,*" etc. The intention of the Palatinate liturgy, therefore, was to give the minister a choice as to which of these two he would like to use.

Datheen's translation, however, had rightly omitted the words, "or thus," and so ended up with the citations from Psalm 103 and Romans 5 serving as an encouragement and preface to the prayer of thanksgiving. Apparently, the 1574 Synod of Dordt didn't understand this, and that's why they determined that a new preface was needed for the prayer.[10]

---

10 Cf. H. H. Kuyper, *De Post-acta of Nahandelingen Van de Nationale Synode Van Dordrecht in 1618 en 1619: Een Historische Studie* [*The Post-Acts or Further Actions of the National Synod of Dordtrecht in 1618-1619: An Historical Study*] (Amsterdam: Höveker & Wormser, 1899), 396, 97ff., also 224–26. Indeed, at

Furthermore, the 1574 synod inserted a change to the words that are spoken with the administration of the supper (the so-called sacramental formula). Following the example of the Palatinate until this time, the Pauline formula from 1 Corinthians 10:16 was used in the Dutch form: *"The bread that we break is the communion of the body of Christ; the cup of thanksgiving for which we give thanks is the communion of the blood of Christ."*[11] The 1574 synod concurred with this formula, but then added a piece that was similar to what is found in Micron's *Christeliche Ordinancien*: *"Take, eat, remember and believe that the body of Jesus Christ was broken unto a complete remission of all our sins."* And with the cup: *"Take, drink ye all of it, remember and believe that the precious blood of Jesus Christ was shed unto the complete remission of all our sins."*

Subsequent synods repeated this resolution.[12] Although the churches appeared to be adhering to synod's decision,[13] Datheen's shorter formula continued to surface in later publications of the liturgy. In the publication that would be submitted to the Reformed churches by Prof. Rutgers and his colleagues, the official formula is restored.

Apart from these, there are no significant modifications in the form worth mentioning.

The 1618–1619 Synod of Dordt did little more than to declare as the pure text the liturgy that was submitted by the Zeeland churches

---

synod's request, Casper Vander Heyden formulated such a preface, but the churches never used it. In all editions of the liturgy, after that which was drafted by Vander Heyden, the new preface was dropped.

11 Ens shares that in some churches the words of institution spoken by Christ that were used "beyond doubt sound like something that came from the mass." Ibid., 227ff. That is why the [earlier] 1571 Synod of Emden had determined that there was freedom to use the words of either Christ or Paul in the distribution of the bread and wine (art. 21).

12 For example, the Synod of 1578 agreed that "the words of the Lord's supper shall be taken from 1 Corinthians 12 and, thereby, to add these words: 'Take, eat...'" The 1582 Synod of Middelburg made the same determination.

13 Cf. H. Kuyper, *De Post-acta*, 397, nt. 3.

(i.e., the 1611 publication of R. Schilders from Middelburg). A synodical advisory committee for liturgical revision had recommended only five insignificant modifications to the form for the Lord's supper. It is known that these changes were not to be included in an official *publication* of the liturgy since they were not actually approved by synod. The result thereof was that some reprints by publishers were handled quite carelessly. Complaints followed at various synods but with no results other than the Particular Synod of South Holland in 1737 that published a somewhat improved (but not officially binding) edition, which generally became the foundation for later publications.

Although the Lord's supper form was, perhaps, the least bungled of all,[14] we have reason nonetheless to be thankful for this form, that stabilization and warrant would come with the publication resulting from the concern of Prof. Rutgers, along with Prof. Bavinck and Prof. A. Kuyper, in 1897.

But then, how is it that we have the book of forms from Prof. Rutgers and his colleagues as an *official* publication of the liturgy? Well, it is a matter of yes and no. If you mean by *official* that it was published under the authority of synod, then I have to say, *no*. If you mean by *official* that every part was reviewed and approved by synod, I would also say, *no*. But, if you mean by *official* that it was *recommended by* synod as the preferred publication, then I can answer in the affirmative.

So what exactly happened?

There has been in existence an authentic text of the liturgy since the Synod of Dordt in 1618–1619. This synod received the 1611 edition liturgical book submitted by Zeeland and appointed a study committee for a revision of the liturgy. They were to determine any changes, if necessary, to be recommended. In 1621, the appointed revisers reported to the churches what modifications they deemed

---

14 In the publication intended for India, Dr. Kuyper mentions in *De Post-acta* that the word "mine" was omitted.

appropriate (thirty-five in total, which were quite miniscule) and, in this way, the *authentic* text was established.

However, the delegates of synod did not provide for the now established text to become an *official* publication. From then on, there was no small measure of arbitrariness in republications of the liturgy. The printers just did what was right in their own eyes.[15] At the initiative of the Particular Synod of South Holland in 1737, a corrected publication was released, but the much-needed stability remained out of reach.

For this reason, professors Dr. Rutgers, Dr. Bavinck, and Dr. A. Kuyper (in no small measure supported by H. H. Kuyper, who authored the Post-Acta) worked together to get the authentic text of the Synod of Dordt back in the hands of the churches. They produced the well-known *Flakkeesche* edition of 1897. Due to not having received an actual synodical mandate for their work, the publication bore no official ecclesiastical stamp. Immediately after the publication of the Reformed church book, congregations felt that they should best go with this edition.

The 1899 Synod of Groningen appointed a trio of deputies, Prof. Biesterveld, Rev. Van Proosdij, and Dr. Honing, to "compare the Forms of Unity and the Liturgy of F. L. Rutgers—published with the help of Dr. H. Bavinck and Dr. A. Kuyper—with the authentic text established by the Synod of Dordt 1618–1619. They were to include in their analysis any proposed linguistic modifications (related to outdated expressions), and to bring advice to the following synod."

The "following Synod" was held in Arnhem in 1902, and indeed the requested report was on the table.[16] In this report, the deputies expounded:

> First, permit us to say, that in our opinion, brothers Dr.
> F. L. Rutgers, Dr. H. H. Kuyper (because all along has been

---

15 Cf. Wielenga, *The Reformed Baptism Form*, 11.
16 Cf. *Bijlage D1* , Art. 24, *De Acta der Generale Synode van Arnhem, 1906.*

known the important role this professor has played in our audited publication), Dr. A. Kuyper and Dr. H. Bavinck, have done the church and the science a great service with the appearance of their edition of the Forms of Unity and the liturgy. The highest degree of effort was dedicated to this publication. Their work was carried out with incredible precision. Uncommon knowledge is displayed in it. A treasure of enlightenment has been added. And what is most evident is that now the General Synod may bring to an end the present commotion in this area. *Therefore, we propose that the General Synod decide to offer her appreciation to these highly esteemed brothers for their accomplished work, and that this publication be regarded from now on as the official edition, and is to be operational in the churches.*

Thus, the praise was ecstatic.

Nevertheless, the deputies did have some comments of their own in which they proposed a number of changes (but of secondary importance). Hence, the last clause of their report was as follows: "A new publication of this work shall only be necessary for inclusion of our suggested modifications should the General Synod find itself in agreement with them."

Noteworthy, however, is that not a single change was proposed for the text of Lord's supper form.

The Synod of Arnhem put this report into the hands of a committee that, in turn, submitted a *report on the report.* This committee also had its own comments. Their sentiments differed regarding a few of the proposed recommendations. Also, they were not of a mind to recommend the Rutgers' publication for approval as the official publication. A stipulation in their report[17] said: "Finally, your commission is not inclined to recommend that the reviewed publication

---

17 *Bijlage, D2, Acta Arnhem.*

be viewed from now on as official, but proposes that this improved, modified version of Dr. F. L. Rutgers and his colleagues be commended to the churches with the expressed desire that it be utilized everywhere."

Synod then moved to discuss the proposed modifications in particular, but it appeared unfeasible to come to a good result. Synod debated, for almost an entire session, just over the word "incomprehensible" in Lord's Day 18 of the Catechism, but with reluctance to arrive at a conclusion.

The president of the synod, Rev. Hoekstra, then made the following proposal:[18]

> The General Synod of Arnhem,
>
> Judging that the way is not clear in our gathering to decide and declare in particular which precise text of the Forms of Unity and the Liturgy is to be esteemed;
>
> Expresses at the same time her gratitude to the delegates of the Synod of Groningen already named for their industry.
>
> Declares the *desire* for the edition of Dr. F. L. Rutgers, delivered with the assistance of Dr. H. Bavinck and Dr. A. Kuyper, *to be received for general usage in our churches,* and that a future publication may take into account the work of the appointed deputies from Groningen, as well as the advice presented at the Synod of Arnhem.

This proposal was adopted unanimously.

Therefore, the Rutgers publication is not *official* (in the strict sense of the word), but the *ecclesiastically recommended* edition. And so, with respect to the Lord's supper form, we employ the text of this publication as the foundation of our discussion.

---

18 Cf. art. 27.

7. TEXT AND OVERVIEW OF THE FORM

Here then is the text of the form, with appropriate notations, as it is found in the ecclesiastically recommended edition:

Regarding Holy Communion[19]

All those who are committed to the congregation of God and desire to be admitted to the Lord's supper, must first be instructed in the articles of the Christian faith from God's word. The form and manner of such instruction in the churches is to be that which is deemed most edifying.

So when they have attained a basic understanding and confession of the articles of the faith, they are to be asked whether there remain any doubts (regarding the doctrine) so that they may be satisfied. If they answer in the affirmative, one tries to satisfy them from the holy Scripture.

When their doubts are dispelled, ask them if they intend to remain committed to the aforesaid doctrine, to forsake the world, and to lead a godly life. Finally, ask if they are also willing to submit themselves to the discipline of the church.

---

19 In the publication of the liturgy of the sixteenth century, the Lord's supper form was preceded by what was in use at the time, *The Short Examination of Faith*, to which was added, "As those who have committed themselves to the Congregation, on the basis of knowing and confessing these articles," etc. So almost literally the same as the above printed text, except for the first line.

In the 1611 publication, the Short Examination had been replaced by the Compendium that the Middelburg Church had instituted for the same purpose. But because this was not yet approved by the churches as a whole, it did not find a place here in the official Liturgy. However, it was placed at the very end. In addition, here are only the published liturgy modifications.

The 1619 Synod of Dordt did decide that the churches could make use of the Compendium, but it was not adopted with ecclesiastical sanction for teaching and for the public profession of faith. So it was included, but in the Liturgy itself, nothing else could precede the Lord's supper form than what the official text provided, that is, that which appears in the edition of 1611, with the change introduced in it by the revisers.

When they have promised this, then admonish them to peace, love, and unity with everyone, and to reconcile with anyone with whom they may have unfinished business.

Form for the Celebration of the Lord's Supper[20]

Beloved in the Lord Jesus Christ, attend to the words of the institution of the holy supper of our Lord Jesus Christ, as they are delivered by the holy apostle Paul. I Cor. 11:23–30.

For I have received of the Lord, that which also I delivered unto you, that the Lord Jesus, the same night in which he was betrayed, took bread; and when he had given thanks, he brake it, and said, Take, eat; this is my body which is broken for you, this do in remembrance of me. And after the same manner also, he took the cup, when he had supped, saying, This cup is the New Testament in my blood; this do ye, as oft as ye drink it in remembrance of me; for as oft as ye eat this bread, and drink this cup, ye do show the Lord's death till he come. Wherefore, whosoever shall eat this bread, or drink this cup of the Lord unworthily, shall be guilty of the body and blood of the Lord. But let a man examine himself, and so let him eat of that bread, and drink of that cup; for he that eateth and drinketh unworthily, eateth and drinketh judgment to himself, if he discern not the body of the Lord.

That we may now celebrate the supper of the Lord to our comfort, it is above all things necessary, first, rightly to examine ourselves; and further, to direct it to that end for

---

20 Also, this form in the text here printed, which naturally is presented as the one officially established, differs in some words and expressions from forms commonly in use. Some variations have been around two and a half centuries, instead of the official form, others simply followed the sixteenth-century edition, and others did not get the requisite attention in reprintings of our day.

which Christ hath ordained and instituted the same, namely, to his remembrance.

The true examination of ourselves consists of these three parts:

First. That every one considers by himself, his sins and accursedness, to the end that he may abhor and humble himself before God: considering that the wrath of God against sin is so great, that (rather than it should go unpunished) he hath punished the same in his beloved Son Jesus Christ, with the bitter and shameful death of the cross.

Secondly. That every one examine his own heart, whether he also believes this sure promise of God, that all his sins are forgiven him only for the sake of the passion and death of Jesus Christ, and that the perfect righteousness of Christ is imputed and freely given him as his own, yea, so perfectly, as if he had satisfied in his own person for all his sins, and fulfilled all righteousness.

Thirdly. That everyone examine his own conscience, whether he is minded henceforth to show true thankfulness to God in his whole life, and to walk uprightly before his face; as also, whether he has laid aside unfeignedly all enmity, hatred, and envy, and earnestly resolves henceforward to walk in true love and peace with his neighbor.

All those, then, who are thus disposed, God will certainly receive in grace, and count them worthy partakers of the table of his Son Jesus Christ. On the contrary, those who do not feel this testimony in their hearts eat and drink judgment to themselves.[21]

---

21 The official text has here, *the judgment,* as in the Scripture from which this

Therefore, we also, according to the command of Christ and the apostle Paul, admonish all those who know themselves defiled with the following egregious sins, to abstain from the table of the Lord, and declare to them that they have no part in the kingdom of Christ; such as all idolaters, all those who invoke deceased saints, angels, or other creatures; all those who show honor to images; all sorcerers and fortune-tellers who bless cattle or humans, together with other things, and all who believe in such blessings; and all despisers of God, and of his word, and of the holy sacraments; all blasphemers; all those who are given to raise discord, sects, and mutiny in churches or society; all perjurers; all those who are disobedient to their parents and superiors; all murderers, quarrelsome persons, and those who live in hatred and envy against their neighbors; all adulterers, whoremongers, drunkards, thieves, usurers, robbers, gamesters, covetous, and all who lead offensive lives.

All these, while they continue in such sins, shall abstain from this food (which Christ has ordained only for his faithful), lest their judgment and condemnation be made the heavier.

But this is not designed (dearly beloved brothers and sisters in the Lord) to discourage the contrite hearts of believers, as if none might come to the supper of the Lord, but those who are without sin; for we do not come to this supper, to testify thereby that we are perfect and righteous in ourselves; but on the contrary, considering that we seek our life outside ourselves in Jesus Christ, we acknowledge that we lie in the midst of death; therefore, notwithstanding we experience many infirmities and miseries in ourselves, as namely, that we have not perfect faith, and that we do not give ourselves

---

expression is borrowed (1 Cor. 11:29) from the old Dutch Bible translation. Now it makes sense to follow the authorized version.

to serve God with that zeal as we are bound, but have daily to strive with the weakness of our faith, and the evil lusts of our flesh; yet, since we are (by the grace of the Holy Spirit) heart-broken for these weaknesses, and desirous to fight against our unbelief, and to live according to all the commandments of God: therefore we rest assured that no sin or infirmity, which still remains in us (against our will) can hinder us from being received of God in grace, and from being made worthy partakers of this heavenly food and drink.

Let us now also consider, to what end the Lord hath instituted his supper, namely, that we do it in remembrance of him. Now after this manner are we to remember him by it:

First. That we are confidently persuaded in our hearts, that our Lord Jesus Christ (according to the promises made from the beginning to our forefathers in the Old Testament) was sent of the Father into the world; that he assumed our flesh and blood; that he bore for us the wrath of God (under which we should have perished everlastingly) from the beginning of his incarnation, to the end of his life upon earth; and that he hath fulfilled, for us, all obedience and righteousness of the divine law; especially, when the weight of our sins and the wrath of God pressed out of him the bloody sweat in the garden, where he was bound that we might be freed from our sins; that he afterwards suffered innumerable reproaches, that we might never be confounded; that he was innocently condemned to death, that we might be acquitted at the judgment-seat of God; yea, that he suffered his blessed body to be nailed to the cross—that he might fix thereon the handwriting of our sins; and has also taken upon himself the curse due to us, that he might fill us with his blessings: and humbled himself unto the deepest reproach and agony of hell, both in body and soul, on the tree of the cross, when he cried out with a loud voice,

"My God, my God! why hast thou forsaken me?" that we might be accepted of God and nevermore be forsaken of him: and finally confirmed with his death and shedding of his blood, the new and eternal testament, that covenant of grace and reconciliation when he said: *"It is finished."*

And that we might firmly believe that we belong to this covenant of grace, *the Lord Jesus Christ, in his last supper, took bread, and when he had given thanks, he brake it, and gave it to his disciples and said, "Take, eat, this is my body which is broken for you, this do in remembrance of me." In like manner after supper he took the cup, gave thanks and gave it to them saying, "Drink ye all of it; this cup is the new Testament in my blood, which is shed for you and for many, for the remission of sins; this do as often as ye drink it in remembrance of me:* that is, as often as ye eat of this bread and drink of this cup, you shall thereby as by a sure remembrance and pledge, be admonished and assured of this my hearty love and faithfulness towards you; that, whereas you should otherwise have suffered eternal death, I have given my body to death on the tree of the cross, and shed my blood for you, and feed and nourish your hungry and thirsty souls with my crucified body and shed blood to everlasting life, as certainly as this bread is broken before your eyes, and this cup is given to you, and you eat and drink the same with your mouth, in remembrance of me.

From this institution of the holy supper of our Lord Jesus Christ, we see that he directs our faith and trust to his perfect sacrifice (once offered on the cross) as to the only ground and foundation of our salvation, wherein he is become to our hungry and thirsty souls, the true food and drink of life eternal. For by his death he hath taken away the cause of our eternal death and misery, namely, sin, and obtained for us the life-giving Spirit, that we by the same (who dwells in Christ as in the head, and in us as his members), might have the true communion with him, and be made partakers of all his riches, of life eternal, righteousness, and glory.

Besides, that we by this same Spirit may also be united as members of one body in true brotherly love, as the holy apostle saith, *"For we, being many, are one bread and one body; for we are all partakers of that one bread." For as out of many grains one meal is ground, and one bread baked, and out of many berries being pressed together, one wine flows, and is mixed together;* so shall we all, who by a true faith are engrafted into Christ, be altogether one body, through brotherly love, for Christ's sake, our beloved Savior, who hath so exceedingly loved us, and not only show this in word, but also in deed towards one another.

Hereto assist us, the almighty, merciful God and Father of our Lord Jesus Christ through his Holy Spirit. Amen.

That we may obtain all this, let us humble ourselves before God, and with true faith implore his grace.

Prayer

O most merciful God and Father, we beseech thee, that thou wilt be pleased in this supper (in which we celebrate the glorious remembrance of the bitter death of thy beloved Son, Jesus Christ) to work in our hearts through thy Holy Spirit, that we may more and more with true confidence, give ourselves up unto thy Son Jesus Christ, that our afflicted and contrite hearts, through the power of the Holy Spirit, may be nourished and refreshed with his true body and blood; yea, with him, true God and man, that only heavenly bread; and that we may no longer live in our sins, but he in us, and we in him, and thus truly be made partakers of the new and everlasting testament and covenant of grace, that we may not doubt but thou wilt forever be our gracious Father, nevermore imputing our sins unto us, and providing us with all things necessary, as well for the body as the soul, as thy beloved children and heirs; grant us also thy grace, that we may take up our cross cheerfully, deny ourselves, confess our Savior, and in all tribulations, with uplifted heads expect our Lord Jesus Christ from heaven, where he will make our mortal bodies like unto his most glorious body, and take us unto him in eternity.

Answer[22] us, O God and merciful Father, through Jesus Christ, who taught us to pray:

> Our Father who art in heaven,
> Hallowed be thy name.
> Thy kingdom come.
> Thy will be done on earth, as it is in heaven.
> Give us this day our daily bread;
> And forgive us our debts, as we forgive our debtors.
> And lead us not into temptation, but deliver us from
>   the evil one.
> For thine is the kingdom, and the power and the glory,
>   forever.

Strengthen us also by this holy supper in the catholic undoubted Christian faith, whereof we make confession with mouth and heart, saying:

> I believe in God, the Father, Almighty, Maker of

---

22 Also here, as elsewhere in the formulary, the edition that was commonly circulated for two and a half centuries, instead of the above official text, followed the sixteenth-century text: so the words that introduce the Lord's prayer are missing and the prayer that precedes is concluded with *Amen.*

heaven and earth; and in Jesus Christ his only begotten Son our Lord; who was conceived by the Holy Ghost, born of the virgin Mary, suffered under Pontius Pilate, was crucified, dead, and buried, he descended into hell: the third day he rose again from the dead, he ascended into heaven, and sitteth at the right hand of God the Father Almighty; from thence he shall come to judge the living and the dead.

I believe in the Holy Ghost; I believe a holy catholic church; the communion of saints; the forgiveness of sins; the resurrection of the body; and life everlasting. Amen.

That we may now be fed with the true heavenly bread, Christ Jesus, let us not cleave with our hearts unto the external bread and wine, but lift up our heartson high in heaven, where Christ Jesus is our Advocate, at the right hand of his heavenly Father, whither all the articles of our faith direct us; not doubting, but we shall as truly be fed and refreshed in our souls through the working of the Holy Ghost, with his body and blood, as we receive the holy bread and wine in remembrance of him.

In breaking and distributing the bread, the minister shall say:

The bread which we break is the communion of the body of Christ. Take,[23] eat, remember, and believe, that the body of our Lord Jesus Christ was broken unto the complete remission of all our sins.

---

23 In the oldest publication of the Liturgy here, and a few lines further, are only the words from 1 Corinthians 10:16. But the 1574 and 1578 Synods of Dordt, as well as the 1581 Synod of Middelburg, determined, and repeated, that the words, "Take, eat," etc. and "Take, drink," etc. should be included (as it is here above). Nevertheless, for around two and a half centuries of publishing the liturgy, also in this place the wording of the oldest text was simply reprinted; and that is the reason these words are missing in the commonly circulated edition.

And when he gives the cup:

The cup of thanksgiving, for which we give thanks, is the communion of the blood of Christ. Take, drink ye all of it, remember and believe that the precious blood of our Lord Jesus Christ was shed unto a complete remission of all our sins.

During the communion, there shall be uplifting singing or something read to serve the remembrance of the death of Christ such as from Isaiah 53 or John 13, 14, 15, 16, 17, 18, or the like.

After the communion, the minister shall say:

Beloved in the Lord, since the Lord hath now nourished our souls at his table, let us therefore jointly praise his holy name with thanksgiving, and everyone say in his heart, thus [Ps. 103]:

1. Bless the Lord, O my soul; and all that is within me, bless his holy name.
2. Bless the Lord, O my soul, and forget not all his benefits.
4. Who redeemeth thy life from destruction; who crowneth thee with lovingkindness and tender mercies.
8. The Lord is merciful and gracious, slow to anger and plenteous in mercy
9. he will not always chide: neither will he keep his anger forever
10. He hath not dealt with us after our sins, nor rewarded us according to our iniquities.
11. For as the heaven is high above the earth, so great is his mercy towards them that fear him.
12. As far as the East is from the West, so far hath he removed our transgressions from us.

13. Like as a father pitieth his children, so the Lord pitieth them that fear him.

Who[24] hath not spared his own Son, but delivered him up for us all, and freely given us all things with him. Therefore God commendeth therewith his love towards us, in that while we were yet sinners, Christ died for us; much more then, being now justified in his blood, we shall be saved from wrath through him: for, if, when we were enemies, we were reconciled to God by the death of his Son; much more being reconciled, we shall be saved by his life. Therefore shall my mouth and heart show forth the praise of the Lord from this time forth for evermore. Amen.

O merciful God and Father, we thank thee with all our hearts, that thou hast of thy infinite mercy, given us thine only begotten Son, for a mediator and a sacrifice for our sins, and to be our food and drink unto life eternal, and that thou givest us a true faith, whereby we are made partakers of such great benefits. Thou hast also been pleased, that thy beloved Son Jesus Christ should institute and ordain the holy supper for the strengthening of that faith. Grant, we beseech thee, O faithful God and Father, that through the operation of thy Holy Spirit, the remembrance of our Lord Jesus Christ and the proclamation of his death may daily increase in us the upright faith, and in blessed fellowship with Christ, through Jesus Christ thy dear Son, in whose name we conclude our prayers, saying as he has taught us:

Our Father who art in heaven,
Hallowed be Thy name;
Thy kingdom come;

---

24 This paragraph consists of Scriptures that the author paraphrases, but here also, the old translation must have been replaced by the Dordt Bible.

Thy will be done in earth, as it is in heaven.
Give us this day our daily bread;
And forgive us our debts, as we forgive our debtors.
And lead us not into temptation, but deliver us from
the evil one.
For Thine is the kingdom, and the power, and the glory,
forever. Amen.

In general, the compilation of the Lord's supper form is like that of the baptism and marriage formularies. It begins with the *Instruction Section*, which expounds the doctrine of the Lord's supper, followed by the *Ritual Section* that takes up everything pertaining to the administration of communion.

Each of these main sections has subsections that together form a complete unit. Here is the outline of the form in order to show how it is constructed. Following the examination of the communicants, it goes like this:

I. Instruction Section

A. *The Words of Institution* ("Beloved in the Lord...")
B. *Sincere Self-Examination*
    1. Reminder of sin ("First. That every one consider...").
    2. Faith in God's promise ("Secondly. That every one examine...").
    3. Commitment to thankfulness ("Thirdly. That everyone examine...").
    4. Warning to the unconverted ("all those who...").
    5. Comfort for the humble ("But this is not...").
C. *The Purpose of the Supper*
    1. Remembrance of Christ's death ("First. That we are confidently...").

2. Strengthening of faith ("and that we might firmly...").
3. Bonding in brotherly love ("Besides, that we by...").

II. Ritual Section

A. *Praefatio*
   1. Prayer ("O most merciful God...").
   2. Urging to sincere celebration ("That we may now...").
B. *Communion*
   1. The sacramental formulas ("The bread which we...").
   2. Administrative rubric ("During the communion...").
C. *Post-communion*
   1. Exhortation to thanksgiving ("Beloved in the Lord, since...").
   2. Prayer of thanksgiving.

---•

Chapter Two

EXAMINATION OF THE FAITH

1. ADMISSION TO GOD'S CONGREGATION

In addition to the actual Lord's supper form in the publication we use is a preceding section that has to do with admission to the Lord's table. It is as follows:

> All those who are committed to the congregation of God and desire to be admitted to the Lord's supper, must first be instructed in the articles of the Christian faith from God's word. The form and manner of such instruction in the churches is to be that which is deemed most edifying.
>
> So when they have attained a basic understanding and confession of the articles of the faith, they are to be asked whether there remain any doubts (regarding the doctrine) so that they may be satisfied. If they answer in the affirmative, one tries to satisfy them from Holy Scripture.
>
> When their doubts are dispelled, ask them if they intend to remain committed to the aforesaid doctrine, to forsake the world, and to lead a godly life.
>
> Finally, ask if they are also willing to submit themselves to the discipline of the church. When they have promised this, then admonish them to peace, love, and unity with everyone, and to reconcile with anyone with whom they may have unfinished business.

This piece is not read at the administration of the supper. In most church books it is not even reprinted so that it is as such unfamiliar to the people. Nevertheless, it is of significance for our church life insofar that here is presented the position of the Reformation church in terms of the making of profession of faith.

That is why it is our task here to provide some remarks regarding this preface and to make some general comments regarding admission to the Lord's supper as ordered according to Reformed principles.

In a note, the revisers of our liturgy (Prof. Rutgers and his colleagues) indicate that the oldest publication had still been preceded with the Short Examination of Faith In the 1611 edition (that later became the official edition). The Short Examination was removed for those who wanted to replace it with the Compendium that had been approved by the Middelburg Church under the influence of Faukelius and his colleagues. However, since the churches in general had not yet adopted this Compendium for use, there was the desire that it not be placed at the beginning of the Lord's supper form, but at the very end, *after* the official liturgy. At the beginning of the communion form remains only the above for the purpose of "liturgical instructions" (the conclusion and summary of the Short Examination).

In light of the fact that the Synod of Dordt did allow the Compendium, and even recommended it as a manual for catechetical instruction, but has not adopted it officially as such, it may not be included in an official publication of the liturgy among the liturgical writings. At best, it may have a special place at the end. It may not precede the Lord's supper form itself other than what is referred to in the 1611 publication, with the (Dordt) revisers' proposed modification,[1] so far, the annotation of Prof. Rutgers and colleagues.

We have these men to thank that the liturgical instruction concerning admission to the Lord's supper regained its rightful place. This short preface is of no small value for the outcome of catechetical

---

1   This modification refers to the word "completed" in the last line, which was replaced with "promised."

instruction to be a clear understanding of the profession of faith. Even more clearly comes to light that our fathers themselves considered *catechetical instruction, profession of faith*, and *the Lord's supper* as constituting an indivisible triad.

In the spirit of true Reformed liberality, they left the actual form or manner of instruction to the churches themselves. However, as a firm tenet of ecclesiastical life in general, they determined that "all those who are committed to the congregation of God and desire to be admitted to the Lord's supper, must first be instructed in the articles of the Christian faith from God's word."

Clearly, the two phrases, "are committed to the congregation of God" and "to be admitted to the Lord's supper," are intended as parallels, in so far that the second phrase completes and explains the first. On the one hand, to desire admittance to the Lord's table involves being received into the congregation of God, and on the other hand, those desiring to be received into the fellowship of the church do so by seeking admission to the holy supper.

It should not be suggested that the form is exclusively, or even primarily, intended for those who are not part of the congregation and now wish to be accepted into the circle of the church.

"Those who are committed to the congregation of the Lord" also applies to baptized children of the congregation, who fundamentally already belong to the church. Though, in principle, belonging to the congregation, they have not yet *committed* themselves to the church as long as they have not yet made the profession of faith. In their inexperienced youth, their parents *brought* them to God's congregation that is the gathered, instituted church. When they are grown, the time comes for them, as members who come of age, publicly to commit to the congregation and to *accept* God's covenant.

So, this *making of a commitment to the congregation, in order to be admitted to the Lord's supper,* according to the Reformed point of view, is identical to (the same as) making profession of faith.

2. THE HISTORY OF CATECHETICAL INSTRUCTION

There was a time, during the first century of the Christian church, when public profession of faith coincided with receiving the sacrament of baptism. These were the days when the church received most of her members from the outside by way of conversion to Christianity.

As a matter of good order, as the church further developed (and the seed of the covenant grew from within), profession of faith was attached to the Lord's supper.

Sad to say, Rome did not, or rather, *wrongly failed* subsequently to sense the connection between profession of faith and communion. From early on, as it became common for the public profession that preceded baptism to take on certain pomp, Rome gradually made the profession of faith of baptized catechumens into a ceremony of its own. They designated such a profession as *confirmation*, also known as *affirmation,* and granted it the character of a *sacramental rite.* The Roman church invoked the statement of Paul: "Now he which stablisheth us with you in Christ, and hath anointed us, is God; Who hath also sealed us, and given the earnest of the Spirit in our hearts" (2 Cor. 1:21–22).

The administration of this new sacrament was at first entrusted only to the bishops. The confirmation ceremony primarily involved the bishop making the sign of the cross, with holy ointments (oil and balsam), upon the forehead of the one confessing and saying: "With the sign of the cross, I seal and confirm you with the oil of salvation in the name of the Father, the Son, and the Holy Ghost." Then there was a laying of hands on the catechumens to symbolize a setting apart and dedication to holy warfare.[2]

Preparation for confirmation was initially quite austere. The church did not involve itself with actual instruction of a child. This was left entirely to the parents and sponsors (godparents). The church

---

2   Cf. P. Biesterveld, *Het Gereformeerde Kerkboek* [*The Reformed Churchbook*] (Kockengen: Het Traktaatgenootschap Filippus, 1903), 232.

did little more than admit children to some religious exercises at which opportunity they were addressed specially in the preaching.

Obviously, with such instruction, the knowledge of the baptized remained scant. Generally, the entire preparation for confirmation was limited to no more than a mechanical recitation of the Apostles' Creed and the Lord's prayer, to which were sometimes added the renunciation formulas and the obligations of baptism.

The Middle Ages brought hardly any changes to this ecclesiastical malaise. There did appear a few catechetical documents (e.g., the Weisenberg Catechism and the exposition of the Apostles' Creed and the Lord's prayer by Alcuin of York). Also, the connection between the church and the child was tightened by involving him in the sacrament of confession. However, a genuine ecclesiastical catechesis was nonexistent. As far as church education went, it bore more the character of training for obedient service to the hierarchy. There occurred virtually nothing more than a perfunctory breeding for submissive membership in the mighty institution.

Also in this respect, the Reformation brought comprehensive and principled change. Over against the violation of the rights and freedom of the individual, the Reformation stood for recognition of the dignity of personhood. Connected to this, the men of the Reformation brought a preparation for profession of faith that was not some sort of training in which essentially the interests of the church were in view, but was a cultivation of the *person* for becoming a mature, thoughtful, and willing member of God's church. And indeed, along this path, the door to the Lord's supper would be opened.

Of all the reformers, this was in no small measure clearly recognized and taught by Calvin.

Luther did react sharply against Rome's confirmation, which in his potent manner he called "monkey business." Also, he strongly championed in-depth instruction, promoted the institution of Christian schools, and even produced more than one catechism himself for such teaching. Nevertheless, he retained confirmation as the goal of catechetical instruction. For him, though, profession of faith was not a mere access to the Lord's supper, but a *Lehr-und Glaubensexamen* (instruction in doctrine and faith) by which the catechumens came to ecclesiastical adulthood.[3]

Calvin also pointedly condemned Rome's confirmation (like Luther, in noteworthy manner, he called it a *singerie*, monkey business), but he went further, to replace the Roman system with a completely different underpinning. He brushed off confirmation, and profession of faith essentially became admittance to the Lord's table. Preparation for profession of faith now occurred chiefly with a catechism that Calvin himself produced. Parents were considered the original, designated instructors of the children. They were to ensure that the children learned the catechism by heart. Then, at appointed times, they would bring them to the minister, who would assess and sharpen their knowledge.

When it came to school-aged children, they would assemble at noon at their school for the teachers to bring them to the catechism class. Moreover, every Sunday afternoon there was a catechism sermon to instruct the youth. Those who ignored this ecclesiastical ordinance would be admonished by the leaders of the congregation. The names of those who failed to respond were reported to the city council.

When it came to catechetical instruction, the reformation in the Netherlands ran along the same Calvinistic line. Already, the 1568 Assembly of Wesel had said that catechization should be considered as belonging to a function of public worship, even declaring this as a practice handed down by the apostles and their disciples.[4] For the Walloon churches, this assembly prescribed the Genevan Catechism, and for the Dutch-speaking churches, the Heidelberg Catechism.

---

3 Cf. P. Biesterveld, *Het karakter der catechese* [*The Character of Catechesis*] (Kampen: J. H. Kok, 1900), 26.
4 *Acta van Wesel*, chap. III, art. 1.

Further, this church gathering, with deep and earnest conviction, made the following, remarkable stipulation:

> That great care be exercised for the children, as appropriate for their age, that they not only externally learn and recite the syllables and words of the catechism, but also can grasp the subject. And that their understanding be not only a matter of the head but also impressed deeply upon their hearts. That is why they should not only be asked to recite the answers but should also be further questioned regarding the clear and complete explanation of the material itself provided by the catechism instructor.
>
> However, highest regard must be given for the catechism to be explained in terms they can process, and for the instruction to take into account the level of the children. There should also be earnest insistence for the parents of the students (the catechumens), as well as their school teachers, that they diligently instruct the children at home and in school, so that what was taught at church will undergo further reflection, and be reinforced with appropriate portions of Scripture.[5]

So, the main purpose of this catechism instruction was now preparation for the Lord's table.

Catechization, profession of faith, and the Lord's supper were like links of one chain, firmly connected, or rather, each developing out of the other like a root, stem, and crown grow into one plant.

Note well what the same Assembly of Wesel determined concerning admission to the Lord's supper:

> No one shall be admitted to holy communion before he has made profession of faith, and has submitted himself to ecclesiastical oversight.

---

5   *Acta van Wesel,* chap. III, art. 3.

Those who desire to be admitted to the Lord's supper shall bring their names to the preacher eight days beforehand. Immediately, an order shall be given in consistory to one or more elders, depending on the circumstances, carefully to inquire concerning their previous life, and thereafter to give opportunity to the consistory in time to speak out if anything stands in the way of admitting these, or on the other hand, continuing the examination.

As to the exam itself, for many reasons it is neither necessary nor advantageous for this to occur in public. It will be sufficient to have it overseen by the ministers, teachers, and itinerant pastors or, if none of these are available, just with elders and the minister. The form in the ecclesiastical liturgy shall direct the procedure.

However, it would not be out of place for the youth who have graduated from catechism to be examined before the entire congregation, eight days before holy communion. Their exam should follow the shorter catechism, to which should be added the main ideas from the large catechism.

Those who are satisfactorily examined, be they youth or be they adults, shall present themselves before the congregation days before the administration of the Lord's supper. Each one shall be confronted with the chief articles of the faith, so that they may express their agreement with them. They at the same time subject themselves to church discipline. Their names are to be inscribed in the book of members of the church. Then, after the congregation has been informed, there being no objections, at a later day they are admitted to the holy supper.[6]

These stipulations from the time of the Reformation reveal not only how seriously they took preparation for profession of faith, but

---

6   *Acta van Wesel,* chap. VI, art. 7–11.

also how close and natural the connection between the profession and the Lord's supper.

This earnest intention also came to light at subsequent synods during the Reformation. In fact, there was hardly any ecclesiastical assembly ever held where there was not some discussion regarding the subject of the *catechization, profession of faith*, and *Lord's supper* trilogy.

The 1574 Synod of Dordt officially decided that catechetical instruction should be based on the Heidelberg Catechism and that it be left to the discretion of the ministers to allow some to be instructed in the Short Examination.[7]

Similar positions were taken by the Synods of Dordt in 1578, Middelburg in 1581, and The Hague in 1586, until this distinguished component was made a permanent regulation at the Great Synod of Dordt (1618–19).

3. CATECHIZATION AND THE SYNOD OF DORDT

It was in the fourteenth session that this subject was first broached and specifically handled in terms of the necessity of catechism preaching when the attendance was particularly meager. By the end of this session, a request was advanced to the synod "to come up with an appropriate way to better instruct the youth and the parents in the Reformed Christian religion."

The foreign theologians submitted their advice in the fifteenth session. And in the seventeenth session, the synodical decision regarding catechism instruction was adopted.

Synod determined that there would be three types of catechism instruction: in the homes by the parents, in the schools by the schoolteachers, and in the churches by the ministers, elders, and pastoral assistants.

The calling of the office of *parents* is to instruct their children

---

7   Here the synod was referring to *The Short Examination of Faith* by à Lasco, which was printed before the Lord's supper form.

in the principles of the Christian faith, to inculcate the fear of the Lord, to require Scripture memorization, to prepare them, with simple explanations from Scripture, for catechism lessons in school, and later to prompt them, and also to go over the sermons with them, especially the Catechism sermons. Parents who appeared to neglect these obligations would be admonished and, if necessary, disciplined.

In the schools as well, the children would be diligently instructed in the fundamentals of the Christian faith. At least twice a week the catechism for the youth should be instilled and explained.

Three catechisms would be used in the schools for this purpose.

The smallest catechism, for the youngest children, would consist of the Apostles' Creed, the ten commandments, and the Lord's prayer, the institution of the sacraments and church discipline, a few prayers, questions pertaining to the catechism, and some Scriptures to inspire godliness.

The second catechism would be the Compendium of the Heidelberg Catechism for the more advanced students.

And finally, the Heidelberg Catechism itself shall be taught.

The instructors should take heed that their instruction makes the sense and substance of the questions well understood. They must also see to it that the children are brought along to hear the sermons and later to review the messages with them. To ensure that all this is happening, the minister with an elder and, when necessary, a government representative shall audit this work.

As far as *ecclesiastical* catechization goes, ministers must so direct their preaching of catechism sermons so that that they can also be understood by the youth. Those in their later years, or any who have never attended school, shall be assembled together every week to be instructed by the minister. And those who intend to join the church shall be instructed frequently and diligently for three to four weeks prior to the administration of the Lord's supper.[8]

---

8   Cf. Biesterveld, *Het karakter der catechese,* 43–44.

What was going on in terms of synod's decision regarding this threefold catechization plan warrants further explanation.

The fact is, for an extended time, the catechism for the youngest children had as good as disappeared. However, the second-level catechism, better known as the Compendium, was in use for catechetical instruction. There were churches where this compendium replaced the main catechism altogether and became the only textbook for instruction. To the contrary, in yet other places, only the catechism itself was esteemed and any use of the Compendium, even as a teaching aid in instruction, was entirely rejected.

So what was going on?

When in the seventeenth session the synod made the decision regarding this threefold catechetical instruction, the delegates from Classis Zeeland appeared to have already indicated that they had in hand an abridgment (i.e., the Compendium) of the catechism used in their churches. This Compendium had been written in 1608 under the direction of the consistory of Middelberg by the ministers of their church (primarily Rev. Faukelius) and was included in the official publication of the confessions and the liturgy (R. Schilders, 1611).[9]

Also, the delegates from the Palatinate appear to have brought to attention their own abridgment of the catechism that was in use.

Synod then decided that a committee they appointed to care for both of the smaller catechisms (Professors Gomarus, Polyander, and Thysinus, and the ministers Faukelius, Lydius, and Udemannus) was to make use of these abridgments in their work but, as much as possible, follow the wording of the large catechism.

In the 177th Session, the appointed committee submitted their report.

---

9   Cf. H. Kuyper, *De Post-acta,* 277ff. Due to the fact that this Compendium lacked ecclesiastical sanction, Faukelius had placed it at the end, after the liturgical documents. The questions for admission to the Lord's supper, to this point, had stood after the Compendium. However, Faukelius placed them, with some modifications, before the Lord's supper in the 1611 edition. So, in the publication of our form (i.e., the Rutgers edition) this is correct order followed.

The Post-Acta mentions what happened:

> It is determined that those delegated by synod for this have
> already recommended the usage of the two smaller cate-
> chisms, instead of the large catechism, in the instruction of
> the tender youth. The smallest is then read and approved,
> with the condition that it be supplemented with material
> from the large catechism. Regarding the other one, that is
> somewhat larger, the president determines that it need not
> be read before the synod for the sake of time. It is then
> approved that the churches may make use of these, or oth-
> ers, such as that which the Middelberg church had drafted
> and distributed.

From these comments, one might assume that the Synod of
Dordt was rather indifferent as to which of the three catechisms
should enjoy preference in the churches. In reality, however, the
synod had established the priority of the large catechism over the
others, by explicit declaration, when it determined that the Heidelberg Catechism is "the most suitable textbook for the youth as well as
the adults" (148th Session).

There appears to be some conflict between this declaration and
the above decision to allow the smaller catechisms.

Indeed, it appears that synod had some hindsight regret regarding the decision they took in the seventeenth session, "that the
churches from now on would use all three catechisms." From the
notes of Heyngius (which were confirmed by Voetius), there is indication that it was not so vague.[10] In any case, Heyngius shares the
following:

> It is to be understood that a small and brief *Extract* was to
> be taken from the *Catechism* and introduced to the grow-
> ing children, and to that yet another, a bit larger, for those

---

10 H. Kuyper, *De Post-acta*, 273–74.

somewhat older, and so begin to be prepared for the Lord's supper. Both in this order were certainly intended by this synod.

But these documents should not be considered by the people as new catechisms, nor cause any confusion in the congregation that would degrade (or discredit) the adopted catechism. So it was approved that, guided by the usual cate-chism, to the ABC book used in the schools, from the small and brief extracts just read, a few questions should be added. And concerning the other, that one, instead of a brief exam-ination, recommend to the churches the form composed to such an end by that of Middelberg.

While not making a declaration *against* the use of an abbreviated catechism and at the same time *recommending* the Compendium of Faukelius, synod was apparently unwilling to draft a new, abbreviated catechism of her own to offer to the churches. From there, the fact that it had been decided that a few questions should supplement the old, already-used little ABC book, and that the already-established Com-pendium of the Zeeland churches had been recommended, synod was in line with the concept submitted by the synodical committee.

The fathers of Dordt were reluctant to do anything that would be able to overshadow the Heidelberg Catechism. Also in future synods, the churches remained faithful to this principle.

When at the 1620 Provincial Synod of South Holland, some were insisting that the form introduced by the committee to the Synod of Dordt was submitted to the churches, it was answered in this way:

It is to be duly noted that the catechization process, above all, according to the decision of the National Synod, be introduced into the churches, with as much harmony and as seamless as possible, for which the synod esteems most expe-dient of all to be that one follow the *course of the Christian catechism*. For all that, in case anyone in particular would prefer to use a resource such as the document of Faukelius, or one from someone else, they are free to do so.

Clearly, the use of the Heidelberg Catechism was established as the *standard*, and the assistance of the Compendium, or another catechism booklet, was indeed left to discretion but not absolutely recommended.[11]

Thus, those who for catechization *replaced the catechism* with the Compendium, and nothing other than this little book was used, also for the adults, were operating in conflict with the spirit and the principle of the fathers of Dordt.

On the other side, however, also unjust and one-sided was condemnation of any use of the Compendium. The little catechism of Faukelius was indeed recognized with approval and recommended as a valid resource. And that the opinion of the churches agreed on this wholeheartedly is evident in that since 1637 the Compendium has received a place among the liturgical documents. Thus, the respectable little book of Faukelius had in a certain sense procured citizenship and could most certainly serve as a resource in catechetical instruction. In some places, it did with justification completely transcend the large catechism (e.g., where under the means of grace, which strengthen faith, it mentions the gospel, which is omitted by the catechism). Indeed, apart from the intrinsic qualities of the Compendium, experience teaches that for many who are somewhat sluggish of comprehension, a certain little book of repetition is indispensable. Merely in few churches is the spiritual development and the intellectual, conceptual abilities so high that a Compendium would be completely superfluous.

Therefore, the Short Examination has received the place she deserved. One does not scorn this little golden book that for centuries accomplished its blessed work, but the *place of honor* is always assigned to the Heidelberg Catechism. And now, as the principle for

---

11 H. Kuyper, *De Post-acta*, 276.

catechetical instruction, *the catechism, standard—the Compendium, supplement.*

4. THE AUTHENTIC CHARACTER OF CATECHIZATION

The care that the Reformation awakened for the upcoming generation was both remarkable and shaming. The instruction extended at cost to the seed of the covenant was as broad as it was deep.

The church was not content only to inculcate the main truths upon the youth; she sought to convince the catechumen of the excellence of the Reformed doctrine, and gave him in hand the response to defend the precious truths of salvation against the enemy.

Voetius and others insisted that the instruction not limit catechization to the basic truths (fundamentals), but also include how to do battle against errors. Otherwise, such ignorance would make the congregation vulnerable.[12] Also, Koelman, in his *Ambt en Plichten der Ouderlingen en Diakenen,*[13] emphasized that the "young men and women" be catechized in the controversies with various religions, such as against the Papists, Socinians, Remonstrants, etc.[14] Many also held that those who already had been permitted to the Lord's supper should have ongoing instruction.

In large measure, under the blessing of God, the Reformed church has owed her exemplary flowering to the conscientious and comprehensive instruction of the youth. Catechization awakened a generation that understood the truth and could follow Reformed preaching in its deepest expeditions. The congregation sensed not only her richness in possessing the Reformed faith, but also in grasping her calling to walk according to those truths *in the life of*

---

12 Gisbertus Voetius, *Politica Ecclesiastica* [*Ecclesiastical Polity*] *I-III* (Amsterdam: Johannem Janssonium á Waesberge, & Elizeum Weyerstraet, 1663). Cf. Biesterveld, *Karakter der Catetechese,* 50–51.

13 Jacobus Koelman, *Het Ambt en de Pligten der Ouderlingen en Diakenen* [*The Office and Duties of Elders and Deacons*], ed. S. Van Velzen ('sGravenhage: J. Van Golverdinge, 1837).

14 Cf. Biesterveld, *Het karakter der catechese,* 52.

the church. Those who professed their faith knew that thereby they were bound to the Lord's supper. Catechization ripened them for the proclamation of the Lord's death in the midst of the congregation. It was not like a little church within the church, or an exclusive club of calibrated piety within a chaos of the unconverted, but a strongly organized *church* of confessing believers who had deliberately placed themselves under the discipline of the Reformed faith.

Nevertheless, there was yet one *misunderstanding* with respect to catechism instruction that the fathers didn't foresee, and that did not a little damage to the proper development of church life. In the days of the Reformation, and for long afterward, the right relationship between the *family, school, and the church* was not envisioned. The school was too often considered a component of church life. The school was a creation and maidservant of the church. And a significant part of catechization was conducted by the school teachers, which the minister, for the most part, merely supervised as to whether the teacher was faithful to his task. For some, it was indeed a question as to whether it belonged to the office of the minister of the word to catechize the youth. In his *Politica Ecclesiastica*, Voetius had to extensively refute various objections that were leveled against the idea of catechization conducted by the minister.

Eventually, true light dawned upon Reformed territory regarding the relationship of the family, school, and church.

The place where instruction originates is in the *family*. Parents are not only responsible for their nurture; they themselves are the nurturers of their own offspring. The baptism form says, "Parents are *in duty bound* further to instruct their children herein when they shall arrive to years of discretion." And in the "Exhortation to the Parents" it says: "Do you promise and intend *to instruct* these children, as soon as they are able to understand, in the aforesaid doctrine, and cause them to be instructed therein."

Now this parental instruction is not only to tell them Bible stories, or even to warn and correct them in case of disobedience, but to have intentional conversations with the children regarding the matter of their baptism, over their *membership* in the covenant of grace and, in connection with this, their enduring responsibilities that this covenant requires. What could be more obvious here than that *they* who present the child for baptism into God's covenant (and thus for the child to progress in the ecclesiastical realm), that they immediately, as it pertains to the child, teach this serious enterprise and guide them into the mindset of the covenant of grace? The men of the Reformation deeply felt and earnestly advocated for parents to assume this responsibility with respect to the children of the covenant.

And so, not only is this involved in the words just cited from the baptism form, but also what the Synod of Dordt determined as *home catechization*. Indeed, the question may be asked as to whether home catechization is still upheld by Reformed families today. That is to say, are parents still *instructing* their children in the substance of the covenant of grace? Do they understand their calling as the natural, God-ordained instructors of their descendants?

A survey regarding the state of home catechization would not deliver encouraging results. Home catechization is not flourishing. In countless families, it is barely recognizable. Its existence and necessity are not presumed by many homes.

Accounting for this situation, it may certainly be noted that the peace of domestic life and therefore home life itself is harmed immeasurably in these restless times. The taskmaster drives us relentlessly in "the battlefield of life." There is no more time for peaceful, intentional devotion to a child in the family.

With this comes the fact that instruction outside the family has picked up its pace. School education is flourishing as never before. Church instruction is exercised more earnestly than ever. Does it not make sense, then, for father and mother to hand their children over to teachers outside the home as much as possible, and that the instruction of the covenant *is left* completely to them?

Clearly, this fact is *understandable*, but it is nonetheless *inexcusable*.

When life's work lays such a burden on a person that he cannot make one hour of room in his week for the children God has entrusted to him, then something in this societal wasteland must change. And so, the question cannot be avoided: In all seriousness, among the most committed parents, are there not few to be found that will take a stand for a peaceful home life? For what did God give his *Sabbath* to mankind?

And further, may the flourishing of education outside the home ever be a ground for neglecting parental instruction? When one organ of the body develops, is another left to die? Or is it not precisely the budding of one branch of learning that stimulates new growth to come to others? With the general progression of culture, improvements in technology, and the advancement of knowledge, parents can and must, more than ever before, make an impression upon the *geest* of their children. In this respect, contemporary society has so much more than former generations. We are better off than our fathers, so let us also devote *more* to our descendants. Let home catechization in Reformed territory experience a complete revival in new power and in the highest degree!

After home catechization comes *school education*.

In a Reformed framework, the school is not an institution of the church, but of the parents. Nevertheless, it is not an extension of the family, but operates on its own basis. It is intended to lead the child into the world-and-life-view sphere of the cosmos[15] (creation living in general). It shapes a person in order to fulfill his calling as a *person* for accomplishing his task in the domain of culture. It has an eye for the work of society. That is why the school may not be a miniature church, much less an evangelistic or correctional agency. She exists

---

15 Abraham Kuyper, *Encyclopaedie der Heilige Godgeleerdheid* [*The Encyclopedia of Sacred Theology*] III (Kampen: J. H. Kok, 1908), 508.

in the territory of common grace and must seek her excellence on those terms.

Naturally, this does not preclude that she also has a task for the life of special grace. How otherwise could it be a *Christian* school? Indirectly, she also cultivates for the church, for the kingdom of God, for heaven. That is why also theological instruction (*sit venia verbo*) must have a place in the school. Children should be taught not only Bible history but also Bible doctrine. Also, the catechism belongs to the instructional material for its teaching, and it is in this sense that there is, and must be, *school catechization.*

Nevertheless, so there is no blurring of the boundaries, this instruction must have its own character, distinguishing it from ecclesiastical catechization. In the school, theological study must have its own department, albeit a division enfolded within the basis for education.[16]

5. THE PURPOSE AND MEANING OF THE EXAMINATION OF FAITH

In light of the foregoing, the purpose and meaning of an "examination" of the faith becomes clear.

Along the lines of Calvinism (with its primacy of the intellect!) falls the emphasis upon *doctrine.*

"All those," as goes the introduction to the Lord's supper formulary, "who are committed to the congregation of God and desire to be admitted to the Lord's supper, must first be instructed in *the articles of the Christian faith* from God's word."

Though our fathers upheld doctrine with rigor (dogma was for them a supreme and inviolable asset), they were yet familiar with restraint regarding the method for instructing that doctrine (i.e., *catechetical* instruction) as evident in what comes next: "The form and

---

16 Biesterveld, Ibid., 61.

manner of such instruction in the churches is to be that which is deemed most edifying."

Following instruction, then, comes *profession.* This is, according to the Reformed conception, basically an affirmation of the doctrine. Nevertheless, it is not along Romish lines of an absolute bowing before the dogma of the church, setting aside the rights of the individual, but a free and personal assent to the doctrine of salvation from a mature, inner conviction.

Therefore follows what is so characteristically Reformed: "So when they have attained a basic understanding and confession of the articles of the faith, they are to be asked whether there remain any doubts (regarding the doctrine) so that they may be satisfied. If they answer in the affirmative, one tries to satisfy them from Holy Scripture."

From this perspective on profession of the faith follows that it includes a promise regarding *life.* Not an intellectual, let alone theoretical, comprehension and profession of doctrine is sufficient. A true profession requires submission of the whole person to true doctrine.

From there is the second question: "When their doubts are dispelled, ask them if they intend to remain committed to the aforesaid doctrine, to forsake the world, and to lead a new, Christian life."

Since the bond between the professed doctrine and the Christian life is monitored and strengthened by discipline that the church exercises among her members, the church then also has the right to request a promise of obedience to ecclesiastical admonition: "Finally, one asks if they are also willing to submit themselves to the discipline of the church."

In expressing the matter this way, it is clear that it was not the intention of the framers to formulate the actual questions that come with profession of faith. We discover here more of a description than a prescription. The churches are free to formulate their own questions while remaining true to the model, namely, that they cover the three subjects of doctrine, life, and discipline.

In some churches, it is common to use the questions from the baptism formulary for adults. Such usage has some attraction because the baptism of adults involves a conscious profession and commitment and grants access to the use of the sacraments. But, with justification, the objection that has been raised regarding the use of these questions is that baptism (including that of adults) first of all concerns a commitment to the church itself. The baptismal candidate is viewed as standing outside the church and now, by profession of faith and baptism, is admitted into the fellowship of the church. However, when it comes to the profession of baptized members, those making their profession are considered as associated with the church in a sense. With profession, they become *mature* members. When asking the same questions for the profession of faith of the seed of the congregation as those used by the baptism of adults, it gives the wrong impression, that one must first make a public profession in order to become a member of the church.[17]

However, should one value profession to operate as much as possible in the language of the fathers, then the last two questions in the baptism form for adults could be taken and divided into three questions as follows:

1. Dost thou assent to all the articles of the Christian religion as they are taught here in this Christian church according to the word of God, and purpose steadfastly to continue in the same doctrine to the end of thy life; and also, dost thou reject all heresies and errors in conflict with this doctrine?

2. Dost thou promise to persevere in the communion of our Christian church, not only in the hearing of the word, but also in the use of the Lord's supper?

3. Hast thou taken a firm resolution always to lead a Christian life; to forsake the world and its evil lusts, as is

---

17 Cf. Biesterveld, *Het Gereformeerde Kerkboek*, 235.

becoming the members of Christ and his church; and to submit thyself to all Christian admonitions?

Voetius provided as an example the following questions (which are still in use by many churches down to the present day):

1. Dost thou declare to hold the doctrine of our church, in so far as[18] thou hast been taught, hath heard and professed, to be the true and saving doctrine, in harmony with the holy Scriptures?
2. Dost thou promise, by the grace of God, to remain fully committed to this profession of the saving doctrine, whether in life or in death?
3. Dost thou promise, in harmony with this doctrine, with constant faithfulness, honesty, and integrity to direct your life, and to adorn your profession with good works?
4. Dost thou promise willingly to subject thyself to the warnings, corrections, and ecclesiastical discipline and shall be submissive should it occur (may God forbid) that thou in doctrine or life should go astray?

It could be noted that in these questions not enough comes out regarding the character of profession as to the acceptance of baptism and one's commitment to the supper of the Lord. With this in view, I offer the following questions that are used in the church of Utrecht, and (I think) are preferable.

1. *Dost thou understand the doctrine contained in the Old and New Testaments, as summarized in the forms of unity of the Reformed churches (the Belgic Confession, Heidelberg Catechism, and Canons of Dordt), and as taught here*

---

18 Cf. Ibid., 236. Prof. Biesterveld has rightly noted that it would be better, in order to preclude limitations in the profession, to read "that" in the place of "in so far as."

> *in this Christian church, without doubt, to be the true and complete doctrine of salvation?*
>
> 2. *Dost thou intend (i.e., by your personal decision) to remain in that doctrine, dependent upon God's grace, and so to seek your life and salvation outside yourself in Christ, to love the God of your baptism, to forsake the world, put to death your old nature, and to confirm this profession of faith with a godly life?*
>
> 3. *Art thou of mind and heart, to seek diligently the administration of the word and sacraments for yourself, as true members of the church of Christ, with the condition that if thou go astray in doctrine or life (may God forbid!), you will submit to the Christian admonition of discipline?*

In my opinion, this strikes it precisely.

It comes out clearly that the profession is acceptance of the doctrine of Scripture, as it is summarized and rendered by *the church* in her formularies. But there is also a tangible connection, on the one hand, between profession and baptism and, on the other hand, between profession and communion. Thus preserved is the continuity and unity of church life.

The point is that if authentic catechesis is an introduction to the reflections-and-ideas world of the church,[19] then also the profession, which can be called the completion and sealing of catechetical instruction, must be a presentation of what the church teaches and establishes. Thus, in the profession of faith, the emphasis falls on the intellect, rather than the will or the emotions of the one professing. Prof. Biesterveld is correct where he deals with catechetical preparation for the profession.[20]

This character of catechization, as leading to the second sacrament, distinguishes us from all subjectivism and methodism. These

---

19 A. Kuyper, *Encyclopaedie*, III, 505.
20 Biesterveld, *Karakter der Catetechese*, 72.

directions would sidetrack catechization into various personal inclinations and prevent giving oneself to the Lord's service. Such emotional stirrings of the soul can then be grounded and directed to the Lord's supper. For here is all of life, rather than the constant repetition of changing emotions, or the frailness of the past. Then, assurance of faith is missing; empowerment for daily living cannot be awakened; existing and thinking as a Christian is consumed by the emotional life.

Therefore, authentic Reformed profession is first of all an act of the intellect, not in the sense of a raw intellectualism, but in the sense of living knowledge that abides in the enlightened and sanctified mind of a Christian.

As the above questions indicate, actions of the will and the emotions are not excluded. The promise, "to confirm this profession of faith with a godly life," can only be realized by an act of the will. The true profession elicits a captivated heart and holy, mystical feelings of personal love for the Lord Jesus Christ. With earnestness, the Reformed church of all ages has warned against a mere historical faith.

Nevertheless, acceptance of the *doctrine* of the church remains primary in the profession of faith. Only then does the real *ecclesiastical character* of profession step into the light to live its enduring obligation unto new godliness. By virtue of the *sacrament of baptism* resting upon the professing one from youth, out of holy responsibility, he also, publicly, comes to celebrate *the Lord's supper* and to participate in all the activities of ecclesiastical life from now on with the congregation of God.

And it is sensed that the profession is not an "acceptance" or "confirmation" of "new members." Rather, it is a public declaration that the *baptized member* of the church is now full-grown to mature membership (*membra completa*).

In this way, the church has God's blessing and can expect a blossoming spiritual life. The church blossoms by *faith*.

And...by *love.*

Authentic profession of faith is a commitment to the church not only as institute, but also as *congregation,* i.e., the gathering of *believers.* Those who publicly connect to the congregation of God connect personally to all her members. The public profession of faith is also a profession of the *communion of the saints.*

That said, well sensed and rightly placed are the final words of the introduction to the Lord's supper form: "When they have promised this, then admonish them to peace, love, and unity with everyone, and to reconcile with anyone with whom they may have unfinished business."

In the heart of a true professor of the faith resounds the echo of the benediction that the Old Testament vocalist proclaims to the Jerusalem of God:

> "Let peace abide in thee for aye,
> May naught disturb thee now or ever."
> By reason of his temple fair
> And for the mercy proffered there,
> Will I invoke thy good forever.[21]

And then shall the King of the church, in answer to this promise, that other psalm confer upon his people:

> So they who dwell in peace no want shall know,
> For there the LORD their God His blessing sends
> And grants the life that never ends.[22]

---

21 Tr. *Genevan Psalter* 122, trans. Dewey Westra.
22 Tr. *Genevan Psalter* 133, trans. Dewey Westra.

Chapter Three

THE COMMENCEMENT OF COMMUNION

1. THE ADDRESS OF THE FORM

Following the introductory remarks regarding the "examination of the faith," the actual form for the Lord's supper begins, and does so with a solemn tone:

> Beloved in the Lord Jesus Christ, attend to the words of the institution of the holy supper of our Lord Jesus Christ, as they are delivered by the holy apostle Paul (1 Cor. 11:23–30).

> *For I have received of the Lord, that which also I delivered unto you, that the Lord Jesus the same night in which he was betrayed, took bread; and when he had given thanks, he brake it, and said, Take, eat; this is my body which is broken for you, this do in remembrance of me. And after the same manner also, he took the cup, when he had supped, saying, This cup is the new testament in my blood; this do ye, as oft as ye drink it in remembrance of me; for as oft as ye eat this bread, and drink this cup, ye do show the Lord's death till he come. Wherefore, whosoever shall eat this bread, or drink this cup of the Lord unworthily, shall be guilty of the body and blood of the Lord. But let a man examine himself, and so let him eat of that bread, and drink of that cup; for he that eateth and drinketh unworthily, eateth and drinketh judgment to himself, if he discern not the body of the Lord.*

This sounds like an overture that is preparing the hearts of the listeners for pure enjoyment.

If an overture is fitting for the piece, then it must not only prepare the way for the soul by setting the right *tonality*, but also by providing preparatory grounding for the coming theme of the music.

Both of these requirements are met in the "prelude" to the holy cantata for the banquet of King Jesus. It not only necessarily ushers the gathered congregation into the broader movement of listening to the Lord's supper form (indeed, a song in prose!), but also in advance is weaving in the theme of the form itself.

Truly, one could not begin celebration of the holy meal with more powerful, richer language than as happens here with Scripture's own language that stands out so beautiful in form, so robust in content.

With this preface of commencement words from Scripture, the Lord's supper form, from a liturgical viewpoint, is more refined and more fully developed than the baptism form that, lacking such an introduction, begins immediately with instruction.[1]

We have Calvin to thank for this fortuitous asset. In his form, after the Apostles' Creed that follows the introductory prayer, begins the actual form: "Attend to the words of the institution of the holy supper of our Lord Jesus Christ, as they were delivered by the holy apostle Paul in the 11th chapter of the First Letter to the Corinthians." In this way, the London form, as well as ours, followed Calvin.

Only with the very first words is there a difference. In our Lord's supper form, the instruction begins with addressing the gathered congregation as *beloved in the Lord Jesus Christ*.

This designation is not without meaning. It provides the standpoint that Reformed believers, those from of old as well as those continuing, are comprised as members of the covenant.

---

1   Cf. Wielenga, *The Reformed Baptism Form,* 23. "It starts abruptly without leading us through a golden gate."

Also, the baptism form begins the admonition to the covenant members (the baptism parents) with the address, "Beloved in Christ the Lord!" While it is true that this expression is not taken literally from Scripture, the idea is pure Scripture. The apostles address the congregation as beloved brothers, called to be saints, believers in Christ Jesus, sanctified in Christ Jesus, beloved of God. It might appear that the address, beloved in Christ Jesus, is weaker than the scriptural titles cited. When Paul calls the believers at Rome *beloved of God*, he expresses the rich thought that the Roman Christians are *loved by God*. But here, the minister expresses that *he himself* loves the congregation. This is the language of the communion of the saints, not first of all that of fellowship with God.[2]

Still, there is more in this designation than a solitary declaration from the side of the minister that he loves his congregation. This has to do here with the love in *the Lord Jesus*. The communion of the saints is in the root, according to the sense of the catechism, a communion with Christ. Therefore, the minister speaks to his listeners as those who have a portion with the King and the Lord of the Lord's supper, not only with respect to the external bond of confession, but also the inner bond of true faith.[3]

Therefore, when the minister begins the reading of the form with the words, *Beloved in the Lord Jesus*, he directs himself to *the people of God*.

---

2   There are those who have different thoughts, for example, Jacobus van Houte in his lengthy explanation of the Lord's supper form, with the title, *Het formulier des heilgen nagtmaals verklaard en praktikaal uitgebreid...* [*The Formulary for Holy Communion Expounded and Practically Explained...*] (Leiden: Joh. Hasebroek en Zoon, 1761), 67ff. Van Houte is remarkably tame with respect to the designation of the forms that he explains as "those who love the Lord Jesus and are loved by him, not only with a love of good intentions, but also with a love of good deeds." There is no insinuation that we here have to do with a noteworthy example of exposition.

3   In stark contrast with this understanding of the declaration of the formulary's designation is Van Houte, who otherwise proposes the supposition that the framers of the expression were intending, in a broad sense, a general love for others that is a primary requirement of the minister for those who need to be affected by the gospel. Also the unconverted would then be embraced by this designation. Ibid., 72ff.

Thus, to *the congregation of Christ*, because the congregation is the people of God. Not that every external member of the congregation is also inwardly a member of Christ—not all who are called Israel are of Israel—but the congregation as such is the gathering of true Christ-believers, washed by the blood of the Lamb. She is not a bifurcated association of converted and unconverted, living and dead, but a *body*, a gathering of true believers, albeit in which also hypocrites are mingled, like wheat mixed with tares. The apostles also spoke of the congregation as the gathering of the living children of God even though, as we all know, the church on earth is not completely pure.

Beloved in the Lord Jesus—so the gentle sound wafts over the gathered multitude. This language conveys that which is deeply personal and warm, an encouragement to embrace with abandonment the riches of the covenant of grace, and to be fully aware of the privilege to be a child of God.

Also, note this, that here the covenant member is not directly called God's beloved. The minister is the one who addresses them as beloved, not only personally, but also officially, that is, in the name of his king. Even in his designation of the congregation is he the messenger of peace, and so here administers the word: How beautiful upon the mountains are the feet of him that bringeth good tidings, those that say unto Zion, your God is King!

2. THE WORDS OF THE INSTITUTION

Attend to the words of the institution of the holy supper of our Lord Jesus Christ.

This too is the language of awakening, which breathes in the enriched aroma of the covenant of grace. Let the word of God—the word entrusted to you, the book of the covenant—tell you how the Lord's supper was instituted, how it was bestowed upon you, what it has for you, and to whom it is given.

Listen, beloved! Incline your soul's ear, not to a man, but to your God. Attention! Your covenantal God speaks!

And what does he say?

Through his instrument—and what a finely tuned instrument—the holy apostle Paul, he reveals the history, the fact, of the institution. When your hungry soul seeks refreshment at this banquet and you do this believing that this means for strengthening your life in grace is ordained by God, then you are not pursuing some artistic, fictitious fables. Paul, led by the Spirit, writes to the Corinthians, to the people of God of all ages:

> *For I have received of the Lord, that which also I delivered unto you, that the Lord Jesus, the same night in which he was betrayed, took bread; and when he had given thanks, he brake it, and said, Take, eat; this is my body which is broken for you, this do in remembrance of me. And after the same manner also, he took the cup, when he had supped, saying, This cup is the new testament in my blood; this do ye, as oft as ye drink it in remembrance of me!*

Obviously, the framers of the words of the institution could have also borrowed from one of the gospel writers (Matt. 36:20–29; Mark 14:22–24; Luke 22:19–20). However, they preferred the further developed word that the apostle received from the ascended Savior and applied to congregational life. However, so that the historical word of the evangelists would not be missing in the formulary, the framers in due course introduce the gospel period where the form says:

> And that we might firmly believe that we belong to this covenant of grace, the Lord Jesus Christ, in his last supper, took bread, and when he had given thanks, he brake it, and gave it to his disciples and said, *"Take, eat, this is my body which is given for you, this do in remembrance of me!"* In like manner after supper he took the cup, gave thanks and gave it to them saying, *"Drink ye all of it; this cup is the new testament in my*

blood, which is shed for you and for many, for the remission of sins; this do as often as ye drink it in remembrance of me!"

These citations from the gospel complete Paul's words. It would have been regrettable had they been absent from the form. But where by way of introduction the *fact* of the institution must be established, certainly the citation from Paul's letter is more appropriate.

One would not here already analyze this rich pericope in every detail. In many respects, we would be getting ahead of the explanation of the form itself. Nevertheless, the Pauline word, which speaks the language of obligation to our mind and heart, must be further elucidated.

3. LORD'S SUPPER AND LOVE FEAST

A primary complaint that the apostle brings up in his letter to the Corinthians dealt with the Lord's supper. Granted, it was not long after the institution itself that the supper was refined and developed by the introduction of love feasts, but in places where spiritual life had in a measure also deteriorated—as was the case in Corinth. And precisely there the refined form of the celebration led to grave abuse.

The practice in those days was that the love feast (*agapé*) preceded the actual Lord's supper. For this meal, the wealthier ones would bring extra food to share so that those who were poor could enjoy the favor of God's blessings. In serving the meal, the practice was representing the unity of God's people with respect to material goods.[4]

When everyone at this feast had been refreshed and their hearts were resonating with joy in the Lord for the wonder of loving fellowship, they eventually went on to the celebration of the spiritual, sacred meal that was instituted by Jesus himself. After they had first enjoyed their love for one another in the communion of the saints,

---

4 In my opinion, Godet is correct where he says that nevertheless, this material, earthly character of the love feast did not rule out that this meal was itself a religious act. Frédéric Louis Godet, *Commentary on St. Paul's First Epistle to the Corinthians*, 2, trans. A. Cusin (Edinburgh: T & T Clark, 1890), 144.

now together they were seeking the greater good, the binding love of Immanuel, with the desire that through the proclamation of the abundant blessing of his death, they would bring honor to the Living Potentate.

Indeed, a high measure of spirituality would be required for such a communion celebration to be truly spiritual. But it was possible because the congregation was filled with the Holy Spirit, and the communion of the saints blossomed in an exemplary manner. The love feast *propelled* them to the Lord of the supper and prepared their hearts for partaking of the sacrament.

Truly, an anticipation (foretaste) of life in heaven itself![5]

The received revelation of the kingdom of heaven also in its external beauty!

But all the greater was the collapse when the glory of that spiritual life in the congregation began to deteriorate and the external form no longer reflected the internal. Then materialized the *corruptio optimi pessima*.[6] The Lord's supper became scandalous when the love feast, abandoning true love, degenerated into a sort of party where the rich

---

5   Gunning, *Waarom niet toegetreden*, 23. Gunning meditates on this in his excellent explanation on the Lord's supper formulary where he writes: "Don't you find the *thought* compelling, disarmingly beautiful? Imagine that our meal times were as such, so personal, so tender that, without blushing, they could conclude with the celebration of the Lord's supper. That we could so enjoy the gifts of God for body and soul, that our affections are so irresistibly drawn to the idea of the Highest Love, that our sharing and unity with one another is elevated! And further—*couldn't* it really be like that? And then, mutual fellowship culminates *precisely* when the Lord sets his seal upon it as we receive the body and blood. Sadly, sadly, we are so stuck in the totality of our everyday lives, that the idea of including an ordinary meal with communion would barely cross our salvation mindset! Today, the Lord's supper exists far *above* our everyday level of existence. Many assume that to get to that higher plain they must first work up a spiritual high by various means. And even more despair of ever reaching such heights, and remain ever behind." How true! But, in my opinion, Gunning goes too far when he entirely aligns the love feast with a regular meal. The agape meal was part of the Lord's supper, the *introduction* and *preparation* for communion. When Paul speaks of the Lord's supper in 1 Corinthians 11, the love feast is therein included.

6   When corruption of the best becomes the worst.

reveled in their abundance and the poor observed in their hunger, anguished in soul by the excessiveness of his brother.

Paul is addressing this situation in the verses of the cited pericope with which our form begins.

"*When you come together*," he says in verse 20, "*this is not to eat the Lord's supper.*"

The "come together" is here the *congregational* gathering for the celebration of communion, as is apparent in verse 18: "When ye come together *in the church*, I hear that..."

But the gatherings as the Corinthians were conducting them were not entitled to the name of the Lord's supper. "*This is not,*" says Paul with deep indignation, "*this is not* to eat the Lord's supper." It is morally impossible to celebrate the supper rightly in this manner.

"*For,*" the apostle continues, "*in eating every one taketh before other his own supper,*" i.e., before the meal was served to all the guests present, some had already begun to eat the provisions they had brought for the occasion. In cross egotism ignoring the others, they immediately dove into their own meal.[7] The result was that the ones, namely the poor, who were counting on the contribution of the rich received nothing—"*the one is hungry.*" And the rich overindulged in lasciviousness—"*and another is drunken.*"

"*What? have ye not houses,*" asks Paul, "*to eat and to drink in? or despise ye the church of God* (you who are conducting yourself offensively), *and shame them that have not?*"

And then further, with harsh irony, this indictment: "*What shall I say to you? shall I praise you in this? I praise you not.*"

This *not-praising* is sharper than a reprimand. It betrays a restrained wrath.

So that the congregation will listen, as to how divine the supper is in its origin and therefore how holy it is in its character. So that the

---

7   The idea that the apostle is referencing the rich who had eaten *before at home* is not accurate. That does not fit the context and conflicts with the prevailing practice of the love feasts.

congregation will yet understand what a tarnishing of the supernatural it is when they reduce the Lord's supper to the natural life.

4. RECEIVED OF THE LORD

For I have received of the Lord, that which also I delivered unto you, that the Lord Jesus the same night in which he was betrayed, took bread.

With clear intention, Paul puts here (in the Greek) the word *I* in the foreground in order personally and genuinely to impart received revelation.

"*Of the Lord,*" from him he had received the doctrine of the Lord's supper that he had delivered unto the Corinthians.

There is difference of opinion as to whether Paul meant a receiving of the revelation by way of tradition, that which was relayed to him by another as to what the mouth of the Lord had spoken on the night of the betrayal, or, indeed, if he had in view a special revelation that was given him. As to the former, the argument appears to be based on the fact that the apostle here uses a preposition (*apo*) that does indicate origin, but not in the sense of direct delivery. Nevertheless, no one need seriously doubt that the apostle is referring here to personal, direct revelation. He adds to the Greek word for *received* a preposition (*para*) that further explains the first preposition and clearly indicates direct reception. Above all, what sense would it make for the apostle to put so strongly in the foreground that he received it personally if he had merely received it from other apostles? So we may think of a direct impartation from God such as mentioned in Galatians: "For I neither received it [the gospel] from man, neither was I taught it, but by the revelation of Jesus Christ" (1:12).

Where and how Christ appeared to him, we don't know. The apostle did not glory in his revelations. But the ascended Lord had given his dear disciple special instruction regarding the Lord's supper in view of his entirely unique mission. It speaks for itself that it is not so much the content of the revelation that is important here as is the form. The content cannot essentially differ from that which the evangelists recall.[8]

Here the old history, by apostolic authority, through special revelation, receives new splendor and power.

Consider then, from where the Lord's supper comes.

The Lord Jesus (Paul now adds *Jesus* to the first designation of *Lord* because it concerns here the historical appearance of the Lord) in that horrible (and, nevertheless, blessed) night of the betrayal took bread,[9] that is, one of the unleavened loaves on the table. Then, with the bread in hand, he gave thanks, as was the practice at the passover celebration. The head of the family spoke these words at the passover: "Blessed is he who created fruit of the earth. Blessed is he who causes the earth to bring forth bread." Perhaps the Lord offered the same words, but in so doing, he would not have left out gratitude for the spiritual bread that the Father has prepared for his children, and of which this earthly bread is symbolic. The thanksgiving of Jesus was a *Glory to God!* because, as mediator, his highest purpose is the glory of the covenantal God. So also must the *prayers* of the Lord's people be of *thankfulness.* By such prayer, the gift is sanctified to proper use. Matthew employs the term "blessed" ("and blessed it and brake it", 26:26), and on this the Dordt scholars note that,

> Luke and Paul, instead of having blessed, use the word having given thanks, like as some Greek copies have here also. So that to bless and thank or give thanks, are taken for one and the same thing, and signify to separate the bread, as also afterward the wine, from the common use, and by

---

8 It most strongly resembles that of Luke, which stands to reason since Luke (Paul's companion) would have heard the revelation from the apostle and so transcribed it as faithfully as possible.

9 In some manuscripts, the article appears before *bread*. The preferred reading is without the article.

thanksgiving to God to sanctify, or apply it to an holy use, as in Gen. 2:3, the seventh day is hallowed and blessed by God.

Jesus *breaks* this blessed-through-thanksgiving bread, not only breaking the bread in order to make distribution possible, but also to symbolize the breaking of his body in death.

And then the Lord says: *"Take, eat, this is my body which is broken for you."* When Jesus says, *take*, therein lies that he first *presents*. The guests cannot take the bread that Jesus has in hand until the Lord *affords* it to them. This offer is symbolic of the bestowal of God's love. There is an entreaty of the covenant member *coming* to God. And the Lord's will is for the house of Jacob to *plead* for his covenantal blessings. But there is also an act of God (indeed, this is primary) upon the sensibilities of the covenant member, so that he shall freely receive. When someone offers something to another with an outstretched arm, such an act symbolizes: "Take it, I grant it, I am giving it to you." To think that God would offer something to a covenant member without true *intention* would be blasphemous and make God out to be a liar.

Therefore, following this *giving* is the *receiving* from the side of the vassal. This is an act of faith. And indeed, an act of appropriating faith. The one *receiving* indicates that he believes the presentation. To receive it is to say *Amen* to God's bestowal of friendship. It is giving symbolic expression to faith in a (paradigmatic) claim on the gift. He who *receives* glorifies the divine attributes of love, truth, and faithfulness.

Nevertheless, in and of itself, this receiving would be meaningless if it were not to lead to the next act of faith, *to eat*. Bread has no other purpose than for nurture. It cannot be saved as a souvenir because it is susceptible to spoilage. It is intended to be eaten. The symbolism of this eating is a deepening and strengthening of the symbol of receiving. He who *takes* appropriates the gift. He who *eats* appropriates the *power* and the *blessing* of the gift. As long as the bread is not consumed, there is no life enrichment. With bread in hand, the vassal could yet die from hunger. But by eating, he is proclaiming that he desires the most heartfelt communion imaginable with respect to the benefits of the covenant of grace.

Indeed, with the Mediator of the covenant himself—because what does Jesus say? *This is my body.* He says this pointing to *bread.* It would make no sense to think Jesus is saying this pointing to his body. Such a declaration would be superfluous, as well as tautological.

But Jesus truly did say of the pieces of bread that he holds in his hand, "*This* is my body." But in what sense?

5. THE SIGN OF THE BREAD

When the Lord says, "*This is my body,*" the particle *is* does not indicate a *synonymic* (identifying) relationship between the bread and body. It does not say, this bread is the very same as my body. And Jesus could never have meant such a substance-equivalence of two different materials. That is unreasonable and impossible. Even Rome does not speak of substance-equivalence but, indeed, of substance-*change.* Rome believes that by the announcement of the sacramental formula, "This is my body," the bread is changed into the body of Jesus. Following this change, the bread is no longer really bread, but has been recreated into a completely different substance.

If, however, the proclamation intended to mean a substance-change, the Lord would have said, "This bread *becomes* or *has become* my body." Therefore, the idea of transubstantiation, already on grammatical grounds, is entirely excluded.

Neither does the particle *is* indicate a *conjoining* (fusion), as Luther taught. For the perspective of this reformer, the Lord would have announced that his body *accompanies* the bread (the so-called consubstantiation). By, with, and under the bread, the actual body of the Lord would then be present. Apart now from the fact that, when the Lord's supper was instituted, Jesus' body was not yet glorified and therefore was not (considering Luther's view) omnipresent, this conception is incongruous for linguistic reasons. The verb *to be* never expresses the idea of a combination.

If one desires not to violate the plain sense of Jesus' words, then one must come to the Reformed perspective, that here a *comparison* is drawn, and indeed of such profound character that both the image and the original are identified as entities having the same character. The bread with which Jesus satisfies his disciples has such properties, and now receives by sacramental action such a meaning, that it *reflects, symbolizes, stands for* the body of the Lord. Along similar lines, it is like pointing to a statue of Prince William, and it is the intention of the sculptor to represent and give attention to his majesty. And in external form, indeed, the resemblance is striking. One can say, that *is* Prince William. So here as well, the relationship between the symbol and that being symbolized can be expressed by the same little word.

This use of language is actually not foreign to Scripture. In the same letter to the Corinthians, Paul says concerning the rock from which the fathers drank: "And that rock *was* Christ." The Dordt scholars note:

> That is, was a *sign* and a *type* of Christ...a phrase usual in the Sacrament as the bread and wine of the Lord's Supper are called the body and blood of Christ, because they are a sign and seal thereof.

A sign *and seal!* The strength of the comparison is not exhausted by saying that there is correspondence between the sign and the intended object. Indeed, otherwise the supper would be destitute of spiritual operation. But when Jesus says, "This *is* my body," he is also presenting the bread with a pledge that he, by way of sacramental nourishment with the bread, will bestow upon the dinner guest the same grace that accrues to the sinner in communion with his body. He who receives the bread of the sacrament receives thereby not only spiritual instruction, a visible gospel proclamation, but also a direct participation in the body of the Lord, that is, to Christ himself. That this statement is valid and scriptural is evident from what the apostle says in the foregoing chapter: "The bread which we break, is it not the *communion* of the body of Christ?" (10:16).

The men of synonymy and combination have no right contemptuously to minimize the Reformed Lord's supper as an act of mere symbolism. Also according to our conviction, there is an *is-ness* of Christ himself in and with the sign. But this *is* is not fleshly tasteable but, rather, spiritually perceptible. Such a spiritual character of our fellowship with Jesus in the sacrament is not diminished to an idealistic, imagined communion exercise, but denotes precisely the highest, most glorious reality of communion with him.

Then, to eliminate any misunderstanding concerning the spiritual character of this fellowship, the apostle adds yet the explanation, "*which is broken for you.*" The text of these words appears not to be definitively established since in some prominent manuscripts the word "*broken*" is absent. That is why newer editions of the Bible have, "*which is for you.*" This reading is not unreasonable. It could be deduced that Jesus would have said this. Contained therein is a certain strength of expression. "*Which is for you*" suggests that it is designated for you, intended for you, that you have a spiritual claim on it, because I *give* it to you.

However, it can't be denied that there is in this reading something problematic in that it does not so purely fit the tone of the passage that previously mentions a *breaking* of the bread. It is more in the spirit of the entire sacramental action if it is read, "which is *broken* for you."

This *breaking* has in view the sacrifice of Christ on the cross. This is not to say that Jesus' body was *actually* broken because the glory of God's faithfulness shines precisely in the fact that the prophecy— no bone of him shall be broken—is fulfilled. But it does indicate the breaking of bodily *living* by death. It concerns the self-offering of Jesus' body, at the cost of his life. So Luke makes a valid point with his variant, "my body, which is *given* for you," i.e., is offered.

Now if the broken body of the Lord in the sacramental manner is to signify true faith-enrichment, then even a direct communion experience with the living, triumphant Savior is not enough. When now the bloody battle has been won and the course of the wounds has ended, it is precisely then, by the congregation's remembrance of the *fact* of this awful curse of death, that she is strengthened in her life of faith. It is not that the night of suffering is now over and *forgotten*, so welcome the new dawn of glory! No, the passion history must forever remain inscribed upon the soul and, according to this history, be refreshed ever more clearly in her awareness, so that she may be brought nearer to the Lord and the Lord nearer to her.

With a view to this Jesus immediately follows the words just recalled with, "*This do in remembrance of me.*"

The Lord intends with these words not first of all glory and gratitude for him by his people. The command originates from the intention that the Lord's supper be performed as richly as possible for his congregation. Without Jesus' remembrance in the celebration the bread cannot be a sign and seal of his body, "which is broken for you." Without remembering, no reawakening! From the *occurrence* of the redemptive fact comes the wonderful power for uplifting the soul.

"*This do* (namely, the entire act of celebrating the Lord's supper—the breaking of the bread, to give, take, and eat) *in remembrance of me.*" From this ordinance, which appears only in Luke (apparently following Paul's) and not in Matthew and Mark, it is seen how great the significance is of the revelation that Paul received. Especially with this command is the Lord's supper inscribed in ecclesiastical tradition as an *abiding institution*. One act of celebrating the Lord's supper cannot be sufficient for the congregation. She must continually and constantly keep doing this in Jesus' remembrance.

From this perspective, the Lord's supper is also a re-creation of the Old Testament passover. In the passover, Israel continually celebrated the remembrance of what happened that miraculous night in Egypt. The passover was also a *meal of remembrance*. The Lord had said: "And this day shall be unto you for a memorial; and ye shall keep it a feast to the Lord throughout your generations; ye shall keep it a feast by an ordinance forever" (Ex. 12:14).

Also, in the last night of Jesus' passion, the passover meal was celebrated in memory of that saving miracle (and indeed, with the passover lamb). But now Jesus turns the attention of the disciples from the passover lamb to his own person, saying: "This do in *remembrance of me.*" Certainly, the remembrance is directed by the sign of the bread first to the broken *body* of the Lord. But this body itself brings the soul into contact with the *person* of the Lord. The act of *deliverance* calls to mind the person of the *deliverer.* The soul elevates from the gift to the divine giver and rests not before it finds rest in the heart of the Mediator. Indeed, true faith first intuitively embraces the Christ of God and at the same time receives from Christ a share in his riches and blessings.

So it is thereby truly evident that celebration of the Lord's supper is also honor to the person of the King. Actually, how could it be otherwise? How could Jesus, who has such unspeakable love for his people, not evoke the personal gratitude of his own? And how could that people celebrate the remembrance of the atoning death, seeing the blessed face of the Man of Sorrows himself, and in spirit not kneel at his feet with a *Rabboni*?

Authentic communion binds your heart to Jesus' heart, strengthens more intimately the bond of the mystical union between the head and the members, and joins the Bridegroom above with the bride here below in a blessed foretaste of the wedding to come for one life together.

With the sacramental ordering of the bread, however, the Lord's supper has not yet come into full bloom. Of itself, the bread would be sufficient for celebration as a sign for remembering Jesus' death. It speaks to us of the complete atoning death of Christ. But in the body of the Lord, which is broken for you, is the blood, and by the breaking of the body flows out the lifeblood. And stronger yet than the breaking of the body is the symbol of pouring out of the lifeblood. Even more so, it is the *proof* of his salvation-rich, redeeming death.

By thus adding another sign to the sign of the bread, which brings to mind the blood, Jesus deepens and enriches the celebration of communion. He makes the salvation mystery of his death sweeter and more precious to the heart.

Just listen: "*And after the same manner also, he took the cup, when he had supped, saying, 'This cup is the New Testament in my blood; this do ye, as oft as ye drink it in remembrance of me.'*"

6. THE SIGN OF THE CUP

Following the institution of the sign of the bread is the institution of the *cup.*

In 1 Corinthians 10, the cup is mentioned prior to the bread where the apostle says: "The cup of blessing which we bless, is it not the communion of the blood of Christ? The bread which we break, is it not the communion of the body of Christ?" The view has been maintained, however, that in 1 Corinthians 10, the apostle is following the order of spiritual experience. Faith first comprehends the forgiveness of sin (i.e., the cup), and then the renewal of life (i.e., the bread).

In 1 Corinthians 11, from which the Scripture in our form is cited, Paul links to the *historical* order as it took place in the institution of the Lord's supper. Christ first took the bread and thereafter the cup: "*And after the same manner also, he took the cup, when he had supped, saying, 'This cup is the New Testament in my blood; this do ye, as oft as ye drink it in remembrance of me.'*"

Concerning the expression, "when he had supped," let there be no mistake. Most understand these words to mean the *New Testament* Lord's supper, the just-instituted meal of remembrance for Jesus' death. However, that which we today call and know as the Lord's supper was not yet fully instituted. The cup was still missing. The term *supper* is therefore to be seen as the Jewish supper, the Old Testament passover. Matthew tells us that Jesus took bread "*as they were eating,*" that is, while the actual passover meal was still in progress. When Paul now says that Jesus took the cup *after* eating the supper, it is given to mean that the *passover meal* was finished.

Apparently, after the Lord had instituted the first sign, he led his disciples into one of his rich and meaningful prophetic discourses, as recorded by John. Jesus spoke of his imminent departure to the Father, the looming sorrow of his disciples, and the approaching struggle with the world. He admonished them to unity and comforted them with his vision of the eventual eternal reunion. Through the thick, dark clouds of trials and travails, he displayed to them the splendorous perspective of the kingdom that is soon to be fulfilled.

As he instructed them with his prophetic wisdom, encouraged them with his priestly love, and upheld them with his royal power, the moment arrived for the meal to be concluded.

Before that, Jesus institutes the second sign as a remembrance of his atonement. And as the first sign was borrowed from the ingredients of the passover meal, so too with the second sign.

Jesus takes the *cup,* after eating the supper.

In the previous chapter, the cup is called the cup of *thanksgiving.* At the passover feast were a total of four (in some views, five) cups that were circulated. Each had its own meaning and led into its own unique hymn or prayer. The last cup was called the cup of thanksgiving, because with this one, the passover meal was concluded with thanksgiving. The presider at the meal extended his hands in blessing, i.e., in thanksgiving, over the cup, and then passed it around to the guests.

The Lord also did the same.

But before he passed the cup to his dinner companions, he consecrated it for sacramental service of the new covenant. "*This cup,*" he says, "*is the new testament in my blood.*"

With these words, Paul and Luke (a follower of the apostles) are the same. Luke yet adds: "*which is shed for you.*"

Matthew and Mark virtually concur: "Because this is my blood of the new testament, which is shed for many."

Thus, there is no essential difference between Paul and the evangelists. However, Paul's language is further developed, more mature. In his formula, Paul brings out that the covenant is based on the blood, and therein derives its power. After all, he speaks of the new testament in, that is, *grounded in*, the blood, while Matthew and Mark only indicate the wine as a sign of the blood of the new testament.

The main idea of the words of the institution that are delivered to us is the idea of the *covenant*. Our translation renders the original (*diathèkè*) as *testament*, but in the Dordt scholars, a comment is added, "*or covenant.*"

These two are not completely synonymous. Originally, in Scripture, there is only reference to *covenant*, and there was no usage in Israel of "testament" as it is now known by us. However, in the Septuagint (the Greek translation of the Old Testament) the Hebrew word for covenant (*berith*) was translated with *diathèkè* that has a primary meaning of a contract, but also the related meaning of *testament*. By the leading of God's providence, this related meaning was taken over by the New Testament and adapted for the covenant that God had established with Israel.

Though the original meaning of *covenant* was retained, in order to characterize the richness of the covenant, here now was also assigned the meaning of *testament*. By so speaking of a testament, it suited the apostles in that in the covenant of grace, God is the giver of all things and Israel only a receiving party. Paul developed this metaphor and applied it in passages such as Hebrews 9:15–18, where it says:

> And for this cause, he is the mediator of the new testament, that by means of death, for the redemption of the transgressions that were under the first testament, they which are called might receive the promise of eternal inheritance. For where a testament is, there must also of necessity be the death of the testator. For a testament is of force after men are dead: otherwise, it is of no strength at all while the testator

liveth. Whereupon neither the first testament was dedicated without blood.

He then quotes Moses himself where he spoke of covenant blood: "This is the blood of the testament which God hath enjoined unto you." Clearly, the intention of the apostle is to further picture and deepen the idea of the covenant by the blood that was typified on Israel's altars and on the cross was shed in definite atonement. This provides evidence of *testamentary legality* for the possessions of the covenant of grace to become the property of God's people. Therefore, in the words of the institution, Paul, under the leading of the Spirit, may render that, "This cup is the new testament in my blood"—the word *testament* receives its full emphasis, while the idea of *covenant* remains as the main idea.

Jesus' intent is to bring to the attention of his church the new phase of development in the dispensation of the covenant. By the obedience of his suffering and death, the covenant of grace enters into another stage with yet richer blessings than previously for the covenantal people. Already, the prophet Jeremiah had proclaimed this new development with God's own words:

> Behold, the days come, saith the Lord, that I will make a new covenant[10] with the house of Israel, and with the house of Judah; Not according to the covenant that I made with their fathers in the day that I took them by the hand to bring them out of the land of Egypt; which my covenant they brake, although I was an husband unto them, saith the Lord: But this shall be the covenant that I will make with the house of Israel; After those days, saith the Lord, I will put my law in their inward parts, and write in their hearts; and will be their God, and they shall be my people. And they shall teach no

---

10 Already from this expression, it can be seen how groundless the opinion is that Paul himself could not have utilized the word *new*, but that this would have been inserted by a later redactor.

more every man his neighbor, and every man his brother, saying, Know the Lord: for they shall all know me, from the least of them unto the greatest of them saith the Lord: for I will forgive their iniquity, and I will remember their sin no more.

Jesus now stands with his disciples as if on the border line between the old and new covenant. The moment has come for the twilight of the old order to make way for the new dawn. The long shadows that proclaimed the rising of the coming light are diminishing. The new covenant shines like a bright summer's day upon this world's vale of tears.

In principle, the new covenant is no different than the old. The fathers of previous times were saved by the same mediator, Jesus. There is no contradistinction as if between a covenant of works and a covenant of grace. The old covenant was a covenant of grace, and long before the Mediator of the atonement came to earth, it conveyed the atonement as the comfort of God's people.

No, the difference between both covenants rests in the *degree of luminosity* of revelation and in connection with this, the *form* of the covenantal dispensation.

The new covenant displays to the world the glory of the cruel cross, and through this cross, the word of grace sparkles like a case of diamonds in the eyes of the children of humanity. It is revealed, even more clearly than in old times, that the way to the Father's house is the way of the forgiveness of sins, and not in the way of obedience to God's law. The congregation of the new covenant has not received the spirit of bondage again to fear, but the spirit of adoption, whereby they cry, "Abba, Father!" Now they see with *unveiled* eyes the glory of the Lord as in a mirror, and receive in its fullness grace upon grace. They glory in a blood that is not a shadow and pattern for redemption but is redemption actually established. And so, Jesus speaks of the *New Testament in his blood* and gives to his church the sign and seal of that blood in the cup of the Lord's supper.

With this understanding begins the sacramental language that resounds spirit and life in the Lord's supper.

"This cup is the new testament in my blood," that is to say, the blood of Christ is the foundation, the power, and the glory of the new dispensation of the covenant. The *cup* is the symbol and the seal of this new dispensation because in the cup is the *wine*, the sign of the blood.

There is a strong sequence of thought. The cup is identified with the wine that is in the cup, so that wine is identified with the new covenant.

Also with the institution of the cup, as with the institution of the bread, Jesus follows with the words: *"This do ye, as oft as ye drink of it in remembrance of me."*

This phrase does not appear in Luke. Matthew and Mark have only, "Drink ye all of it." Here is additional proof as to how meaningful the revelation was that Paul had received.

This do, says the Lord, and thereby he intends not only the taking and drinking of the cup, but the entire sacramental institution, thus also the *giving* of the cup and the pronouncement of the sacramental formula.

Rightly, the words *"as oft as"* have been interpreted that the Lord intended for the drinking of the cup from now on, and not to be limited to an annual observance as with the passover. This brings up the matter of how often the congregation may partake of the cup. One should not infer that here Jesus would have condoned that whenever we have a glass of wine (also when there is opportunity), thereby a sacramental ceremony is being observed. That might be true if the pronoun *ye* were absent and in the text was literally, *"as oft as you drink it."* But, correctly, our translation utilizes the pronoun *ye*, because the correlation is clear that Jesus intended that cup. Above all, if the congregation were commanded to celebrate the remembrance of Jesus' death with every meal, or also at every customary festivity, the border between the natural and spiritual lives would thereby be confused and the sacrament lose its special meaning.

So, *"as oft as ye drink of it"* has a view to the official ecclesiastical administration of the supper of the Lord and intends to provide admonishment for the congregation not to betray this ecclesiastical usage.

7. PROCLAIMING THE LORD'S DEATH

The words that now follow are not those of Jesus himself, but of the apostle. The discourse indeed flows from the same line of thought, but there is no doubt that Paul departs from the quoted words of Jesus with his conclusion that now presents a deduction, *"For as oft as ye eat this bread, and drink this cup, ye do show the Lord's death till he come."*

The relationship with the foregoing is not immediately evident. Nevertheless, one would not have expected a deduction beginning with *for* but with *therefore* because here the conclusion would be appropriate. That is why some have thought here to be a typographical error and read the text as, *"Therefore, as oft..."* However, when it is taken into consideration that the phrase connects with that which immediately precedes—*"This do in remembrance of me"*—there need be no objection.

Paul is drawing special attention to the *person* of Christ and is admonishing the congregation: "You must not be thinking of anything else, least of all worldly matters, but of Jesus alone. *For* (and now comes the deduction), as oft as ye eat this bread, and drink this cup, you proclaim *the Lord's death,* till he come."

However, when one maintains that the deductive *for* is original, there is cause to adjust in a sense the translation of the Authorized Version that has been transmitted to us. Our translation renders the imperative form as *"so proclaim"* the Lord's death till he come. The word here for *to proclaim* can also be understood in a demonstrative sense, *you proclaim.* And this translation is preferable here where the apostle provides not as much a command as an *impetus* for why the congregation must celebrate the supper in remembrance of *Jesus*. He says, then, that it here is about the *person* of Christ, because as oft as you drink this cup, you must proclaim the Lord's death.

In order to move the hearts of the Corinthians and to broach the admonishment to reverence for the Lord's supper, he so points the congregation to the genuine character of the celebration of communion. It is not befitting to offer banalities regarding the Lord's table; here pending are matters of especially grievous sin with dreadful consequences, because to come near to sit at this meal, you are in fact to proclaim the death of the Lord.

From this conception appears at the same time what the apostle intends with the proclamation of the Lord's death.

Certainly, the idea of a literal and auditory proclamation is not completely excluded. Especially in the early days when the Spirit of God also granted gifts of prophecy, there often would come to expression tongues that were released at the Lord's supper from prophetically gifted guests. Wonderful things were spoken regarding the precious, redemptive death of the Messiah. In some ancient liturgies (e.g., in the *Liturgia Jacobi*), one also comes across *die profetische lofprijzingen*[11] of Jesus' death. Also our Dordt scholars indicate in their notes the declaring of this word that ministers spoke with auditory voice at the Lord's supper, by which they instructed the people "that this broken bread, and this wine, is a sign and sealing of the bitter death of Christ on the cross, and of the benefits procured for us thereby."

So, although the idea of a verbal (word-based) proclamation was not completely excluded, firmly in this context the *action* of symbolic preaching remained primary. Even though the Corinthians irreverently attended the administration, nevertheless their presence yet directed them to the *act* of the proclamation of the Lord's death, which was for the express purpose that through this death

---

11 Tr. Prophetical chants or songs of praise, perhaps from earlier prophetic utterances.

proclamation, so desperately needed, holy earnestness and peaceful tranquility would govern their souls.

With regard to this symbolic proclamation, then, it depends as much upon the form as the content. Already the rising up and going to the Lord's supper meal in order to partake of the seals of the covenant is of itself a preaching of the death of the Lord. Who does so indeed cries out this death in the middle of the congregation and before the face of the world, that the death of Christ is the ground of my hope, the source of my salvation!

> Jesus, priceless treasure;
> Source of purest pleasure.[12]

Thousands today still walk by the cross indifferent or with reproach. Those who go to the meal, where the signs of the crucifixion are provided as medicine for the soul—these proclaim:

> Bearing shame and scoffing rude,
> In my place condemned he stood;
> Sealed my pardon with his blood.
> Hallelujah! What a Savior![13]

But with the external act belongs inner conviction. The soul must commit to centering its thoughts upon Christ in holy contemplation. There must be internal wondering, lamenting, thanking, praising. Or, as the Dordt scholars say: "The Lord's death must be proclaimed from those who savor the Lord's supper. There in their hearts they must reflect, believe, and confess with thanksgiving that Christ the Lord died for them for redemption from eternal death unto salvation."

And this proclamation is one that is such a glorious, operational action that it lasts "*till he come*" (literally, until he shall come again). The congregation shows forth the proclamation until Jesus shall

---

12   Tr. Lyrics by Johann Franck, Trans. Catherine Winkworth.
13   Tr. Hymn by Philip P. Bliss.

reveal himself for the second time. Not that this shall end this salvation work, because this work endures through all eternity. But with Jesus' coming, the sacrament comes to an end because the congregation will walk no more by faith, but by sight.

The Lord's supper binds the first coming of Jesus in the flesh to his second coming upon the clouds. Regarding the first coming, the supper is remembrance. Regarding the second coming, it is prophecy. Therefore, when the Lord comes, the prophecy is neutralized, because it is fulfilled. And the proclamation of the Lord's death will then not be a sacramental preaching, but a never-ending, jubilant praising of the Lamb. "Thou, God, hath purchased us with your blood from every family and tongue and people and nation."

8. WHO EATS UNWORTHILY

After impartation of the *institution* of the Lord's supper that Paul had received from the Lord (1 Cor. 11:23–25), and from there to a conclusion as to what concerns the *character* of the commemoration of communion (v. 26), the apostle now comes to his admonishment in addressing the Corinthians. What Paul had written so far was preparation for the admonishment so that it would be delivered with the strength of being well-grounded and reasonable.

If all this is so, that the Lord Jesus in the night in which he was betrayed took the bread and ordered the Lord's supper in the manner described so far, and it is true that thereby eating this bread and drinking this cup actually proclaims the Lord's death, then it follows that, "*Wherefore, whosoever shall eat this bread, and drink this cup of the Lord unworthily, shall be guilty of the body and blood of the Lord.*"

An important question regarding the declaration of these words is, what are we to understand by the word "*unworthily*"?

In general, the exegesis of this word has been too frequently generalized, losing sight of its uniqueness. When it is said that unworthily eating and drinking is to partake of the Lord's supper without genuine repentance or without sufficient self-examination, this is true in a general sense. But it does not get at the apostle's intent with this word.

By the word *unworthily*, we have to think especially about the diminishing of the Lord's supper celebration in the Corinthian congregation. This diminishment consisted in everyone's eating of the love feast before each partook of the supper, so that when gathering at the Lord's meal, the one was hungry and another was drunk (vv. 20–21). The Lord's supper was debased to the unconsecrated, natural life.

Naturally, such a communion celebration conformed to neither the *character* nor the *purpose* of the Lord's supper. The apostle indicated to the congregation that the genuine *character* of the supper had to do with the blood and the body of Christ (10:16). He described the *purpose* of the Lord's supper as eating and drinking in remembrance of the Lord Jesus. When by the frivolous manner of conducting the supper the sacrament *cannot* come to its own, then such a celebration of the Lord's supper must be branded with the mark: *unworthily*.

Due to not interpreting this expression directly from its context, over time an incalculable, severe misunderstanding has arisen to the detriment of ecclesiastical life. Many have so conceptualized the word as if it refers to the *person* of the Lord's supper participant himself. No one, then, would be able to come to the supper other than he who verifies himself as *worthy* to eat the bread and drink of the cup. Overly sensitive and somewhat unsure Christians, who feel *unworthy* of such a royal honor as to sit with Jesus at the holy banquet, are therefore kept at a respectful distance.

A deep, erroneous idea!

Because if the worthiness of the *person* is established as the measure for admittance to the Lord's table, then there is no hope for even the most advanced Christians. In this sense, even the apostle Paul was not a worthy partaker of the supper, who testified of himself: "O wretched man that I am!"

No. If worthiness of the person were the issue, then he would be the most worthy Lord's supper participant who personally confesses most fervently to be *unworthy*.

Nevertheless, the apostle intends here not first the person but the method, the manner of celebrating the Lord's supper. Here it is about the *gestalt*, external as well as internal, of the participant. The question is *how* it is done and *when* it is done. If one celebrates the supper like the Corinthians here described, then he is doing it unworthily, even though as a person he is a true child of God. From this perspective, it is evident that a committed disciple of the Lord, by way of a tragic lapse into worldliness, can unworthily celebrate the supper and so seriously commit sin.

Comprehending the word of Paul in this way bears a richer meaning and a more rigorous significance that summons the *entire* congregation to self-examination.

Provided that this exposition, in which the word of the apostle is given its special due, is left unimpaired, there is no objection to providing a further extension to the sense, as for example that of the Dordt scholars:

> This unworthily eating and drinking comes to pass when the persons are not rightly disposed to go to the Lord's supper, being either publicly scandalous persons, which also be kept from it, or close hypocrites, and standing in the strife with their neighbors, and laden with hatred, envy, covetousness, and unrighteousness; or else when the faithful themselves have not duly prepared themselves thereunto, or do not receive the same with due consideration.

According to these words, any person at the meal who is unconverted (that is, a public or private sinner) attends the supper *unworthily*. But also, the believer who has not sufficiently prepared himself, or who participates in the meal itself without his heart purposed for holy matters, eats and drinks unworthily.

"Whosoever shall eat this bread or drink this cup of the Lord

unworthily..." Peculiar that here in verse 27 as in verse 29, the apostle doesn't have eat *and* drink of the cup, but eat *or* drink. Rome has drawn the conclusion from this distinction that the celebration of communion under one kind (*communion sub una*) would be sufficient. In practice, Rome ordinarily limited itself to the eating of the bread. This is completely unjustified, as in the previous verse the connecting word *and* appears.

Apparently, it was the intention of the apostle to express the possibility of taking the *bread* worthily, but not the *cup*. When the communion celebration was lengthy, and finally the wine—always the symbol of joy—was distributed, an initially spiritually attuned soul could surrender attention and drink the cup *unworthily*. But whether one eats the bread unworthily or only drinks the cup of the Lord unworthily, he "*shall be guilty of the body and blood of the Lord.*"

This to *be guilty* means *to be bound by guilt* of the body and blood of the Lord. See, says Rome (and Lutherans concur), that the bread and wine of the Lord's supper are something else than a sign or seal? How would Paul otherwise state that he who unworthily eats and drinks of the *body* and *blood* of the Lord is guilty? The body of the Lord must therefore actually and literally be present in the Lord's supper.

What must be kept in mind, however, is that eating and drinking unworthily, according to the intention of the apostles, cannot be a sin against the *substance*. The sinful deviation is hidden in the heart, which does not climb from the substantive signs to Christ himself. Who thus eats or drinks unworthily sins against the person of Christ and is guilty with respect to his body and blood. Those who treat the symbol as reality violate that which is represented by the symbol. Those who are careless with the royal instructions deride the king. Those who desecrate the Bible are guilty of sinning against the divine author. Those who unworthily eat or drink are guilty of the body and blood of the Lord.

And God shall by no means declare the guilty innocent.

9. THE SELF-EXAMINATION

"But let a man examine himself, and so let him eat of that bread, and drink of that cup."

The most beneficial preventive means against unworthy participation at the Lord's supper is self-examination. If ever it is necessary, then it is here for the soul to be brought into fitting "frame of mind," unattached and beyond the sphere of the natural life and enveloped by the sphere of spiritual, heavenly matters. The moral act of testing the heart for the authentic disposition is necessary for celebrating the supper in a way that is commensurate with the character and purpose of communion. For this is required honest accountability regarding the question of whether the soul's passion by means of the supper is making a constantly deeper separation between you and the world, between the table of the Lord and the table of demons.

The criterion for true self-examination is personal integrity. Resounding when God established the covenant with Abraham was: "Walk before me, and be thou *perfect.*"

There may be in the soul no bifurcation or hobbling between two opinions. The prevailing tone of the heart must be that of power over sin, faith in Christ, and thankfulness toward God.

Even though the apostle dealt especially with testing the soul with respect to the sin at Corinth, preserved in his admonishment in seed form is the requirement for Christian scrutiny of the entire spiritual life. The Dordt scholars had the right exegesis:

> That is, search his mind and conscience, whether he feels in his heart a true sorrow and grief for sins, as also a firm faith and confidence in the merits of Jesus Christ, and moreover an unstained purpose to die from sins more and more. And to walk before God in new godly life.

The Dordt scholars provide here an outline for true self-examination that we will later come across in the Lord's supper form where in particular the examination is discussed. The trinity of guilt, grace, and gratitude summarizes our entire doctrine of salvation.

"But let a man examine himself, and so let him eat of that bread, and drink of that cup." Nearly every word of this sentence contains an idea.

The *man* examines himself. The apostle is indicating that no one is excused from the ordeal of self-examination because the word for *man* provides the most general description. Not only the hesitating soul, but also the courageous Christian whose testimony may burn like a bright light is summoned to self-examination.

The word for *man* also includes the idea of smallness and weakness. The word speaks of evanescence, sinfulness, and misery. He who examines himself does this with humble awareness that nothing of man, in the sense of nothing evil, is foreign to him, because the *man*-Christian knows that in him, i.e., in his flesh, nothing good lives.

A man examines *himself*. Also, this word is here by no accident. For the attentive reader, there is a clue for striving against the born tendency to judge *others*. The man must examine *himself*. Pull the weeds from his own garden. Point the finger at his own chest.

Let a man examine himself *and*... To speak in this way, the apostle does not intend that *every* self-examination must result in an entrance to the Lord's table. The self-examination can occasionally lead to *self-discipline* that consists of a Christian refraining from participation at the Lord's supper. There *can* be a moment that comes in the Christian life that he will deny himself the sacrament due to his sin or lack of spirituality.

But the rule for the Christian life cannot be anything other than this—that *authentic* self-examination is followed by the eating and drinking of the Lord's supper. To self-inspection also belongs confession, and true confession flows from the atonement. Self-examination is not merely a constant rehearsal of one or another spiritual fault. It also includes the wrestling of the soul to be liberated from these faults, bringing to God on bended knee, "Forgive me! Cleanse me!"

And provided this prayer is sincere, no sin need hinder the approach to the signs of the covenant. Also, the so-called examination sermon (currently referred to as the preparatory message) does not have as its purpose to discourage entrance to the table, but to eliminate all hindrances that can stand in the way of blessed communion.

And so one eats of the bread and drinks of the cup. The phrase *and so* does not mean to prescribe a particular manner of communion celebration. Here the phrase *and so* has the meaning of *and then*. When a man has examined himself, *then* he eats and drinks.

Therefore, the *and so* serves even more strongly the result that the calling of the Christian to celebrate communion remains unweakened. And the reigning question for preparation is not, "Can I find a reason to refrain?" but, "How can I so pave the way that I, despite the aberrations of my soul, may nevertheless draw near to the sacrament?"

However, above all, the self-examination must be deep and sincere. It is (from the viewpoint of human perspective) better not to go to the Lord's supper than to attend on the wrong basis: "For he that *eateth and drinketh unworthily, eateth and drinketh judgment to himself, if he discern not the body of the Lord.*"

In some prominent manuscripts, the word *unworthily* is absent. Warrant for removal of the word appears correct. The verse is then: "For he that *eateth and drinketh* (i.e., the one who eats and drinks) *eateth and drinketh judgment to himself, if he discern not the body of the Lord.*"

The sense of the words remains the same because even if *unworthily* might not belong in the text, the strength of the connection to verse 27, where eating and drinking *unworthily* is referenced, nonetheless provides the basis for the idea in this verse.

10. THEY EAT AND DRINK JUDGMENT TO THEMSELVES

So hears the congregation the strong language that any person who does not make use of the covenantal symbols in the proper manner eats and drinks *a judgment.*

A language, indeed, that is frightening to the anxious heart!

Yes, but this is read with inattention. Some who do not give sufficient account to Paul's words read a threat here, that he who celebrates the supper unworthily is as good as inviting eternal judgment upon himself. Therefore, out of fear of bringing on themselves the unavoidable judgment of condemnation, they stay away from the Lord's supper.

However, the apostle is not speaking here of the judgment of eternal condemnation. Certainly, this judgment that rests upon every *unrepentant sinner* can be made heavier by unworthy participation in communion. The Dordt scholars are not entirely wrong when they speak here of eternal punishment *in respect of hypocrites.* Nevertheless, such judgment is not the consequence of the erroneous celebration of the Lord's supper, but is the fruit of the unconverted state in which a man remains hardened.

That is why Paul intended something else with the term *judgment.* He refers here to the chastisements with which the Lord disciplines his people when those people deviate from his ways into disobedience. Such afflictions can apply to body and soul; they can reveal themselves in the deprivation of earthly blessing and in the withholding of spiritual fortune. In light of the following verse, the apostle especially has physical chastisement in view. He says: *"For this cause, many are weak and sickly among you, and many sleep."* These words must not be interpreted spiritually but naturally. In the Corinthian congregation, many had succumbed to physical deterioration and disease, and many had even passed away (many *sleep*), as punishment from God upon the unworthy celebration of the Lord's supper.

So that the attentive reader would not forget what he is saying, Paul is not speaking of *the* judgment but *a* judgment that a person can eat and drink to himself. Also, the warning is already serious enough, because when the hand of the Lord strikes, it strikes sharply and causes the disobedient child to lament with woe. Even for the

Lord's own people, it is a fearful thing to fall in the hands of the living God.

The apostle describes the sin that God visits, in order to preserve the holiness of his supper, as a failure *to discern of the body of the Lord*.

The word transmitted as *to discern* can also be translated by *regard*. Some prefer this translation. And it holds some attraction. One who participates in the sacrament without preparation and lacking thoughtful consideration demonstrates thereby that he does not esteem the body of the Lord, the signs of which he is utilizing. That which is holy, he is treating as profane. He is toying with the treasures of the covenant of grace, like a child who plays with gold without knowing its value.

However, also the rendition here, *discern not*, makes good sense; indeed, we choose this translation above the other. The admonition of the apostle is confronting the Corinthian misdeed, which consisted of celebrating the supper as if it were a *common* meal. They were not *discerning* between the bread of the supper and the bread of a casual meal. They were not viewing the bread as a sign and reflection of the Lord's body. Those who celebrate the Lord's supper in such a way are tarnishing its holy character. Those who so eat and drink, eat and drink a judgment unto themselves.

The purpose of the admonition is that the Lord's supper participant, softly and tenderly, draws near to the divine meal, and that the congregation experiences a deep impression within the heart with respect to the exalted, spiritual sacrament.

God's people can never be encouraged enough in this: to celebrate the Lord's supper is coming to God, for intentional communion with Jesus, being drawn into the holy mystery of the covenant of peace.

---•

Chapter Four

THE AUTHENTIC EXAMINATION

1. THE LORD'S SUPPER FOR OUR COMFORT

Following the prologue, in which the word of God itself addresses the congregation, begins now the actual instruction regarding the Lord's supper. Apparently, without transitioning, the formulary continues:

> That we may now celebrate the supper of the Lord to our comfort, it is above all things necessary, first, rightly to examine ourselves; and further, to direct it to that end for which Christ hath ordained and instituted the same, namely, to his remembrance.

One would expect that first the cited Scripture passage would be explained with a few words, or at least the main idea, with a view to explaining the proper celebration of the Lord's supper. However, the formulary does nothing else than to render objectively the words in 1 Corinthians 11, in order, without any comment, to go to the teaching portion.

Calvin did make a transition in his form. After quoting 1 Corinthians 11:23–29: "Here we have heard, dear brothers, how the Lord kept the supper with his disciples, in order thereby to teach us that they who are outside the congregation of believers may not be admitted; therefore we follow this rule." And then the author proceeds, in the name of the Lord, to exclude from the Christian congregation all those who are publicly leading a sinful life.

We do not now decide whether a similar exclusion (excommunication) indeed may be viewed as the main thought of Paul's word or also can be viewed only as direct conclusions of this word. Our interest in the citation has to do with the fact itself that Calvin makes an attempt to connect the prologue to the form.

We cannot say with certainty why this did not happen in our form. Apparently, the framers were of the opinion that although the transition was not indicated in so many words, the connection would still be felt by the attentive listener.

And, indeed, the connection *is* there for those paying attention.

The quotation from 1 Corinthians 11 forms not more than a premise with which one makes sidelong acquaintance in order then to move into the instruction itself. We have already identified this passage as an overture in which the *theme* of the formulary is presented. And so, it is true. The prologue pioneers the entire formulary. It provides not only the *material* but also the *train of thought* for the whole piece. This happens in reverse order. The self-examination that is the apostle's last admonishment, the form brings first to the table. The character and meaning of the celebration of the Lord's supper that the apostle describes first, the form explicates further in the second part.

It would certainly have been desirable had this connection been indicated with a few words such as: "*So we see from the word of the apostle* that to keep the Lord's supper unto our comfort, before anything else, we must rightly prove ourselves; and so direct it to the purpose for which Christ the Lord had instituted."

Now that this did not happen, it is even more necessary for the congregation to pay attention to the connection and train of thought in the form.

The Lord's supper formulary has *the word of God* as its foundation and is built upon this foundation.

The beginning of the demonstrative portion of the formula is surprising.

In the baptism form, it is frugal, almost austere: "The principal parts of the doctrine of holy baptism are these three."

The Lord's supper form begins immediately with the warm tone: "That we may now celebrate the supper of the Lord to our comfort."

This immediately evidences the character of the formulary. If the catechism is the *manual* of comfort, then our Lord's supper form provides for us the *liturgy* of comfort. Perhaps we would have found it pleasant, more appropriate sounding, had the purpose of *God's glory* been positioned in the foreground. In the preface to the prayer in the baptism form, it rings so beautifully: "That therefore this holy ordinance of God may be administered to *his glory*, to our comfort, and to the edification of his church." Perhaps one would be inclined to consider this "concealment" of God's glory as the main purpose of the Lord's supper as a flaw.

One remembers, however, that the design of the Lord's supper form is different from that of the form for baptism. First the section on self-examination is mentioned, and then the second part, which applies the purpose and character of the sacrament, is in order. Note that the second part of the form exhibits well the obligation to understand the glorification of God because *the end* for which the Lord Jesus instituted the supper is designated as "*in remembrance of him.*" Here resonates in the form the *Soli Deo Gloria*.

And upon reflection—does one consider that when our catechism deals with sin, it chooses its point of departure from the only comfort in life and death? Not always, but in the book of comfort shines brightly the sunlight, that the most prominent element of the comfort is this: how we shall be thankful to God for such deliverance. The outcome of the book of comfort is also *glory to God!*

We regard it precisely a profitable discovery in the Heidelberg Catechism that he begins his instruction with the mention of comfort. This is the real-human (and at the same time, the real-divine) in the Christian religion, which places the saving of the man on the foreground. In the carrying out of this is found the secret of the popularity of the catechism.

So also is the case in our Lord's supper form. It is not in the first place dogmatic and theoretical, but *paraenetic,* applicable. It is not first directed to the head, but to the heart. It seeks to bring the soul into the frame of mind necessary for the true celebration. And isn't it true that the Lord Jesus gave this holy meal for the *comfort* of his people? He instituted the supper so that the grieving disciples, soon after his departure, would be refreshed by the sacrament. He gifted it to his bride so that in the time of the Bridegroom's absence, the heavy-laden and troubled heart of his own would be strengthened. And no matter how many frightening life situations, the Lord's supper of the church is there for extraordinary comfort.

In Rome's dismal catacombs, the oppressed disciples of Jesus ate the bread and drank the wine *comforted* in order to soon take up the martyr's cross. In remote shelters, the persecuted children of the Reformation arranged the meal, and in their suffering, God's goodness radiated upon them, his power undergirded them.

Eternity will reveal what a blessing the *comfort* of the Lord's supper was for God's inheritance when they were languishing in the unfolding course of the ages.

2. THE MAIN THOUGHT OF THE DOCTRINE OF THE SUPPER

However, even though this supper was given to us so that we would keep it unto our comfort, this is not to say that it only pertains to the mystical state of the soul. True comfort indeed flows within the heart, but it reaches the heart by way of *understanding*! In distinction from other churches, the Reformed church of all times has professed the primacy of the intellect (the priority of understanding). When the catechism discusses the only comfort in life and death, the path then to this comfort is sought through *knowledge*. After all, the question follows: How many things are necessary for you to *know*, that you in this comfort may live and die happily?

The same goes for our Lord's supper formulary. So that we may keep the Lord's supper for our comfort, presented to us is material for *reflection*, seeking to reach our heart through the portal of understandable exposition.

Before anything else, that is, before we draw near to the table to eat and to drink, to seek communion with Jesus, to proclaim God's honor—before *all* things it is necessary that in advance we test our right for that which the Lord Jesus has ordered and instituted, and also that we direct it to that end to which the Lord Christ has ordered and instituted it.

The principal doctrine of the Lord's supper is apportioned in two parts. First is the *preparation* for the supper and then *the Lord's supper itself* is handled. The order could have been reversed. In the catechism, first the doctrine of the supper is explained, and it then concludes with bringing the preparation into view. In general, this order is preferable because the preparation can be truly grounded and effective when previously the awareness of the purpose and character of the Lord's supper is lively. That the form diverges from this usual order (which Paul also follows in 1 Corinthians 11) is certainly not baseless. The form follows a practical rather than a logical order. It addresses the congregation that is not unfamiliar with matters pertaining to the Lord's supper. When it begins with the self-examination, the Lord's people immediately comprehend the intention. And placing the self-examination beforehand presupposes this instantaneous awareness of the congregation: it has to do here not as much with theoretical reflection as practical enjoyment of the Lord's supper. Here it pertains to the faith not as a system, but as life itself. And it is not possible to live the faith if the heart and affections are not prepared for sanctified action by way of self-examination.

3. THE SELF-EXAMINATION REQUIREMENT AND ROME'S CONFESSION

So the first part that the form presents to the congregation for reflection is that of *self-examination*.

We mentioned that the admonishment to self-examination immediately connects with the word that Paul directed to the Corinthians, especially that last, "*But let a man examine himself.*"

There are those who repudiate this. Mensinga[1] and others assert that the requirement for self-examination is not dependent on 1 Corinthians 11 because there is an enormous difference between the ecclesiastical preparation that is conducted by us and the special preparation intended by Paul. He says quite crassly:

> By the way, it goes without saying that in light of plain history, and free from the influence of ecclesiastical hermeneutics, that the quoted Pauline passage, as a proof text for the self-examination, must be completely discarded.

How then did the framers of our formulary get to place so much emphasis on the part of the self-examination?

Indeed, answers Mensinga, the self-examination is nothing other than an ecclesiastical practice, indeed a residue of the Roman Catholic sacrament of confession that used to be in place prior to communion, which also is still kept by the Lutherans. This preparatory penance originates

> ...from the increasingly lofty esteem for the high and holy mystery of the consecration, the symbolic drama of Christ's suffering and death—the center point of the entire worship service—that finally, became a daily repeated appearance, a continual sacrifice of the Lamb of God, and the material and bodily consumption of the flesh and blood, of the God-man as the slaughtered sacrificial lamb. Since such could allow no unworthy participation, a man must beforehand attain to a state of grace that itself must be received by an earnest mouth.

Mensinga presents it in such a way that the reformers themselves were unable to let go of such things, "engrained from their youth,

---

1   Mensinga, *Over de Liturgische Schriften*, 247–50.

already developed since the first centuries in the church, by thousands of symbolic and allegorical expressions endorsed by notions of the ancient church fathers."

In order to cover the communion-penance inherited from Rome with a statement (that sounds like it is) based on the Bible, the framers would interpolate the cited portion of Scripture. Mensinga sees here nothing other than an attempt to dress up the ecclesiastical practice with words from the Bible, "something that took place too frequently among our reformers than that we should have to do more then remember it."

Finally, Mr. Mensinga is so kind as to explain that by this criticism he has said nothing about the value and the usefulness of the ecclesiastical practice of preparation for the Lord's supper as such. "We regard it," he says, "as with so many other ecclesiastical ordinances, very useful and beneficial; except, one must not say that it is prescribed in the Bible."

For the framers of the formulary, the judgment of this liturgist is not now designed to be a compliment. They must have been gullible men for a Romish communion-penance to get injected into a Protestant Lord's supper ceremony, unbeknownst to them that they had merged two heterogeneous elements.

However, whether intended as a compliment or not, the judgment of Mensinga strikes us entirely wrong. The penance of Rome and the preparation of Protestantism differ not only in form but also in essence. With Rome, penance is a preemptive purification (acquittal), in order to receive the blessings of communion and the mass. With us, the preparation is a self-examination destined for the desired cleansing and atonement. And in so far that also with us there is mention of doing away with sin prior to the Lord's supper, this signifies the putting away of offenses so that afterward the Spirit of God is not hindered and the King of the Lord's supper may travel on smooth terrain.

Undoubtedly, it also goes without saying that the notion is wrong that the preparation by way of self-examination is not found in Scripture. The apostle in 1 Corinthians 11 does deal with the unique circumstances of the Corinthians, but he deals with this special case precisely for application of the rule in general. Where would we be if we denied broader significance for the special words of the holy writers? Are not all of the apostolic letters written with an eye for special circumstances? So the admonishment of Paul—but let a man examine himself—has divine authority for the church of all ages. So the self-examination for preparation to which the Lord's supper formulary alerts us is to be seen as a pure reflection of this word.

4. THE SELF-EXAMINATION REQUIREMENT IN THE COVENANT OF GRACE

The requirement for self-examination is not only *Pauline* in the narrow sense of the word, it is also scriptural through and through. The whole Bible breathes with the idea that before any holy deed, the heart must be prepared. The soul must be ordered to meet God. First, it must go into the hiding place of the spiritual life, to examine whether everything is ready for receiving the King. This ordinance is woven throughout the entire ceremonial law. Israel must sanctify itself before God establishes the covenant with his people in the wilderness. They must sanctify themselves before holding the feast day or coming with an offering. And this sanctifying is not only an external break with sin, but also subordination of the internal life of the soul, eloquent evidence of which is provided for us in the Psalms. For here you approach the inner chambers of God's saints, you witness the soul-wrestling that takes place before the covenant between God and the soul is renewed.

Note that this is the right idea of self-examination necessary for one to have insight into the mystery of the *covenant*. The covenant by its nature is a *gift* of God, but it is also an *ordinance* of God and presupposes action not only from the divine but also the human side. The Lord God comes with the covenant to man, so that from man's side it would be *acknowledged* and received. When at Horeb the ceremony for sealing the covenant took place, the people must first *sanctify* themselves. And when Moses descends with the commandments from God to the multitude, the people must say *Amen* to the covenant and must *choose* for the Lord.

This action of acknowledgment in the covenant is not only communal, but also personal. Every Israelite is called for himself to undertake the choice and the bond between God and him personally, to confirm it with a deliberate inception.

Also, this action is not by itself a one-time standing event in the history of God's church or in the personal life of the devout. The nature of the covenant brings with it that this action be continuously renewed. From the side of a man, the covenant is always broken repeatedly by sin and iniquity. Then by contrite, penitent return to the Lord must the covenant be sought anew.

Flowing from this perspective of the covenant is that from the side of man, self-examination is necessary throughout one's entire life.

That said, this especially applies with respect to the Lord's supper.

The sacrament of *baptism* runs parallel with the sacrament of circumcision. Here God *grants* the covenant, and the covenant member is passive (i.e., with respect to the baptism of children). Baptism is the sacrament of *regeneration*, the immediate action of the sovereign grace of God.

The Lord's supper, however, runs parallel with the Old Testament *passover*. Here is the divinely administered covenant by way of public, intentional receiving. Here the covenant member is *active*. The Lord's supper is the sacrament of *conversion*. As conversion is not an action that is accomplished in a certain moment for a lifetime, but must constantly be renewed and resumed, therein is the reason that meticulous preparation is fitting prior to every Lord's supper celebration, principally existing in the self-examination. Communion summons the faith-consciousness of the covenant member and requires anew the choice for God.

What Samuel said to Jesse and his sons before he offered the sacrifice, "*Sanctify* yourselves, and come with me to the sacrifice" (1 Sam. 16:5)—that is the summons of the minister to the congregation before every Lord's supper. He does this in the so-called *examination sermon* or *preparatory message* that mainly invokes self-examination and shows the way to self-examination.

But also, the call to self-examination emanates from the formulary itself. The fact that the instruction of the form begins with the foregoing is not a fault, but a virtue. It shows how clearly our fathers grasped the nature of the *covenant*, and how greatly they esteemed its significance, that the congregation's Lord's supper celebration would be viewed in the light of the covenant of grace.

Those like Mensinga, outstanding as they may be as historians and experts of the liturgy, do not understand these matters of the formulary, because they are strangers to the doctrine of the covenant.

For people who know and love the Reformed confessions, precisely this portion of the communion form is more strongly valued.

5. THE END FOR WHICH THE LORD'S SUPPER IS INSTITUTED

"That we may now celebrate the supper of the Lord to our comfort, it is above all things necessary, first, rightly to examine ourselves; and further, *to direct it to that end for which Christ hath ordained and instituted the same, namely, to his remembrance.*"

Authentic Lord's supper participation requires a twofold knowledge; knowledge first of the person (the *subject*) who comes to the supper. This is knowledge that is gained by way of self-examination. But then, also knowledge of the supper itself (the *object*) for which one has prepared to celebrate. Subjective preparation alone is groundless. Objective preparation alone is heartless. They need each other, exert reciprocal action upon the other, and are two sides of the same coin.

Pure objective knowledge includes a correct perspective regarding the purpose of the Lord's supper. He who knows what the Lord's supper is about, what the *end* is to which the supper is *directed*, also has clear insight on the nature and structure of the sacrament. The one is impossible without the other. Therefore, our form, from a position of objective knowledge alone, directs the supper to the end for which the Lord Jesus had ordained and instituted without identifying it as the knowledge of the character or the historical origin of the supper.

And what is now that end for which Christ ordained the supper?

As one could have expected, the form has identified a purpose of the celebration as the *strengthening of faith.*

After all, the sacrament is a sealing that services to fasten the covenantal promises to the faith awareness of the covenant member.

However, our form takes the position that the strengthening of faith is *secondary* (in second place), and that *primary* (foremost) is the glory of God. The end to which Christ has ordained the supper is *to his remembrance*, that is, his glory, and in him the glory of the triune God. At the supper, the covenant member is called to rekindle in his awareness the remembrance of the suffering and death of Jesus Christ. By this remembrance, he exercises communion with the *person* of the Lord Jesus. And by this communion exercise, he brings the honor of a deeply affected soul to the *name* of the Lord.

This is the Reformed, the biblical, and the God-glorifying point of view with respect to the celebration of the Lord's supper.

In its most profound sense, it is not about man, but about God. The first question is not, will I experience comfort, but how may I serve my King? The supper is not in the first place a matter of *need*, but rather of *obedience*. The question is not first of all, what does God *grant* me, but what does God *require* of me?

The Lord's supper is ordained *to his remembrance.*

But precisely in this way, it is for comfort. The entering into the work and person of Christ *cannot* leave the soul empty. He who glorifies God opens his heart for the descending flow of benefits within the covenant of grace. The glory of God is the blessedness of the sinner, as is the rescue of the sinner the hallowing of God's name.

Our form brings this connection clearly to light as the circumstance for the *comfort* of the supper is established that its celebration be unto Jesus' remembrance.

6. THREE THINGS NECESSARY

First of all, then, the "*authentic testing of ourselves*" (the subjective preparation) is presented.

We have previously mentioned that self-examination prior to the supper is required by the nature of the sacrament. Already in the baptismal formulary is indicated that in every covenant are contained two parts. More emphatically displayed than in baptism is the *second* side (the human, subjective side) of the covenant in the Lord's supper. Or rather, the second part of the covenant, which in baptism is consequential, comes first in the Lord's supper celebration truly to its own. The mature covenant member shows from his side acknowledgment of the covenant and the "new obedience," to which baptism "admonishes and obliges" him to practice, in dedicating himself to the supper of the Lord. Communion celebration is covenantal capitulation. Lord's supper celebration is baptismal application. That is the reason the Lord's supper form is so closely related to the baptism form. That is why the Lord's supper form begins with self-examination.

When we realize that Calvin supplied the content and Olevianus the form for the self-examination, then we are not surprised that this portion consists of *three parts.*

The co-author of the catechism has inserted, as it were, the three things of which knowledge is necessary for the only comfort into the Lord's supper form, and this has also again narrowed the connection of this form to the baptism form. Also in this latter form, the same three parts are included. After all, it begins with: "The principal parts of the doctrine of holy baptism are these three." And then follows the explanation of *misery* that makes necessary the washing away of sin, *salvation* that is guaranteed by the promises of the covenant, and *gratitude* that is displayed in the life of the new obedience.

It is unavoidable that also here, where it revolves around the question of whether the covenant member has made the doctrine of salvation his own, these three parts again come into view. It happens here in a manner that the subjective element of self-examination comes to its own and joins itself to the supper. The three parts are beautifully elaborated, pastorally and eloquently. The composer displays his mastery of covenantal communications.

7. A PERSONAL CONTEMPLATION OF ONE'S SINS AND ACCURSEDNESS

First, laudably, is that it (in harmony with the character of an authentic Lord's supper celebration) immediately brings the self-examination into connection with the bitter and atoning death of the Lord.

> First. That every one considers by himself, his sins and accursedness, to the end that he may abhor and humble himself before God: considering that the wrath of God against sin is so great, that (rather than it should go unpunished) he hath punished the same in his beloved Son Jesus Christ, with the bitter and shameful death of the cross.

A close analysis of this passage is instructive and pleasant.

How delightfully and movingly is here developed the simple description that the catechism gives ("How great are my sins and miseries"). And how encouraging it is already in itself by the fact that the communion participant may begin with giving an account for his sin. A pharisaically ordered Lord's supper would commence with, "First, that everyone considers by himself, his faith and good works." *Our* form begins with the attitude of the tax collector and reckons with the reality of life.

At the entrance to the supper, the words of Jesus shine: "Blessed are they that mourn, for they shall be comforted."

Consider well, that the prompt here for considering sin is not intended for the unconverted sinner, but for the child of the Lord.

At the beginning of the form, we were addressed as, "Beloved in the Lord Jesus Christ!" Therefore, it is the *devout* who are called to regard their sin. Indeed, in the path of life there is a twofold knowledge of sin. There is an initial discovery that precedes conversion and leads to the arms of Jesus. But also there is a progressive knowledge, the fruit of discovering the truth and, unfortunately, also the practice of life. Even after his conversion, God's child proceeds to sin. It is precisely this sin, *after* having discovered God's peace, and *contrary* to the better knowledge and profession, that even more strongly brings into view "how great are our sins and miseries."

That is the reason every Lord's supper celebration requires covenantal renewal, and every covenantal renewal, the recognition and confession of guilt.

Here also, nearly every word has a particular emphasis.

"*That everyone*" considers his sins.

Not only the young in faith, who for the first time, with reticence, newly approaches the covenantal meal. But also the elder Christian who has become accustomed to this holy activity.

Not only the "troubled one," who is restrained by a thousand hesitations, but also the one firmly established who by grace may give an account of what God has done for his soul.

That everyone considers his sins, and he does this *by himself.* Our Christian life-sustenance does not preclude a person's *conversation* with others regarding his sin. For self-control, an outpouring of the soul to the ear of a brother can be spiritually healthy. Even in the good practice of pastoral visitation in the congregation prior to the Lord's supper is such conversation regarding God's way sought and encouraged.

However, this framework for *conversation* about sin does not exclude but includes the obligation for personal reflection. The one without the other is impossible. No one knows what goes on with a man as the soul of a man that is within. The life of our soul is a mystery, and unfortunately, frequently for us, unsolvable. And while the Protestant concept now requires the preservation of the right and dignity of a man over against the church community, there yet rests upon a man among the believers the personal obligation to give an account of his soul's condition. He must *personally* be at peace with God. The church cannot save him. He himself (with the support of the church) must learn to believe and to be saved by faith.

So one can see how far the Lord's supper form has kept itself from all Romanist stain, and how here it contradicts in particular vis-à-vis Rome's practice of penance.

The authentic communion participant must consider by himself his *sins and accursedness.*

There stands not *sin,* but *sins,* in order to indicate that true testing concerns actual living. The admonishment to self-examination comes, as we have mentioned, to the "beloved in the Lord Jesus Christ," that is, to the people who already at the beginning *stand* exposed before God in their sinful condition, but now further also lead the entire life by the fight against sin, and alas!, stumble into many. The call to the Lord's supper is the summons on account of God that this people shall examine its "ways" and inspect its "paths" and shall give an account of itself for the *sins* by which the covenant was desecrated and the God of the covenant grieved.

This self-examination must not happen casually, but with intention. It must, as the word itself suggests, be an *examination,* a recollection in one's conscience of the past, a testing of previous living, in accordance with the obligations of the covenant of grace. There are moments of life that remain inscribed in the memory. These are moments in life of elevated enjoyment, moments when a man won glory, but the moments when he sank and suffered shame will involuntarily be eliminated from the soul's consciousness. An English philosopher once said that the soul of a man is a large cemetery with many buried memories. Every gravestone has an etching engraved upon it, but on most, the etchings have become unreadable.

The requirement of authentic self-examination involves a man walking among the graves of his memories, most of all where the sins are buried, and seeking to decipher the engraving and to *reflect* on it.

He *considers* his sins. This is not to say merely to call to mind the sins of the rapidly paced life (and how *few* sinful failures he would recall!), but that the impression of their *existence* be activated. It is not about keeping score but weighing in. The consideration of *sins* is to become aware of *sin*. He who can say with the psalmist, "I thought on my ways," will at last come to the conviction, "Behold, I was shapen in iniquity; and in sin did my mother conceive me." There is nothing that so revives awareness of the corrupt nature as pondering *daily* sins. To know that I have again and so frequently transgressed, despite my solemn promise, despite enjoyment of blessings, despite holy admonitions—onward to a deeper insight into *inborn* wickedness. David never felt so alive within than when he recognized that in his flesh he contained no good, and *was able* to come to terms with the mortal sin with Bathsheba. He did not know that he was so depraved, the swamp of his unrighteousness was so deep, the inborn wickedness so poisonous.

Thus, a personal consideration by himself of his *sins*.

This is not to say that a person must be cognizant of *every* sin before he may approach the Lord's table.

Neither does it mean to say that he must be cognizant of his sins *to a particular measure*.

A Christian is a lifelong learner in the school of the Holy Spirit and never graduates from the question of *how great* are my sins and misery.

Yet, when the heart is in the right place as far as sin is concerned, it is not only lacking knowledge as to the depths of sin and that so many sins are performed without a thought. Also, this consideration of *sins* leads to the knowledge of *sin*; even more so with the sense of barrenness and deadness of the soul that makes evident the spiritually pitiful state into which man by nature had sunk.

However, although it is not stated how many of your sins you must know or how far in the school of the knowledge of sin you must advance, the form nevertheless does indeed provide certain marks whereby a Christian can know whether his consideration of sin is sufficient. For even an unspiritual man can have somewhat of a notion of his sin. Even Cain cried out that his iniquity is greater than that which can be forgiven. Saul testified that he had transgressed against the Lord. Judas cried that he had sinned, betraying innocent blood.

No wonder that God's child would ask: "Is not my sin awareness like that of the children of the world? How can I assess whether my notion of sin is bestowed by the Holy Spirit?"

The formulary presents a valuable guide in matters pertaining to the spiritual life. The word *sins* is immediately followed by *accursedness,* and thereby indicates in what light a person must see his sins, in order to see them aright. There is knowledge of sin that remains limited to the unvarnished continuation of wickedness. The world also recognizes sins (from a psychological perspective) but, not sensing guilt before God, does not see her sins as *accursedness.* By design, the form employs the strongest word that Scripture offers, in order to bring to light the *damnable character of sin.* But it is not the sin itself that is the subject of God's curse; through sin, the *person* becomes a curse. The Lord says: "Cursed is *everyone* that continueth not in all things which are written in the book of the law to do them."

Let us not take this lightly: to be a curse of God!

This is to say that in one's deepest, internal existence, to be an object of divine displeasure means to be a vessel of wrath. To be despised, condemned, and forsaken. To stand at the gateway to hell. To totter on the rim of the eternal abyss!

Those who identify themselves as accursed, who recognize the death sentence signed by the hand of the divine judge.

Those who cry out: "I am lost! I am damned!"

8. TO THE END THAT HE MAY ABHOR AND HUMBLE HIMSELF BEFORE GOD

Moreover, there is a second criterion that our form provides for the right knowledge of sin, and that is immediately connected to the foregoing.

Even in the unconverted there can be, to a certain measure, a knowledge of sin that is attached to a knowledge of accursedness. Judas felt the curse in his unredeemed soul when he saw his iniquity in the lightning bolts of God's wrath. He recognized that he was accursed.

But where did that knowledge bring him?

It did not cause him to fall on his knees before God. Even though he knew himself to be guilty before God, he did not surrender. He indeed confessed his sins before the world, but not before the Holy One. Rather than to beg yet for grace, he leaped into the arms of death. He chose for the dwelling place of demons rather than the footstool of God's throne.

In the knowledge of his accursedness, the soul of the sinner remains unbroken. His *ego* stands firm. He holds up in resistance against God.

In the heart where grace has entered, this is entirely different.

Here, following the consideration of sins and accursedness, is that a man *abhors himself* and *humbles himself before God.*

This is the true mile marker for the knowledge of misery. Such language also resounds in other places of our holy, beautiful liturgy. In the baptism form, it is that the sprinkling with water teaches us, whereby the impurity of our souls is signified, "and we are admonished to loathe and humble ourselves before God."[2]

The knowledge of sin by the godless man leads to *feeling sorry* for himself. He blames the circumstances. He designates God as the origin of his misery. But he does not abhor himself.

Only the Spirit of God teaches a man to take responsibility for *himself* for his sin. He reveals the vile source of all his shady business. And that source is one's own heart from which sin "always issues forth as water from a contaminated fountain" (Belgic Confession, article 15).

Fundamentally, by this self-loathing, the Spirit puts to work regeneration. From this, he produces repentance, but strengthens it in sanctification. God's child must be constantly nurtured in this self-abhorrence.

---

2   Cf. Wielenga, *The Reformed Baptism Form*, 38–42.

In proportion to a devout soul's spiritual maturing, he presses deeper into the abyss of his sinful *existence* before God. He will continue to disappoint himself and recognize, I did not know that I was so depraved. In proportion to the luminosity of revelation shining brightly in the soul, the more the spiritual eye sees the *hidden* sins. When Job, despite having already learned self-knowledge earlier, then arrives at the end of the trials, he cries out: "Wherefore I abhor myself, and repent in dust and ashes."

So closely belong the two ideas of *self-abhorrence* and *humiliation* together. Precisely in the combination of these two is the hidden power of testing the spiritual life.

Still, also among the children of the world does one encounter a certain self-loathing. Deeply resounds in the heathen authors the tone of self-detesting and blunt speaking of how small, how poor, and how miserable they are. Also in our times, parallel to the language of self-esteem, especially among the artists, is the language of self-effacement. Schopenhauer, the philosopher of pessimism, traveled the world for the self-detesting of human life. And what is suicide, which he recommends, if nothing else than the consequence of an undefined self-abhorrence. In spite of all his pride and arrogance, modern man often gets a profound, momentary glance at the pitiful misery of his own existence. His scientific discoveries, his own experience of life, his conscience speak to him of his lack of courage and capacity.

He sighs with the devout: "I am a miserable person!"

But the self-abhorrence is not combined with *humiliation*. The sight of his insignificance does not make him insignificant but fills him with exasperation.

Indeed, the self-abhorrence concerns his life and his existence, but not his inner *self.* Although he recognizes his vices and frailties, he does not concede *himself* as lost. And so when he, despairing of himself, takes his own life, then that suicide has no other basis than that his self-loathing sought release by way of self-annihilation.

Note well how the "transformed" person also sees these things *differently.* When the Word and Spirit at work within shine light in the darkness of the spiritual condition of death, then for the exposed sinner there is no creature to detest so deeply as *himself.* The red face of sin-consideration covers his face, and he becomes *astonished* and *grieved* by the realization of the contradiction between his *being* and *appearance.* And without a sickly mysticism that takes a certain pleasure in self-loathing and values the self-abhorrence as something that is of itself desirable, he recognizes this abhorrence as itself a work of God's Spirit. He says with the prophet: "*After that I was instructed, I smote upon my thigh*" (Jer. 31:19).

And that is why combined with the gift of self-loathing is *humiliation.* He senses it as a great pity to be so disappointed in himself and to be such a profoundly detestable creature. But this knowledge does not fill him with exasperation. The self-abhorrence does not make him bitter toward life or his fate. It makes him tiny and fearful and drives him to his knees before the Lord. The transformed person displays his broken heart and slain spirit to the Holy One.

Neither among the wise nor the scholars of this age but in the school of the spirit of grace and prayer he has learned his self-abhorrence. There David also learned such, as he testifies:

> For well aware am I of my great shame;
> These evil deeds upon my heart are weighing,
> Thus have I erred and now deserve your blame,
> Since your commands I have not been obeying.
> Your righteous judgment I have surely earned,
> Nor could I hope to flee your harshest sentence.[3]

It definitely costs tears for a child of God as he kneels down in the valley of humility. His flesh and blood wrestle against any self-humiliation. Even in his self-abhorrence a man does not want to give up hope in *himself.* He concedes an initial defeat when God proves too strong for him, and the Spirit overpowers him.

---

3 Tr. *Genevan Psalter* 51, trans. David Koyziz.

But in the valley of humility itself is good.

To the measure that the more deeply a man devalues his own value, the more—amazingly!—he is closer to God.

To the measure he senses that in himself he is lost, the nearer he is to God.

The valley of humiliation borders on the mountains from where the help comes.

The *humiliation* of self-abhorrence soon leads to the *exaltation* of faith authentication.

To such little ones, the Lord accommodates his hand. He invites them to his covenantal meal. He provides them with the wedding garment.

That which is nothing, God has chosen, in order that he might bring to nothing that which is something.

The Lord's supper is for the sick, those who know themselves to be sick: the maimed, the crippled, and the blind! The Lord's supper is the hospital where the miserable seek healing for incurable ills. Here the Great Physician anoints blind eyes. Into the ears of the deaf, he cries out his *ephphatha!* He makes the crippled spring like a deer. And to the leprous he says: "Be clean."

Because Jesus has not come to call the *righteous* but *sinners* to repentance.

"All they that go down to the dust shall bow before him: and none can keep alive his own soul" (Ps. 22:29).

9. CONSIDERING THAT THE WRATH OF GOD AGAINST SIN IS SO GREAT

What has been said thus far in relation to the first part of the form should be sufficient.

With these few words, the way to self-examination and the criteria for self-examination are clearly indicated.

That every one considers by himself, his sins and accursedness, to the end that he may abhor and humble himself before God.

He who understands this well will not go astray.

Nevertheless, the formulary now, in harmony with its pastoral character, here yet adds something. It brings to bear upon the self-examination a logic of sorts, as a warning to take this matter seriously.

And so follows immediately,

> ...considering that the wrath of God against sin is so great, that (rather than it should go unpunished) he hath punished the same in his beloved Son Jesus Christ, with the bitter and shameful death of the cross.

Strictly taken, this is already contained in the foregoing exposition. Those who rightly consider their sins and *accursedness* bring themselves near to the foot of the cross and look up to Jesus, who displayed in his suffering the curse of sin.

But it is good that our formulary yet remarks on this matter in particular, so that the communion participant grasps deeply that his misery is *guilt before God*.

Because he knows that he never *humbles* himself before God deeply enough and can never be sufficiently displeased with himself.

Sin is not a fate, but a deed.

The sinner is not only pitiful, but damnable.

Certainly, it is from the law, indeed first from the law, that God's child learns of sin. From Sinai, "amid thunders and lightnings," he says that the Lord does not tolerate the unholy. From the peak of Horeb, the thunder of God's wrath rumbles in the ears, as it blasts that *cursed* is he who confirmeth not all the words of this law to do them.

But no less than Sinai, another mountain on earth instructs concerning the essence of *sin*. It is Mount Calvary, the tiny hill of Calvary. The cross proclaims *love*; indeed, it is a *symbol* of God's love, but it also proclaims wrath, as it is the focal point where the lightning bolts of the Judge's anger converge. The cross establishes the tone for how God judges sin, how he condemns it in accordance with his incorruptible justice. If ever, here would have been a reason for the Righteous to moderate the wrath, to temper the furious intensity of his anger, because he in whom God punished sin was the only begotten, eternally beloved, his own Son. It was his holy child, Jesus, in whom God was well pleased. Every shriek of pain that was heard from the cross, every quiver of pain that trembled through the brutally tortured body, pained the Father's heart.

But God held back nothing of the weight of the wrath that Jesus had to bear.

So great, according to the nature of the holy divine being, is the wrath of God against sin that (rather than it should go unpunished) *he hath punished the same in his beloved Son Jesus Christ, with the bitter and shameful death of the cross.*

10. THE SECOND PART OF SELF-EXAMINATION

The second part of true self-examination concerns the knowledge of *redemption*. More than both of the others, this has attracted the attention of Reformed people, and has become the subject of the exchange of ideas. In potent and weighty style, the formulary says:

> Secondly. That every one examine his own heart, whether he also believes this sure promise of God, that all his sins are forgiven him only for the sake of the passion and death of Jesus Christ, and that the perfect righteousness of Christ is imputed and freely given him as his own, yea, so perfectly, as if he had satisfied in his own person for all his sins, and fulfilled all righteousness.

In this language, you recognize the church of the Reformation. Here blasts the trumpet of faith her unmistakable sound. So say the heroes who dare combat on the battlefield of life, braving the devil, the world, and the flesh.

There stand the men, our fathers, who gird their loins with truth. On their arm hangs the shield of faith, with which they quench the fiery darts of the wicked. In their hand glitters the sword of the Spirit. And on their head glimmers the helmet of salvation.

In order now to get to the true sense of this mostly misunderstood section, one tends to think that here the Lord's supper participant is longing for nothing much different from what is essentially the requirement of the foregoing passage. The fact is that one could give a heartfelt amen to the first passage and be at odds with the second. And even worse, a yet unconverted person could accede to the first part, but the second passage can only be affirmed by the people of God.

Our exposition of the first section showed that it is about the beginning or knowledge of the *faith*, which is the fruit from the root of regeneration. No one can abhor and humble himself before God, *unless he believes*. And so also in the second passage, that no one can have a part in the redemption that is in Christ *except through faith*. Therefore, the second part is not (forgive the expression) *easier* than the first. Both are equally difficult, indeed completely unattainable, unless God's Spirit manifests the miracle of faith in the soul. Man is incapable of achieving his own faith-knowledge, as it pertains to that punishment according to the righteousness of God, or the love of God that is bestowed—unless he is regenerate.

In the first section, the knowledge of the faith has more to do with the strict justice of God in the reckoning of sins. In the second, faith stretches itself out to the *mercy* of God in the forgiveness of sins.

With this established in the foreground, we grant that in the order of the sections there is clear progression. In the second part, there is a higher degree of faith activity required than in the first. Or, rather, there is advancement, development in the life of faith, when it comes from the knowledge of sin to the knowledge of Christ, when the soul by agony over the reckoning of God's righteousness is driven to the cross of Golgotha, and there discovers peace.

11. THAT EVERY ONE EXAMINE HIS OWN HEART

Notice how pure and powerful the test is that the formulary provides for this level of the life of faith.

That every one examines *his own heart*. In essence, this is nothing other than the consideration *of oneself,* which is in the foreground, the examination *of the conscience,* which is addressed in the next section. There is a mere variation in expression, but it is not arbitrary. Here it has to do with dedication to the Lord by trusting in his promises. Scripture intentionally points to the *heart* as the location for this confidence. With the mouth one confesses unto salvation, but with the *heart* one believes unto righteousness (Rom. 10:10).

Naturally, the intellect is not excluded in this activity of faith—faith is always a certain *knowing,* indeed, in faith itself is the intellect primary—but the deeper, hidden desire, the holy passion, the constant energizing source of faith enclosed in the heart, is that which is unveiled in life. The intellect is the portal to the soul, by which faith enters the world of the affections.

That every one examines thus his own *heart,* whether he also believes *the sure promise of God.*

This is finely perceived and well said. By this manner of speaking, you recognize the valiant, perspicuous profession of our ancestors.

This is truly scriptural, this is—if I may say so—truly Reformed, for faith to seek its grounding in the *promise.* In essence, the promise is nothing other than the word itself. And the word of God is the *gospel.* The gospel is always the promise, so that the entire holy Scripture is summarized and locates its objective and expression in the promise.

Herein is first stated that the ground of faith can never lie in a pleasant experience, special signs, or personal emotions. Faith is not in itself the ground, but it is the foot, that indeed *stands* upon the ground of the promise. Faith is the hand that clings to the rock of the promise. It is the anchor that attaches itself to the bedrock of promise.

To the question, how do you know, and on what do you rest your conviction, the Christian points time and again to the word of his God. He echoes the refrain of the psalmist: I have hoped in thy word!

You can now see how this language of the form relates to the revelation of the *covenant*. The content of the covenant is always the promise, like the sacrament is a covenantal seal of the promise. When God establishes his covenant with you, he comes to you with his promises. The central promise is: "I will be your God!" And from this life-giving root sprouts all God's promises that in Jesus Christ are yea and amen. The most precious and most comforting of all these promises is indeed this, that God wills to pour out upon his covenantal child *the forgiveness of sins*. Baptism testifies of this, indeed seals this in powerful symbolic language. Baptism *witnesses and seals unto us*, says the baptismal form, *the washing away of our sins through Jesus Christ*. And further developed, the form says:

> And when we are baptized in the name of the Son, the Son sealeth unto us that he doth wash us in his blood from all our sin, incorporating us into the fellowship of his death and resurrection, *so that we are freed from all our sins and accounted righteous before God.*

This same promise is now identified in the communion form as the promise that must be embraced by faith. There must be a personal examination of one's heart as to whether he believes this sure promise of God, *that all his sins are forgiven him only for the sake of the passion and death of Jesus Christ, and that the perfect righteousness of Christ is imputed and freely given him as his own.* And in further indication as to how complete and absolute this forgiveness is, there is even added for your comfort, *yea, so perfectly, as if he had satisfied in his own person for all his sins, and fulfilled all righteousness.*

One could make the observation that the Lord's supper form did not need to limit itself to identifying the one promise of the forgiveness of sins. True faith does grasp in principle all the promises of God, and these pledges to the abundance of priceless blessings are appropriated by him. One might suggest that an oversight may be charged to our communion form that to the promise of the forgiveness of sins at least the other, matching promise, of the renewing of life, was not listed. In the baptism form, the forgiveness of sins is nonetheless named in the same breath as the *incorporation into Christ*, that is, the new birth. And soon, later in the further elucidation of the Lord's supper form, the recollection of the life-giving Spirit is named as the great benefit of the covenant of grace.

However, nothing can be said here of an essential error because the promise of the forgiveness of sins, i.e., the imputation of the righteousness of Christ, in principle includes in itself that other promise. Those to whom the Lord bestows and imputes the righteousness of Christ, from the same merits of Christ to them he also bestows life and salvation.

And reflecting on this observation, how remarkable is the similarity of both formularies in this regard. It is as if the one is made-to-measure for the other. There is stirring harmony, perhaps not in a literal phrasing but, nonetheless, in content and meaning.

Such is no accident.

The harmony of the forms is the fruit of a harmony in the concept of life and the consideration of life in *the covenant.* Both forms, all portions of our liturgy, are inspired by the covenantal idea.

That is why faith in the promises of God is regarded in connection with the obligation of the covenant of grace.

> Whereas in every covenant there are contained two parts, therefore are we...admonished of and obliged unto new obedience, namely, that we cleave to this one God, Father, Son and Holy Spirit; that we *trust* in him and love him with our whole hearts.

Baptism seals not only the promise, but also the obligation to faith in the promise. Since the celebration of the Lord's supper is a public receiving and experience of the covenant, then is also foremost the question in the preparatory self-examination as to whether there is present obedience to the obligation of the covenant: *faith in the promises of God.*

From this point of view, it appears for many to put such a "critical" part of the self-examination in another light.

The emphasis here rests not in the believing *subject* (the person), but in the faith *object* (the subject matter of faith).

Many read the words of the following this way (and from there flows misunderstanding), as if it says: "That every one examine his own heart, whether he also *surely* believes this promise of God..." However, it reads: "That every one examine his own heart, whether he also believes this *sure* promise of God..."

Even the simplest reading can sense that the latter is something totally different than the former.

In the first case, the word for *sure* belongs with the not yet fully developed faith of a Christian. Then the requirement would be that a person must come to the supper possessing a fully guaranteed and crystal-clear conscience.

In the second case, which repeats the language of the formulary, the word *sure* belongs with the ground of faith and serves for consolation for the "afflicted and contrite" heart, thereto indicating that the promise of God *an sich* (in itself) is unshakably certain and inflexibly firm. The requirement is not that one comes to the supper because his own faith is indubitably certain, but that he comes in the *confidence* that has to do with a God whose testimony is eternally certain, whose covenant is firm, and whose promise is unassailable.

Those who come to God may not doubt whether he has to do with *truthfulness*, whose promises—there are so many—in Christ are yea and amen. Because those who do not believe God make him a liar.

In the heart of the believer, ongoing doubt regarding the integrity of his own life of faith may not be entirely driven out. But he may not be drawn in to doubt as to whether God's promises are *sure and certain*.

Perhaps an anxious reader will suggest that we, in making a distinction between the subject and the object of faith, are replacing true, saving faith with the so-called historical faith. For that reason, one should indeed understand that when dealing with the objective character of faith, we therewith are referring only to a particular aspect of true faith. The "upright faith" of God's child can be distinguished in terms of its operations in relation to the word (the apprehensional aspect) and its operations in relation to the conscience (the appropriational aspect). But a truly apprehensional faith can be nothing other than appropriational at the same time.

Nevertheless, here is not spoken of faith in respect to the word but faith in the *promise*. A certain holding-as-true of the word (historical faith) you can sometimes also find in the ungifted heart. Faith in the *promise* (that is the same word, but now meant as *gospel*) is revealed only in the regenerated soul.

In his *Institutes* (III.2.29), Calvin notes this:

> We make the freely given promise of God the foundation of faith... Faith is certain that God is true in all things... Nevertheless, faith properly begins with the promise, rests in it, and ends in it...the gracious and unconditional promise of his mercy... Since this is the ministry of reconciliation, no other sufficiently firm testimony of God's benevolence to us exists... Believers embrace and grasp the word of God in every respect: *but we point out the promise of mercy as the proper goal of faith...* If someone believes that God both justly commands all that he commands and truly threatens, shall he therefore be called a believer? By no means! Therefore, there can be no firm condition of faith unless it *rests upon God's mercy...*its particular effect and, as a distinction, subordinating to the class that special mark which separates believers from unbelievers.

With this, Calvin indicates the principle of the pure psychology (*zielkunde*) of faith.

Faith takes its starting point in the word. In its initial functionality, faith is purely objective. It receives what the word says regarding the avenging righteousness of God, and this knowledge guides the soul into a profound agony. Yet enduring, faith takes hold of the word of God with its seed of life and seizes the promise, the sweet honey of the gospel from the divine testimony.

Not that the gospel of the word is *diffused* (as the ethicists teach) like golden granules in ore—the word is entirely gospel. All of it is gold. *Everything* that was previously written was written for our instruction and salvation. But the eye of those without grace does not see this. Only the eye of true believers sees the word as *promise*, perceives from that word the vision of the gospel.

How the formulary describes the promise of God is striking. The formulary could have sufficiently stated: "That everyone examine his own heart, whether he also believes the sure promise (or *promises*) of God." In harmony with its pleasant, mystical character, it speaks in the warm language of how the promise of God sounds. It is the promise,

That all his sins are forgiven him only for the sake of the passion and death of Jesus Christ, and that the perfect righteousness of Christ is imputed and freely given him as his own, yea, so perfectly, as if he had satisfied in his own person for all his sins, and fulfilled all righteousness.

We have already established that the formulary, by referencing one from the rich treasure of the promises, does not thereby set the others into the background. We considered that the formulary flows as a whole from the idea of the *covenant* and the *seal* of the covenant. The promise in particular that God in his covenant bestows, and by the sacrament authenticates, is that of the forgiveness of sins. Similarly, this comes to expression in the baptismal form: "Secondly, holy baptism witnesseth and sealeth unto us the washing away of our sins through Jesus Christ." Although in another way, the supper promises the same thing. The broken bread and poured out wine witness the atonement, forgiveness and *justification*. Justification is the double benefit: the acquittal from guilt and punishment and the right granted unto eternal life. In this dual benefit contains *every* saving possession that God in the covenant has pledged to his people.

The formulary in this place, so as not to select one promise as an example from the abundance of promises, rather identifies the *fundamental promise*, the *central promise*, in order thereby to characterize the entire covenant with its total content.

Perhaps there are grounds to suggest that the form here in a sense describes too broadly this one sure promise. The parts of self-examination are about *arriving at* an exact and precise description of the matter.

By a few insertions, the entirety is to some extent in tow. Especially the last, "yea, so perfectly, as if..." provides the sense that it would be too much and therefore (for the weak in spirit) belaboring. So frugality was more effective.

But apart from this formal observation, how gospel-filled and beautiful it sounds here. How warmly and richly spoken! And also, how everything is included by the idea of the celebration of the Lord's supper itself. When speaking about the forgiveness of sins, in one breath is added, *only for the sake of the passion and death of Jesus Christ*. Do not suppose that the ground of your faith lies within your faith itself, but know that it lies outside you in the salvation fact of the atoning death, and absolutely in that salvation fact, resolutely and completely.

The form, upon declaration of the forgiveness of sins, follows with explanation and completion, *that the perfect righteousness of Christ is imputed and freely given him as his own*. The forgiveness of sins occurs *because of* the death of Christ and happens by the imputation of Christ's righteousness. The first is the gracious action of *Christ*. The latter is the redemptive action of the Father. Christ *fulfills*, and that is why the Father is *propitiated*. Christ purchases salvation, and the Father reckons it to the sinner. He sets aside his wrath and grants entry to the Father's house with its treasures of love.

The once damnation-worthy and God-dishonoring sinner becomes a member of the covenant and an heir. Indeed, the righteousness that the Father imputes and bestows is the fruit of the great gift that the Father granted to the lost world, *his only begotten Son.* The deepest ground for this *pardon* is *predestination.* The atonement is rooted in the eternal council. "For God so loved the world, that he gave his only begotten Son, that whosoever believeth in him should not perish, but have eternal life."

So we note that the certainty of faith is not rooted in the appropriation but in the apprehension of the faith. Like a ship that is adrift cannot be anchored to itself, but to an anchor that grips sea bottom, so the anchor of faith is not found *within* but *without* the person. His anchor is in the heavenly sanctuary.

Nevertheless, it must also be remembered that certainty lies not entirely outside the appropriated knowledge. The anchor that grips the sea bottom cannot hold the ship unless the anchor rope is fastened to the ship itself. Thus, there is also what is called the subjective side of faith. And when the form admonishes us to examine ourselves as to whether we believe the promise of God, this examination must consider that appropriation factor. After all, we shall examine our *heart*, whether faith in the promise is present.

However, there is a distinction to be made here.

The appropriated certainty of the faith is not something that is experienced separate from faith as some *extraordinary work* of the Spirit. The certainty of faith rests in the faith itself. It is a part of the faith, or rather, an activity of faith that originates from its nature. According to the description of the Heidelberg Catechism, faith is certain *knowledge*, whereby the believer holds for truth all that God has revealed in his word, and a *heartfelt confidence* that all his sins are forgiven him. Any activity of the soul related to doubt or distrust of God is not some lower level of faith, but exists outside faith, goes *against* faith, is *not faith.*

Faith itself involves (includes) the *consciousness* of faith.

The *certainty* of faith is the *intuition* (immediate act) of faith.

The more this faith is healthy and strong, the less the believer reflects on whether it is certain. A person with excellent vision *uses* his eyes without constantly getting into the question of whether his sense of seeing is trustworthy. He *sees* without pondering over the character or the nature of seeing. One could even say that the majority of people use their sensory organs for their entire lives, and if perception is reliably clear, do so without even something of a rudimentary understanding of the senses. To the question, do you know for sure whether your eyes are deceiving you?, they would answer, *I see what I see.*

So it is, as long as the senses are working *normally*, and no effects of disease are weakening the organs. With debilitation, immediately arises doubt, and calls for the help of counteracting medication.

It is the same thing with faith.

In faith, God grants the person an *organ*, a new, wonderful, spiritual sense by which he perceives the promises of his God. As long as this organ is healthy and strong, the man uses this new organ without asking, is it not failing me? He says with the blind man, in sanctified soul-sensation: "One thing I know, that, whereas I was blind, *now I see.*" As for going through a lengthy series of marks and tests and categories of marks, and then more categories of the categories (as they are sometimes analyzed and advanced)—he has not the least of need. He finds all such investigating of marks as such superfluous, as superfluous as if on a bright, summer morning you were seeing the sun shine in all her glory, and you would delve deeply into the question of whether your eyes are deceiving you.

So what is going on here?

The miracle of faith that is in itself good and beautiful is in its working being hampered by enemy forces. The tiny divine plant of faith is in a place where evil influences from within and without are obstructing and hindering its development. As long as a Christian remains in this life, also his faith will be less than vigorous and wanting in strength. When he believes, the entreaty ascends to God to come, help my unbelief.

To those hindering factors belongs first of all the earthly flesh, the old man, who lusts *against* the Spirit. The flesh says *no* when God says *yes* and makes God out to be a liar.

Such evil activity is fortified when the temperament, the disposition, of a person is beset with doubt. There are resolute natures, strong dispositions that once having taken something on, do not waver in their conviction. Such men who have been transformed by the Spirit of God will also evidence something of that resoluteness in their faith. These are the Peter-Christians, who say: "Thou art the Christ, the Son of the living God."

But there are also hesitant, wavering, and heavy-laden dispositions, men who in every matter first look for the downside and will hesitate ten times before daring to come to a decision. When such people are indwelt by the Spirit, their disposition (that by grace is indeed sanctified, but not altered) provides no support, but a harmful influence upon their faith. Satan, who sees this character weakness, right there goes to work, and with a battering ram pounds against the fortress of a man's soul, to shake it to its foundation. Such a Christian will be swayed to and fro by thousands of questions and fears, with no taste of spiritual joy in his life. Indeed, he *lives*, but he does not *enjoy* life, because he doubts in the living.

Naturally, such Christians are not to be dealt with harshly. They must be led with gentleness. They are the bruised reed that is not broken, the smoking flax that is not quenched. These are the ones the good Shepherd desires to carry in his arms. However, they must indeed be told that the root of their doubt is in *the sinful flesh*, and they must be earnestly encouraged to fight against these sinful elements.

Of even more significance than this natural tendency of the flesh and innate character flaw may be the *upbringing and spiritual nurture* under which a Christian in great measure is provided. If a person was raised in an environment where a rigid legalism was practiced that damaged the budding faith of fragile sprouts, then doubt will ultimately shoulder a pathologically chronic character. There are circles in which a direction dominates where doubt is *cultivated*, in which doubt is presented not as a weed but as a *mark* of faith; circles wherein that so-called concern is cultivated, is valued, and as *the ideal* is proposed and preached. One who dares to express his faith is like a Pharisee, or in any case, identified and judged as a natural man. If the seeking soul has not made its way through a predetermined sequence of soul-struggles, and they cannot give a particular reasonable account of what God has done in them and accomplish the broad array of "marks" that count as such for them, then is the soul not encouraged but admonished "to have appropriated" nothing to itself. The man who, as proof of his faith dares to propose the immediate certainty, *"one thing* I know, that I *was* blind and *now* I see," is therefore an unknown, or at least one of no account. In short, there the *gospel* in its richness and glorious beauty is unknown.

Is it any wonder that a person raised in such ungospel-like circles, whose soul is constantly laden with dread, without the sowing of seeds of joy, languishes in the spiritual life and dares not to emerge in the certainty that cries, I know that my Redeemer lives?

That is why it is of such great importance to have a healthy scriptural upbringing, a covenantal preaching, from the start for the children of the covenant of grace that leads in the right path of faith. It is necessary to identify the foolishness, the dangers, that beguile the spiritual life—woe to those who cry peace! peace! when there is no peace—but also that the complete gospel is delivered, to the encouragement of timid souls, driving them to the certainty of faith. Our people must again learn that anxiety over the spiritual condition is not normal, but that normal is a *certain* knowledge of God and his promises and a *heartfelt* confidence that in Christ all my sins are forgiven.

Finally, a reason that must be identified for the self-examination prior to the Lord's supper is the *influence of Satan*.

There are two methods with which the evil one seeks to destroy mankind. His favorite is the method of audacious *unbelief* or also, indeed, dead indifference to God. By far and away the greatest number of Satan's spiritual children end up in this territory.

However, if this method does not take, and a person under the influence of upbringing or the preaching indicates a certain inclination toward God, the force of darkness attempts to corrupt him with a fictitious or *counterfeit faith*. He concedes to the person a certain level of religiosity, allows him to stroll in the attire of external religion, and he approves that he lives in a delusion of being favored by God and an heir of heaven. But the fact of the matter is that this man is all along as much an enemy of God as the public opponent of religion.

Our fathers spoke of the distinction between true, saving faith and that of *miraculous faith*, *historical faith*, and *temporary faith*. Considered by itself, here is spiritual activity that with these labels indicates something that is correct. In itself, it is priceless to believe in the miraculous power of God, in the historical truth of Scripture, or also to have the intention with heart and soul to be dedicated to God. However, when these three actions of the soul are considered the activity of true, saving faith, there is said to be a *counterfeit faith*.

It is similar in the material realm to the counterfeiting of gold. There is a metal alloy that so remarkably resembles gold, only the eye of an expert can tell the difference. By itself, this alloy has value in society, but the instant it is issued as the real metal it must be stamped with the label *fool's gold* and banned.

Thus, the Christian must take care. Art is known to imitate nature in a deceitfully beautiful manner. The reproduced flower can surpass in prettiness the form and color of the real flower. Humanly derived faith can frequently appear to the eye as a faith worked by God's Spirit, as one drop of water compared to another. Sometimes pseudo faith even exceeds true faith with regard to its external glow. Therefore, there is every reason for the admonishment that he who confesses Christ examines *his heart* as to whether it may be gauged as true faith.

And how must he then test his faith?

We have already discussed an immediate sense, an intuition of faith, whereby a man knows of himself whether the activity in the soul is real or not. This intuition exists only among the healthy believers, the oak trees of righteousness.

As a rule, it is necessary to inspect faith with respect to its fruit, as also the confession says: "that every one may be assured in himself of his faith by the fruits thereof" (Heidelberg Catechism, question and answer 86). Life, the practice of godliness, is the test for the sum of faith. Self-reflection, self-psychology (studying one's own inner life), can often lead people into a circular maze. Marks of faith that are defined by some therapists also require the self to review such marks, because also counterfeit faith can provide some marks (remorse, affliction, apparent truths) that the true believer experiences in the life of his soul.

However, we will soon come to this subject when the third part of self-examination is handled. For those wondering, may the explanation to this point regarding the second part be sufficient.

The main idea for much misunderstanding is hidden herein, due to the times in which we live, also on the spiritual terrain, that are so much different than the age in which the form was given birth. Our forefathers could use courageous language because they dared to believe. And they dared to believe because in the frightening struggle with the powers, Zion fortified the spiritual life like steel. Over against the fierce activity of unbelief stood the mighty activity of faith. Over against the brutal storming of hellish powers was the majestic liberated soul, with the energy of faith that says, I know that my Redeemer lives. Not only the entire confession, but also the liturgy, reflects this faith. Not with the sign of anxiety but with the sign of glory was the great battle fought.

This was also kept in view by the Lord's supper formulary.

We have already mentioned in our introduction that a formulary, with respect to the second part of the examination, would sound differently today if presented in our faith language and according to the requirements of our faith life. We intend right up front, the duly established *principle, namely,* that the Lord's supper being ordained only for *believers* may not be conceded in any single way. It is also our conviction that the confession may not deteriorate to the lower level of spiritual life in which the church of God has sunk. The confessions and the forms must stand above the level of our faith. We must not tear down the confessions, but they must build us up, awaken us, and instruct us. However, with this placed in the foreground, we do nevertheless desire a change in the formulation of the second enquiry. If the form will raise us up to a higher level of faith, then the first requirement would be that the language be understandable for all, and misunderstanding be mitigated. Then it would be necessary to come out clearly in the form that not a *sure* faith but an *upright* faith is required for entrance to the supper. And this upright faith need not be present only in sustaining development, but also the *early stage* of faith is sufficient for approaching the covenantal meal. Also, the soul that, convicted of sin, knows no other refuge than the cross of Christ, and in its needs and deeds comes forth to cry out to the Man of sorrows—that he be invited to the supper. Not only the fat of the earth come to the king's meal, but also those who are groveling in the dust, and *whose soul is hanging on for dear life.*

We do not deny that in the Lord's supper formulary this spiritual situation is not explicitly taken into account. Our fathers, however, were sufficiently knowledgeable in the life of the soul than that they would have excluded the weak of faith. Imitating the gospel, in the form is also the outstretched hand to the little ones. There is spoken of the burdened and heavy-laden heart. And especially after the lengthy summary of sins that exclude people from the table, the tone is warm and comforting. The covenant member, so it rings there, should not take it to mean, "as if none might come to the supper of the Lord, but those who are without sin." The Lord will surely receive in grace those who strive daily against their sinful nature, also *against their unbelief.*

For the careful reader, therefore, the tone of the form is not discouraging but encouraging, not refusing but inviting.

This unmistakable fact, however, does not diminish from our observation that the formulation of the second part of the self-examination can lead one to misunderstanding and, indeed, even more than might be supposed, to refrain from the supper. The writer feels this himself when reading the form in the official worship service, that when he gets to this part he gets an urge to cry out to the congregation: "Don't misunderstand this, you timid ones; the form is not excluding you."

Above all, one must not forget that in a significant sector of Reformed circles, for many generations, this part of the Lord's supper was wrongly taught. More than Methodism, faith that was suggested as a kind of emotional decision, to which a person at any moment of his life can come, and that indeed with complete certainty, has one foot in mysticism that damaged the spiritual life. The one-sided preaching of a doctrine of passivity, the representation as if true faith was only the possession of those who were led on a particular "path," and especially, that the Lord's supper is the place where only the "affirmed" Christian has entrance, is so deeply engrained in a portion of our people that it still leaves many refraining from the Lord's supper in a hardened guilt.

There is reasonable desire for a revised Lord's supper form in which the scriptural requirement of God regarding the sacrament comes out stronger, and to bring about direction and healing upon the ignorance and insanity of our spiritual, ecclesiastical life.

12. THE THIRD PART OF SELF-EXAMINATION

The third part of authentic examination is the most critical as it lies most purely in line with the idea of the Lord's supper.

Thirdly. That everyone examine his own conscience, whether he is minded henceforth to show true thankfulness to God in his whole life, and to walk uprightly before his face; as also, whether he has laid aside unfeignedly all enmity, hatred, and envy, and earnestly resolves henceforward to walk in true love and peace with his neighbor.

The purpose of every divine declaration of grace to man, of every vivifying action upon the soul, *is to evoke thankfulness to God.*

Every gracious work of God in the heart is preparation: *means.* Thankfulness itself is the crown and the *fruit.*

This is especially the case where it concerns the Lord's supper. Communion is the meal of the *covenant,* i.e., not only the gift of the covenant but also an affirmation, a realization, an accomplishment of the covenant. In the supper, the covenant comes into its own. Because in every covenant, as we hear in the baptism form, there contains two parts: and the second part consists herein, that the covenant member lives in *new obedience,* namely that we cleave to this God of the covenant, Father, Son, and Holy Spirit, that we trust in him, and love him with all our hearts and with all our strength. The second part of the covenant is to forsake the world, crucify our old nature, and walk in a new and holy life. When this covenant so functions, when in the two parts it is *complete,* the Lord's supper meets its objective. Requisite for the right celebration of the Lord's supper is thankfulness, love, and obedience. And because this part of the examination speaks of gratitude, we see it as the most critical, the purest interpretation of the communion idea.

The precise manner in which the form arrived at this point is noteworthy. The language of the formulary is quite articulate and serious, but at the same time, sensitive and tender.

That everyone examine his own conscience, whether he is minded henceforth to show *true thankfulness* to the Lord God. True thankfulness is not the natural emotion of joy regarding earthly blessings. To a certain extent, the feeling of thankfulness also tingles in an unconverted heart. Even in a senseless animal one sees faint indications of what could be labeled as gratitude. *True* thankfulness, however, is the state of mind regarding one's disposition that is awakened by the Spirit of God that comes in connection with granting us the great gift of the only begotten One. Gratitude is the emotion that is attached to a personal, saving faith in Christ Jesus. The thankfulness here intended is the third part of the only comfort in life and in death. Such is born in the heart that "believes this sure promise of God, that all his sins are forgiven him only for the sake of the passion and death of Jesus Christ."

No one should suggest, however, that Christian gratitude is nothing more than a devout feeling of the heart, a mystical stirring of the senses. The seat of thankfulness is most certainly the *heart*, and thankfulness itself is an emotion of the heart, but true thankfulness extends *beyond* this or that inner happening whether by word or deed. That is why the form says true gratitude *shows* and indeed, *in his whole life.* The thankfulness that the Lord God requires of his covenant member and dinner guest is therefore *obedience* to his law, conformity to his will, and restoration according to his image.

The form develops this thought further by saying, "and to walk uprightly before his face." This is covenantal language, language derived from God's conversation with Abraham, when the covenantal relationship was imposed: "I am the Almighty God; *walk before my face*, and be thou perfect." For his covenantal child, the Lord is heading to life restoration and creation renewal. And before that, the covenant member bears worthily his honorable name, approaches the table, and experiences the fellowship of a banquet with the God of the covenant, where also his sin-desecrated image is reformed into external beauty. The covenant member has sorrow for sin *before* God, and that is why he feels, thinks, and *lives* for God. And his life is not only an existence, not a mere *being*, but a *walking*, like the text here says, that is stretching oneself to a certain life purpose that is busy in a certain occupation, pursuing a particular objective. It is therefore the supreme revelation of life, the most splendid blossoming of life, and this not unconsciously like a dumb animal, and even less a self-seeking venture for man alone, but *before the face of God*, in the here-and-now, before his holy face, unto his glory.

And then, this walking before the face of God is also not according to human laws or according to human motives, but *uprightness*, that is, according to God's righteousness, subjectively *sincere* and objectively *validated*. Because Scripture says of the true covenant member, who has learned to show true thankfulness with respect to the Lord God:

Blessed are the undefiled in the way, who walk in the law of the Lord. Blessed are they that keep his testimonies and that seek him with the whole heart. They also do no iniquity: they walk in his ways. (Ps. 119:1–3)

You say, this requires much. It is not an insignificant matter to keep God's testimonies, to seek him with the whole heart, and to walk in his ways, like the psalm says. Who is the man who presumes to fear the Lord and show him gratitude?

But understand what the formulary requires of you. The form is a way of life and is real enough not to require that you *will* or *are able* to show such thankfulness with your *whole* life, but that the *intention* lives within your heart as such to be and to do. It is therefore stated that everyone examine his own conscience, whether he is *minded* to show this thankfulness to God.

On the one hand, this language makes the obligation to self-examination more profound and more difficult. The form is a requirement that concerns the hidden life of the soul, the innermost self of a man. It seeks the testing within you that depends at least upon your cognitive perception. It is not *about* you or *regarding* you that is required, but *you yourself*, your *soul*, your *person* that is caught in the crosshairs of the self-examination. For the godless, the imperfect, this requirement is absolutely precluded. Anything that is not sincere before God is hereby dismissed. For the Pharisee, though pretty in his external walk he may parade before the eyes of men, entrance to the Lord's supper is denied.

The requirement of the innermost self of a person makes the requirement of self-examination a heavy matter. But, on the other hand, precisely this requirement makes the self-examination light for the upright in the Lord. For in the heart where there is effectual grace, wherein even the slightest flicker of true life glimmers, there is now hope. What is to the dismay of the insincere may be to your comfort, people of God, that "the Lord *looketh on the heart.*" Certainly, he sees also the external life that the world sees. In addition, he most certainly hears the confession of your lips. But God tests you according to your inward *self.* He hearkens at the portals of your heart. He perceives the tenderness of your soul. He inclines his ear to every sigh that wells up from your bosom. He asks whether you are also *mindful* to show true thankfulness toward your Lord and your God, whether along with Peter, whose external walk so tragically contradicted his confession, the soul *gestalt* within you is stirring so that you declare: "Lord, thou knowest all things, thou knowest that I love thee."

You see, with all the evil inclinations that yet remain in your heart, all the leftovers from the roots of wickedness, there is nevertheless that *longing* to live for God. Your soul is always homesick for God. It is your resolve to be conformed to him. And of all the possessions and treasures in heaven and on earth, this is the greatest possession, the richest treasure for you, to be a pure and holy child of God. Well, that is who you are—despite your countless defects and countless more of your shortcomings—the covenant member whom the Lord invites to his supper.

However, to avoid self-delusion here, it also serves well to make some careful distinctions. The work of self-examination is so delicate and the heart of the covenant member is so cunning that we may indeed daily inquire: "Search me, O God, and know my heart; try me, and know my thoughts." And it is so important to check whether the mindfulness we detect in our soul is a temporary agitation of our state of mind or an ongoing work of the Spirit. It is necessary to know whether that mindfulness is an (always presumptuous) intention of the natural heart, or an authentic desire of the regenerate soul. In your self-examination, you must be objective and alert. Because what is more difficult than to evaluate your *emotions*? Today something happens, and you rejoice; tomorrow it is different, and you weep.

The formulary deals with this danger of self-deception and says therefore, wisely and correctly, that everyone examine his "conscience," whether he is minded to thankfulness. I concur that soul awareness is among the most difficult issues to figure out: what the conscience is and how it is involved in our spiritual life. Our soul is a unity and indivisible but, nevertheless, has various capacities. There is an intellect and a heart, a cognitive capacity and a yearning capacity. And this yearning capacity is again distinguishable in terms of higher and lower desires. Who is to say where the borders are? Or are there no borders? And who can put a finger on the place in your emotional life that is the voice of your conscience?

We are putting this forward, for the purpose of this explanation (also for the sake of everyday usage), as much as possible from a practical standpoint and at the same time with an intention to shed sufficient light.

The conscience is, as conceived in the definition by Amesius:[4] "*the judgment of a person over himself, in so far that it is subjected to God's judgment.*" The conscience then is an act (deed) of the intellect (understanding), but this intellectual judgment extends to the

---

4 A Reformed theologian (1576–1633), known for his work *Vijf boeken van de conscientie en haar recht of gevallen*, republished in 1896 by W. Geesink (Amsterdam: J. A. Wormser) [*Conscience With the Power and Cases Thereof: Divided Into V Bookes* (London: Forgotten Books, 2018)]. Interesting is Dr. Geesink's foreword in which he indicates that Amesius incorrectly posits the operational primacy of the conscience upon the will above the intellect. In this light, Dr. Geesink also clarifies here, according to the time-honored Reformed position, that the primacy of the intellect must be maintained. The volition of a man is dependent upon making a choice, and every choice is an act of the intellect.

volitional life of the man himself. Our conscience tells us who we inwardly are and dissects every particular deed for the verdict as to its guilt or innocence (Rom. 2:15). This conscience is presently as an action of the intellect depraved by sin.

The conscience can err and acquiesce in the most hideous deeds. But by God's Spirit in regeneration and sanctification the conscience is also renewed. This priceless organ of the soul is purified and refined and helps us in the struggle to triumph in holiness. That is why Paul could say, "I have lived in all good conscience before God until this day" (Acts 23:1) and testify, "Herein do I exercise myself, to have always a conscience void of offence toward God, and toward men" (24:16). Indeed, so much does Scripture consider the conscience as the pure reflection (mirror image) of the ethical life, that in some pronouncements, effort and conscience are interchangeable. So it is in Hebrews 10:22: "Let us draw near with a true heart in full assurance of faith, having our hearts sprinkled from an evil conscience."

So it is the calling of the Christian, if he were to honestly test himself before God, to consult with this conscience. In the first part of the self-examination is heard the requirement: "consider *by yourselves.*" In the second part came the demand: "examine *your heart.*" Now is the calling rendered: "examine *your conscience.*" Ask not first, then, how people judge you. It could be that those around you judge you—he is unconverted, while you nevertheless in your conscience are upright before God. But it can also happen the other way around. The world may adore you as a radiant light, while your conscience says, "You are a phony."

In this way, examine your *conscience.* But for this self-examination, concerning your intimate life, the deepest secrets of your soul's existence, it is fitting that you have the conscience go to work, to seek its cleansing in the bathwater of the word, and to let it speak with utter precision. Do not sedate your conscience, but unleash it. Do not be like those who have their conscience seared as with a hot iron (1 Tim. 4:2), but put your God-given organ into action and bend under its judgment—indeed, the judgment of your God—in simple humility.

13. THE CRITERIA FOR LOVING YOUR NEIGHBOR

This self-examination in principle determines the question as to whether you are a worthy guest at the table of the Lord.

Nevertheless, our formulary does not present only this one litmus test—authentic gratitude toward God—but provides yet another criterion that brings us to the second table of the divine law: *as also, whether he has laid aside unfeignedly all enmity, hatred, and envy, and earnestly resolves henceforward to walk in true love and peace with his neighbor.*

Rightly the form also prescribes this for the Lord's supper participant. Jesus did say the second command, *like unto it,* is that thou shalt love thy neighbor as thyself. So this measure for self-examination is also in complete harmony with the communion idea.

Celebrating the Lord's supper is certainly first of all a matter of exercising fellowship with Christ, the living head in heaven. But it is also about seeking unity with the congregation, the members of Christ's body on earth. This is the beauty, this is the triumph of the feast of communion, that what by sin is broken, in Christ is brought together. That which is separated every day in societal life is gathered together to a higher, spiritual unity. That which by the tragic reality of difficult living is widened from each other and crumbles, is united in the one King to one people, in the one Father to one household.

Bringing this unity to expression, this realization of reconciliation, is next to the goal of thankfulness to God, the highest purpose of the celebration of the Lord's supper.

The fact is that no one may go to the supper who does not comprehend this idea. There is no place at the meal of peace for those who have not set aside all enmity, hatred, and covetousness. There is no place at the love feast for those who fail to live with their neighbor in true love and harmony.

Where enmity triumphs against a neighbor, there can never be gratitude toward God.

Where there is a revolution of hatred in the soul, there can never come the Spirit of God, the dove of heaven.

Who then is qualified for this holy supper? So asks a troubled person who in his soul searching, although grace lets its beams of light appear, discovers roots of envy and enmity. Who can, as the requirement states, set aside all enmity, hate, and covetousness? Who can pass for a worthy participant of the Lord's supper?

Notice how also in this place the form deals with you in a truly practical and psychologically appropriate manner. The instructor in the liturgy is not some expert who stands above the people and does not reckon with his own weakness. Rather, he is a friend who follows the example of him who knows your frame and is mindful that you are dust. It is not asked of you whether in actuality (in every deed) you have already set aside all enmity and already walk in true love, but whether you have *an earnest resolve* to attempt to do so with your innermost soul in motion, stretching for its accomplishment. Not having attained the ideal, but a quest for the ideal proposed to you as the standard. And this may serve as a comfort for you when in your self-examination so much must reflect God's displeasure. This may bring you solace when in this territory you still discover much brokenness and misery within you. God will surely receive you in grace as your heart is inclined to the true love and you crave to live in accord with your neighbor.

But here then is also the real test. Precisely because not any external deed is made the standard but that of the inward state of the soul, only the regenerate heart can fulfill God's requirement. The unconverted man can indeed display friendliness, and even sparkle with external politeness and polish, but he does not walk in *genuine* love. For that love he has no *earnest resolve*. And if he has a resolve, even this is not *without some pretentiousness*. Therefore, pay close attention to the self-examination. It is not whether you can work up to a certain level of pleasantness. It is not a demand for a feeling to well up within you for softening your anger or postponing your animosity. You may not identify a particular sentiment as inward grace, as you resolve to set aside all hatred and envy, but you secretly leave the back door open so that as soon as the Lord's supper is over, the temporarily banned enemy is allowed back inside again. Your resolve must be honest and earnest. You must examine yourself before the knower of hearts who sees whether your state of mind "is feeding something bitter, something bad."

And besides, do not forget that when your resolve is earnest—there is then also in *principle* the new life of obedience. It is impossible that you, without any hypocrisy, would stand in peace and, in reality, would live in hate and envy with your neighbor. That which dawns inside must shine on the outside. Love is not a kind of worldview that leaves your existence untouched, it is *life itself.* That is why you have the uprightness of your *resolve* to inspect the reality of your walk.

14. SELF-EXAMINATION AND THE POWER OF THE KEYS

The part of self-examination is herewith not yet concluded. Now follows a portion that one could call the ministration, the application of that which precedes. On the basis of the three identified marks of self-examination is now described, first, who is a worthy participant at the table of Christ; then those who, under penalty of God's judgment, must refrain from the table. By way of an appendix to this administration follows then yet a further exposition of the first part for comforting the convicted heart of those hesitating (beginning with, "But this is not designed, dearly beloved brothers and sisters in the Lord, to discourage...").

Our attention now will first be part of the afterthought. It is as follows:

All those, then, who are thus disposed, God will certainly receive in grace, and count them worthy partakers of the table of his Son Jesus Christ. On the contrary, those who do not feel this testimony in their hearts eat and drink judgment to themselves.

Therefore, we also, according to the command of Christ and the apostle Paul, admonish all those who know themselves defiled with the following egregious sins, to abstain from the table of the Lord, and declare to them that they have no part in the kingdom of Christ; such as all idolaters, all those who invoke deceased saints, angels or other creatures; all those who show honor to images; all sorcerers and fortune-tellers who bless cattle or humans, together with other things, and all who believe in such blessings; and all despisers of God, and of his word, and of the holy sacraments; all blasphemers; all those who are given to raise discord, sects, and mutiny in churches or society; all perjurers; all those who are disobedient to their parents and superiors; all murderers, quarrelsome persons, and those who live in hatred and envy against their neighbors; all adulterers, whoremongers, drunkards, thieves, usurers, robbers, gamesters, covetous, and all who lead offensive lives.

All these, while they continue in such sins, shall abstain from this food (which Christ has ordained only for his faithful), lest their judgment and condemnation be made the heavier.

We call this part a *ministration* of the preceding. Following the form, you meet here the ministration of—as identified by our fathers—the first key of the kingdom of heaven, the proclamation of the holy gospel. With this key, says the Heidelberg Catechism,

According to the command of Christ it is declared and publicly testified to all and every believer, that, whenever they receive the promise of the gospel by a true faith, all their sins are really forgiven them of God, for the sake of Christ's merits; and on the contrary, when it is declared and testified to all unbelievers, and such as do not sincerely repent, that they stand exposed to the wrath of God and eternal condemnation, so long as they are unconverted.[5]

In his form, Calvin expresses this character regarding the ministration of the power of the keys even more sharply than in our form. He explicitly pronounces the excommunication of the unconverted: "I exclude them from the Christian congregation."

In essence, the purpose of our form is not different than that of Calvin. There is also a solemn declaration regarding who does or does not have part in the kingdom of Christ. It strikes us that the softer version is overall better for a Lord's supper formulary.

15. WHO ARE INCLUDED BY THE KEYS

So there is first the *inclusion* in the kingdom of God: "*All those, then, who are thus disposed, God will certainly receive in grace, and count them worthy partakers of the table of his Son Jesus Christ.*" Truly, this is benevolent and comforting language. Unfortunately, too often, the preparation for Jesus' meal is bothered by the question, "What do people think about me?" What will the congregation, and especially that deeply respected Christian, that far-advanced brother of mine, say when I stand up and go to partake of the supper? Many are held back from the blessing due to fear of men. That is why you must listen to what the form says to you in the Lord's name. What counts is not what men think about you; what you think of yourself (by the light of God's word and under the leading of his Spirit) is the measure of your actions.

All those *thus* minded—as above is briefly reviewed—all those who have learned to consider their sins and accursedness, and so therefore have learned to humble themselves before the face of God; all who with their heart have learned to depend upon the sure promise of their God, principally the promise of the forgiveness of sins; all who in their conscience are of a mind to earnestly walk in the ways of

---

5　Heidelberg Catechism, question and answer 84.

the Lord; all such God will *certainly* receive in grace and count them as *worthy* partakers.

I am aware that this says much. But not too much. The above-mentioned condition of the soul is the mark of election. Whoever is thus established and disposed bears the marks of a child of God. He has that wedding garment. He has free access to the banquet. He need not be ashamed to be seated as a guest at the table of God's Son, Jesus Christ. He belongs there. This is his place. Here the king looks upon him with pleasure, serves him from the fountain, feeds him from the delectable storerooms of salvation.

In this manner, by the key of the heavenly kingdom, the formulary opens the gate of the royal palace where eternal joy lives for poor and miserable sinners. And see, "led by light divine, they come." They come and sing:

> Then, at thy sacred altar bending,
> My heart to God in prayer I'll raise.
> With harp and voice, in worship bending,
> Thy courts resound; while psalms ascending
> To God, my highest joy, bring praise
> For all his wondrous ways.[6]

We were right to call the language of the formulary here benevolent and comforting. However, it comes as no surprise to us that it is precisely this part of the form that raises objections. There are those who suggest that here not only the test, but also the *basis* is laid for reception in man, and that it smells like Remonstrantism, so deeply an unworthy creature as man is, though in his heart already lives grace, to call him a *worthy* guest at the table of the Lord.[7]

---

6   Tr. *Genevan Psalter* 43, trans. William Kuipers.

7   See the worthwhile discussion in the *Kamper Kerkbode* [Kampen Church Messenger] (April 23, 1904, and following issues), between Rev. Elzenga and a reader who identifies himself as H. A. Rev. Elzenga reviews the form for the assailant in an efficient and compelling manner.

This has to do here only with an accurate and objective reading of the text. It is indeed said that God receives in grace the person who possesses a certain disposition. But with this it is not said that such a disposition is also thereby the *cause* for the acceptance. The disposition itself, as that which is already new life flowing in a man, is a gift of God. When Scripture testifies of justification by faith, and that those who believe are partakers of eternal life, hereby, nevertheless, the faith of a child of God is not established as the *ground* for the partaking. The truth is, it is as if our form preempted the charges against the Remonstrants because, to allay all suspicion, it speaks of receiving such a state of mind *in grace*. Without a doubt, if it is from grace, then it is not from works. Otherwise grace is no longer grace.

Also, the insinuation that the expression *worthy partaker* fails to do justice to Reformed truth does not carry an ounce of strength. It is not spoken here of worthiness *in itself* (of its own), but of a relative worthiness that the sinner does not have, and that is the possession only of the gifted man. The Scripture itself speaks of this "worthiness" of people, for example where Jesus says to his disciples:

> And into whatsoever city or town ye shall enter, enquire who in it is *worthy* and there abide till ye go thence. And when ye come into an house, salute it. And if the house be worthy, let your peace come upon it: but if it be not *worthy*, let your peace return to you.

By the word *worthy*, the Dordt scholars comment: "That is to say, who will willingly embrace the gospel, which worthiness no man hath of himself, but he that the Lord by his Spirit makes worthy and meet for it."

Consequently, here also, as in many times with such objections, the case for such charges must not be directed toward the interpreter of Scripture, but toward the holy word of God itself. Also here, the formulary does not abrogate—and this is the secret of its beauty and strength—its scriptural character.

16. WHO ARE EXCLUDED BY THE KEYS

With the same way, according to the ministration of the power of the keys, it is now also declared which covenant member is *not worthy* to partake at the table of Christ: *On the contrary, those who do not feel this testimony in their hearts eat and drink judgment to themselves.*

Here you hear the repercussions of that which is said regarding the criterion of the self-examination. This criterion appeals to the conscience, namely the renewed and sanctified conscience. This conscience is in a particular sense the testimony of the Holy Spirit in the heart of the devout. After all, the Holy Spirit *bears witness* with their spirit that they are the children of God. In connection with this the form now says that those who do *not* feel this testimony in their hearts (and thereby lack the mark of divine sonship) eat and drink a judgment to themselves. The line of demarcation that is drawn in the Lord's supper therefore runs parallel with the boundary that exists between the converted and the unconverted man. Naturally here is not denied that there can come also a time when one who is *converted*, by going to the Lord's meal, would eat and drink judgment to himself. The child of God who has fallen into grave sin and, before confessing the sin to God and reconciling himself with God, allows himself to the supper would indeed thereby desecrate the holy meal. Also, the converted must repent of his sins before every Lord's supper celebration, and especially to check whether he, without any enmity, has an earnest intention to live in true love and harmony with his neighbor.

Allowing for these exceptions, the border for celebrating the Lord's supper goes along the line between the spiritual man and the natural man. No matter who you are, what position you hold in the church of God, which office you bear, how high of esteem people have for you—if you don't feel "this testimony" in your heart, you eat and drink a judgment to yourself.

It is not a public judgment of people, but your own judgment over your hidden being that decides. It has to do with the testimony. That is why it is also not the question of whether there is in the heart that occasional feeling of grief over sin, a deep sense of the majesty of Christ, or even a desire to improve your living. No, *this* special testimony must exist that you are *minded henceforth to show true thankfulness to God in your whole life.* If there is even a measure of light in the intellectual understanding and yet some warmth in the mystical affections, but this *testimony* is absent, such a man is not a worthy participant at the Lord's table but a sounding brass and a tinkling cymbal. Note the contradiction between Romish Pharisaism that seeks the mark of life, at least the judgment regarding that life, in the external glory of good works, and what is the depth and the truth of Protestantism, especially the Reformed faith: *the testimony of the heart decides regarding one's life in God's eyes.*

It is not intended thereby that not having this testimony is only a matter of a sin of *omission.* Those *lacking* this testimony are also guilty of the sin of *commission.* While it is true that the testimony is a gift of God, lacking the sense of this testimony is a sin of man. It indicates his unbelief and enmity. It indicates his unwillingness and hardening. It holds him guilty in unclean estimation with respect to the atoning blood of Christ. It arises from one who makes God out to be a liar. Indeed, he who lacks this testimony, and who being raised under the word possess some knowledge of the truth, must be of a mind that he lives a sinful, unsanctified, anti-God life.

Therefore, in addition, the formulary does not here repel those lacking courage. It excludes only hypocrites and the unrepentant. The determination here is not regarding a momentary subjective feeling of appropriation but a constant objective being. Also, although the feeling of the witness in your heart is for the moment not living, whenever merely in the course of your life feeling has the upper hand, you can be assured that God will certainly receive you in grace. In his exposition of the Lord's supper form, Dr. Gunning also rightly states concerning this passage:

Grasp this well and clear, reader, that with these words, "those who do not feel this testimony in their hearts," is absolutely not indicating some kind of experiential condition, even less so that you may misuse these words to distort what they mean by saying, "Since I *do not* feel a special calling to attend, should I not then remain at home?" Because I am telling you that with all your "feeling" and your pious talk you have succumbed straight out *against* God's command. This is the clear unvarnished meaning of these words: all who are clearly and completely of a mind, that they are intentional offenders of God's law, that they the testimony of a longing for the Lord, "do *not* feel in their hearts," because their heart takes a stand for Satan rather than for Christ, and they prefer to make a home with the devil rather than the Holy Spirit, those who belong at the table of the Lord but remain away—such are in deliberate disobedience unless they repent.[8]

17. THOSE WHO KNOW THEMSELVES POLLUTED WITH GRIEVOUS SIN

That our formulary with "the testimony" the covenant member must sense in his heart does not intend a certain pious emotion or mystical resonance of affections, but indeed means really the state of men before God, appears all the more from the following large swath of sinners that is identified for whom entrance to the supper is forbidden. According to the command of Christ and of the apostle Paul are all who know themselves stained with grievous sins admonished to abstain themselves from the table of the Lord, and it is proclaimed to them that they have no part in the kingdom of Christ.

First arises the question as to whether in the word a command of Christ regarding the holy abstention from his supper is actually

---

8   Gunning, *Waarom niet toegetreden.*

found. Barger denies this.[9] And, according to the letter, he is correct. One does not come across anywhere in the discourses of the Lord a church orderly declaration in the ordinary sense of the word. For that reason, the principle, upon which the admonishment of the formulary is drawn, is indeed truly in the Savior's word. There is contained in principle a *command* of Christ concerning the celebration of the Lord's supper in the word of exhortation: "Give not that which is holy unto the dogs, neither cast ye your pearls before swine" (Matt. 7:6). Also it is contained in the word of the apocalypse: "For without are dogs, and sorcerers, and whoremongers, and murderers, and idolaters, and whosoever loveth and maketh a lie" (Rev. 22:15). And above all, all that Jesus has said, and not less what he has done, is the constant denunciation of sin and a testimony that the holy and the unholy are incompatible. Jesus came into the world unto a judgment, a crisis, and a division. No man can serve *two* masters: for he will hate the one and love the other. Ye cannot serve God and mammon.

It is evident that Paul, who by virtue of his apostolic work came into more contact with ecclesiastical life than the Savior himself, does nothing other than to build upon Jesus' instruction when he, for example, says: "Neither fornicators, nor idolaters, nor adulterers, nor effeminate, nor abusers of themselves with mankind, nor thieves, nor covetous, nor drunkards, not revilers, nor extortioners, shall inherit the kingdom of God" (1 Cor. 6:9–10). And especially where he admonishes: "Ye cannot drink the cup of the Lord, and the cup of devils; ye cannot be partakers of the Lord's table, and of the table of devils" (10:21).

The form is entirely in the right to speak of a command of the Lord and of the apostle Paul.

Also here, the form is *scriptural.*

As regards the character of the admonitions, the observation is in order how plainly exactly at this place the administration of the

---

9   Barger, *Ons Kerkboek,* 218.

key-power appears. Fully in the style of the form regarding excommunication is the offender not only admonished to abstain from the table of the Lord, but it is also declared to him that he has *no part in the kingdom of Christ*. In other words, he is publicly and officially excluded from the kingdom of heaven. And seeing that this exclusion happens according to the command of Christ, this exclusion on earth is at the same time exclusion in heaven. Those who here are legally and in the name of the Lord excluded from the table of the covenant shall also at the same time be excluded from the table where Abraham, Isaac, and Jacob are seated at the wedding banquet hall above.

See how the Lord's supper already in this life is drawing the line of demarcation. Note how Christ in his supper is already now a judgment, a crisis. The Lord's supper stands as a judicial bench in the midst of the world. Those unworthy of sitting at the table *here* are also not worthy of a place at the wedding banquet of the Lamb. For the sinner, the supper is the stone of stumbling and a rock of offense. Exclusion *here* is *eternal* exclusion!

With this clear grasp that is required regarding the character of the admonishment, we will also understand the portion of the form that now follows, in which for consideration arises a large array of sinners who are excluded as outside the kingdom of God.

We will first sketch a brief overview of the sins dictated and then attempt to capture the precise meaning of the list as a whole.

The first group is identified as, *all idolaters, all those who invoke deceased saints, angels or other creatures; all those who show honor to images; all sorcerers and fortune-tellers who bless cattle or humans, together with other things, and all who believe in such blessings.* What is clearly referred to here are the first two commandments of the law. The first commandment deals with the character of the faith: no other object of worship than God! The second commandment declares God's will regarding the worship; the form of religion prohibits the use of images but requires worship in spirit and in truth. The first commandment tells us *who* we must worship: only God! The second command tells us *how* we must worship this God: according to his word!

Because these two commandments are so closely related that in many ways they are intertwined, it is no wonder that the enumeration in our form does not occur strictly according to the order of the commandments. So, following *those who show honor to images* (that is the second commandment) is presented *sorcerers and fortune-tellers*, those who are more definitely violators of the first command. After all, the catechism answers the question: "What doth God enjoin in the first commandment? That I, as sincerely as I desire the salvation of my own soul, avoid and flee from all idolatry, sorcery, soothsaying, superstition, invocation of saints, or any other creatures" (Heidelberg Catechism, question and answer 94).

Here is not the place to deal extensively in a distinctive manner with every type of sin identified. The wording is virtually identical to that of the catechism, and our people are familiar with this language. Only an observation may be made regarding the unique expansion that our form gives on the concepts of sorcery and fortune telling, namely to note those *who bless cattle or humans, together with other things, and all who believe in such blessings*. This specification is not found in the catechism, and perhaps it would have been better had this particular reference in our communion form been removed, mostly because giving such a brief specification gives the impression of incompleteness. The field of magic (witchcraft) is so broad that a mere mention of those who bless cattle or humans is inadequate. And above all, a stark mention of those who administer such blessings is insufficient, unclear, and thus can lead to misunderstanding.

Just in recent years has there been a measure of light shed upon the dark field of the *occult* (the doctrine of mysterious things), and the study of these apparitions is showing that much of what in earlier times passed for sorcery and satanism must be ascribed to natural occurrences and the yet undetermined abilities of the man himself. What the most recent science has learned with regard to magic and hypnotism, by observation, is that one with an inclination toward sorcery serves well to be extremely cautious. Perhaps with a revision of the form, this phrase would be the first to be highlighted for possible enlightenment.

Nevertheless, the formulary has a right to speak in so far that it does appear unmistakable that the phenomena in the territory of magic, hypnotism, the paranormal, and especially spiritism are being put increasingly into the service of the kingdom of antichrist. They are used not to the elevation of the true religion, but for the obfuscation, indeed the contesting, of the true worship by a non-Christian world. They can only serve to place people under a spell for *another* way to a state of peace than the way to Golgotha. The occult is for many the pitiful surrogate (a disguised means) for the "mystery of godliness." And especially the occultic phenomenon mentioned in our form is exploited contrary to the Christian's God in Christ. With the *blessing* of the cattle or humans, is meant the so-called laying on of hands, to the end thereby to heal wounds and broken bones without any medication or medical attention.

In and of itself, this laying on of hands does not have to be something anti-Christian. It is very well possible that in a few especially gifted men are housed charismatic powers, by which these are in a position to bring about a sudden change in the physical organism. But it also cannot be denied that these "hand layers" in general practice their art outside or against service to God. Especially in the old days (but also yet today), the laying on of hands was accompanied by a particular incantation or magic formula (the term "blessings" already conveys this) whereby was called upon not the living God but Satan or his accomplices. This enterprise bears completely the stamp of the kingdom of darkness and brings to mind the word of the apostle in 2 Thessalonians 2:9, where he describes the working of Satan as "with all power and signs and lying wonders." These manifestations, according to the opinions of various observers, are part fictitious, part authentic. And it must be understood that under the permission of God, the antichrist (always the mighty instrument of Satan) utilizes splendid innate powers of his own for advancing his kingdom and amazing humanity with his miracles and thereby shackling them to himself.

Thus, the form, judged materially, may not be up to the speed of modern science, but judged according to form and principle, it has it right. Those *who bless cattle or humans, together with other things, and all who believe in such blessings,* are to be denied the Lord's supper and excluded from the kingdom of Christ.

The next sequence of sins signaled here directs our thoughts to the next three commandments of the Lord's law. Without following the particular order, here are indicated those who take God's name in vain (the third command), desecrate the Sabbath (the fourth command), and are disobedient to those in established authority (the fifth command). The form speaks of

> all despisers of God, and of his word, and of the holy sacraments; all blasphemers; all those who are given to raise discord, sects and mutiny in churches or society; all perjurers; all those who are disobedient to their parents and superiors.

Considering *the third command* according to the exposition of the catechism, we then must understand offenders of this command to be *all blasphemers* and *all perjurers.*

The violators of *the fourth command* are *all despisers of God, and of his word, and of the holy sacraments.* Indeed, the catechism interprets the requirement of God in the fourth command this way: "that I, especially on the sabbath, that is, on the day of rest, diligently frequent the church of God, *to hear His word,* to use *the sacraments, publicly to call upon the Lord.*" It is noteworthy how also in the form, our fathers conceptualized the fourth command in a spiritual manner. Undoubtedly, in our day, the formulation would be different and would first identify offenders of the fourth commandment as *those who conduct work on the Sabbath.* In the practice of ecclesiastical life, a significant portion of those who have been banned from the supper has taken the shape of Sunday laborers. An extremely precarious and difficult, yet unresolved, problem!

Among the transgressors of the fifth commandment must be listed *all those who are given to raise discord, sects and mutiny in churches or society, and all those who are disobedient to their parents and superiors.* On the same line are placed those who reject authority in the home, in the church, and in the state. In this connection, it serves to note how seriously our fathers viewed the sin of sectarianism.

The second group of "grievous sins" belongs more particularly in the territory of the second table of the law. Also here they are not handled systematically in the precise order of the ten commandments. In a motley, sinister row are *all murderers, quarrelsome persons, and those who live in hatred and envy against their neighbors; all adulterers, whoremongers, drunkards, thieves, usurers, robbers, gamesters.* In crass, popular terms, all sins are branded that are against the profound word: thou shalt love thy neighbor as thyself. However, because the framers sensed that the violation is as wide as God's command and that even the most complete and realistic portrayal, due to the pluriformity of sinful life, nevertheless in reality is always incomplete or according to the changing times *will be* incomplete, they conclude the list of sins very correctly with the all-encompassing, *and all who lead offensive lives.* From the foregoing no one needs to remain in doubt as to what the form means by this "offensive lives." It is not the "secret faults" known by God alone. It is the external walking in unrighteousness that afflicts the true people of God. And as the world gets older, more comes to light the truth of God's judgment: "He that is unjust, let him be unjust still; and he which is filthy, let him be filthy still" (Rev. 22:11). Because there is also a climax to evil, there is likewise an evolution in unrighteousness.

Now taking the series of sins as a whole into perspective, the historical notation must first be made that this part of the form was borrowed from the Basel formulary (1529). From this form, the sin series was first taken over by Farel, and then Calvin took it over from Farel. So as is familiar to our readers, our form in its turn was drawn from Calvin. Comparison with the various formularies shows the list in our form to be the shortest. In the Basel formulary were also identified:

> those in which matters of the faith will not allow themselves to be corrected from the word of God, healthy and strong panhandlers who by their laziness are a burden upon their neighbors, malicious tongues, and those who undermine justice.

By omitting these, however, we miss little. In the form of Calvin also appeared *heretics and those belonging to heretical sects, whereby causing division to the bond and unity of the church, those who lust for power, assassins, gluttons.* We agree with Barger that the elimination of "heretics" is noteworthy. Though these sinners can perhaps be included under the "despisers of God's word," an explicit mention would have its place.

Regarding the character and meaning of the list of sins, as they appear in the Reformed formulary in general, it is not easy to form a perfect opinion. There is more than one perspective giving weight to objections levelled against such a publication of grievous sins. It has been noted that such a summary is not edifying for the church and does not provide a flattering testimony for the handling of church discipline.[10] One concerned brother writes:

> Here the form hits its lowest note with respect to violating the law. As if we are still living in the Middle Ages. As if we are still experiencing life under the dictatorship of Rome. As if we live among the heathen. There is still speaking of

---

10 Compare, among others, the already-mentioned articles of Rev. Elzenga in the *Kamper Kerkbode* and the discussion which follows, 1904:17, and following.

idolatry, worshiping idols, calling upon deceased saints, angels, and other creatures; witchcraft and fortune-telling, murder and manslaughter and piracy, and many other sins that are unknown in the church, nor even tolerated. And after that heavy note of sins is played, comfort is extended to the believer that this must not be taken so strongly as if to mean that only one who has no sin may come to the Lord's supper. But should there have been brought these outlandish sins, that in the territory of the church are totally foreign, a significant unleashing of consternation to believers as communion participants? I think that a great majority of those who are committed to the form, of whom those belonging to the liberated Christian church would find entirely strange, leans more to justification than condemnation. If one is to move the conscience of the Christian people then it serves to let them hear the law in a more finely tuned form that coincides with the sins to which those in a Christian congregation are accustomed. Above all, such a register of sins, read from the pulpit, is not laudible for a free Reformed church as it thereby might become a lead for the civil authorities to investigate hideous deeds that may be taking place among the people within the borders of the Reformed church.

There is a measure of legitimacy in this complaint. The objections mentioned, though expressed in rather aggressive language, are actually not imaginary. The formulary is not speaking to a mixed crowd, to a *volkskerk*, a chaotic mob, but to the institutional church, the people of the covenant, the living, holy, freely purchased congregation of the Lord. Indeed, it is in some sense peculiar when it is said to the gathering of called saints, in the form no less of the administration of the power of the keys, that idolaters, sorcerers, and bandits must absent themselves from the table of the Lord. Come to think even more of the fact that when such classified are already judged by the world as sinners without a hint of a conscience, such a summary gives the appearance that this is how the discipline of the church is in general, and the medieval situation—that church and general public are the same—is still in force.

Naturally it is not to determine to what extent in reality the tradition of the Roman church had survived with the framers of the communion form and had influenced the construction of the formulary. To their defense, in the very early days of the Reformation, many are gone out with whom Rome's practices were still deeply rooted in flesh and blood. Rome admitted anyone and everyone to the mass. A holy commemoration of the sacrament was almost unheard. People had no idea about a self-check or self-examination before partaking of the sacrament.

That is why it is apparent, even explainable, that the men of the Reformation in their form cause to be heard the heavy sound of what sometimes calls for the big artillery. Certainly, a revised form would take a different tone and thereby be more to the point.

However, this being recognized, the other side of the matter must also warn for misunderstanding and excessiveness. To form a proper judgment, it is not sufficient to get a certain sound, but it is necessary to press to the spirit of the language. The external form of the language that is judged difficult and "aggressive" is also in the law of the Lord that is read to the congregation every Sabbath. The law also speaks of idolatry, image worship, murder, and adultery. But what the spiritual kernel is in this form of language is taught to us in the catechism where it says, among other things, that idolatry is "instead of, or besides that one true God who has manifested himself in his word, to contrive or have any other object in which men place their trust" (Heidelberg Catechism, question and answer 95).

Thus, when our Lord's supper formulary, that from the same time and the same circles was birthed as from where our catechism originated, warns the idolater to abstain himself from the table of the Lord, then that branding must be seen in this historical light. And in this way indeed it hits a tender spot in the conscience. The same also goes for the bandit, murderer, adulterer, and thief.

When one observes against this that being judged according to the spiritual kernel, *no one* is free from blame, because even the very best before God is an idolater and murderer, and tested according to this measure should not be admitted to the table of the Lord—so it is heartily granted and willingly recognized that our form *in principle* alludes to the *sinful deeds*, the breaking out of unrighteous deeds. But then do not forget that the sinful deed, even in the most gruesome form, albeit sporadically, also comes to expression in the circle of those who profess the true religion. Also in the territory of Christ's church are actual sorcerers, blasphemers, perjurers, whoremongers, and drunkards, offenders not only in principle but also according to the *deed*. Insofar that the church is aware of these, she shall condemn them, and by discipline deny them the supper.

However, the sinful deed can disguise itself behind the mask of hypocrisy. Sometimes it can go very far with a sinner before his scandalous business is revealed, especially when the evil doing can be easily hidden from the eye of man. That is why the form says, prior to enumerating the series of sins, that intended are those who are *defiled* by these grievous sins, that is, those who may be viewed as respectable by the world but in secret have soiled themselves with this evil, and therefore stand guilty before God.

From this point of view, it is judged that the heavy note of the formulary is not entirely out of place in the church of the Lord, and we may be thankful for the clear sound of the trumpet.

Finally, also here the form does not deny itself the comforting and consoling character. The form is not to be rebuffed in that it displays the sins so explicitly only to make them enticing. It appears conspicuously now, does it not, what the life is of those fallen away from God, in order that the true people of God may know themselves not in pharisaical pride, but in humble thankfulness in their original holy character. The true people of God have no desire for the way of sinners nor delight in the seat of the scornful. By grace they have a desire for the law of the Lord and a sincere resolution to live not only according to some, but all of the commandments of God. Though stumbling daily in many ways, the true child of God has an inward distaste for unrighteousness. He can *fall* into sin but cannot *live* in it.

It is in order to put this clearly in the light that the formulary concludes its interrogation this way: *All these, while they continue in such sins, shall abstain from this food (which Christ has ordained only for his faithful), lest their judgment and condemnation be made the heavier.* The criterion for self-discipline lies not so much in the sin itself (even the magistrate does this), but in a certain kind of sin, namely, constant ongoing wickedness, or as the form expresses it, to *continue in such sins.* With a true member of the covenant it can happen that he out of weakness (not according to his new nature) falls into sin, but he will not thereby despair of God's grace, *nor continue in sin,* knowing that he has an eternal covenant of grace with God (cf. the form for baptism).

Therefore, the expression utilized in the beginning, "all those who know themselves *defiled* with the following egregious sins," here finds its further explanation and elaboration. The term "defiled," by itself, does not appear to bear a poignant indictment. Who can say that his soul has been preserved undefiled in this world? Who dares to say, "I am uncontaminated by sin"? In a certain sense, even the most sanctified child of God is "defiled," and daily the devout defiles himself again.

However, the form, considering the broad summation of wickedness, means the word "defile" in a special, extremely vexatious sense. It means defilement in its most gripping, infectious, and deadly operations. When an epidemic is declared in a particular population center, one can be certain that hardly anyone will be completely free of the contamination. Everyone touching contaminated material with certainty comes into contact with the contamination. But not every person experiences the contamination infectiously.

In many, indeed, in most cases, the body of the person (on average) is strong enough to reverse the harmful effects of the bacteria. In the battle between a healthy cell and the infestation, inherent vitality wins. Otherwise, there is a "casualty." They are seized as a vessel for the contamination. They become affected. The sickness overcomes them, and soon they are hanging on for dear life. Experience teaches, for the most part, that a person can be defiled and nevertheless not be *defiled*, namely, when his healthy constitution responds in a measured reaction against the clinging virus, so that it does not trigger any damaging effects. But others, mostly the physically weak, lack sufficient immunity. For them to *become defiled*, at the same time means a *weakening*, and *weakening* ultimately to their demise.

And so also in the world of invisible things. From a certain perspective every person is touched by the contamination of sin, with which they infect themselves by walking with the foot, touching with the hand, or taking in with the eye. Indeed, the entirety of life in all its aspects is defiled by sin. However, God's child has in regeneration received new life power by which (also in indirect ways) he is in a position to react victoriously against spiritual defilement. In a certain sense, regeneration provides immunity against defilement. One who is born of God sins not (according to the new man), and he *cannot* sin. It is true that out of weakness the devout frequently falls into sin, and sometimes evil in horrible ways (consider David) gets the upper hand. And as long as this is happening, this fallen child of God must also refrain from the table of the Lord; but this process of the disease does not keep going, it does not *overcome,* it does not overwhelm. Soon comes the reaction of the new life, the virus is driven out, and the stricken rises up.

It is entirely different with the natural man. For him, sin's defilement leads to sin's death. Due to his defilement, he is a slave to sin, a casualty of sin; because he is defiled, he is overcome by evil, like one who is terminally ill, tyrannized by a viral infection relentlessly burrowing through his veins. Due to his defilement, he is completely incapacitated for any good and prone to all manner of wickedness.

A natural man, in spite of his inherent defilement, can be preserved from various external crashing-throughs of evil. Through the influence of a learned perspective on life, by the restraint of an external culture, he manages, in the eyes of the world, to stay on course, indeed, in a particular sense to live correctly. But he is still judged not only according to the pathology of sin, but also by the deed of sin, offensive before God, and the Lord's supper form excludes him as outside the kingdom of heaven. That is why in the foregoing list of sins, before all other sins violations against the first table of the law are identified, namely, serving idols and holding contempt for God's word and sacrament. According to the measure of the world, a man can be considered a moral and virtuous person but yet be defiled with the egregious sins of rejecting God and denying Scripture. The sword of God's testimony, wielded by the church in her formulary, cuts not only wide but also deep. The natural man cannot escape the verdict coming down on him. He cannot excuse himself in the face of the law so clearly spoken. "All these, while they continue in such sins, shall abstain from this food (which Christ has ordained only for his faithful), lest their judgment and condemnation be made the heavier."

It goes without saying that this formal excommunication from the supper (and its accompanying exclusion from the kingdom of God) is not yet an absolute excommunication from Christ. It is not forbidden the sinner, even the most refined, the most strongly operative sinner, to come near to Christ in order to seek communion with his defilement-purifying, guilt-cleansing, atoning blood. To the contrary, also to the one who has strayed the farthest sounds from the gospel the call, the obligation to conversion and consequently to salvation.

Only, the saving power of Jesus' sacrifice comes to him not by virtue of a sudden reach of the hand for the symbols of Jesus' sacrificial death. He may seek communion with Christ but not in this way. A pilfered Jesus cannot benefit him. He may not climb up some other way into the sheepfold. The way of salvation goes through the "door" of the sheep. Those who, without first repenting, seek redemption through a mechanical, external contact with the holy things, defile the holy things, nullify the cross, and make their guilt the more severe.

It is the purpose of the form thereby to indicate that it is beneficial for the person to distance himself from a false supper celebration that would cause him harm. When the covenant member is living in grievous sins and not refraining from Jesus' food, he makes his judgment and condemnation heavier. Just as the word that is heard, neither is the visible gospel ever void. It is a matter of either a savor of life unto life or a savor of death unto death; either a rock whereupon the sinking foot stands unto salvation or a shoal upon which the careless and rudderless shipwreck suffers disaster. Those who *grasp* God's sacred things with the hand of faith shall be saved, but those who *grab* God's sacred things by groping with the hand of unbelief are rebuked as pagan fetishists whom God shall punish. Even an Uzzah who impulsively put out his hand to steady the slipping ark is struck down by God. Who here self-righteously procures entrance to the banquet of the covenant shall God definitively exclude from what is light and joyful. The blade of God's judgment shall turn against him, and unspeakable must be the disillusionment and disappointment as he views from afar Abraham, Isaac, and Jacob, his family, his devout parents and godly friends, sitting at the table—and himself withering—in the eternal radiance. It must be painful beyond words to have grasped for the treasure of the gospel with thievish hand, and then to be struck down in double measure. To have been so close to Jesus that the hem of his garment could be touched, and then to be cast out into outer darkness. To eat the food of Christ here on earth as forbidden fruit will make hell the more hellish.

The language of the form here sounds harsh and frightening, but notice how the word in all of its strength is nevertheless tender.

Strength, providing it is authentic, is always charitable, saving. The formulary does not threaten here with a heavier judgment and doom in order to repel and destroy, but to warn and thus to rescue. Note how through the law the gospel glimmers where it says *while they continue in such sins*, and within this restriction is hidden a soul-attracting invitation. Therein lies: Oh! Then, *continue* not in your sin. Forsake the world, crucify your old nature, and walk in a new and holy life. Therein lies: Repent. There is hope for you. Also, there is yet a place for you. Whenever you come beseeching and weeping, then shall God lead you to streams of water. Remove the sour grapes from between your teeth, and come, come drink of the wine and eat the bread, and your soul shall live.

Truly, so is the power of the keys exercised according to the word of God, and according to the intention of the Spirit.

18. THE STRICKEN HEART IS COMFORTED

The form considers its task of introducing the section of self-examination as not yet completed. In broad terms and in full strength, it identified the marks of the unrighteous, but now the framer feels yet the need to speak a word to the devout, especially to feed pastorally the "little ones." Moreover, when it is said in the beginning that those "who are thus disposed" God will certainly receive in grace and count them worthy partakers of the table of his Son Jesus Christ, in fact the theme is indicated that still must be further elaborated, upon which the actual composition must follow. Otherwise there would be a structural disproportionality. The grounds for exclusion to deter and distance covenant members are gauged extensively. The other side of *inclusion* must be no less emphatic and powerful. The formulary must be sure that not one gentle soul be discouraged by misguided fear to exclude itself. Now, after the heavy organ tone of judgment, it must release the finest tone of the gospel flute. It must now show in its most generous measure the love of Christ, the greatness of the gospel. It would be a pity for the church of the Lord if it were actually discovered that even one timid soul missed the meal precisely by raising objections in the heart. For here comes the true, comforting, encouraging, and faith-strengthening character of the supper to its own.

That is why the form goes further, and in contrast with the just-heard thunder claps, here sounds a whisper like the gentle breeze through the twilight woods.

> But this is not designed (dearly beloved brothers and sisters in the Lord) to discourage the contrite hearts of believers, as if none might come to the supper of the Lord, but those who are without sin; for we do not come to this supper, to testify thereby that we are perfect and righteous in ourselves; but on the contrary, considering that we seek our life outside ourselves in Jesus Christ, we acknowledge that we lie in the midst of death; therefore, notwithstanding we experience many infirmities and miseries in ourselves, as namely, that we have not perfect faith, and that we do not give ourselves to serve God with that zeal as we are bound, but have daily to strive with the weakness of our faith, and the evil lusts of our flesh; yet, since we are (by the grace of the Holy Spirit) heart-broken for these weaknesses, and desirous to fight against our unbelief, and to live according to all the commandments of God: therefore we rest assured that no sin or infirmity, which still remains in us (against our will) can hinder us from being received of God in grace, and from being made worthy partakers of this heavenly food and drink.

For sure, a splendid portion of liturgy! An example of how the keys of the kingdom must be handled for *opening* the door of the kingdom. This is pure *gospel* proclamation, a joyous message for the meek.

We have already previously recalled that this portion in great measure was borrowed from the formulary of Calvin.[11] This richly instrumental reformer had learned from his great master what it is to heal the brokenhearted.

Immediately in the address is the tone of the form worshipful and uplifting. The congregation is entitled "beloved brothers and sisters." Ens notes that in the older editions, following the form of Micron, are only the words *beloved brothers*—until the new translation of the Bible was published, and in the new edition in place of *beloved brothers* the Dordt revisors had set down, *Dearly beloved brothers and sisters in the Lord.* He adds: "With justification because the title is emphatically directed to all communion participants, as also the Palatinate says, *dear Christians,* that includes men and women."[12]

The meaning of this address, with its encouraging sound igniting warm benevolence, lies herein, that the form intends as the outcome, and indeed from its tender side, *the communion of the saints.* Comfort as well as admonishment only have authority when it is established up front that it is *love* that binds the unity between children belonging to the same household. The power of the word is dependent upon the deep source from which the word wells. Behold how pleasant it is for brothers (and sisters) to dwell together. It is like the precious ointment upon the head that ran down upon the beard, even Aaron's beard, which went down to the skirts of his garments.

But like the true communion of the saints is not first of all or mostly the bond between fellow believers, but the bond of the saints together with respect to Christ, in the sharing of his treasures and gifts, so also here addressing the people of God as brothers and sisters is for lifting up the hearts to the same Father of the great household, who in Christ is a propitiated, a loving, a merciful Father.

Fear not, beloved, we have one God and Father, who is above all and in you all! He knows your frame, he remembers that you are dust.

---

11 *Supra,* I:5.
12 Ens, *Historisch bericht,* 222.

Already the address is contrived to inspire the troubled heart to calmness, at least to attentiveness. But listen now to how the children of the Father are carefully led.

That which was said above regarding those who must refrain from the table of the Lord is not designed to discourage the contrite hearts of believers. Indeed, there is a root cause to be discouraged after the lengthy series of sins because in such a wide-ranging list every listener will discover his innermost sin against which he has thus far wrestled in vain, which at any rate has not been eradicated from his heart. And with terror he hears in that sinner's name his own name and says: "That is me!"

Know then, that this summation does not count for the contrite hearts of believers. They should, at least at this moment, not hear the law. They have already heard it, and the law has exposed, wounded, and broken them. From there it is that their hearts are made *contrite*. The heart of the unconverted sinner is not contrite, *cannot* be contrite. The unrepentant sinner *stands* and *fights* against God, persistently resists. The man in whom grace triumphs surrenders the battle, he declares himself defeated, and his heart is crushed, *contrite*.

The word *contrite* appears in Scripture in the sense of *amazed*. In Luke 9:43 we read: "And they were all *made contrite* at the mighty power of God. But while they *wondered* every one at all things which Jesus did." In contemporary idiom, we could replace contrite here with perplexed, that is staggered, whereby the highest degree of amazement is indicated.

When our form speaks of the *contrite* hearts, this word is used in an entirely different sense. And indeed, it is in this sense that the psalm makes use of it: "The Lord is nigh unto them that are of a broken heart; and saveth such as be of a *contrite* spirit" (Ps. 34:18). Especially what must come to mind is that classic event on Pentecost Sunday when the word of the Spirit spoken through Peter struck the hearts of thousands and of these was testified: "Now when they heard this, they were *made contrite* in their heart, and said unto Peter and to the rest of the apostles, 'Men and brethren, what shall we do?'" (Acts 2:37).

Now, it is never the intention of God's word to make afraid or to discourage the hearts of those who in this sense are made contrite. Who is truly broken is not by God *broken off.* The bruised reed God does not break. To the contrary, when the law strikes wounds, even if they be ever so small, the gospel comes with its healing ointment. As soon as the schoolmaster has whipped to sorrow, the great Comforter comes to wash away the tears. Nowhere is it given in Scripture that a certain measure of sorrow or contriteness must be reached, a particular volume of tears from the soul must be wailed, before there may be gospel healing and sacramental shelter. With the first and smallest beginnings of sorrow before God is Jesus ready to be *Jesus.* With the first discovering of poverty in spirit, wrenching of the soul, crushing of the heart, is Jesus rich in mercy ready to extend his hand. God be praised that it depends not on the measure but on the beginning of remorsefulness, and that is why the already contrite heart may never be debased even more.

Understand, that discouraging contrite hearts is not a work of God, but a work of the *devil.* With empty reasoning, Satan keeps you far from Jesus and his means of grace, by disputing that the work of grace is really in your soul. He takes a stand between Jesus and you and conceals Jesus from you.

Especially he seeks to discourage the contrite heart with the delusion: *as if none might come to the supper of the Lord, but those who are without sin.* Naturally, in the literal sense, no one, at least among us Reformed, takes it as if absolute sinlessness is required in order to be a true Lord's supper participant. But yet the heart has a tendency somewhat to believe that one must have reached a certain level of holiness before he has a right to the supper.

This too is an error. Those thus minded misunderstand the character of the covenant and especially of the establishment of the covenant indicated by the Lord's supper.

For we do not come to this supper, to testify thereby that we are perfect and righteous in ourselves. The Lord's supper is not a show-place where a Christian displays the assets of his spiritual life. It is not an assembly where the king reviews his troops to determine who is the most advanced. Even more so you should not imagine that he who goes to the supper must have in advance discovered in himself a ground for righteousness.

But on the contrary, considering that we seek our life outside ourselves in Jesus Christ, we acknowledge that we lie in the midst of death.

In theory, without doubt, any Reformed person would readily agree. He knows and teaches that salvation is found outside himself in Christ alone. Christ does not call the righteous but sinners to repentance. Wisdom extends her invitation to the eating of her bread and to drink of the wine she has mingled (Prov. 9:4–5).

But in everyday life, the heart so easily wanders from her paths. Under the external guise of dogmatic orthodoxy is yet a fret and worry first to be something before God. Those who seek to ground their Lord's supper participation in a certain practice of virtue would readily be called a Pharisee. But you overlook the Pharisaism in your own heart when you seek the ground of your participation in the *knowledge* of your sin, in the *consciousness* of your guilt, in the *feeling* of your unworthiness. This all must indeed be present in the soul of the covenant member to a certain degree, but if it is present, then is this not of your doing, but Christ's work in you. Then the ground of life is not in you, but outside you in Christ Jesus.

Indeed, so far from our being perfect and righteous in ourselves, we recognize by our coming to the supper *that we lie in the midst of death.* A powerful expression, against which some have objected. Some have made the observation that with regeneration (and this is meant when mention is made of the contrite heart of the believer) there is no speaking of a being or lying in death, considering the word of John, that he has passed from death into life (1 John 3:14), and according to Paul's instruction, that he has been made free from the law of death (Rom. 8:2).

Is here then perhaps intended a lying in natural death in the sense of being under the law of perishability? This is a truth, however, that also applies to the believer, that his life (according to the blunt language of the baptism form) is nothing but a constant death. Death encompasses him. He walks in the shadow of death. And he does not get out of that until he is awakened on the last day.

Or perhaps under *death* must be understood the sphere of death in which the believer walks upon earth, because he is surrounded by a dead world? In a particular sense he lives in the middle of death, in the midst of a dead society, the *living dead.*

Neither of these are intended by our formulary. From the context, where various flaws that still cleave to the believer are enumerated, it is clearly evident that here is spoken of *spiritual* death. But note well that it is not said (and from there the misunderstanding!) that the believer *is* spiritually dead, but that he *lies* in death. The believer himself is *alive*, but the living believer, so long as he is on earth, is in the midst of death. Death here must then be thought of as a stream in which he lies down struggling, or as a dungeon in which he lies outstretched. Certainly, by the outpouring of new life in his heart is he *free*, truly free, eternally free. However, this freedom is objectively juridically secured in Christ, and in so far as it is subjectively applied, holds only in principle. The liberated Christian must therefore with Paul yet lament and appeal: "O wretched man that I am! who shall deliver me from the body of this death?" (Rom. 7:24). It appears that the form borrowed its manner of expression from this classic word of Paul. Paul felt himself to be a prisoner. The prison in which he groaned was the body of death. According to the context, he meant with this body of death, as the Dordt scholars comment: "the remainders of sin and of the old man, which are called the body of sin." After all, in Romans 6:6 the apostle says: "Knowing this, that our old man is crucified with him, that the body of sin might be destroyed." Sinful desires, inclinations, and actions are all connected, stemming from one principle, together forming one organism. This organism is usually referred to as a *man*, and indeed the old man, but as evident in the cited texts, this organism is also indicated with the label of *body*.

Consequently, our form has every right to speak of the believer who lies in the midst of death. The believer has with himself, carries with himself always, the members who are on earth, the man that is corrupt according to the deceitful lusts (Eph. 4:22). Truly, when Paul admonishes to put off the old man (like someone takes off a coat), it therefore follows that he thinks of the believer as being in the old man. Perhaps from this comes the old engraving of Jan Luyken that portrays a large skeleton wherein a living man is held captive.

In the midst of death! That is the somber, ominous reality, the tragic truth. And in that death the living one is wrestling, with that death the living one is fighting, from death the living one is calling.

To whom is he calling? He calls to Christ. He seeks Christ. Death oppresses him. Death distresses him. He bears an aversion to the dead members, as there is "anger, wrath, malice, blaspheming, filthy communication out of your mouth, fornication, uncleanness, inordinate affection, evil concupiscence, and covetousness, which is idolatry" (Col. 5:8–9). The body of sin and death disgusts him, as if appalled by a rotten corpse. And considering that he is powerless against this encircling death, he seeks his life *outside himself in Christ Jesus*. And in this seeking, he confesses and acknowledges that he of himself cannot find life, in other words, that he lies in the midst of death.

Do we now understand the language of the formulary and feel its comforting strength? Is it not also now clear that the form is not speaking of an exceptional situation in which only a very weak or far-wandering believer should be converted, but that this bitter, dreadful language, *in the midst of death*, regards also the greatest heroes of faith and those most sanctified? Are we aware that life on earth brings with it this reality, and that it can be no other way as long as we bear image of the earthly?

Well now, then listen further to what the form says to you, in order to allure you to the medicine of the covenant that must heal you.

The formulary, after the matter in question has been first introduced with only a sentence, now goes into the matter itself, working it out in a practical way for the congregation. It brings up a few facts from the reality of the Christian life, by which he can see what that is: to lie in the midst of death, but also how this fact cannot hinder us from partaking of the heavenly food and drink.

Here the formulary gives us a fine piece of spiritual psychology (pastoral care). Sometimes fun is made of the psychology that our fathers have served us in their enormous books, and indeed there was in their life-analysis a bit of scholasticism now and then or also a touch of mysticism. But now appreciate this example of healthy congeniality. It is true, in the style of the fathers, the sentence is long and difficult, but the content is sweet and tender and does not neglect to revive the heart of those who hunger for righteousness.

The chief fault of the "troubled" one is, as we have already noted, that he is looking for the standpoint of his faith within the confines of the life of his soul. The basis for the life of faith may and can only be Christ. Now when the "troubled" believer counters that he nevertheless must investigate the life in his soul, so that he shall roam uninhibited among Jesus' friends, then is the answer: "Certainly, but that life is and may only be a *mark* of your faith, not its *ground*." And then, you may not seek this mark of faith in terms of the *process* but in the *principle* of life. With the principle of life in your heart can be connected, even factually connected, *many faults and miseries.*

The form sums up three shortcomings for you. The first concerns the *awareness of faith.* A child of God never has a mature, full-grown faith on this earth. His knowing is a knowing in part, his prophesying is a prophesying in part. Not only is his faith in strife with unbelief, coupled with unbelief, so that to the confession: I believe, must attach the petition together: so come help my unbelief, Lord!—but faith itself is weak, it complains illegitimately, it blooms poorly. The plant of faith stands in dry ground and is encompassed by a freezing atmosphere. That is why no matter how sanctified, how beautiful, how godly faith is in itself as a miraculous work of the Spirit, it does not *function* well as long as you are in this life.

In not realizing this truth hides the main source of spiritual foolery, especially when the certainty of one's salvation is marked as a special gift that the Spirit attaches to faith. Scripture teaches that faith *itself* includes knowledge and certainty. If a man believes, then he is also assured. By the measure of his faith, he is also convinced. But when Christian experience teaches that faith is small and imperfect, then follows from this that also certainty is imperfect. There are times when heaven appears far away, the presence of Christ fades, and the cross darkens. Moments come when divine billows and waves overwhelm and you do not see the fatherly hand. Or, what is worse, your heart has waxed so cold that any feeling there seems extinguished and the desire for grace seems dead.

Certainly, such disposition of a soul is dismal and we are obligated to humble ourselves before the face of God, but do not think that the imperfection of faith excludes you. It does not concern your state before God, but your condition. It concerns not the being, but the wellbeing of the life of your soul. Even though you cannot refer to times in your life when you could rejoice in the knowledge that your Redeemer lives, also though on your pilgrim's journey you have seen nothing other than the twilight, also then the weakness of your faith may not cause you to doubt your standing of righteousness before God. Weak faith cannot fight with fact, the fact that you live. One who is weak is not dead. The dead are not weak, they are nothing at all. The imperfection of faith is, dare I say it, a *normal* occurrence. At any rate, it is not abnormal, uncommon for someone who yet lies in the midst of death, that here on earth he is like a teetering, tottering toddler, like a reed that is bent to and fro by the wind.

Further, the second shortcoming that the believer experiences within, and to which Satan directs him in order to keep him from the supper, concerns his *duties of faith*. Constantly, *we do not give ourselves to serve God with that zeal as we are bound.*

True faith is not only for taking refuge but also for bearing fruit. Faith holds to Christ but also works from Christ. It does not do this first when it has come to full maturity, but at once when it becomes active. It is of the nature of faith to go to work, to serve God. As it is impossible for a burning fire not to give off heat, so it is impossible for a living faith not to be zealous in the service of the Lord. Where faith is exceptionally alive, there sounds the gallant language of the apostles: "We cannot but speak the things which we have seen and heard." There is the testimony of Da Costa, that he wants the whole earth to resound with God's praise.

Correctly then may, indeed must, one conclude that those in whom devotion for the things of the Lord is entirely absent are yet unconverted. Those who feel nothing, with no interests for the kingdom of God, or who are merely passionate with a pharisaical zeal, out of pride, in order to be seen by men, for building a temple to themselves, are yet in their sin.

However, be warned regarding the opposite conclusion, that only those who always have an unwavering, burning devotion for service to God would be a child of God. Also, here determinative is not the degree but the principle. Suppose that in only one moment of your life—which of itself is, fortunately, impossible—you sensed a weak cherishing of love in your heart for the things of Jesus, and this devout love was upright. By this you already may know that you are in and not out. Like when a baby heaves the one cry, no matter how weak and even if barely audible, it is a sign of life. The *dead* do not breathe, they do not sigh, and they have no zeal.

Therefore, do not hold in view (at least not in this connection) the mighty heroes who have been so zealous that in their life was actualized the word, "The zeal of thine house hath eaten me up,"— but consider what God's Spirit has wrought within you. And do not despise the day of small beginnings—though there is much deadness and lack of love in your heart, you know nevertheless times when something burned in your soul for the honor of your God, that within you something ignited a passion for his glorious kingdom. There was something within that *compelled* you to prayer. You were led to God's word and had consumed the words of life. And you sat under the preaching teary-eyed and with an overwhelmingly convicted heart. Must you now not say with the men of Emmaus that your heart was burning within you?

The zeal is there, the Spirit of God not leaving himself without a witness; only it is not about zeal for which you are *guilty*. You come to this in part, not more. Indeed, ninety-nine percent short. But that this is less than perfect does not take away from the fact that it is real. And the reality is this: a dead person has no zeal!

Whereby then in the third place is called the shortcoming in *spiritual warfare*. True zeal of the heart made alive directs itself not only to advancing the things of the Lord, but also to one's personal maturation of life. Faith seeks not only to expel Satan from the fortress of God's *church*, but also from the castle of your own *heart*. And when a Christian recognizes this task of life, he then perceives that he is yet daily to *strive with the weakness of our faith, and the evil lusts of our flesh*.

The here-mentioned matter concerns particularly the life of sanctification. In the battle about spiritual freedom, the true believer desires not to be worsted, but offers resistance in order to keep the upper hand.

Also at this point the truth holds, that he who is a slave of his sinful passions feeds his evil desires publicly or secretly, and only does not yield to them in so far as the external circumstances prevent him, but as the opportunity offers itself gives free rein to sinful passion. Also, here it holds of such a one that he stands outside the kingdom of God, and at the same time outside the table of the Lord. A fleshly existence is absolutely incompatible with the highly spiritual character of the holy sacrament. For believers the Pauline word truly is that they walk not after the flesh, but after the Spirit. For they who are after the flesh do mind the things of the flesh; but they who are after the Spirit the things of the Spirit. For to be carnally minded is death; but to be spiritually minded is life and peace.

However, also be careful here of the opposite conclusion, as if the complete absence of any stirrings of the flesh is necessary for being a child of God. No, the believer also must do battle with the evil lusts of his flesh. Or rather, *only* the believer has to do battle with this. The unbeliever does not fight with it. He loves his desires. He nourishes them. At least, he doesn't hate them. And if he does suppress them, it is only because it is what necessity requires of him.

Strife is a sign of life, even though the strife is merely an endeavor. The dead do not strive but are buried. Also here is the principle that is decisive for you. And also, the small beginning of obedience may be a sign for you that God has begun a good work in you. Certainly, there is a gradation (ascending) in sanctification. There are those far ahead on the way as Job, who in his infirmities praised God—and you may be jealous of these saints and long to reach their heights— but the Shepherd also tends to the weak sheep, the good Shepherd is also determined to lead the little lambs.

Behold what a guide of faith he is.

It is his voice that resounds in these words: *therefore, notwithstanding* such things as these, *you rest assured of being received of God in grace, and of being made worthy partakers of this heavenly food and drink.*

This is gospel. The merciful God establishes his *nevertheless* over against all your misgivings, over against the fact of your profound lostness, your despicable depravity. In the midst of death—*nevertheless! notwithstanding!* This is the triumph of redemption over the mighty threesome of Satan, sin, and death.

Watch, however, that with this triumphant gospel you heed the noteworthy parenthesis that our formulary here inserts so as to administer the key of the word purely. As it says in the catechism, it is declared and publicly testified to all and every believer, that *whenever they receive the promise of the gospel by a true faith,* all their sins are really forgiven them of God, for the sake of Christ's merits.

The presentation of the gospel is bound to, in a certain sense one can say is dependent on, true faith. Where there is no faith, there is no forgiveness, also no comfort. That is why in our form is also embedded this portion: *yet, since we are (by the grace of the Holy Spirit) heart-broken for these weaknesses, and desirous to fight against our unbelief, and to live according to all the commandments of God.*

Especially tenderly and encouragingly is the contrite of heart here addressed, and at the same time a difficulty that weighs upon him is met. Previously, the shortcomings were identified that still cleave to him: small faith, sluggishness, lust of the flesh. Of itself comes the objection: is not the presence of this evil evidence that I have imagined in vain to be a partaker of grace?

This certainly could be the case because how lightly the heart of the Pharisee appropriates wellbeing along ways of vanity. But in the first place, this is decidedly not the question: what have you done and which shortcomings do you yet have, but: *where are you heading*, what are you thinking, how do you feel deep down about it?

Should you be heartbroken for such weaknesses, and if you are desirous to fight against your unbelief and to live according to all the commandments of God, then take courage, for the work of God has begun in you. No sin or infirmity, which still remains in you (against your will), can hinder you from being received of God.

From the perspective of language, a comment must be made regarding the last part of the sentence of this pericope that strikes us as somewhat strange.

One would expect to read that no sin nor infirmity, which still remains in us (against our will), can hinder *God*, that he in grace would receive us. However, there stands: can hinder *us*. So we get a linguistic sense that the sentence does not run smoothly, because following the words *can hinder us* should then be, "from approaching God" or, "from receiving God's grace." However, we have here to do with a *praegnante* (compression), a rhetorical device. To be understood here must be inserted: *in faith* or *in trust*. The sentence then goes well as: "Therefore we rest assured that no weakness or infirmity, which still remains in us (against our will), can hinder us *in trusting* that our God would (not) receive us in grace." It speaks for itself that in either case the particle *not* must be dropped, otherwise there would be a double negative.

Going forward, we shall refrain from further detailing of the spiritual situations that our formulary raises. Certainly, the usefulness cannot be doubted of what one could call a Reformed faith psychology. Especially in our days with its objective glory is the concern to make the man more and more known to himself and to concern himself that in word and writing the people are exactly instructed concerning the "experiential life." However, no less may the eye be opened for the impending danger that exactly by too much psychology the heart is not jerked from its sphere and loses its certainty. It is simply impossible to heal the ailments and sicknesses of the spiritual life by psychology, no matter how finely constructed and how ingeniously specialized. The ground of faith is never a soul experience within us but is Christ the Lord outside us. The secret of the certainty of faith is not hidden in a certain self-reflection, but lies therein, "that we seek our life outside ourselves in Jesus Christ." And insofar that faith must nevertheless be a personal experience, so is certainty an *immediate* possession, a holy intuition, that is not learned in a school, but is granted by the Spirit. Undoubtedly, Christ provides us his word and sacrament for building up the spiritual life, and thus also to enlighten the consciousness of faith. But this enlightening happens not through constant discussion of the topic of the certainty of faith, but through the simple preaching of the gospel itself, by the administration of the word of God in all its richness. To the measure a man increasingly partakes of the bread of life, according to that measure shall he be strengthened, and thus also his perspective become more sure and clear.

Moreover, experience teaches that especially the extensive summation of the so-called marks of faith in the end spiritually brings a man no further, in part because the unconverted also have faith criteria such as sorrow, need, shame, gladness, desire. In order to serve as marks for the basis of faith, further marks are then needed whereby we can test the marks, and so, with the praiseworthy intention to guard the soul against self-deceit, the poor soul is dangled among these countless marks. The little fellow bobs hopelessly on the uncertain bars of psychology of feeling, when he could be so firmly anchored if his certainty were sought outside himself in him who is our hope.

Especially with a view to the Lord's supper may there be an earnest watching that the emotional life does not dominate. More than emotion is a person's *will*. By the will is a man obedient, and obedience is the principal rule in the kingdom of God, as it surpasses in importance even the sacrifice. And the will is in turn directed by the intellect, with which a man is also called to serve his God. So that not one activity of the soul, but the whole man must be tested as to whether he is a Christian and thus a worthy partaker of the Lord's supper. He who at the cost of the other "faculties of the soul" (allow me yet once this expression that is contested in our times) forces one to the foreground, shatters the harmony of the soul and loses directive control over his life.

The obedience of the covenant, which baptism requires, and which the Lord's supper summons, is always *that we cleave to this one God, Father, Son and Holy Spirit, that we trust in him and love him with our whole hearts, our whole soul, our whole mind and with all our strength.*

To these strengths belong not only the emotions and the will, but also *the intellect* (see Matt. 22:37).

Chapter Five

IN REMEMBRANCE OF HIM

1. THE MEANING AND FORM OF THIS SECTION

Now before us is the last section of the doctrinal portion of the Lord's supper formulary. We are instructed regarding the purpose and character of the celebration of the Lord's supper. It unfolds for us the scriptural idea regarding the meaning and the use of this covenantal treasure.

Strictly taken, this is the main portion of the form, and everything that precedes was introduction and preparation. In the baptismal form, the doctrinal section exists only from an instruction concerning the meaning of the sacrament itself. Absent is instruction that serves for the preparation of self-examination. Yet the form for baptism does not direct itself in the first instance to the little child who receives the sacrament, but to the parents who seek the sacrament for the little child.

In the Lord's supper formulary, this character of the instruction is switched. Here is the congregation itself receiving the sacrament and thus summoned to a testing of the faith, namely faith not in general (because this faith is also required of the parents of the baptized child) but faith specifically in connection with the celebration of the banquet meal of the New Testament.

Thus, it is logical and practical that in this last form an extensive testing of faith precedes. And as we have noted, in this examination there lies, as our form presents it, already many a valuable lesson regarding the authentic character that celebration of the supper involves, so that we do not enter unprepared from the narthex of the formula into the holy place itself.

A few remarks are in order concerning the architecture of this part.

As we already explained in our introduction,[1] this portion is divided into three sections. The purpose and meaning of the supper is first indicated by characterizing the supper as a remembrance of the death of the Lord. This section begins with: *First. That we are confidently persuaded in our hearts...*; and ends with the words, *that covenant of grace and reconciliation when he said: It is finished.*

Following this *first*, one would now expect a *second* or *next*. But you would find a distinguishing particle as such to be absent. The second section, in which we are instructed concerning the character of the sacrament in terms of what it means for the strengthening of faith, begins with the words, *And that we might firmly believe that we belong to this covenant of grace*, and concludes with, *and be made partakers of all his riches, of life eternal, righteousness, and glory.*

The third section is clearly delineated, though not with a *thirdly*, but beginning in this way, "*Besides, that we by this same Spirit...*" The end of this portion falls naturally with the conclusion of this entire doctrinal part, indicated by, "*and not only show this in word, but also in deed towards one another.*" Whereupon yet the formula bears the character of a benediction: "*Hereto assist us, the Almighty God and Father of our Lord Jesus Christ through his Holy Spirit. Amen.*"

That is the structure of the main portion of our formulary.

With this might now appear inharmonious the heading above this section, which is, *Let us now also consider, to what end the Lord hath instituted his supper, namely, that we do it in remembrance of him.* At the beginning of the form, virtually the same words are written:

That we may now celebrate the supper of the Lord to our comfort, it is above all things necessary, first, rightly to

1 See beginning of chapter II.

examine ourselves; *and further, to direct it to that end for which Christ hath ordained and instituted the same, namely, to his remembrance.*

Inadvertently, one is tempted to question: but is the celebration of the supper only for the purpose of the remembrance of Christ? Is not its goal, indeed its chief purpose, wherefore Christ has instituted this sacrament, the strengthening of faith in communion with the living Christ? Is this not virtually assumed by the form itself, when it devotes an important pericope, namely, the second above written part, to the exposition of this effectuation of the sacrament upon the life of faith?

Such questions are fair and reasonable. And we admit that it would have been desirable if it were plainly noted in the heading above this section that the Lord has also instituted his supper for us to enrich spiritual life in the exercise of communion with Jesus. A revision of the form may do well to give attention to this point.

One should not forget, however, in order to establish a sound judgment, two things.

First, that in the institution of the supper, the Lord himself has given the purpose of the ordinance no otherwise than by saying, do this in remembrance of me. And Paul, recalling these words, adds by way of explanation: "Ye do show the Lord's death till he come."

Therefore, our form confines itself to the actual, sober wording of Scripture.

But in the second place should one consider that in these sober words are contained, as in seed form, the entire doctrine of the Lord's supper. First of all, the Lord's supper bears true fruit when it strengthens the relationship between Christ and the believer. The conscious union experienced in the supper also comes to expression in the intentional remembering of the suretyship of the dying Christ. If that faith-remembrance is there, there is rapport between Christ and you. And if this rapport is there, the Lord's supper *cannot* fail to strengthen your faith. It is absolutely impossible for the supper to foster blessing without remembrance of Christ. But in contrast, it is also impossible that we should contemplate Christ in faith without thereby being blessed.

It is therefore the matter being conceived *in principle*, not at all incomplete, when the form says that the Lord has instituted the supper to the end that we do it in remembrance of him, and then provides guidance for this remembrance with further instruction. Only, what in principle is correct can be pressed by *formal* objections. And so is it here according to our conviction. It would be worthwhile to the words, "that we do it in remembrance of him," to add the words, "so that we may be strengthened in our faith through communion with Christ." Or also that one use this formula: "The Lord hath instituted for us his supper, so that our faith be strengthened through communion with him. Such occurs in this way, that we celebrate the supper in remembrance of him."

Such a heading would undoubtedly better cover the further content of the doctrine of the supper that is presented to us in the form. Nevertheless, obviously the form shows that true celebration of the supper is not only a matter of remembering the fact, to have knowledge of the death of the Lord, but also a faith-rapport with the triumphant Savior.

Zwingli esteemed, as is known, the first to be sufficient as to the celebration of the meal. According to him the main idea of the covenantal meal was a return to the historical event of the deliverance through Jesus' atonement. For him, the horizontal and historical was virtually the sole line. Calvin taught that the supper also concerns a working of faith that happens in connection with the heavenly Christ. To the horizontal line he thus added the vertical or mystical line.[2]

And in our formulary, both of these lines are clearly taken into account.

---

2   See A. Kuyper, *E voto Dordraceno: toelichting op den Heidelergschen catechismus,* III (Amsterdam: Höverker & Wormser, 1904), 133ff.

The first part summons remembrance of the fact of the deliverance through Christ's atoning suffering and death. Here runs the horizontal.

In the second part that exercise of remembrance in connection with Jesus' own words of the institution is further drawn out and deepened while directing the eye of faith on high, as the form says, that we by the life-giving Spirit, who dwells in Christ as in the head, and in us as his members, might have true communion with him, and be made partakers of all his riches.

Because we will soon return to explaining this matter of the sacramental working of the supper, in order to document it with historical evidence, this introductory word may for now be sufficient for getting into the character of this second main portion in our formulary.

2. THE REMEMBRANCE OF CHRIST'S SUFFERING AND DEATH

Now we transition to handling the first part of this section, which is as follows:

First. That we are confidently persuaded in our hearts, that our Lord Jesus Christ (according to the promises made from the beginning to our forefathers in the Old Testament) was sent of the Father into the world; that he assumed our flesh and blood; that he bore for us the wrath of God (under which we should have perished everlastingly) from the beginning of his incarnation, to the end of his life upon earth; and that he hath fulfilled, for us, all obedience and righteousness of the divine law; especially, when the weight of our sins and the wrath of God pressed out of him the bloody sweat in the garden, where he was bound that we might be freed from our sins; that he afterwards suffered innumerable reproaches, that we might never be confounded; that he was innocently condemned to death, that we might be acquitted at the judgment seat of God; yea, that he suffered his blessed body to be nailed to the cross—that he might fix thereon the handwriting of our sins; and has also taken upon himself the curse due to us, that he might fill us with his blessings: and humbled himself unto the deepest reproach and agony of hell, both in body and soul, on the tree of the cross, when he cried out with a loud voice, *My God, my God! why hast thou forsaken me?* that we might be accepted of God and nevermore be forsaken of him: and finally confirmed with his death and shedding of his blood, the new and eternal testament, that covenant of grace and reconciliation, when he said: *It is finished.*

In this part is clearly and eloquently presented the straightforward purpose of the Lord's supper celebration, namely, the remembrance of Christ.

This pericope is indeed quite noteworthy for our form. The fact is that in Calvin such a passage does not appear, and also it is not found in the London formulary. Thus, we have here to do with Olevianus' own contribution. And it indeed speaks well of him, for it is a contribution that depicts the entire character of the Reformation. It would be difficult to point to any one writing of the men of the Reformation wherein the suffering of Christ as a surety, a definitive substitutionary suffering, is depicted as here, so inspired and clear and detailed.

Here, clearly and beautifully, reverberates those portions of our confession wherein also the substitutionary atonement (*satisfactio vicaria*) is confessed. For example, questions 17 and especially 37 of the Catechism are cited almost verbatim with what we have in our form, that "all the time that he lived on earth, but especially at the end of his life, Christ sustained in body and soul the wrath of God against the sins of all mankind..." We also encounter the same language in articles 20–23 of our Belgic Confession.

So it strikes us as rather odd to hear Mensinga's claim that "here appears to be taught a superficial perception of the substitutionary atonement" that "upon closer consideration" one would see "that it is not solid." And especially it goes against the grain when Mensinga says that the analysis of the sufferings of Christ is rather verbose and pleonastic (excessive).[3]

How can the vicarious character of the Lord be more intensively and amply attested than by the constantly repeated contrast between "he" and "us"? That in our consideration of Christ not only in the moment of his death, but upon all his way, and in all his actions and suffering, he should be viewed as a *surety*, that the suretyship character in the various phases of his sufferings is displayed to us. And truly, those with Reformed sensitivities know that precisely the suretyship is the heart of the gospel and the ground for faith, and that this analysis is neither verbose nor exhausting. Rather, this language is a *frisch*, an invigorating gospel bath wherein the soul is immersed.

Certainly, it must be agreed that not every expression utilized here is taken directly from Scripture. More than one of the thoughts is *inferred* rather than *drawn* from the word. Also, it is true that in the circle of the Reformed in the area of this inference, especially in preaching, it occasionally went too far. For a time, it was in vogue as to contemplation on the suffering to see a special meaning in every part of it, e.g., that Christ suffered thirst in order to expiate the sin of drunkenness, and he was naked on the cross in order to atone for the sin of outlandish apparel, etc. But there is solid ground for disputation that the Lord's supper formulary may also be faulted at this point.

Right from the beginning it is already beneficent.

In this introduction is mentioned, by way of leading into the portrayal of suffering, the character of the incarnation, as well as the fact and purpose of Jesus coming to earth. There is here offered, in a sense in abbreviated, *pregnant* style, a summary of the entire history of salvation. These salvation facts, however, we must not merely

---

3   Cf. Mensinga, 52ff., as well as in other places.

accept intellectually as history but must receive these into our hearts *as truths*. From there comes that kindhearted benevolent beginning: that we are confidently persuaded in our hearts. When it concerns one or another fact in secular history, we can with our intellect receive it as an actual event without it speaking to our heart. No historian will require of you more than an intellectual faith when it comes to the history of Alexander or Caesar. With the history of salvation, it is different. It concerns your salvation. It is a personal matter. It has to do with your life or death. It weighs as the history of *your* Christ, with whom you are bound through living faith, and in whose communion with you for all eternity your redemption is secured.

That is why you must *trust* and indeed be persuaded *in your heart* that *our Lord Jesus Christ* (how distinguished this summary of Jesus' great titles, and how warmly appropriate that preface of ours!) *was sent of the Father into the world*.

According to the Reformed method, the work of salvation is viewed as proceeding from the Father. God himself took the initiative. Christ is the mediator *from* God. Hence is he with all his people, indeed with the whole creation, *unto* God.

Also markedly Reformed is the view of Christ in Old Testament light, from the perspective of the promise, that is, from God's eternal *counsel*. After all, by way of a parenthesis it states: *according to the promises made from the beginning to our forefathers in the Old Testament*. With this the form witnesses to the divinity of the old dispensation, which nowadays is so reviled and criticized. It summons us: read and reread the old promises beginning with Adam. See how they are fulfilled in history. Grasp them firmly, and let them solidify your faith for an inner-deep confidence in the truth of Christ.

And then consider further that this Christ, who is *sent* into the world, thus as an apostle that as ambassador came to you, *assumed our flesh and blood*, whereby fulfilling the condition he *must* meet to be our mediator, since there must be essential oneness and communion between him and the people of God if he shall be for that people the surety, and to take upon himself the wrath of God against the human nature and then from himself bear life in his own.

The incarnation, the coming into the world, is thus already the basis of redemption (that is why the joyful song of Christmas sounds so beautiful!), but it is not itself redemption. This can be realized in no other way than that the mediator *bore for us the wrath of God from the beginning of his incarnation, to the end of his life upon earth.* Note-worthy is here also a parenthesis inserted for further description of the wrath of God: *under which we should have perished everlastingly.* In the catechism, the addition sounds somewhat different where it says that Christ "sustained in body and soul the wrath of God against the sins of all mankind" (Heidelberg Catechism, question and answer 37). The form has a more personal expression all about the individual, compelling shame and humility, but at the same time also drawing faith and trust. After all, you can get relief from the burden of the guilt if you know that the wrath that Jesus bore is the same as the wrath under which you should have perished everlastingly. What Jesus bore for you can no longer harm you. He paid the penalty for *your* sin. Where there is no sin, there is no more wrath, and where there is no wrath, there is God once again everything for the person. For in truth the prophet spoke: "Your iniquities have separated between you and God" (Isa. 59:2). When the sin is gone, the separation is lifted, and God is with you, and he regards the very best as not too good for his child, whom he had made in his image. He opens heaven for you with its treasures, indeed, the Father unlocks for you the depths of his own heart. Then is the promise of the covenant completely fulfilled: I will be *your* God.

Indeed, the form is using old-fashioned language here, a language that so many advanced "pious" people these days refuse to hear anymore. Or they esteem it an insult to God to speak of a *wrath* of God whereunder a person must perish everlastingly and Christ actually perished. They therefore prefer to sail in the pantheist's stream in which one thus denies personality to God and therefore also the will to be angry, and teaches that the wrath of God exists only in the disillusioned imagination of man.

That is why one prefers to view things along a pantheistic line by which he denies a personal God, and thus also his anger, and teaches that the wrath of God exists only in the disillusioned imagination of man.

But the congregation of Christ still loves precisely this old language. They hear, even *feel*, the truth in it. They know that God himself has so testified to such in his own word, where this word reveals Christ to us, who was *made to be sin for us* (cf. 2 Cor. 5:21). Only in the old doctrine of the suretyship finds the soul her peace.

To a complete consideration of Christ belongs also that we pay attention to the obedience in deed by which he earned salvation for us. Thus, the work of Christ is not only the negative, repelling and consuming the divine wrath, but also positive, obtaining heaven for us, the eternal blessing. That is why it says *that he hath fulfilled, for us, all obedience and righteousness of the divine law.* Certainly, the atoning passion is also a result of Jesus' submission under the law of his Father. The sin that Jesus bore was mighty due to the law. However, by this passive obedience the relationship to the law was indirect. By the active obedience the relationship is *immediate.* Here stands Jesus face-to-face with the holy law and upon him rested the requirement to fulfill that law for us in all its breadth and depth. Here Jesus has the task to accomplish the work that Adam, the head of the covenant of works, so scandalously left undone. Through the obedience and righteousness in fulfilling the holy, salvation-bringing law, Christ had restored the violated covenant of works and seized for us the crown of eternal life.

This active obedience is not a separate part of Jesus' life. It stands not readily distinguishable and categorized for us because Jesus' life is one at the root, as a whole, and in the fruit. The active and passive obedience are as it were intertwined and developed together. They are as two sides of the same coin. And with a view to Jesus' work, clearly evident is the passion element standing in the foreground—life was always a burden for him—that the form suffices mainly to paint this submissive suffering.

And is it not true that this happens in heart-stirring language? This passage in the form does not allow the making of a mystical impression on the congregation. Here brings the form the frame of mind, the emotion, precisely that soul-affection, that is necessary for celebration of the Lord's supper. Awakened within you is empathy for the supreme victim, an empathy that is not an emotional disorder but a movement of faith, because the supreme victim described here before our eyes is Immanuel, God with us.

The momentum of Jesus' suffering that the form puts forward is not arbitrarily chosen. It is precisely those scenes wherein passion contemplation so vividly highlights passion realism (if we may so describe it) and also passion symbolism. It is not some striking passion play in the unspeakable passion drama; no, in it is his suffering events wherein the spiritual instruction and spiritual fruit of suffering accrue abundance for the congregation.

These events include the wrestling in Gethsemane where the exhaustion of the Savior's soul pressed out of him the bloody sweat; the libelous apprehension whereby his arms were cuffed with coarse twine; enduring ridicule before Caiaphas, Herod, and Pilate in which not only his body was violated and tortured but also his sensitive soul wounded by innumerable accusations; the unjust, unlawful conviction and the death sentence whereby the enmity of the people and the hellish violence of their hatred for him triumphed; his being nailed to the cross, by which he took upon himself all the accursedness, and endured the deepest reproach and humiliating agony, of hell; and finally, the catastrophic death wherein bearing the scorn was completed, but also the disgrace of the suffering was portrayed most vividly.

For sure, this is a summary and vivid portrayal of the entire way of the cross. And although it would not be difficult to add yet other moments in this graphic preaching (such as the betrayal, the kiss, the denials, the disrobing, the thirst, etc.), we may say that our formulary succeeds with relatively few words in placing before the eyes of the congregation the man of sorrows in the melancholic glory of his humiliation as in a complete image.

Noteworthy is that with this passion description, rather than the cause as to why Jesus must suffer all this is named the purpose *for which* he suffered. The formulary could have chosen to follow the usual way passion accounts go by underscoring the spiritual-moral misery that necessitated such humiliation. For example, it could say: Because we were bound by sin as in captivity, Jesus was bound. Because we were confounded by sin, Jesus suffered innumerable reproaches. Seeing that due to our disobedience we deserved death, Jesus was condemned to death, etc.

In this way also the indisputable connection between the suffering of Christ and his congregation would be placed clearly in the light.

However, the form makes a preference for another way.

The outcome is the relationship between Jesus' way of the cross and our *redemption*, between the suffering and the fruits of the suffering, and isn't it true, for those who look carefully, that in the purpose at the same time is indicated the cause? Principle and purpose are as two sides of the same coin. It is impossible to have a purpose without having established the principle, and it cannot be otherwise than that one whose starting point is from a principle pursues a purpose.

So when it is here said that Jesus was bound so that we might be freed, at the same time is indicated the *cause* of Christ's suffering, namely, that we are bound by the dominion of sin. The same goes for the other passion elements.

We want briefly to set aside the gist of what we mean, so that we can attempt to understand it more thoroughly.

That said, the question to be weighed first has to do with whether the form correctly differentiates the passion phases and the application thereof to the various phases of redemption. We already noted that with regard to this "application" a mistake has been made by some *virtuosos* in the area of exposition (here the word *eisegesis* applies). But the question remains as to whether such usage itself is justifiable.

In the foreground stands unwaveringly firm that the suffering of Christ is a unity, like an organism is one. One cannot stand by a tree and point to a branch or root and say: "This is now the tree." One cannot point to a single part of the human body and say: "This is the man." The passion of Jesus is an organic whole. Nothing from the suffering can be omitted, not a single part, no matter how minute it may appear, but neither may it be said of any single passion segment: now this is it, this only!

Also, the passion is one as to its cause. The *why* of Jesus' sufferings is this: our transgression, our unrighteousness. He was wounded for our transgressions, he was bruised for our iniquities.

In the same way the passion is one as to its purpose, namely, redemption, salvation. The Son of Man came into the world to save sinners.

But to avoid misunderstanding with this at the foreground, there indeed may, on the other hand, be differentiation in this one passion in order to instruct the congregation regarding the depth and the breadth of the misery that made the suffering necessary, and the significant accomplishment that the passion effectuated. The misery is one and yet manifold. The result is one and yet multifaceted.

Sin is a being bound, a lying in shame, a being condemned, a being cursed and abandoned of God, and so much more.

And redemption is a being liberated, a release from shame, justification, a being accepted by God, and much more.

Provided it is firmly remembered that, for example, our being loosed is the result of the entire passion of Christ. Therefore, not of a single isolated fact, such as Jesus being cuffed in Gethsemane, may it be said and strongly emphasized in the instruction to the congregation that Jesus was bound in order that we may be loosed. Did nothing other happen to Jesus than this single fact of the apprehension, there would be no redemption. But in connection with the one great suffering event, this binding throws light on our being imprisoned by sin, and also our being delivered by Christ from that incarceration.

Certainly, the Scripture itself makes this distinction for us.

Isaiah saw prophetically that Jesus would be whipped and that his body would bear the stripes of the whippings. And he rejoices: knowing now that our sins also wound but that redemption is a healing from those wounds, *and with his stripes we are healed* (Isa. 53:5).

Remember then your Christ in the grievous humiliation of his being bound. Jesus was not only once but repeatedly bound. First in Gethsemane: "Then the band," says John, "and the captain and officers of the Jews took Jesus, and bound him" (John 18:12).

But as if Jesus was a fiercely dangerous scoundrel, a flight risk no less, they fettered him again and again after every hearing when he had to be moved. Annas sent him bound to Caiaphas (John 18:24). Also after the hearing before the Sanhedrin he was bound. "And they bound him and led him away and delivered him over to Pilate the governor" (Matt. 27:2). We can be certain that Jesus was additionally bound while he was beaten, and then when he was required to carry the cross.

Imagine how painful this was for Jesus' body and also for his soul. For him to be bound gives the idea that we cannot trust him for a second. He is a dangerous individual. Keep an eye on him. This binding meant powerlessness for Jesus, life cut short, indeed, *death*. Because one who is bound is as one who is dead.

Also your sin is a binding, an incapacity, death. It is not being able with regard to what you must be able to do. It is a being a slave where you were called to be king.

However, redemption brings you freedom to will and to do. He who is in Christ is not the son of a bondwoman but of the free. If the Son shall make you free, you shall be free indeed.

Jesus also bore reproaches. The reproaches of those who reproach God fell upon him (Ps. 69:10). This reproach was being belittled, humiliated by word and maltreating deed. One reproaches only what one hates and scorns. In this reproach, the hostile world cools down her rage against God, who is stronger than they. But this frenzy of reproach they brought upon Jesus, whom they assumed was weaker than they. Under such reproach was Jesus shamed, and this shame hurt to the core. He felt in this suffering the communion with his sinful people, who because of their reviling of God lay deep in shame.

Surely our sin is shame. Adam's shame at the moment when he hid from God was not the shame of a silly bashfulness, but the shame of lost innocence. And the end of this self-imposed humiliation is the eternal blushing with shame and becoming shame as God strips mankind of all his imagined glory.

Redemption in Christ preserves you from the crushing blow of God's condemnation because Jesus suffered innumerable reproaches, that you might never be confounded. In connection with this then is also the condemnation of Jesus so that you might be acquitted.

In the judgment of God over sin is not only disparagement (one can disparage someone without punishing him), but also adjudication, punishment. God continues to recognize his image in the fallen human and therefore vindicates in him his righteousness. Jesus' passion was also the verdict, the official and just sending to death. In this judgment, that of itself was unjust and thus was vile and offensive, not only did Jesus experience personal insult, but also triumph of the holiness of God over sin, God's vindication of himself over against the dethronement of God, to which the sinner had presumed.

Nonetheless, sin lies under judgment; sin is damnation.

The end point of the way of sinners is the judgment seat, where the irrevocable ruling resounds: away, away you accursed!

Consequently, redemption is: never again to come into the judgment of God. It is to be free from the law, righteous, innocent, holy. It is to have peace with God through our Lord Jesus Christ.

But Jesus bore and carried yet more. His path ran yet deeper, his misery climbed yet higher. His blessed body—indeed, his body was consecrated by God and in a literal sense blessed by the grateful redeemed, who anointed his body with oil and sprinkled it with tears—he suffered to be nailed to the cross, and with that cross took upon himself the curse. And by that accursedness he sank, he sank into the deepest agony of hell, so that from his indescribable and unbearable pain-pierced soul the scream of damnation cried out: "My God, my God, why hast thou forsaken me?"

This must Jesus suffer because sin is to be cursed not only to be shame and judgment, but also to be cursed. In the curse is declared personal abomination. The earthly judge declares his verdict, but he does not curse. He administers justice but exhibits no hatred or enmity. The heavenly judge also includes his personal dissatisfaction in his sentencing. He hates those who hate him. He is an enemy of those who bear enmity against him. It is a fearful thing to fall into the hands of the living God.

But against this dark background redemption is so luminous and comforting!

On that same cross upon which Jesus' body hung, nailed like a bloody trophy of the seemingly triumphant powers of hell, is affixed another victory sign: the handwriting of your sins, the lengthy, terrifying obligation upon which now is written in blood: forever paid in full!

From the same cross where the accursed one bent himself, now drops the treasure of blessings of Jesus of which you are heir. The tree of the curse becomes the tree of life upon which fruit grows that fills you with life and blessing.

Indeed, from that same tree upon which Jesus cried out, "*Eli, Eli, lama sabachtani*," now sweetly sounds the word of salvation: I shall be God to you, and you shall be my sons and daughters. No more agony. You are accepted of God in order nevermore to be forsaken by him.

There is direct correspondence between the suffering of Christ and the redemption of those of God's favor. On the one hand, as deep as the scale of his humiliation descends, on the other hand rises as high, on high, the scale of your redemption.

As horrible as the fact is that Jesus was spiked down on the stake of disgrace, so salvation-splendorous and glorious is the fact that on the same cross was hung the acquittal for your guilt.

As heavy as the damnation was under which reproaches and agony Jesus submitted his own soul, so rich are the blessings that stream to us by his suffering like a river.

As deep and painful as the lament of God's abandonment sounded, so high sounds forth the jubilant song of divine friendship and reconciliation.

But Jesus' humiliation by the torments of hell was not the end of the "My God." If Jesus would empty the cup, then he could not be spared the great catastrophe of dying. To fulfill the righteousness of God to the complete payment for our sin, the Son of God must humble himself unto *death*. Death is the termination point and, if it does not sound paradoxical, we would say the *crowning* of the passion.

Because Christ, says the form, finally confirmed with his death and shedding of his blood, the new and eternal testament, that covenant of grace and reconciliation, when he said: *It is finished.*

This is authentic Reformed language. With words like these our fathers speak from their heart their core idea.

Time and again here also it comes out that the fathers themselves present redemption in Christ in (the always biblical) terms of the covenant. Their entire salvation doctrine is covenantal. The idea of the covenant is the silver lining that runs through all their writings. The baptism form is structured rigorously in a covenantal manner. But also the Lord's supper form discloses the idea of the covenant. Here the atoning death of the Lord is identified as the decisive point, i.e., the fulfillment and sealing of the covenant of grace and reconciliation.

From a comprehensive point of view here also is added the term *testament*. Testament and covenant are two different words for the same entity, or rather, the word *testament* indicates the covenant as viewed from a particular perspective, namely the covenant as an *inheritance* in connection with the death of the formulators of the testament. That is why Jesus called the cup of the Lord's supper *the new testament in his blood.* In this manner of expression was brought out in measure a certain contrast with the Old Testament. There the blood of sacrifices constituted the seal of the testament. Now the sacrificial blood of Christ has become the seal and surety of the testament. The expression "new testament" is placed here in order to coordinate it with "the covenant of grace" in general. Here is intended the entire covenantal dispensation as it culminates in this last and highest stage.

After all, history teaches the covenant developed in various phases to what it is now. In principle, God established the covenant of grace already with Adam (after he had hopelessly wrecked the covenant of works) with the promise of the seed of the woman. Further in history, the covenant is revealed as a progressive unfolding in breadth and richness with Noah, Abraham, and Mount Sinai, and finally in the appearance of Christ himself the covenant is brought to the supreme revelation. Thus, history recognizes many covenants that are covenantal dispensations, but because the last dispensation, the dispensation of fulfillment, differs in character from the previous covenants, it is called the *new* covenant or testament. So what is called the new testament also includes the previous covenants of which it is the development and culmination. Noteworthy, the form says that Christ, by his death and shedding of his blood, has *confirmed* the new and eternal testament by which is confessed that no higher stage of development is possible because the stipulations of the covenant have been fulfilled. The new testament is now an *eternal* testament. It is now the testament of the full administration of the gospel, of the complete atonement. And in order for the church clearly to visualize this and for it to sink into her mind, Jesus' death and shedding of blood, whereby the testament is finally confirmed, are signified and sealed in the Lord's supper.

3. THE STRENGTHENING OF FAITH

Appropriately, the next part of the form now links the recollection and explanation of the words of the institution to the next goal of the celebration of the Lord's supper, described as strengthening of faith that we belong to *this covenant of grace.*

This happens in the following description:

And that we might firmly believe that we belong to this covenant of grace, *the Lord Jesus Christ,* in his last supper, *took bread, and when he had given thanks, he brake it, and gave it to his disciples and said, "Take, eat, this is my body which is broken for you, this do in remembrance of me." In like manner after supper he took the cup, gave thanks and gave it to them saying, "Drink ye all of it; this cup is the New Testament in my blood, which is shed for you and for many, for the remission of sins; this do as often as ye drink it in remembrance of me:* that is, as often as ye eat of this bread and drink of this cup, you shall thereby as by a sure remembrance and pledge, be admonished and assured of this my hearty love and faithfulness towards you; that, whereas you should otherwise have suffered eternal death, I have given my body to death on the tree of the cross, and shed my blood for you, and feed and nourish your hungry and thirsty souls with my crucified body and shed blood to everlasting life, as certainly as this bread is broken before your eyes, and this cup is given to you, and you eat and drink the same with your mouth, in remembrance of me.

From this institution of the holy supper of our Lord Jesus Christ, we see that he directs our faith and trust to his perfect sacrifice (once offered on the cross) as to the only ground and foundation of our salvation, wherein he is become to our hungry and thirsty souls, the true food and drink of life eternal. For by his death he hath taken away the cause of our eternal death and misery, namely, sin, and obtained for us the life-giving Spirit, that we by the same (who dwells in Christ as in the head, and in us as his members), might have the true communion with him, and be made partakers of all his riches, of life eternal, righteousness, and glory.

In this part the formulary comes to the real instruction regarding the essence and purpose of the supper. Here the real Lord's supper doctrine is proclaimed to us, and precisely the dogmatic character of this portion is important for understanding the Lord's supper controversy that in the days of the Reformation caused such deep-seated and heated dispositions.

Noteworthy is the fact that such an explanation of the purpose of the celebration of the Lord's supper does not appear in the Lord's supper formulary of Calvin. However, it should not be forgotten that with Calvin the instruction regarding the supper happened in the sermon that preceded the celebration of the supper. Naturally, there is also something to be said for this method. In the regular sermon, the minister has the opportunity to provide the necessary instruction that coincides with the developmental level of his listeners and also in connection with the spiritual-ethical situation of the congregation. However, in the end, instruction by the form itself will be preferable because expounding in this manner excludes what would be prompted by arbitrary insight of the preacher. In terms of the ecclesiastical (and consequently, also *spiritual*) life, when dealing with such a weighty matter as the celebration of the Lord's supper, it is of supreme importance that a steadfast line be drawn. It concerns what is said concerning the Lord's supper as bearing a confessional and thus a uniting-together character.

So, we may be thankful to the framers for the inclusion of this dogmatically rich pericope.

There is not complete certainty as to the origin of this section. Some are inclined that the framers here borrowed the idea from the Lutheran liturgy and indeed particularly the Württemberg formulary. This is certainly not entirely unlikely, because in the Lutheran liturgy one generally encounters precisely such explanations of the words of the institution as are found in our form.

By a comparison, the reader can judge for himself.

In the meditation before the supper that appears in the Württemberg church order of 1561 (which is in great measure still used by the Lutherans in our country,) the section in question, in which the doctrine of the Lord's supper occurs, runs thus, being translated:

Therefore, our dear Lord Jesus Christ impoverished himself for us and purposed to become man for our sins, so that he would fulfill the law and the entire will of God unto our salvation, and that by his death he would take upon himself and would suffer for our salvation all the judgment that we loaded upon ourselves by our sins.

And so that we might firmly believe, and by faith may joyfully desire to live for him, after supper he took the bread, gave thanks, and broke it, saying, take and eat, this is my body that was given for you, that is, I became man. And everything that I do and suffer, it all belongs to you, happened for you, and is for your good. That is why I give you a sure sign and pledge, that you might always remain and live in me, and I in you.

In like manner he took also the cup and said, Take and drink ye all of it; this cup is the New Testament in my blood, which is shed for you and for many, for the remission of sins; so as often as you do this, shall be in remembrance of me. That is, because I have taken you as my own and have taken upon me your sin, I freely offer myself in death for sin. With my shed blood, I purchased for you grace and forgiveness. And I established a New Testament in which sin is forgiven and nevermore comes to mind. By this I give you my blood to drink as a sure sign and pledge and for the strengthening and advancement of my life in you. He who eats this bread and drinks of this cup, and also firmly believes these words that he hears from Christ, and receives this sacrament unto a remembrance and strengthening of his faith, such remains in Christ the Lord and Christ in him unto everlasting life.

In this way we now remember and proclaim his death, namely that he died for our sins, and was raised again for our justification, that we might give him eternal praise and thanksgiving as each takes up his cross and follows him. And according to his command, we love one another as he has loved us because we are all together one bread and one body, since we all are partakers of one bread and drink from one cup.

Certainly, there is no speaking of a word-for-word adoption of this section into our liturgy. The example from the Lutheran liturgy may have inspired the Palatinate framers to a similar braiding of profound language that was borrowed for the words of the institution, but it was not copied. It is a free and independent version that they offer us and with which they essentially enriched the Reformed liturgy.

Indeed, to a certain measure, from a formal perspective, the correctness of Barger's remark can be acknowledged, that the repeating of the words of institution, which (be it in the Pauline form) are already mentioned in the beginning, give to the whole a somewhat halting appearance.[4] In such a brief compass, to repeat some of the same words may indeed not be considered advisable. But we differ completely from the judgment of Barger when he

---

4   Barger, 220ff.

calls the explanation of the words of the institution dark and ineffectual. He asks, what should a simple congregant understand by these things? It is true, when a simple member of the congregation is asked to give a clear description of the expression, *to feed and nourish with his crucified body and blood,* he would likely falter for a precise formulation, but with his spiritual instinct he senses very well what these words intend, namely, *to be a partaker by faith in Christ and his benefits.*

We hereby have come near to what one can identify as the heart or the kernel of the form, and Mensinga was correct, in our opinion, to say that "this part, namely the symbolism of the supper, is the most important part of the entire form with respect to dogmatic history."[5]

So it lies before us, and certainly also with regard to the spirit of our readers, that when we explain this part of the form, we not fail to consider the Lord's supper debate at the time of the Reformation.

4. THE WORDS OF THE INSTITUTION

First, however, it serves to mention something regarding the words of the institution themselves as they are here encountered.

We have already in our consideration drawn the fine connection of the form between this part and the foregoing.

The previous section concluded with the solemn testimony that Jesus Christ, with his death and shed blood, fulfilled the covenant of grace and reconciliation when he said: "It is finished."

According to its specifically Reformed character, the form concentrates the confession ultimately in the covenant of grace. To this covenantal doctrine the form now also connects the authentic Lord's supper doctrine as it continues, *that we might firmly believe that we belong to this covenant of grace, etc.*

For sure, these are noteworthy words, noteworthy precisely in contrast with the related Lutheran formulary where, as we saw, the

---

5   Mensinga, 324ff.

connection is placed in these somber words: "And so that this we might firmly believe."

Both are similar in so far that with both is expressed that the purpose of the supper is the strengthening of faith. In the foregoing, the communion celebrant was depicted as one who is of contrite heart and who recognizes that he lies in the midst of death. His weak faith need not keep him from approaching this covenantal meal as long as he has the yearning of his small faith to be saved and to *firmly believe*. Only firm faith liberates and strengthens the covenant member to be fitting for the work, courageous in the strife. Only a firm believer is a joyful believer, and in his assured faith God is glorified.

Precisely here the form touches the sacramental character of the supper. After all, the sacrament is the institution of the covenant of grace whereby God wills to strengthen the already implanted life of faith.

The uniquely Reformed character of the formulary rests precisely in its directing of faith awareness to the covenant. In the abstract, other words could also be imagined. For example, there might be, "That we might firmly believe that we belong to *Christ*," or "that our sins are forgiven" (see the second part of the self-examination of this form: "Secondly, whether he believes...that all his sins are forgiven, etc."), or "that we are God's children." Rather, here is, "that we belong *to this covenant of grace*." And in this formulation, all the others are encapsulated because the covenant is the way in which God imparts himself according to the promise: I will be your God. In the covenant is the forgiveness of sins, adoption by God, all of Christ. That is precisely why the remembrance of the covenant is so striking, because it not only brings the Lord's supper participant under the conviction of the certainty of salvation (for what is stronger than a divine bond?), but also because it thereby presents the life of faith as a life of obedience. He who is a member of a covenant (albeit a covenant of *grace*) has covenantal obligations. He must walk in new obedience.

Indeed brief, and thereby lacking clarity in some measure, is now the transition from the indicated *purpose* of the supper as the strengthening of faith to the statement of the *institution* of the supper. Here is, "that we might firmly believe that we belong to this covenant of grace, *the Lord Jesus Christ took bread, etc.*" More clearly, and therefore improved, would have been, "That we might firmly believe, Jesus instituted the supper for us. The institution occurred in this manner: In the last supper, the Lord Jesus, etc."

The words of the institution here recalled do not come this time from the epistles but from the gospels, and indeed in such a way that it was not taken from just one of the evangelists. Rather, various phrases from the synoptics (Matthew, Mark, Luke) are weaved into one complete narrative.

In Matthew, the words of the institution are as follows: "And as they were eating, Jesus took bread and blessed it, *and brake it, and gave it to the disciples, and said Take, eat; this is my body.* And he took the cup, and *gave thanks, and gave it to them, saying, Drink ye all of it;* for this is my blood of the new testament *which is shed for many for the remission of sins*" (Matt. 26:26–28).

In Mark: "And as they did eat, Jesus took bread, and blessed, and *brake it*, and gave to them, and said, *Take, eat; this is my body.* And he took the cup, and *when he had given thanks, he gave it to them*: and they all drank of it.

"And he said unto them, 'This is my blood of the new testament which is shed for many'" (Mark 14:22–24).

And in Luke: "And he took bread, and *gave thanks, and brake it,* and gave unto them, saying, *This is my body which is given for you; this do in remembrance of me.*

"Likewise also the cup *after supper*, saying, *This cup is the new testament in my blood, which is shed for you*" (Luke 22:19-20).

With italics I have indicated which words of the gospels were borrowed. The material was provided primarily from Matthew and Luke. Notably from Matthew comes, among other things, "gave thanks, and gave it to them, saying, Drink ye all of it." And further, "which is shed for many for the remission of sins."

From Luke comes the familiar expression, "*which is given for you; this do in remembrance of me*," as well as, "This cup is the new testament in my blood."

How tightly constructed the combination is, is evident in the phrase at the end, "for you and for many," that comes partly from Matthew and partly from Luke. *For you* is from Luke, *for many* is from Matthew.

The final words, "this do as often as ye drink it in remembrance of me," come from 1 Corinthians 11.

One senses that nothing is forced here. Rather, a systematic deliberation is presented, and the whole bears the imprint of thoughtfulness.

The question as to why, after the more developed words from 1 Corinthians 11, the less developed words from the gospels are here, is not difficult to answer.

We have already acknowledged that the repetition of the words of the institution leaves a somewhat halting impression of the whole, but this does not hinder us from lauding the good intention.

That is, that Paul's words of the institution are so constructed, that in the apostle's account they precede the admonishment to self-examination, and the framers of the Lord's supper form had prior need of this admonishment for preparing for the instruction in self-examination that the form offers.

But it further serves to note, on the one hand, that while as a whole the words of Paul are more developed as to what concerns the instruction for self-examination, on the other hand, the language of the gospels details words of Jesus that Paul does not recount. There is, for example, the phrase *had given thanks* with the institution of the cup. Also, the command *drink ye all of it.* And lastly, *which is shed for you and for many for the remission of sins.* We would rather not miss these very words of Jesus in our form and are therefore grateful to the framers for intentionally making room for what the evangelists reported.

No express explanation of the words of Scripture that have been quoted can be expected for us here concerning the essential agreement of the words mentioned here with the beginning of the form. For this explanation we point to the third chapter.[6]

It serves to focus here only upon one thought. Whereas in Paul's letter it is said that Jesus instituted the Lord's supper *the same night in which he was betrayed*, it indicates here that Jesus, *in his last supper*, broke bread. The term *supper* naturally points to the *passover* that preceded and is ostensibly meant for keeping in mind that the New Testament sacrament blossomed from the Old Testament. To rightly understand the Lord's supper, it is necessary to maintain a strong hold on this connection. The critical theologians deny such a connection and say that Paul, rather than Jesus, instituted the supper. According to them, it is unthinkable that Jesus would have "linked the bread and wine with his death, much less have given them to eat as signs of his body and blood," since these requirements "could only arise when in the church a certain view about the person and death of Jesus had taken shape."[7]

Firmly contradicting this is the historically settled argument that, in his letter, Paul is proceeding from the assumption that the celebration of the Lord's supper as the institution of Christ was already a common occurrence in the Christian church. Thus, it is impossible that it was invented and imported by him. But most of all the error of the deniers lies in their inability to sense the continuity (the continuation) of the covenant, and therefore they also do not understand the connection between the passover and the Lord's supper. Not only the blood payment that must yet come at Jesus' death, but also the blood payment that preceded in the passover, as well as in the entire

---

6 Cf. III.1–6.
7 Bavinck, *Reformed Dogmatics*, Vol. IV, 544ff.

ceremonial dispensation, gave Jesus immediate cause and material for the institution of the sign for his blood.

Let us bring to mind the celebration of the passover of the Jews that was also prominent as celebrated by Jesus in his last supper. We borrow our explanation from the concise elucidation of Dr. Bavinck's *Dogmatics*:

> At the approach of the feast, thousands upon thousands of Israelites traveled to Jerusalem; there they purchased lambs, and had them slaughtered in the temple court by the Levites the afternoon of the fourteenth of Nisan. In this context, the priests stood ready to catch the blood in silver and gold basins, which they passed on from one to another and finally, in a single act, poured out over the altar. In the meantime, while the Levites sang the Hallel, the priest strung up the animals, removed their intestines, and brought them in a vessel to the altar. Then those who had brought the lamb to be slaughtered, who usually numbered somewhere between ten and twenty men, took the slaughtered lamb with them to a private dwelling and roasted it there without being permitted to break a single bone. The meal itself began with a cup of wine circulating around the room and with thanksgiving. Then the bitter herbs and a bowl of puree were brought to the table and eaten, whereupon the lamb was put with the unleavened cakes. Before it was eaten, however, the father, or later the official reader, related the story of the Exodus, the celebrants sang the first part (Pss. 113–14) of the Hallel (Pss. 113–18), and the second cup was passed around. At that point the actual meal began. When it was finished, the third cup was blessed by the father and emptied by him and all the participants. The whole event was then concluded with the pouring of the fourth cup, the singing of the second part of the Hallel (Pss. 115–18), the blessing of the fourth cup by the father with the words of Psalm 118:26, and the cup's

emptying by the guests sitting around the table. These four cups were required for this meal, but sometimes a fifth went around while the celebrants sang Psalms 120–37.[8]

We do not know for certain at which moment in this commemoration meal Jesus instituted the Lord's supper, and the sacrament of the shadows was deliberately fulfilled. In the words that our form cites, it first says that Jesus *in* his last supper took the bread. Next it states that *after* the supper, Jesus took the cup. Apparently, the first phrase is intended generally, indicating the entire sacramental gathering. The gospels say *and as they were eating* Jesus took the bread, in other words, when they were together at the meal. Regarding the institution of the cup, Paul imparts to us explicitly that this happened after eating the supper, in order to show that the sign of the wine *follows* the sign of the bread. The term *supper* refers here not to the New Testament Lord's supper, but to the Old Testament passover,[9] and, indeed, that part of the supper that consisted of the eating of the lamb. Perhaps we may so present the order of the commemoration meal as such that at the moment that the passover lamb was consumed, Jesus took the bread, and right after the passover lamb was finished, the cup of the New Testament circulated. It is certainly imaginable that this happened in connection with the third cup, the cup of thanksgiving, that immediately followed the meal.[10]

There is no doubt that the Lord Jesus took of the unleavened bread that was on the passover plate, without thereby also binding his church from now on to using this particular type of bread. In the same way, Jesus took of the wine that was generally consumed in Israel (also among the people) and that so generously flowed at the

8 Bavinck, *Reformed Dogmatics*, Vol. IV, 545-546.
9 *Supra,* III.6.
10 Bavinck, *Reformed Dogmatics*, Vol. IV, 546.

passover. So the Lord sought or did nothing unusual regarding the selection of the signs but appropriated what was available to him.

Although the gospel writers are quite sober in their reports regarding the setting of the supper—certainly because Jesus himself was sober as well in what he did as in his manner of speaking—it is nevertheless abundantly clear that he instituted the mentioned signs in connection with his upcoming suffering and death. There yet remained the portions from the lamb that was slaughtered, sacrificed, as a sign of the atonement, that only by the shedding of blood could be brought about, and was eaten as a sign of salvation-rich communion with God that flowed from the atonement. Christ knew and saw himself as the true passover lamb. The dreadful altar (the cross!) was already prepared for him. Soon the lifeblood would pour out from his wounds. And by his horrible, atoning death, he laid the foundation for the covenant, he extinguished God's wrath, he broke and banished the power of sin, he was victorious over the devil, he saved his people.

Though we cannot establish that Jesus literally said these precise words, nor any others (except for the various ones reported by the gospel writers), the main idea is indubitably certain, and our form has already given such a description of the words of the Lord such that the atonement idea, and the believing acceptance of the fact of the atonement, stands clearly in the foreground.

5. DESCRIPTION OF THE WORDS OF THE INSTITUTION

The literary form of this paraphrase is unique. It is not an objective, scholarly rendition but a subjective oration from Jesus' own mouth. As if the Lord himself is speaking, it proceeds:

> That is, as often as ye eat of this bread and drink of this cup, you shall thereby as by a sure remembrance and pledge, be admonished and assured of this *my* hearty love and faithfulness towards you; that, whereas you should otherwise have

suffered eternal death, *I* have given *my* body to death on the tree of the cross, etc.

The entirety receives thereby something warm and touching that does not neglect to move the heart of the congregation.

But also, the content of the declaration deserves praise and is worthy of close consideration.

The formulary begins with the quotation from the earlier cited words of Paul (1 Cor. 11). In the Pauline words of institution at the least clearly comes to light that Jesus had the intention to institute a *sacrament*. Some so-called interpreters doubt this and contend that Jesus intended for that one occasion to break the bread and present the cup in order to prophesy his death. What Paul imparts as received from the Lord, however, removes even the tiniest shadow of doubt, because there is: *as often* as ye eat of this bread and drink of this cup. Thus, Jesus had in mind a *recurrent* usage, a usage according to a fixed arrangement, as a *sacrament*. And these words the form presents ahead of the testimony of the gospels (which do not exactly include these words) to express: *that is, as often as ye eat of this bread and drink of this cup.*

Therefore, the sacramental character of the Lord's supper is first of all scripturally confirmed.

We proceed further.

You shall *thereby*—not by bread and wine in and of itself, but by the sacramental breaking and eating of the bread, and by the sacramental taking and drinking of the wine—*as a sure remembrance and pledge* (note that the word *remembrance* refers to the sacrament as a sign, specifically as a sign for remembering, and the word *pledge* expresses a seal of guarantee) *be admonished and assured.*

The word *admonish* is particularly a favorite term in our liturgy. It appears in the baptism formula: "and we admonished to loath and humble ourselves." And later: "therefore are we by God, through baptism, admonished of and obliged." Given the connection in the Lord's supper form with these, the word does not have the severe connotation of punishment, but of powerful and compelling instruction, binding the heart, convicting. Hence, the addition of the word *assured* makes good synonymous sense. Notwithstanding, we should not desire to overlook the connotation of reprimand that the word *admonish* continues to have in our everyday language. It is certainly far from superfluous that the congregation again and again is made to sense the disgrace and shame of all unbelief, indeed also of small faith. Jesus admonishes his disciples, when they merely hesitate, and calls them on it: "Why are ye timorous, O ye of little faith?"

And what is the content of the admonishment?

First, in general, the covenant member at the Lord's supper is assured of Jesus' hearty love and faithfulness toward him.

Though the Lord did not himself speak these particular words as such, they are nevertheless spoken according to his Spirit. They breathe the Christ, who not only loves his own, but also seeks his own faith in his love. True love wills to be recognized, seeks a sense of awareness and communion. Christ is the bridegroom who seeks the *heart* of his bride, not only because he himself thirsts for her love, but also that he wills the good for her. And this good is missed without verifiable knowledge that Jesus loves me with a heartfelt love, and that he is faithful to me and *remains* faithful to me.

We might want to ask how it is possible, with such a passage before our eyes, to deny that our Reformed liturgy has an intentional and mystical warmth. Certainly, the Reformed faith salutes the primacy of the intellect and is afraid of the incitement of emotions that are so easily moved. But there is always room for a healthy mysticism in its religion. After all, the word of God itself is mystical. Jesus' parting words to his disciples tremble with the powerful emotions of his deeply moved heart. Therefore at the meal of the Lord's supper (the foreshadowing of that great marriage feast), the plucking of the strings of the emotional life is not missing. Here celebrates love in the highest. Here the bride says,

Let him kiss me with the kisses of his mouth; for thy love is better than wine. Because of the savor of thy good ointments thy name is as ointment poured forth, therefore do the virgins love thee. Draw me, we will run after thee: the king hath brought me into his chambers: we will be glad and rejoice in thee, we will remember thy love more than wine: the upright love thee. (Song of Sol. 1:2–4)

However, in order that the love of the bride may be not a one-sided love affair, but a *faith love*, the subject matter of faith is further described. The congregation is admonished and assured of that love of Jesus that was revealed in that matchless self-surrender to the cross: *that, whereas you should otherwise have suffered eternal death, I have given my body to death on the tree of the cross, and shed my blood for you.*

The death of Christ is not otherwise to be explained than as the death-surety, the death-payment, the death in the place of his people. There was an alternative (the one or the other): either Jesus must die or we must die. The death of Christ is not to be explained as a sealing of the truth, nor a triumphant martyrdom, much less an inevitable course of nature. His death was a deed, an act of God the Father, who *gave* his Son, and of the Son who gave himself, "because, with respect to the justice and truth of God, satisfaction for our sins could be made no otherwise than by the death of the Son of God."

And this sacrifice of Christ was not only an act of obedience with respect to the Father, which flows from nothing but his love to the sender; no, it was also—and here appears this sacrificial death in an especially tender, mystical light—rooted in the love of Christ for his people. And indeed, this love may be called a *hearty* love, because scarcely would anyone give the existence of his life for his friends. Thus, how deep, how genuine, how divine the love of Jesus, that he offers his life for them who were yet enemies. Jesus (in a certain sense) preferred his people over himself. Given the choice: they must die or you must die, he denied, destroyed, and obliterated himself and tossed himself into the ocean of death and doom, so that his guilty people could go free.

On the entire way in relentless descending depths, Jesus was inspired by this wholly unique love. The thought, *I for you*, carried him step by step to bear the shame and reproach. For the joy that was set before him, namely, the rejoicing of his redeemed people and his reunion with them, he endured the cross and despised the shame.

True celebration of the Lord's supper is to exercise remembrance of this fact, this sacrifice, this deed of love, that brought redemption. The supper directs faith back to this event, in order therein to ground itself, thereto to cling, therefrom to draw the blood of life.

But at this place the celebrating congregation may not be satisfied.

Jesus did more for his people, and that is why he promises and stipulates more.

Not only an objective atonement came with the death of the cross. Jesus' death speaks not only of history that has passed, but also of a reality that is present. Through the cross springs the font of power that recreates the congregation and pours out new life within her. Jesus' crucifixion is not only of history gone by but also of a reality that is now present. This death witnesses not only to what Jesus has done, but also what he is now doing and shall continue to do. With other words, the cross is not only the cause of our justification, but also of our regeneration and sanctification. And this side of the work of redemption through the Lord's supper is no less signified and sealed.

Just listen further to what the form puts in the mouth of Jesus: *and nourish and refresh your hungry and thirsty souls with my crucified body and shed blood to everlasting life, as certainly as this bread is broken before your eyes and this cup is given to you, and you eat and drink with your mouth in remembrance of me.*

The sense of these words is clear.

There exists a spiritual rapport between the living Christ and his bride. This rapport has its ground and cause in the atonement. From there we may say that fellowship has a place with the *crucified*

Christ. The essence and content of this fellowship can be described as a grafting of the believer in Christ and of Christ in him. By this relationship life flows from the head to the members, and with this life the benevolence of the covenant. Because there is also this imparting of the riches of life and the benefits as fruit of the cross, specifically of the breaking of his body and the flowing of his blood, it can be said metaphorically that we are nourished and refreshed with Jesus' *crucified* body and *shed* blood to everlasting life.

This strong, and we may well say bold, imagery is not directly in the words of the institution, for Jesus did say: "Take, eat, this is my body which was given for you." But the command to eat refers directly to the *bread* in his hand. In the familiar address that John delivered to us, it is stated in a somewhat different form: "I am the living bread which came down from heaven: if any man eat of this bread, he shall live forever: and the bread that I will give is my flesh, which I will give for the life of the world" (John 6:51).

And when the Jews debated among themselves, saying, "How can this one give us his flesh to eat?" Jesus spoke further: "Verily, verily, I say unto you, except ye eat the flesh of the Son of man, and drink his blood, ye have no life in you. Whoso eateth my flesh, and drinketh my blood hath eternal life; and I will raise him up at the last day" (John 6:53–54).

Placing these words in connection with the former, in verse 35 where Jesus says, "I am the bread of life: he that cometh to me shall never *hunger*; and he that believeth on me shall never *thirst*," then there need be no doubt as to what our fathers were thinking with the words of this part of the form. While there may be truth in the observation that Jesus did not intend in his address (John 6) to refer directly to the eating and drinking of the Lord's supper, certainly it cannot be argued that the full light of this glowing metaphor is thereby extinguished with respect to the Lord's supper.

When the Lord says in verse 51, "The bread that I will give is my flesh, *which I will give for the life of the world*," he is prophesying his sacrificial death on the cross. That is why the Dordt scholars correctly note by the word *flesh*: "That is, my human nature, that I will give up on the cross, for a sacrifice of reconciliation, for the sins of the elect throughout the whole world, that they may therefore obtain remission of sins and everlasting life."[11]

And when Jesus says, "Except ye eat the flesh of the Son of man, and drink his blood, ye have no life in you,"[12] the comments explain this very precisely:

> That is, except ye believe in me, who am I to give up my body to death on the cross, and shed blood for the forgiveness of sin. For Christ speaketh not here of the outward eating, which is done in the Lord's supper, seeing that was not yet instituted at that time, but of the spiritual eating, i.e. receiving of Christ by true faith, and by thereby being united unto him, *which is signified and sealed by the outward eating in the Lord's supper.*[13]

In other words, the eating of Jesus' body, which is spoken of in John 6, served the purpose of Jesus with respect to faith in general, while the sacramental eating at the Lord's supper meal means that special faith communion and reality that Christ has specially attached to this sacrament.

However, in principle, the meaning of the metaphor remains the same. In both cases, the *sacrifice* of Christ must be remembered as the object of faith, and the communion of faith itself must be viewed as one that realized in a spiritual sphere what happens in the natural sphere by the taking of food and drink into the body. As in the natural, food and drink that is consumed by the mouth become one with our flesh and blood and thus united to our flesh, and further, by this becoming one with us strengthen and gladden our weak life, also in

---

11 *DBC*, Vol. V, John 6:51.

12 John 6:53.

13 *DBC*, Vol. V, John 6:53 (italics added).

a spiritual manner there is a union of the mediator Jesus, God and man, and that man in soul and body, in a way such that these two lives (of Christ and the covenant member) become one, and by this unity the life of faith is awakened to higher action.

6. THE SYMBOLISM OF THE SIGNS

We now will first give attention to the signs as such, and thereafter to what happens with the signs. The signs first speak of themselves.

Jesus doesn't offer flesh, but *bread*. Flesh is life built to its completion, that which exists by the food. With bread flesh grows. The natural food for man is not meat. God gave the animals to Adam to govern them. Adam had dominion over the birds of the air, the fish of the sea, and the animals on earth. A king does not eat his subordinates but protects and governs them. But due to our *sinful* will the animals are also cursed, and by the curse became nourishment for man.

In the slaughter of animals by Israel's altars, God prophesied and symbolized for centuries the accursed death of the great sacrificial lamb that would come. That is why under the old covenant the sacrament was bloody, and the sacrificial meal was meat. The people had to know: the sacrifice of the atonement is to come but *is* not yet come.

Now that the sacrifice has come, Jesus does away with meat and for it puts bread in its place. It is as if the Lord also took away the curse with the meat and restores man in his dominion. By introducing bread in place of meat, Jesus raises man to a higher level, brings him closer to paradise, directs the history of creation further to its completion.

However, the fulfillment itself is not yet. Bread is indeed a natural nourishment, but it was not the food of paradise that Adam ate. Adam ate that which nature itself (i.e., God in nature) had brought forth for him as prepared, namely, the fruits of the trees of the garden and the herbs bearing seed. All that he had to do was to keep the garden and to cultivate the earth (Gen. 1:29; 2:15) so that they would bear more and even better fruit for him.

The bread that we eat certainly speaks of a significant culture that would be noteworthy as a gift of God. However, at the same time bread speaks of the fall and its miserable aftermath. After the fall it is, "In the sweat of thy face shalt thou eat bread" (Gen. 3:19). Bread must be grappled from the ground, wrestled from nature, as the result of strife with a stubborn creation. Hence, the future heavenly life is not pictured as a banquet where this food is presented, but as living under the tree of life, bearing twelve kinds of fruit, yielding fruit every month (Rev. 22:2). As God directly provides food, so luscious, so succulent, so nutritious, man with all his creativity and energy can never discover or prepare it.

It is for sound reason that Jesus now institutes not the fruit of nature but the bread of cultivation as signs of his sacrificial body.

After all, bread in its essence pictures the sacrificing of Christ. The first moment in the production of bread is the death of the wheat in the ground. When the grain is ripened, then comes the sharp sickle that cuts it off. On the threshing floor it is beaten until the husks release the noble kernels. With mill stones the corn is crushed and powdered into meal. This meal, after it has been seasoned, is put into a hot oven, and only then does it become food for man. It is a long-suffering path that the natural product goes through before it is displayed as food on our tables.

That this manner of preparation is symbolic with respect to the suffering road of the Lord, Jesus himself taught when he, with the eye on his approaching death, spoke of the corn of wheat that must fall to the ground and die in order to bring forth fruit. We may further develop and present this image by saying that when the corn of the wheat is not cut off, crushed, smashed, and beaten, it brings forth no fruit. Jesus became Christ for us in going through every stage of the God-ordained way of passion. Through what happened in Gethsemane, by Gabbata, at Golgotha, he became spiritual food for us.

However, the *presentation* of this sign by Jesus was not enough.

The bread is *broken* before the eyes. Of itself, bread is already broken fruit. But with this special ritual, the congregation is specifically reminded that Jesus' body was broken.

Understand what is going on here.

In the sense of breaking and crushing, it cannot be said that Jesus' body was broken. We note precisely that the fact that the Lord's body on the cross was not broken by the soldiers was a faithful fulfillment of what was foreshadowed by the passover lamb: nothing may be broken but was to be brought as a whole to the table. The body of Christ was broken in an entirely different sense. The life of the body broke off, its propelling power that drives the body forward, that sustaining strength capacity. That said, we know that when life leaves the body, or even for a moment subsides, the body immediately experiences the effect. Without the soul, the body is a corpse. Without the soul, the body is rotting stuff, the ingenious edifice a revolting carcass.

In that sense, Jesus' body was broken, the life in that body was broken. The mysterious connection that the soul and body form together as a unity of life was broken. And this process of separation that was completed in the hour of death was quietly at work for Jesus' entire time of life on earth. Jesus' life was a constant dying. His life grew older and was subject to nature's law of perishability. Jesus had assumed the Adamic life that is perishable. He bore in all points like as we are (yet without sin) an earthly frame, and thus *could* die, yes, *must* die, unless he *willed* not to die.

Thereby came the horrible burden of suffering that was exerted upon the entire life of the man of sorrows. All the powers of hell directed their violence upon this life in order to break it. And to the extent these powers succeeded, Jesus lost human strength. His body was broken when the bloody sweat was pressed out of him in the garden. It broke him when he was reproached in countless ways, when his back was thrashed with the stripes, when he was shouldered with the heavy beams of the cross, when his hands and feet were spiked through and the lukewarm lifeblood spilled from the cracks in his earthly tabernacle.

Then was his body broken. So every death is the breaking of the human body, also the body of children of God. For we know that when our earthly house of this tabernacle is *broken*, we have a building from God, a house not made with hands, eternal in the heavens (2 Cor. 5:1).

And see, in order for the immeasurable, redemption-bringing event of the breaking of Jesus' body to be made clearly mindful for the congregation, the bread of the sacrament is broken before your eyes. You may not doubt the reality of this salvation fact. The process is completed. As in the breaking the bread falls in irreconcilable parts, so was the man Jesus broken apart in two pieces. His body was separated from the life source, the soul, radically and completely.

In the light of this consideration, the breaking of the bread is thus witnessed as a ritual of enormous, symbolic, sacramental meaning.

In order to gauge in full measure to his congregation, Jesus added to the sign of the bread the sign of the *wine*. In itself, it could be judged that one sign in the sacrament should be sufficient. After all, baptism has only one sign: water. So would only bread already make the Lord's supper a richly expressive language of visual communication for the covenantal people. The bread already speaks clearly enough that Jesus was broken, was dead, and in this way that he became food for our souls of eternal life.

However, consider that in the Lord's supper, Jesus himself includes that which naturally comes with a meal and thereby according to the creation order concerning the nourishment of human life. Human life is supported not only by food but also by drink. And the most exalted of all drinks that God has ordered for mankind is wine that gladdens the heart of man.

That is why Christ, in his spiritual meal, to the nourishment of bread added the nourishment of drink, wine.

Also here, at first the sign speaks for itself. But after that the symbolic act also happens with the sign.

In distinction from the bread, the sign of the wine does not bear a character specific only to the New Testament. With the first sign we noted a contrast between the Old Testament sign of lamb's meat that involved shed blood, and the bread of the new covenant that signifies the fulfillment of the atonement work. In contrast to this, the wine is brought over from the passover meal to the Lord's supper table. And this is evidence that the sign of the wine bears a secondary (consequential) character.

Nevertheless, does this sign not also speak volumes?

Wine is not a direct gift of creation. In this way, it is on the same line as the bread. The immediate gift of nature is the grape that grows from the grapevine. Wine comes then first from the grape, when the grape is crushed and pressed, and the retrieved juice, by a chemical process, undergoes an essential change. Thus, for the wine the grapes must be broken down, and to that extent also speaks to us of the atoning passion and sacrificial death of our Lord Jesus Christ.

But also, when it comes to the sign of the wine at the Lord's supper, there occurs another instructional image. Just as the Lord did not limit himself with the sign of the bread only to display this sign, but also to *break* it, to make the symbolism yet clearer and more striking, so is something also more to be *done* with the wine to bring out all the more the power of the sign. The bread must be *broken* so that it can serve as food. The wine must be *poured* in order to be drunk. It must flow, first *into* the cup that is filled, and thereafter *from* the cup that is emptied.

Indeed, in not so many words in the institution of the Lord's supper there is a message provided in this dispensing or pouring of the wine. It is stated that Jesus *broke* the bread, but of the cup it is only said that this Jesus *took* and *gave*. Of the *in-pouring* of the cup (the counterpart to the breaking of the bread), the Scripture does not speak. But it nevertheless stands to reason that this pouring of the wine also took place. After all, in the explanation of the sign the Lord speaks of the body that is broken. This *breaking* Jesus does before, which he pictures in the breaking of the bread. And now Jesus speaks also of his blood that is *shed*. What lies more at hand than that this outpouring is also symbolized by filling the chalice from the jug, and thus to teach the viewer that like the purple wave floods into the cup, so also from Jesus' cruel wounds flows the blood of the atonement.

The bestowing or pouring of the wine is thus to be regarded as a logical antitype to the breaking of the bread. At the celebration of the Lord's supper it is worthwhile therefore that the minister fills at least one of the cups before the eyes of the seated guests, prior to pronouncing the sacramental words. Then is more beautifully pictured the cross of Christ for the remembrance-celebration of the congregation, and it better suits the purpose of the feast of faith.

We refer to the Lord's supper as a *feast of faith*, which brings us now to that part of the Lord's supper celebration that deals with the communicants (those who partake of the meal).

By the work of the atonement of Christ something happens from *outside* a man and *for* a man, namely the sacrifice of Christ.

This work outside and for a man is sacramentally reflected in the breaking of the bread and the dispensing of the wine.

But the work of redemption also captures something that takes place *within* a man, something that takes place *by* a man, namely the receiving of, the depending upon the sacrifice of Christ by faith.

This last is also pictured in the finely organized celebration of the supper. There is here to do not only with what Christ does in the meal (with reference to the minister), but also is intended something for the believers to do.

Christ breaks and gives the bread. The believer *takes* and *eats* it.

Christ pours and gives the cup. The believer *takes this* and *drinks from it*.

So, let us give some attention to this rich act of faith by God's people. For hereby comes the sacrament into its right: it becomes the meal of the *covenant*. That is because every covenant contains *two* parts. The one part is God, who gives. The other is his child, who receives and believes. Through acceptance in faith, the covenant is fulfilled from the human side. From his side, God seals the covenant with the bestowal of the sacrament. Man seals the covenant through use of the sacrament. We can say here, with a variation on the word of the gospel, that he who receives has sealed that God is faithful.

This reception is a response to the giving. In the story of the institution it is expressly said, with the bread as well as the wine, that Jesus *gave.* When the Lord stretches out the hand to his disciples, he *presents* the signs, and in order to facilitate the reception of the sacrament, with this he says, *take.*

Soon, the ministers of the word would do the same as Jesus in the administration of the supper.

And hereby is not only symbolized that God comes to meet his people in the covenant, but much more, that he has definite intentions for his people. When someone offers bread to the hungry, he can do it in two ways. He can point the suffering one to the basket of bread and say: "Get the bread there." But he can also himself take a piece of bread from the provision, hold it before the poor guy, and say: "Look here, take it." In this last case comes much more powerfully the love-filled disposition, the genuinely intended character of the offer, and it makes it much easier for the starving man to take the food. In the first case, he may yet doubt as to whether the bread would really be *granted.* In the second case, hesitation in receiving would be almost an insult. The giver could say: "What do you think? That I am kidding with you? That I would pull my arm back when you reach to take it?"

By giving as Jesus gave to his disciples in the Lord's supper is the possibility, at any rate the likelihood, of rejection as good as excluded. Also, practically and factually, no one refuses the sign that is extended by the minister. Those who refuse would make the minister, and in him God himself, out to be a liar.

So, by this *giving* and *presenting*, God teaches his people that his covenant is true and his love well-meaning. As surely as God lives, he has no pleasure in the death of his covenantal child, but in his living.

The word that is illustrated in the supper is a faithful word and worthy of all acceptation. The Lord's supper is "a sure remembrance and pledge, wherein we are admonished and assured of the Lord's hearty love and faithfulness towards us."

The giving is an assurance: be at peace! It is also an admonishment: be sure to do it!

That is why there is no place where the *meek and lowly* love of God is so clearly exhibited than at this meal of the sacrament. Here God descends to his people most deeply, approaches most nearly, makes himself most familiar.

By this love-filled, divine presentation is thus prepared and evoked the sacramental compliance that is necessary from the side of the covenant members. God doesn't wait until we want to ask, "Father, grant me this bread!" He approaches us preemptively, goes to meet us, presents bread to us, and says, "Take!"

Deeply foundational and principally regarded then is also the second side of the covenant, the reception by faith, which is a divine issue. God himself awakens the faith of his people with his irresistible love. He sets it in motion, yes, he himself in advance planted it in the soul by his Spirit. Most profoundly, the covenant is not two-sided (bilateral) but one-sided (unilateral). From God and through God are all things.

However, this miraculous fact of grace takes not away that the covenantal child is responsible for this second part of the covenant, the compliance. He is *admonished* and *obliged* unto new obedience, namely, to the complete love of all his soul, the total expression of faith in all his heart. And as he believes and professes, then is this—though made possible by God's gracious working—nevertheless his act and so, a divinely designed love response.

So, you can see how also this comes into view at the table of the Lord.

Christ, the host, gives. The child of the covenant, the guest, receives. This taking is an essential component for the celebration of the sacrament that we dare not miss. By Rome, the wafer is placed on the tongue of the communicant by the priest (so that no crumbs of the "body" of the Lord are dropped). By the Reformed supper, the covenant member himself is active; he stretches out his hand and *takes.*

In doing this he is saying symbolically: "Lord, I believe. I desire to be cleansed by you." By doing this he is symbolizing: "O Lord, save my soul."

By receiving this sacrament, he is professing in deed: "I believe the forgiveness of sins."

The outstretched hand is to say *amen* to the promise. It is the confirmation of the tendered friendship of God. It is a renewal affirmation of the covenant.

That said, it doesn't stop here.

The believer, when he has received the bread, brings it to the mouth and tastes and eats it, that is, he incorporates it to his own body, with his life and blood.

In part, this absorption happens consciously and intentionally—*to eat* is an *action* of the person—and in part is here also an unaware working of nature, namely, in so far that food is consumed by the body, digested, and processed in the biological system.

Also in the appropriation of faith at the supper, there is a twofold action. The believer not only receives Christ unto himself, takes for himself the bread of heaven, makes himself one with his work, his person, but also there is a subconscious soul activity (by the indwelt power of the Holy Spirit) that the conscious faith-action sets in motion and accomplishes, and that bonds the Christian more closely to his Savior. However, with the first *deliberate* act we are dealing with an emphasis. Soon, when the form points us to the dwelling of the Holy Spirit, in Christ as in the head and in us as his members, it speaks especially of the quiet action.

That means that first must be asked, what does faith do in the sacramental appropriation of Christ?

As it appears from the wording of the Lord's supper formulary, faith in the first instance is active with respect to a deed, a fact, an event, namely, that Christ offered his body to the wood of the cross unto death and shed his blood. By eating, the covenant member celebrates in striking manner remembrance of the salvation-fact of the sacrificial death. He exerts remembrance with respect to the humiliated, priestly Jesus.

The form refers to this with these words: "you eat and drink with your mouth *in remembrance of me.*" There can also certainly be a remembrance of Jesus' atoning death by quiet contemplation (meditation) of the mystically disposed heart. There are moments in life wherein the sacred thoughts erupt and the soul is swept into the effects of wonder and worship. But these moments of inspiration are seldom and unpredictable. The usual level upon which a Christian lives is lower. As a rule, his soul has no need of a bridle but a spur. He needs to tell his soul, "Wake up! Nourish the ancient faith again!" And also, he is obliged, watching out for the cooling and flagging of the spiritual life, to take hold of the ordinary means, that is, the means of grace that God has ordered for him.

You see, when he approaches the supper table and he takes the bread in the mouth and *eats*, when he clasps the cup and *drinks* the sip of wine, then he *compels* his sluggish, forgetful soul to think on Jesus, as the man of sorrows. It is spiritually impossible to celebrate the supper and *not* to reflect on the suffering of Christ. And especially, in that sacred, memorable moment, with the holy covenantal seal in your mouth and then traversing into your body, which is so intimately engaged with the most delicate parts of your body, is the soul thereby directed to what happened with Jesus. This eating is a symbolic *honoring, extolling* of Jesus. It is a symbolic hosanna to the crucified one. The congregation that eats and drinks at the table of the Lord presents an offering to the suffering Savior.

But the faith of the fellow guest at the Lord's meal does more.

By eating and drinking of the bread and wine with his mouth, he directs faith itself to action for a higher certainty. Christ grants bread and wine to the communicant in order by sensory affirmation to bring assurance to the faith.

Those who *see* the bread and wine may by viewing the visible be drawn and secured by the invisible. Time and again, it is: *as certainly* as you see this is the invisible verified.

And so then, "*as certainly* as this bread is broken before your eyes and this cup is given to you, and *you eat and drink with your mouth in remembrance of me.*" There is here a clear ascent in sensory affirmation, and thus also in the certainty of faith. First, the minister breaks the bread before the eyes of the guest. The eye of the supper guest *sees* this. His eye does not deceive him as this is what he actually sees. So now he may depend upon the reality of the atonement.

However, the sacrament comes to him yet closer. He himself takes it in hand, brings it to the mouth, it enters the body, and now every doubt should be foolishness. That the eye of a man can mislead is not entirely excluded. Sometimes we think we see something that in reality does not exist. And sometimes something is actually there that nevertheless we do not see.

But when it comes to touching something with the hand, and that is in our mouth, feeling it with the delicate instrument of the tongue, there may exist complete certainty. Here reaches certainty its zenith. Here works the sacrament its highest operation. And the believer makes the application: *as certainly* as I eat and drink this bread and wine with my mouth in remembrance of Jesus, has he given his body to the wood of the cross and shed his blood for me, *and nourishes and refreshes my hungry and thirsty soul with this his crucified body and shed blood to everlasting life.*

Also, it serves well to note what comes with this last; yes, precisely with this last is so strikingly revealed what the sacrament says.

We have noted that in the eating and drinking a remembrance is celebrated to the honor of Immanuel. However, there is no symbolic agreement between the eating and the death of Jesus. There is here only a correlation for certainty.

However, there is a symbolic correspondence with directing faith to the immediate action of Christ in the present.

After all, there must be a distinction made between what Christ has done and what he does now. Christ gave his body unto death. This is a salvation fact that occurred before us. That is an event of *history*. But Christ also gives something in the present. On the ground of and in connection with his priestly self-sacrifice, he wills now to nourish and refresh our souls unto eternal life, i.e., he wills by the working of the Holy Spirit to grant us a share of his own life, his gifts, his person.

Wherefore, this sharing of himself is signified and sealed unto us by the eating and drinking. What one eats he takes into his body as life-sustaining. You are united with the food and it with you. It takes effect for strength that nourishes you and goes into your living.

At the moment the Christian eats (and, naturally, also afterward as he intentionally recalls this moment), he may come to the salvific conclusion that what bodily and materially happens with this bread and this wine, happens spiritually and for my soul with Christ in my heart. The mystical union comes into play. The branch is united to the vine. He abides in you and you in him (John 15:4). Because you are crucified with Christ, nevertheless you live; yet not you, but Christ lives in you. And the life that you now live in the flesh you live by the faith of the Son of God, who loved you and gave himself for you (Gal. 2:20).

7. THE REFORMED LORD'S SUPPER IDEA

In that which now follows in the form, this rich sacramental language is yet more precisely nuanced. Knowing that it here concerns the essence of the Lord's supper idea, the framers endeavor to faithfully enlighten the congregation.

From now on the form of the direct discourse is abandoned, and for it is substituted again the objective or demonstrative manner of speaking.

As if a conclusion is being drawn from the previous—indeed that which is now said is in part further explanatory, but yet more inferential—it proceeds:

> From this institution of the holy supper of our Lord Jesus Christ, we see that he directs our faith and trust to his perfect sacrifice (once offered on the cross) as to the only ground and foundation of our salvation, wherein he is become to our hungry and thirsty souls, the true food and drink of life eternal. For by his death he hath taken away the cause of our eternal death and misery, namely, sin, and obtained for us the life-giving Spirit, that we by the same (who dwells in Christ as in the head, and in us as his members), might have the true communion with him, and be made partakers of all his riches, of life eternal, righteousness, and glory.

The form does not bring a new subject with these tenderly presented sentences. Indeed, a new thought is not introduced. Rather, the foregoing is clarified, expanded, and deepened.

There is also a clear sense that the form in a cautious manner (because in a form such as this it would not be the appropriate place) chooses to position itself against errors that threatened the church of those days regarding the Lord's supper.

Rome directed faith and trust of the flock to a fantasy sacrifice that would take place in the mass.

Our formulary causes us to see, from the institution of the sacred supper of our Lord Jesus Christ, that Christ directs our faith and trust to his perfect sacrifice, *once offered on the cross*, as to the only ground and foundation of our salvation. Clearly the emphasis falls here on the words: once offered on the cross. Of course, Rome does not deny the central meaning of the sacrifice on the cross, but by the continual, repeated sacrifice of Christ in the mass, this fundamental fact recedes to the background in the awareness of the believer. And there is actually even a pushing of Jesus' sacrifice into the background in so far that the sacrifice of the mass must serve to complete and activate the sacrifice of the cross for the believer. From this perspective, the sacrifice of Christ is neither a *perfect* sacrifice *once offered* on the cross, nor, for the Roman Christian, the only ground and foundation of their salvation.

In the foregoing exposition of the words of the institution, the form clearly indicated that Rome's perspective was defective. Christ spoke nothing, in fact not one word, of a continual sacrifice. Christ points to his body, which was given for his own, and to his blood, which was shed for many, and only requires of his people the remembrance celebration of this wonder of grace when he says: "This do ye, as oft as ye drink it in remembrance of me." The congregation invests its faith and trust not first of all in what God is doing now, but in what God has done. This is the specifically Reformed idea that the Lord's supper form is expressing, and that we refuse to see damaged or diminished at any price.

The victory cry of believers joins with Paul: our passover lamb *was* slain for us! The jubilance of the elect is: God was in Christ reconciling the world unto himself and has committed to us the word of reconciliation. Entrance to the throne of grace need not be opened, it is unlocked, and we may have access with a true heart and in full assurance of faith. The mediator's atoning death is and remains as the point of rest for our heart, and therefore also always remains, as we all, abandoning all, in contriteness draw near to his comfort.

However, there is still another onesidedness against which the form establishes the whole truth. In the Palatinate, where our form was birthed, were not a few followers of Zwingli, who in the doctrine of the Lord's supper deviated significantly from the Calvinist conception. According to the perspective of Zwingli, the main purpose of the celebration of the supper was a referral back to the death of Christ, so that the supper itself was a *memorial meal*. The calling of the believer was by faith to recall the hour of Jesus' death, and thus to exercise communion with the crucified Jesus in an historical sense.

It is also undoubtedly implied that the form, (exercising discretion) without naming names, reacts against the Zwinglian reversal of the sacrament and leads the congregation to a deeper, Reformed view when, mentioning the historical foundation of our salvation, it follows with, *whereby he is become to our hungry and thirsty souls the true food and drink of life eternal.*

Next to the historical fact of the atonement, the form at the same time establishes the (flowing-from-this) reality of the present, namely, that Christ *is become* for us (not *became*) our nourishment of life. *After* Christ gave his body and shed his blood, he also *gives* his body and blood. In other words, in the supper is interwoven not only a bond of historical remembering of the crucified Christ, but also a bond of a living communion with the now living and glorified Christ. Indeed—and herein also the Reformed faith stands unyielding—the historical fact of Jesus' crucifixion is the fountain of salvation. At Golgotha reconciliation was accomplished, finished. There the foundation of salvation was laid. For the justification of the congregation Jesus has *nothing* more to supply. In this sense, his work is totally finished. But yet is this accomplished redemption just then become our salvific possession when Jesus deliberately applies it to us in the present by our receiving it as his members and possessing it with his mediator's life.

This happens now in the supper.

Of itself it could be imagined that the table of the Lord grants only remembrance in the manner that the passover once did. And even then, the meal would not be without some influence for the life of faith. But according to the Reformed conception, the supper does more. It brings us into a faith rapport with the victorious Lord. It nourishes and feeds us with Christ. Through him, it administers life to us.

However, are the words of institution in the form then correct to speak of the eating and drinking *in remembrance of Jesus*, as if to exclude that there is intended the eating and drinking *of Jesus' body*, that is, to exercise communion with Jesus himself?

Note how deeply and beautifully the formulary grasps the thought of Scripture and develops the embraced idea. First it is said that Jesus, by the sacrifice of the cross, *is become* for us true food and drink for our souls, which the form has every right to say, especially when consideration is given to his own, and already quoted by us, speaking in John.

But then the form paints more on this canvas and explains further how by the death of Jesus the now-living Christ is become food for us.

By his death, Christ *hath taken away the cause of our eternal death and misery, namely, sin, and obtained for us the life-giving Spirit.* This is splendid, classic language of our fathers that we recognize. Here it is materialized that he who digs deeply can also build high. The form plumbs Christ's sacrifice of reconciliation to the depths. Christ has not achieved the possibility of salvation. Neither has he softened nor minimized the distress of life. He has in principle taken away the *cause* of our misery. That was his blessed triumph of the cross.

It must be granted that the quick transition from the one image to the other strikes as not ideal, at least not perfectly harmonious. In the phrase that immediately precedes the one here is mention of *hungry and thirsty* souls. Meant is the hunger for salvation that stems from regeneration, the appetite for life, why Jesus says in the sermon on the mount that such are blessed.

But now in this connection the form suddenly makes mention of an eternal hunger, which is the same as trouble and as a miserable outcome of sin. This hunger makes a man miserable, shall torment him horribly in the state of damnation where there is no satisfaction. From a literary point of view, it is not a good idea in such rapid succession to use the word *hunger* in such completely different, indeed opposite, senses. But apart from this formal objection, how deep and pure is the tone that the formulary causes to spring from the word of the gospel! How appropriate and deep the knife here cuts the bread of life for the congregation. How clearly this tried-and-true language brings to the light the eternal salvation-rich outcomes of the messianic sufferings. Certainly, with the supper, the memory of the covenantal people goes back to Golgotha, but in order out of that history that is far in the past to draw the comforting conclusion for today. There, with the breaking of Jesus' life, with the pouring out of his blood, is the *cause* of our misery taken away. There we are in principle saved. Indeed, this is the false help to the world, that it merely plasters over the wounds, hides the deformity under its paints. With its appearance of beauty, it narcotizes its conscience, and it anesthetizes the weeping homesickness forever.

In the gaping abyss of life's distress, they toss in the worthless toys of its culture. To alleviate the misery, it gives that which intensifies the suffering. And what they provide to relieve the starvation produces even greater cries of hunger. The poor man spends money for that which is not bread and labors for that which cannot satisfy. For what is seen is temporary, but what is unseen is eternal.

There, the great Sovereign of life comes near, the Lord, your Great Physician. He sees the deep cause of your soul's infirmity and prescribes medicine for you, stopping in its tracks the hellish effects of your toxic blood. He takes away that which caused you for so long to wither, suffer, and struggle, and that which soon would kill you for eternity—the root evil, the source of the poison, namely, *sin.*

He takes that sin away by taking it upon himself. He who knew no sin *was made to be sin.* He pays the debt and sets you free. He bears the guilt for sin, and as a result wipes away the stain, pulls it out by the root, eliminates the source of sin.

Do not forget this last one in order to understand well the benefit of the supper.

The table speaks to you not only of *justification* that was earned outside you by the death of Christ and that you received through faith, but just as much about *sanctification* that was also acquired by Jesus' sacrifice and applied to you in the redeeming present.

Viewed rightly, sanctification is an aspect of justification. That is because justification involves a double benefit: the acquittal from guilt and punishment, as well as the granting of the right to eternal life.

It is good to see this positive side of the judicial grace as a distinctive benefit. Christ removes the cause of our hunger and misery then only in the applicatory, actual way when he takes away the sin *in us*, purges evil from the heart, pours life into us, in a word, when he grants us the most sublime of all his gifts, *the Holy Spirit*.

Note that the formulary also says this: that Christ *obtained for us the life-giving Spirit*.

Truly, the covenantal benefit of the supper increases with this addition in beautiful completeness. It becomes all the richer, broader, and deeper.

In the words of the institution itself the working of the Holy Spirit is not mentioned. But the form explains Scripture with Scripture. By virtue of the organic unity of Scripture, this is included in the words of Jesus, and we may correctly infer from them, we may say: from the institution of the holy supper it follows that he makes us partakers of the life-giving Spirit. Feeding and refreshing our souls with his body and blood, Jesus does not otherwise and could do no other way than by the life-giving Spirit.

Truly, the words regarding the working of the Spirit shed light that makes it all the more clear that authentic celebration of the Lord's supper is not limited to a remembrance exercise.

It is noteworthy that God the Spirit is here called the *life-giving* Spirit.

This name he bears on account of the work that he produces. His work already at creation is to infuse the power of life into lifelessness. At the dawn of creation, upon the formless and void, this Spirit moved upon the waters. And into the dead stuff he bred life (in the Hebrew of Genesis 1:2 is a word that indicates a brooding). Also in the existing nature he constantly awakens life anew. When God sends forth his Spirit, things are as it were created anew, and he renews the face of the earth.

But in the work of redemption is first directly revealed the immeasurable power of the Spirit. Here his task concerns not merely the lifeless, but the *dead*. It is about making alive that which lies bound by the power of death. And also, this is what he accomplishes. Jesus himself witnesses in his discourse where before the astonished crowd he identifies himself as *the bread of life* (John 6) and says that he who eats of this bread has eternal life. When Jesus notes that the listeners are understanding these things materially, at least naturally, he says: "It is the Spirit that quickeneth; the flesh profiteth nothing: the words that I speak unto you, they are spirit, and they are life" (v. 63). According to the Dordt scholars, Christ here is indicating a spiritual eating "which is accomplished by the power of his Spirit, and that produceth life."

The result is like the cause. He who produces the eating is the *Spirit*; thus is the fruit of the food also *spiritual*. By eating, a man becomes spiritually living. The nourishment happens *unto life eternal*.

However, when the Holy Spirit reveals himself here as the life-giving Spirit, he never grants this life outside Christ. Jesus is the vine, and we are the branches. And the Spirit of truth speaks (and we add to this: works) of himself, "Because," says Jesus, "he shall receive of mine, and shall shew it unto you" (John 16:14).

The formulary describes the relationship between Christ and his people, that by the Spirit is accomplished, thus: *that we by the same Spirit (who dwells in Christ as in the head, and in us as his members), might have the true communion with him, and be made partakers of all his riches, of life eternal, righteousness and glory.*

This is spoken intimately and earnestly. The image of the relationship of life between Christ and his church is depicted hereby clearly and fully. Herein lies the secret of the mystical union, that the Holy Spirit dwells as well in Christ as in his members.

Let us understand this well.

Christ does not contain the Spirit according to his divinity, but (with the Father) he causes the Spirit to proceed from himself.

As mediator, Jesus is anointed by the Spirit in immeasurable richness. Especially when he was glorified and received the promise of the Holy Spirit (Acts 2:23), he received gifts.

But he received these gifts in order to share them, in order to shower them upon his people, and thus also to enliven with his life his body that is upon earth.

By nature of the matter, this bond of living communion need not be applied from the side of Christ. From his fullness streams life as from an inexhaustible fountain. But indeed, living rapport must be applied to the side of the elect who of themselves are dead objects. If there shall be a relationship not only *of* Christ but also *unto* Christ, then the Spirit of God must cleanse and *graft* us into Christ. He must deposit the power to believe into our veins. He must administer in the blood the mysterious cravings for love, and in this manner open our heart for the outpourings of grace from the heart of the mediator.

Therefore, it is so that we by this Spirit "might have true communion with Christ, and be made partakers of all his riches, of life eternal, righteousness and glory."

The form depicts the relationship between Christ and his own with the biblical image of the unity of the body. The members of the body are united by the power that springs from one source. Sometimes this life origin is seen as in the heart, from which are the issues of life. But there is also reason to seek the center of life in the head, from where countless nerves and fibers run through the entire body, animate it, and direct it. In a certain sense Christ is the heart of his people, where the engine of life works, but he is also the head. And the Holy Spirit is he *"who dwells in Christ as in the head, and in us as his members."* In this imagery the Holy Spirit functions not as the blood, but much more intimately, here his place and mission in the body operates as the *soul* of the person. According to the Reformed conception, the soul is present not in one little place of the body, but it is *tota in toto corpore,* i.e., wholly present in every part of the body. It is, however, not present in the various parts of the body in the same strength and glory. In the fingertips, which are extremely sensitive, the soul is present more than in the arm. The hand, which directs the pen, so that it practically by itself sets the thoughts of the head on paper with its countless small, fine movements—it is indeed one of the most life-inspired, mental organs. Keeping in mind what the hand does in obedience to the spirit, one might begin to imagine at the same time what the spiritual body will be like, of which Paul (1 Cor. 15) makes mention, that will bear fully the image of the heavenly,

This symbolism sheds all the more light upon the mysterious work of the Holy Spirit.

In our natural, earthly existence we are material, shackled, dead. According, however, as the union comes to existence between Christ and his members, our existence becomes all the more spiritual, that is, adroit, powerful, refined, and rich. The Holy Spirit *spiritualizes* the sluggish, listless flesh, our lowly, frail existence. And he does so by granting to us "all of the riches" of Christ.

The form names only three riches from Jesus' treasure: life eternal, righteousness, and glory. In these three in summary fashion, all of the riches are identified whereby Jesus, who is wealthy, wills to make his poor people rich. But no human understanding can apprehend the extent of the length and breadth and depth and height and comprehend the love of Christ that surpasses knowledge. It is a tremendous—impossible to appreciate—work that the Holy Spirit accomplishes in us to enrich us, more than we according to human ability could ever conceptualize.

Noteworthy is the relationship that exists in this regard in the presentations of our Lord's supper and baptism formularies.

We see how the last form replenishes and explains the first, like the sacrament of the Lord's supper itself completes and confirms baptism.

Speaking of the promise of the Son, the baptism form says that Christ "incorporates us into the fellowship of his death and resurrection." Then it expresses that this incorporation happens by the work of the Holy Spirit. The Holy Spirit assures us that he will sanctify us to be members of Christ, *applying unto us that which we have in Christ.* This last expression corresponds with what our Lord's supper form calls the becoming partakers of all the blessings of Jesus by communion with him.

Judicially we already *have* in Jesus all the riches that belong to his own, but experientially there is yet but a small portion in our possession. The work of the abundant love of the merciful Spirit is to make us as rich as possible, *to make us partakers* of all that is ours.

Therefore, his work is not completed until we, "at last, with the congregation of the elect, shall be presented spotless in life eternal." Then for the first time, the life-giving Spirit lives in all the members with the full glory to which these members are entitled. Then for the first time, the whole body has the true fellowship with the head, which is necessary unto the full blooming beauty of the body, and Christ is glorified in the highest in his own.

It serves also to observe that the Heidelberg Catechism brings out the same thought. As well as in the confessional as in the liturgical fruit of the Calvinist Reformation, there reigns a unity of the spirit, even in the language of the symbolism.

To the doctrine of the Lord's supper in the catechism, Ursinus and Olevianus devoted their noblest theological gifts. For the purpose of their composition was to provide steady, dogmatic guidance in the face of troubling notions regarding the Lord's supper in the Palatinate.

In question 75, the distinction is first made between the operation of faith with a view to the historical fact of the atonement and the operation of faith with respect to the now living and glorified Christ.

Even so, Christ, as it says there, has commanded me and all believers to eat this broken bread and to drink of this cup unto his remembrance, and thereby promises: *first, that his body was offered and broken on the cross for me, and his blood shed for me, as certainly as I see with the eyes, etc.* This is the strengthening of faith by the sacramental remembrance of the salvation fact. And further,

> *that he himself feeds and nourishes my soul with his crucified body and shed blood to everlasting life, as assuredly as I receive from the hands of the minister, and taste with my mouth the bread and cup of the Lord, as certain signs of the body and blood of Christ.*

Here the catechism establishes for us the sacramental operation of the Lord's supper by which is realized the mystical union with the living Christ. This emerges further in the explanation that question 76 gives of the symbolic words: to eat the crucified body of Christ and to drink his shed blood. Hereby we nevertheless understand that it is not only

> *to embrace with a believing heart all the sufferings and death of Christ, and thereby to obtain the pardon of sin and life eternal; but also, besides that, to become more and more united to his sacred body by the Holy Ghost, who dwells both in Christ and in us; so that we, though Christ is in heaven and we on earth, are notwithstanding flesh of his flesh, and bone of his bone; and that we live and are governed forever by one Spirit, as members of the same body are by one soul.*

Thus, the congruence is not only in the idea, but also in the choice of words. It is no wonder that when we take notice, the same pen of Olevianus that wrote the Lord's supper form also applied its influence in the catechism. Especially the line of thought is drawn that the symbolism of the communion between Christ and his members in the catechism is further developed and elucidated. The Lord's supper form only makes a distinction between Christ, *the head*, and us, *his members*. The catechism speaks of a being unified with *the holy body* of Christ with the outcome that Christ, with whom we are united, is not only head but is the whole body.

Above all, the catechism is more clearly aimed at the danger (or fault?) that was alleged from the Romish side against the Reformed Lord's supper doctrine, namely that in the Reformed supper there is never an essential communion with Christ of which can be spoken, seeing that Christ is and remains in heaven while the believers remain on earth. The catechism answers by pointing to the mystical body. Although Christ is in heaven and although we are on earth, nevertheless, we are flesh of his flesh and bone of his bone. And this mystical communion is grounded in the fact that the same Spirit penetrates and permeates all the members of this body, like the same soul gives life to all the members of the human body. In the Lord's supper is such grace poured out upon believers that the operation of that Spirit (through the exercise of faith) becomes more powerful and profound, and thereby the union with Christ closer.

Seeing that we know of no richer and more affectionate elucidation regarding this working of the Spirit than what Dr. Kuyper provides with almost lyrical prose in his *E Voto*,[14] we shall take the liberty to borrow this exalted quotation to gain for further enjoyment and instruction, with an apology (certainly to be reasonably accepted by the reader) for the lengthiness of the citation:

> The idea of the mystical body of the Lord here therefore may not be relinquished for even a second. Though you do not see the body, it nonetheless exists. It is there. You belong to it. You are a member of it, and a member of it shall you forever remain. And while in this body are many members, as Paul speaks of a foot and a hand, so this body has also a head and a Spirit of life that is pervasive and enlivening. That head is the now exalted Mediator, and that life force in the mystical body is the Holy Spirit. In the common, material body, your foot or your hand or the tip of your finger has its communion with your head by the life force of your body.

---

14 Kuyper, *E voto*, III, 164–65.

When by narcotic anesthetizing the working of this life force within you is arrested, one can amputate your foot without your head taking notice. Only when that life force of your body binds with all your members is the body healthy and resilient.

So too in the body of Christ. Also, in this body there is no fellowship of the members with the head than by the living force of the body and this living force of the body is the Holy Spirit. In Paradise, God first created Adam's body and then breathed into him the breath of life, and so became Adam a living soul. In a similar way, on Pentecost, the body of Christ stood ready, but first thing on Pentecost Sunday God breathed into this body the Holy Spirit, and so it became the living, animated body of the Lord. Also, from that moment on, the Holy Spirit is never absent from this body of Christ. To think that the Holy Spirit is at work in this body only now and then is completely at odds with the clear instruction of the Holy Scriptures. The Bible teaches us time and again that the Holy Spirit came to live in us and to remain in us, and that we are his *temple*, so that this Holy Spirit *within* us never *can* depart. Should the Holy Spirit ever leave the body of the Lord for even a second, this body would at the same second expire and die, something which the eternal value of Christ's sacrifice and the unchangeability of God's election makes unthinkable and impossible.

What can happen and does happen is that this life force is hindered from working powerfully in the body, or also he recedes from some members for a certain time almost entirely. Our earthly, material body provides enough example of this. We all know the moments when our bodies don't feel well; when we feel completely miserable, and the weary parts of our body drudge along with nothing but difficulty. Then we are not fresh, bright, alert, or content. We drag ourselves along but feel that we are losing our disposition and are crippled by a general malaise. Well, what is this other than that the life force of our body is still there (because otherwise we would have passed away) but nevertheless, that life force no longer strongly resonates in every vessel of our nervous system and in every drop of our blood. And that continues until a remedy brings relief or our vigor happens to return. Then all of a sudden that life force that had been in hiding is pushing out into the foreground. Our pulse strengthens. Our nervous system awakens. Everything in us reactivates. And suddenly we feel rich and exuberant again. Although our language does not express this first not withdrawing and presently returning of the life force with regard to our material body, precisely in our word, "radiance" so picturesquely, "I have no radiance," it does say, so graphically: "the life force is indeed still there, but it does not penetrate."

Take this in terms of the mystical body of the Lord and what do you have? It is this, is it not, that there shall be times when the church of God declines into a lusterless dull state, through which the life force of the Body did not depart, but *nevertheless drew back.* In contrast are other times when the church of God will be *inspired* and filled with holy *exaltation* because that same living-giving Spirit that before had withdrawn himself now again *reverberates through* the entire body with holy energy. Then the head works again upon all the members of the body, and all the members of the body react quickly and with inspiration again unto the only head; and the glorious delight is experienced as streams of life and blessing descend in grace from the head and while praise and thanksgiving ascend again from the members to the head.

Such rich, glorious days were experienced by the first Christian church of Jerusalem and happened time again, especially known also in the days of the Reformation. And though since then things have been going downhill, nevertheless, in the revival and other spiritual movements in this century significant glorious renewal has been evident; blessed moments wherein the flock of the Lord feels refreshingly united with her head and Savior.

Of much interest is it that precisely at this portion of our formulary, the full light falls not only for the inner value of this piece itself, where the holiest intimacy of the sacrament is described, but also for the antithetical conceptions to which it has given occasion.

With some interpreters of our liturgical writings, you discover a certain honestly intended, but nevertheless not entirely purified of bias, effort to externalize the intimate language of our form. Namely, the goal appears to be to deny the specifically Calvinistic character of our formulary and as much as possible to place a Zwinglian stamp on it.

We hear, for example, what Mensinga judges in his earlier cited work:

> With lack of historical certainty concerning origin, the question naturally comes as to the spirit, whether it be Calvinist, Zwinglian, or Lutheran... One cannot miss that another spirit is voiced there than that in the Lutheran formulary. Neither is it straight-up Calvinism. Thus, it could be Zwinglian. Not that Lutherans or Calvinists would have something to object but certainly, Zwingli standing on the least intensive and negative side, agreed with him in the positive part of his theory. But it is nevertheless a manner of presentation that we find neither in their formularies nor in their dogmatic and exegetical writings, *there, where it matters,* to explain *the true symbolical nature of the supper.*[15] Truly, it would come as no surprise that also a Zwinglian portion were taken up into

---

15 Emphasis added.

the Lord's supper form. There were always many Zwinglians in the Palatinate, as well as Melanchtonian theologians who were related to them in spirit, whose case one gladly would promote, and whose presence can have had influence on the composition of the form.[16]

Indeed, Mensinga sees "even more specific proof" for the Zwinglian spirit in this portion of our form:

Precisely in taking its exposition as a whole: the chief purpose for the Lord's supper is to point to the death of Christ; particularly at the cross is he become the food and drink unto eternal life for us; it has to do with what was there accomplished and procured for us, and to what our eating and drinking of bread and wine is directed; that presentation is the genuine and particular criterion of Zwinglism.[17]

In order "to place this important point in the full light of day," the author reaches into his treasure chest to pull out all kinds of historical material to show us.

His reasoning is as follows: that according to the "latest" and "deepest" studies of the writings of the reformers it would appear that Calvin and Zwingli stood much closer than has been imagined for a long time. One historian, Schweizer, goes so far as to say that Zwingli like Calvin recognized the entire, living unity of the members with Christ the head as the highest level of sanctification, and that it is compatible with their doctrine in viewing it as a symbol of the *unio mystica* (mystical union). To pass a proper judgment, however, it is necessary to distinguish properly between the matters themselves and the *presentation* of the matters. It is evident that the reformers utilize the same terminology, but nevertheless intend something different. Calvin and Zwingli both speak of a spiritual eating and drinking of

---

16 Mensinga, 235ff.
17 Ibid., 236.

the body and blood of the Lord, but they do not attach the same ideas to these expressions. With Zwingli, the body and blood of the Lord is only the *crucified* body and *shed* blood. And the eating of this body and drinking of this blood intends only to say: *believe* that the body was crucified and the blood was shed.[18]

In contrast, with Calvin the *body* and *blood* are not only the crucified Christ, but the entire Christ, in his divine-human nature as he is glorified in heaven. And eating and drinking this Christ means to be with him united, assimilated to him, not only through the conscious working of faith, but particularly by the Holy Spirit who is the agent of this supernatural and incomprehensive participation.[19]

We come across one of Calvin's most characteristic expressions in terms of this mystical, spiritual operation in his explanation of 1 Corinthians 11:24 ("And when he had given thanks, brake it and said, 'Take, eat, that is my body, that is broken for you; do this in remembrance of me'"). Here Calvin says:

> Let us see in what manner Christ's body is given to us. Some explain, that it is given to us, when we are made partakers of all the blessings which Christ has procured for us in his body—when, I say, we by faith embrace Christ as crucified for us, and raised up from the dead, and in this way are effectually made partakers of all his benefits. [Here Calvin is referring to, among others, the Zwinglians.] As for those who are of this opinion, I have no objection to their holding such a view. As for myself, I acknowledge that it is only when we obtain Christ himself that we come to partake of Christ's benefits. He is, however, obtained, I affirm, not only when we believe that he was made an offering for us, but when he dwells in us, when he is one with us, when we are members of his flesh, when, in fine, we are incorporated with him

18 Ibid., 237ff.
19 Ibid.

(so to speak) into one life and substance. Besides, I attend to the import of the word, for Christ does not simply present to us the benefit of his death and resurrection, but the very body in which he suffered and rose again. I conclude that Christ's body is really (as the common expression is), that is, truly given to us in the supper, to be wholesome food for our souls. I use the common form of expression, but my meaning is, that our souls are nourished by the substance of the body, that we may truly be made one with him, or, what amounts to the same thing, that a life-giving virtue from Christ's flesh is poured into us by the Spirit, though it is at a great distance from us, and is not mixed with us... That Christ, while remaining in heaven, is received by us. For as to his communicating himself to us, that is effectuated through the secret virtue of his Holy Spirit, which cannot merely bring together, but join in one, things that are separated by distance of place, and far remote. But in order that we may be capable of this participation, we must rise heavenward. Here, therefore, faith must be our resource, when all the bodily senses have failed.

After this striking citation in which clearly comes out that the difference between Calvin and Zwingli is truly more than a difference of emphasis, Mensinga arrives at the conclusion that our Lord's supper form, especially where the doctrine of the supper is presented and the meaning of the symbolic action of Jesus is developed, gives that idea that "with Calvin in his form itself was touched only faintly. And so, regarding the matter it remains with Zwinglism and does not rise to Calvinism."

As to the question regarding what reason the framers of our formulary may have had for setting such a Zwinglianist tone precisely at this noteworthy point, the learned liturgist also has an answer, that the thought was foremost to complete, or rather, to improve the form of Calvin. According to the convictions of the composers, neither the form of Calvin nor that of Micron satisfied the demands that one could rightly place upon the Lord's supper form. By them there is what "is considered an essential defect that in the form of Calvin, and especially that of Melanchton, so extremely little is ventured on the very fruit of his love, about the touching and moving institution of the Lord's supper."

In general, Prof. Gooszen defends the same point of view in his book. He submits in this writing the impression that the difference between the conception of Calvin and that of the old-Reformed view was especially advocated by Bullinger. Calvin alone would see in the supper the most intimately thinkable union of the soul with Christ, a union considered "quite physical." In the old-Reformed conception, the union of Christ with the believers is indeed not overlooked, but is nevertheless considered more as a union by faith. The historical fact of the suffering of Jesus, and as it pertains to what he procured for us, stands hereby in the foreground. Further, in this old-Reformed view, more emphasis is laid on the symbolism of the breaking of the bread whereby the supper takes on the character of an agape, to which symbolism Calvin attached little worth.

According to Prof. Gooszen, although our Lord's supper formulary would have some Calvinistic expressions, largely prominent is the old-Reformed conception.

Barger, who gives this professorial elucidation a brief overview in a footnote, indicates there somewhat tongue-in-cheek:

> The question of whether on the point of the Lord's supper there exists such in depth material difference between the named conceptions, that they are contradictory, or are even to be distinguished, we reckon to the eloquence that is reserved for the history scholars.[20]

Indeed, this is also our opinion, and we are convinced that an extended and in-depth study over the subject would be out of place

---

20 Barger, 216–17.

here for our readers who mainly have to do with opening the choice of language of the Lord's supper form, and would feel little interest in a question that bears well-nigh an exclusively academic character.

Consequently, we shall not require all that much of the interest capacities of our readers on these matters.

That being said, it is extremely difficult to make out with complete certainty in an expression of our form as to what extent the framers desired to relay a more Zwinglian than Calvinist idea, seeing that both reformers sometimes marvelously agreed, but nevertheless did not mean exactly the same thing. We have already established the idea of the fact that Calvin and Zwingli both speak of the true body and blood of Christ, which believers eat and drink in a spiritual manner.[21]

Whereby yet comes that in neither can be found such consistency and similarity of expression that one with certainty and in particular can describe their intentions.

Mensinga recognizes of Zwinglians: "When it comes down to it, to expressing it precisely, they were not in agreement, indeed, Zwingli himself would be vacillating."[22]

And in his dogmatics, Dr. Bavinck expresses the same charge against Calvin.

The relationship between the Zwinglian and Calvinist perspective is explained by this historical dogmatician in the following way:

> At the suggestion of Honius, Zwingli interpreted the words
> of institution figuratively and explained the vocable "is" [in

---

21 Mensinga provides a few noteworthy quotations from Zwingli's writings (borrowed from Schweizer), e.g., this Calvinist-sounding statement: *Credo in S. Coena verum Christi corpus adesse fideï contempalatione*, i.e., "I believe that in the Lord's supper the true body of Christ is present for the contemplation of faith." However, the same Zwingli also says: *Spiritualiter edere corps Christi, nihil aliud est, quam spiritu ac mente niti misericordia Deï, per Christum*, i.e., "to eat the body of Christ in a spiritual way says nothing other than the spirit and the understanding standing upon the mercy of God, by Christ" (cf. Bavinck, *Dogmatics*, IV, 557).

22 Mensinga, 239, nt. 20.

the phrase, "This is my body"—B.W.] by the word "means," a recurrent practice also elsewhere in Scripture: Gen. 41:26; John 10:9; 15:1, for example. The bread and wine in the Lord's supper, therefore, are the signs and reminders of Christ's death, and believers, trusting in that reality, partake of the body and blood of Christ in these signs. Zwingli definitely rejected the physical presence of Christ in the Lord's supper, but in so doing he by no means denied that Christ is spiritually present in it to believers. On the contrary, Christ is very definitely received in the Lord's supper, as John 6 clearly teaches, but Christ is present in the supper and is received there in no other way than he is present in the word and by faith, that is, spiritually. This reception of Christ consists in nothing other than in trusting in his death.

Dr. Bavinck then follows with our already-mentioned citation wherein Zwingli explains that the spiritual eating of Christ is nothing other than that with the spiritual trust in God's mercy, and risking strife, that a collapse ignited between the German and Swiss reformations in terms of the Lord's supper.

When Calvin appeared on the scene, there was no longer any hope of reconciliation, although with his doctrine of the Lord's supper he took a position between and above the two parties. Calvin was absolutely on Zwingli's side insofar as he firmly rejected any kind of physical, local, and substantial presence of Christ in the signs of bread and wine. Such a presence, after all, is inconsistent with the nature of a body, with the true humanity of Christ, with Christ's ascension, with the nature of the communion that exists between Christ and his own, and is vastly different from an unprofitable eating with the mouth (*oralis manducatio*).

But Calvin also clearly revealed the antithesis between him and Zwingli. He had against Zwingli "that all too much allows the gift of

God in the Lord's supper to recede behind what believers do in it and hence one-sidedly views the Lord's supper as an act of confession," and further, "that in the eating of Christ's body, Zwingli sees nothing other and higher than believing in his name, the act of trusting in his death."

In a certain sense, therefore, Calvin put himself on the side of Luther and said

> that Christ is present in the supper and is received there—not physically and locally, to be sure, but certainly truly and essentially, with his whole person, including his body and blood. Between him and Luther there was disagreement not over the fact but only over the manner of that presence. And the eating of Christ's body in the supper is not exhausted by believing in him, by relying on his death. Eating is not identical with believing, even though it always only comes about by believing, but is rather the fruit of it, just as in Ephesians 3:17 Christ's indwelling in us, though it happens by faith, is nevertheless distinct from that faith. Calvin's concern evidently was the mystical union, the communion of believers with the whole person of Christ. While this communion does not come into being first of all by the supper, for Christ is the bread of our soul already in the word, it is nevertheless granted "more distinctly" in the Lord's supper and sealed and confirmed in the signs of bread and wine. In the supper there is not only a participation in the benefits but also communion with the person of Christ, and in not only with his divine but also with his human nature, his own body and blood, and this communion is called an "eating."

In the conclusion of his argument, Dr. Bavinck says:

> Calvin's representation is not clear in every respect, especially not as it concerns communion with the true flesh and blood of Christ and the life that flows from them. Utenhove

therefore asked him with some justice to abstain from the use of more or less obscure expressions when he dealt with the Lord's supper. So also in the confession and doctrine of Reformed churches and theologians there occasionally were different ways of expressing the truth about the Lord's supper. Some, like Bucer, seeking to get closer to Luther's view, said that "substantially," that is, "with respect to its substance," Christ's body was present in the supper.

The foundational idea of Calvin found entrance into the Reformed churches.

But Calvin's main idea—that in the Lord's supper, by the Holy Spirit, believers experience spiritual fellowship with the person of Christ and hence also with the body and blood of Christ and are thereby nourished and refreshed unto eternal life—has been taken over in the various Reformed confessions and become the common property of Reformed theology.

This last undoubtedly counts also for our Lord's supper form. It does not breathe the spirit of Zwinglianism but of Calvinism. We submitted the extensive citation from the fitting dogmatic-historical description of Dr. Bavinck, because here clearly comes to the light how it is possible that so many different sentiments can arise over the character of our formulary. "Calvin's representation is not clear in every respect;" note there an important factor that may also be neglected in the appraisal of our form. Not that we ourselves would hesitate in our convictions. In our opinion, there need be no doubt regarding the Calvinistic caliber of our form. The language, especially in the last part that we discussed, is clear where true communion with Christ in the supper is presented as a communion between head and members of the body. It is not the spirit of Zwingli speaking here but the spirit of Calvin.

It deserves attention that even a man like Mensinga, who has exerted so much of himself to depict our form as Zwinglian, in spite of himself must repeatedly acknowledge the Calvinistic elements in the form, and thus in a measure contradicts himself.

After first admitting that the broad depiction that our form gives of the suffering and death of Christ with the fruits that are connected with them (which must serve as evidence of the Zwinglian character) in no single respect can be judged by a Calvinist as here not being suitable. Mensinga himself points out that in the prayer and in the *Sursum Corda* which precede the communion, exactly the "strongly Calvinist-colored expressions" from Calvin's form are adopted. Especially the expression, "Be nourished with him, true God and man," would have to give offense to a Zwinglian.[23]

Therefore, it is truly unnecessary to judge our form as at fault whenever by some a more Zwinglian than Calvinistic idea presides in the Reformed churches. Of itself, the more intellectually disposed nature tends toward the Zwinglian side. Also, ignorance concerning the Bible, history, and confessions causes error. And not the least, shallowness and superficiality in the spiritual life is cause that the Lord's supper says so little to many and on many has so little effect.

That is why it cannot be overestimated as to the value of Dr. Kuyper in his exposition of the Reformed Lord's supper conception in his *E Voto*; he spares nothing in chopping down any leveling and cooling down of the Calvinistic idea of the Lord's supper. There can be a difference of sentiment concerning the question as to whether the origin of the intellectualistic conception of many Reformed got the message from Zwingli himself, but it certainly should be respected that Calvin, and we repeat, also our form, may not be faulted.

Undoubtedly, the reader will thank us as also here we recall the upbuilding and inspiring words of Dr. Kuyper. In no small measure it can contribute to "enlightenment" regarding the vastly differing opinions regarding the passage in our Lord's supper form.

First comes a sharp judgment regarding Zwingli himself:

---

23 Mensinga, 243–44, etc.

Zwingli therefore deviates the furthest, in so far that he denies *any* operations of grace in an extraordinary sense, and hereby takes a stand against Rome, Luther, and Calvin. Yes, one can say that Zwingli actually denied all sacraments as such. According to Zwingli's original presentation God chose his own; knowing for certain one is elect, he calls to faith; this faith must show itself in works, and to these works belong also the sacrament: an obligation wherein, also according to his own clear statements, God does not do something for us, but we do something for God. Not God but man is the working person in the sacrament. One receives nothing in the sacrament, but comes to fulfill his obligation, and to witness to his faith. Later in his letter to Francis I, Zwingli allowed that the holy sacrament *strengthens faith*, but he admits this only in the sense that the signs of the holy supper alert our senses in a holy manner where they otherwise might be cluttered with sinful thoughts. In the Reformation era one did not express it imprecisely by saying that Zwingli, with regard to sacramental elements, saw only *nuda signa,* i.e., nothing but a sign. And actually, which difficulty Zwingli himself may also have given, to hold the holy supper yet in honor ecclesiastically. That fact stands fast once and for all that for him it was *not* a sacrament; that there is consequently no sacramental power extended upon the soul; and that on that account it comes to stand on one line with various phenomena that can make an edifying impression on us, like the universe, a death bed, a praying child, and what not more.[24]

Kuyper also lets it be known why for our people it is necessary for him to send out such a sharp signal regarding Zwingli's doctrine of the Lord's supper.

---

24 Kuyper, *E Voto*, III, 127.

It would be almost unnecessary to even invest thought on this drab and dull Zwinglian perspective if it were not from of old that such an opinion was advocated here. There is in Dutch society a trait of character that exhibits a strong connection, and the best way to describe it, as a too scant thirst for the ideal. Not as if in times of high stress of the spirit also in the Swiss and Hollanders cannot be inspired. History teaches us quite the opposite. But this does not diminish that there is nevertheless in both nationalities as such something flat, something low, that is had neither by the Italians, the French, the Germans, nor the British to such an extent. We are stuck with the tendency, with our rather businesslike understanding, the desire to examine everything, and what does not fit within the frame of the businesslike understanding we tend to mock or to dismiss. From there that even the unbelief of the common citizens among us bears a so much more unpleasant character than by our neighbors near and far. And this now was the origin that, without agreement, in both Switzerland and in our country, an even more businesslike and low conception of the sacrament found entrance, that is there held yet by thousands and that found a spokesman in Prof. Doedes of Utrecht yet even in the last decade.[25]

So decisively does Dr. Kuyper state the criterion that he says:

Those who stand with Zwingli, that in baptism and the Lord's supper there is indeed an action by the believer to the glory of God but not in principle an action of God that takes place for the benefit of the believer—do not belong with us; with such we can have no ecclesiastical fellowship as they belong rather with the followers of Sozzini, also in their 19th century form.

---

25 Kuyper, *E Voto*, III, 127–28.

In a following chapter where Dr. Kuyper comes to the positive exposition of his view on the Lord's supper, he embroiders further on this same theme that he apparently held with extraordinary conviction:

Those sober believers who are devoid of all mysticism, who find their primary interpretation in Zwingli, see in the Lord's supper only *what can be seen by the eyes.* They see a few people gathering around a plate. They see one who takes the lead to break the bread on that plate and to pass around a cup of wine. They hear a few words spoken. And they see those sitting at the table take the bread and drink the wine. But they see nothing more. They see nothing of Christ. Nothing of the Holy Spirit. They comprehend nothing of any *divine* action taking place. All that takes place is an action by *people.* Man does something, God does nothing. Or to express it with Zwingli's own words: The one partaking of the supper comes to the Lord's supper indeed to witness to something, to declare something, to confess something *to* God, but not in order to receive something *from* God, and inwardly to be enriched by his God.

Thereupon Dr. Kuyper closely relates this characterization of our ecclesiastical life:

This Zwinglian stance is constantly contested and rejected by the Reformed, so much so that the Swiss, before Calvin appeared, already expressed themselves much more warmly in their Confession of Basel. *Though all of our churches in their Catechism and Confession, have set themselves entirely against this dead and dry Zwinglianism,* nevertheless this Zwinglian conception continues always to spread among us in two ways. First, by worldly church members who averse to any spiritual mystery because they have no eye for it. And second, and is more regrettable, by many devout children of God who yet always think that one comes to the holy supper only to bring something to God, or testify to God, instead of coming to receive something *from* their God and to allow himself to be witnessed to by his God; and who find this same testimony not powerful enough in their own soul on this account, and so year in and year out refrain from the holy supper.

It is known how Dr. Kuyper in his *E Voto* develops in an extensive argument the idea that at the supper an *action* from the divine side takes place, and indeed the threefold action of the Father, the Son, and the Holy Spirit.

These who yet might doubt which spirit is rendered in our Lord's supper form, just dive into our Reformed Lord's supper literature, and it will heal them of their unbelief. He shall know that our form, though by nature conciliatory rather than polemical, expresses the healthy mysticism of Calvinism.

In our form not only thinks the head, but also beats the heart of the Reformation. It speaks not only of a historical Christ who works his deeds of salvation for us, but also of the eternal living Christ who is one with his people by the indwelling of the Holy Spirit. It calls the Christian in the supper not only to proclaim the Lord's death, but also testifies to the love of God that satisfies the hungry souls of his own with the salvation benefits of the covenant.

True, the form describes the character of the Lord's supper celebration in the main as a commemoration unto Jesus' *remembrance* (and it is primarily this terminology that has led some critics astray). But when we are instructed: *after this manner are we to remember him by it*, comes clearly to light that this remembrance goes back into history only so the hearts can better be lifted up "in heaven, where Christ Jesus is our Advocate, at the right hand of his heavenly Father," in order to be more intimately bound to him by the mystical working of the life-giving Spirit, and of his fullness to receive grace for grace.

Chapter Six

ALTOGETHER ONE BODY

1. CHARACTER AND PLACE OF THIS SECTION

Factually, with the portion that up to now we have explained, the form has concluded its program (at least the doctrinal portion).

"So that we may celebrate the supper of the Lord to our comfort it was necessary in the first place for right examination, and further that we direct the Lord's supper to the end whereto the Lord Jesus has ordained and instituted it, namely, to his remembrance."

The form faithfully expounded that which is necessary for the examination as for the remembrance, and then with respect to the last part the instruction went deep, more deeply than the subject indicates; the form delivers more than promised with the program. Authentic Lord's supper celebration consists not only in the remembrance of Jesus' atoning death, but also in the exercise of fellowship with the living Christ.

Now notice that the form touches upon (is it by way of concession?) yet another subject that we must also consider before we come to the table of the Lord. It concerns not the exercise of fellowship with Christ, but that with the members of Christ, thus a matter that not directly but only consequently belongs to the use of the sacrament.

Besides, that we by this same Spirit may also be united as members of one body in true brotherly love, as the holy Apostle saith, *For we, being many, are one bread and one body; for we are all partakers of that one bread.* For as out of many grains one meal is ground, and one bread baked, and out of many berries being pressed together, one wine flows, and is mixed together; so shall we all, who by a true faith are engrafted into Christ, be altogether one body, through brotherly love, for Christ's sake, our beloved Savior, who hath so exceedingly loved us, and not only show this in word, but also in deed towards one another. Hereto assist us, the Almighty God and Father of our Lord Jesus Christ through his Holy Spirit. Amen.

This part even in its formulation is of Lutheran origin. In the Württemberg liturgy is

as out of many berries, pressed together, one wine flows and is mixed together, and from many grains one meal is ground and bread baked so shall we all who by true faith are incorporated into Christ be all together one body, through brotherly love, for Christ our dear Savior's sake, who before has so exceedingly loved us. And show this towards one another, as John teaches, not only in words but also in deeds. May the almighty, merciful God and Father of our dear Lord Jesus Christ help us in this, through his Holy Spirit. Amen.[1]

There is thus enough literal agreement regarding the content of this piece, though the motivation for the insertion is different. In the Lutheran form, this part is detached from the previous section; our form in a logical manner incorporates it with that which precedes. There was spoken of the mystical union of believers with Christ. This union was presented in terms of the biblical image of the body in which all members are one with the head. However, from this mystical union also follows that the members are bound to each other unto a marvelous, spiritual unity. Of itself the discourse flows in the same channel when it says that we by the same Spirit are united with each other as members of one body in true brotherly love.

---

1 *Supra*, I.5, where this was first flagged from the German text.

We admit that here in fact a new idea (though it be a conclusion of the preceding) is introduced.

Noteworthy is that in the Romish and also in Calvin's liturgy one looks in vain for such a passage.

That in Rome's liturgy the communion of the saints is not mentioned is obvious. The Lord's supper degenerates there in the sacrament of the altar, and genuine communion is driven completely into the background. There is found not even a trace of the fellowship in sitting at the same table. Likewise, the symbol of brotherly accord is entirely fallen away.

Moreover, what says more, also in the form of Calvin one finds no explicit mention of this holy aim of the celebration of the Lord's supper.

In our Reformed confessions we get only a hint of it here and there.

In question 75 of the catechism it is said that "Christ has commanded *me and all believers* to eat of this broken bread and to drink of the cup in remembrance of him." And at the end of question 76 we have "that we live and are governed forever by one Spirit, as members of the same body are by one soul."

And in article 35 of our Belgic Confession is the only place where the communion of the saints is indicated: "In a word, we are excited by the use of this holy sacrament to a fervent love towards God and our neighbor."

How then are we to account for this unique passage in our Lord's supper formulary? Does it belong there, or not?

We did note that, logically, the subject of brotherly love connects firmly to the theme of the mystical union. But from there it does not yet follow that mentioning it here is the logical place. Not all corollaries have a right to insertion. Without agreement with Mensinga, who calls this "the weakest place in our form,"[2] we must nevertheless

---

2 Mensinga, 260.

certify that weighty consideration can be raised against this passage from the perspective of literary symmetry and balance.

Regardless, that there be brotherly unity is partly condition, partly fruit of the celebration of the supper. Condition it is in so far as the stipulation comes to the covenant member to examine himself before the supper as to "whether he has laid aside unfeignedly all enmity, hatred, and envy, and earnestly resolves henceforward to walk in true love and peace with his neighbor." And fruit it is in so far as the supper of God is ordained unto the strengthening of the life of faith and that this strengthening comes to good expression. I believe the communion of the saints.

Strictly speaking, the communion of the saints, weighty as it is of itself, is nevertheless only a secondary component of the Christian faith and the Christian life. The sphere of influence of the Lord's supper reaches much further still than strengthening the bond of love between covenant members. The supper beams the rays of its blessings over the entire area of the life of faith and stimulates the Christian to activate all the ordinances of the Lord.

Thus, from this perspective there is warrant for objection to taking up in our form the pericope regarding brother love. Caution always serves to avoid anything that could distract from the idea of the one, unspeakable primary truth: union with the head, Jesus Christ, triumphant at the right hand of the Father!

However, allowing this objection, on the other hand the reasonableness must also be tested.

While it is true that strengthening the bond of brotherhood is only one of the fruits of celebrating the Lord's supper, yet this fruit does stand out in an entirely unique way with respect to the symbolism of the supper. It belongs to the supper like the end to the means. And this end is the first and closest at hand when the believer on this point consciously treats sacramentally.

Certainly, in defense of our formulary one could also observe that the fellowship of the communion of the saints is one of the richest fruits, perhaps *the* richest fruit of the supper, and is by far the highest measure of ecclesiastical life. Whoever for whom this observation counts has certainly a powerful ally in the apostle John, who in the most engaging and penetrating notes intones the necessity, glory, and worthiness of Christian love; who postulates brotherly love as a criterion of regeneration, indeed absorbs virtually the entire spiritual life in the life of a fellowship of believers mutually.

Not easily (indeed, especially in our cynical, shrewdly self-seeking age) can the congregation be over-reminded of the essential importance of believers living in unity. And already on account of this single fact, an intentional mention and instruction concerning this matter, as this found in our form for the Lord's supper, would deserve excuse, if not appreciation.

2. AS ONE BREAD, ONE BODY

However, for the correct judgment regarding this passage, attention must be given to the symbolism of the Lord's supper.

In the structure and character of the sacrament itself there is an introduction to the message of this article of faith.

Scripture draws it to our attention.

Because we have to consider in the Lord's supper how we also by the same Spirit are bound to each other as members of one body in true love, the holy apostle speaks of this: *"For we, being many, are one bread and one body; for we are all partakers of that one bread."*

The apostle who says this is Paul. It is right there in 1 Corinthians 10:17.

There has been much to-do over this text.

If we compare verse 17 with the immediately preceding verse, then we see that our form takes the lead from Paul himself regarding the communion of the saints in the symbolism of the supper. Even so, in verse 16 the apostle says: "The cup of blessing which we bless [*give thanks*], is it not a communion of the blood of Christ? The bread which we break, is it not the communion of the body of Christ?"

And then follows: "For (it is) one bread, (so) are we many one body: seeing we are all partakers of one bread."

So Paul binds the unity of believers immediately to communion with the body of Christ.

This much is clear.

However, difficulty arises regarding the correct translation of the text.

In no less than three ways this text can be grammatically construed.[3] Here is not the place to provide an exegetical treatise on the text. It is enough for us to share what is primarily going on with the question as to whether the inserted words "it is" and "so" actually belong in the text. Our Dordt commentary also provides another translation without these insertions, "for we many are one bread, and one body."[4] Herein appears that our translators did hold some sympathy for both options but gave priority to the first.

Especially among the more recent exegetes this translation finds support.

Godet translates: "Seeing that there is only one bread, we, being many, are one body: for we are all partakers of one bread."[5]

In general, this rendition is the same as our Dordt Bible. Perhaps it is preferable for superior correctness. Godet regards the consequential *for* or *because* as the beginning of a new phrase and takes it as a subordinate clause. The words, "For there is one bread," are dependent upon the following words that form the main idea: "We, who are many, are one body."

In our Dordt Bible the entire verse is thus dependently tied directly to the preceding. Godet takes this dependence more indirectly. The primary thought, however, is the same in both translations. This idea is that all who sit at the table of the Lord, through receiving the same bread, are thereby, in a moral sense, bound to one

---

3   Cf. Godet, *Commentary on St. Paul's First Epistle to the Corinthians*, II, 83ff.
4   This translation is also followed by the old Dutch translation (Emden, 1562).
5   Godet, 75.

and the same body. "The bond which thus unites them to Jesus as their common head, unites them also to one another as members of the same body."[6] Paul weaves into his argument the idea of the mutually being bound as a secondary concern that is to be included with the primary motif. The apostle provides that primary motif in verse 16 with the classic words: "The cup of blessing which we bless, is it not a communion of the blood of Christ? The bread which we break, is it not the communion of the body of Christ?" He desires to bring to light that it is not possible to take part in idolatrous meals without thereby entering into communion with the god of the heathen, that is, the devil. The Corinthians are warned: "Flee from idolatry" (v. 16), because in the eating of the sacrifice, the symbolism of communion with the god of the sacrifice lurks. Let no one say that the idol of the heathen is a fallacy (an illusion) because, "I say, that the things which the Gentiles sacrifice, they sacrifice to devils, and not to God: and I would not that ye should have fellowship with devils" (v. 20).

This is the main idea.

But inadvertently, Paul now raises this correlative thought that by the sacrifice there comes about not only communion with the god of the sacrifice, but also with the participants at the sacrificial meal. He who honors the god of the heathen, casts his lot with the heathen themselves. He becomes a participant, a covenant member of that people. He becomes one body with them.

To resolve this contradiction, and thus to raise the gravity of his admonishment, the apostle now says: "For we being many are one bread, and one body: for we are all partakers of that one bread" (v. 17).

The idea of the one bread, of which all are participants, by gathering at the same meal, gets him to the idea of the one body, into which all the guests are incorporated. It deserves observation that the word "body" here is being used in a different sense than in the preceding verse. When Paul asks, "The bread which we break, is it

---

6   Godet, 84–85.

not the communion of the *body* of Christ?" he intends here the sacrificial body of Christ, the body in the actual sense from which flowed the blood of the atonement. However, when he says, "We who are many are one *body*," then he is using the word in a figurative, spiritual sense. Both ideas indeed hang closely together because participation in the actual body of Christ involves also communion with the mystical body of the Lord, but that is also why a distinction nevertheless must be made between the ideas.

What a glorious and joyful thought, the idea of the communion of the saints into one corporate entity, one body!

Already in a compelling and moving way it is presented to the eye when everyone is seen at the same table, to see everyone eating of the same bread, drinking from the same cup.

It might come as a surprise that Paul here indeed speaks of the communion in the same bread, but does not mention the no less impressive fact that all sip from the same cup. Is such surprise the origin for the insertion by some Bible translations of the expression regarding the cup?

The fact is that a special mention of the cup is unnecessary as the single image of the bread already clearly expresses the intimacy of the fellowship. According to the conception of Scripture, the bread is a reflection of the body of Christ, and this image is of itself complete.

But this does not take away from the fact that the cup, which passes from hand to hand, also movingly symbolizes the unity of the covenant members, and that God's people must give ear no less to this symbolical message.

Because is it not true that there is also so much in this life that divides the children of God? Among them also burns opposition. There are the wealthy, entirely enriched, and the poor of spirit and possessions. There is an Abraham, who enjoys the affluence of earthly blessings, and there is a Lazarus who lies festering at the gate of the rich. The lack of parity in societal life of the devout often creates division. No wonder! How different are the various tables around which they sit! How meager is the meal of the poor, endowed by the deaconate, a young mother in her miserable attic room. And how the crystal and silver glisten, how the wine sparkles, on the table of the affluent who gathers his friends to the feast. Here is one of God's choice guests who in order to live must continually struggle and in that struggle suffers near to death. There is another who, overseeing his blossoming fortune, says, "God has made me wealthy."

And what differences there are also in talents, in disposition, in aptitude!

What a disparity between the unlettered who murmurs his psalm verse, and the theologian who with the fruits of his sanctified power of thinking nourishes his fellow pilgrims.

What a disparity between the doubter who in dreary gloom stumbles along his narrow path, and the assured one who knows that nothing separates him from the love of God.

What a disparity between Onesimus who in the eleventh hour is saved like an ember from the fire, and a Timothy whose devout life bears fruit ever since his early youth.

What endless differences to consider in terms of intellect, desires, and actions; in conviction, comprehension, and insight; in life's beginning, sequence, and ending.

And yet they are all one!

Yet they all gather at the one table, eating the one bread, and plant their lips on the one cup!

No, we do not desire sinful homogeneity that is the curse of modern life. Inequality, also among God's children, is to some degree ordered by God. Even in eternity there is no uniformity in glory, because the one star that shines in the heavens throughout the ages differs in glory from the other star.

At the same time, we abhor sinful inequality, the other extreme, which is the fruit of corruption, and which is all the more pointed and deepened due to the hatred of men.

Just as much we fight the drive of selfishness that on the one hand deifies the powerful and, on the other hand, dehumanizes the weak.

Indeed, *distinction* but no *division* among those who are children of the same father.

Indeed, variation but no *opposition*.

And to warn and to arm the congregation regarding this sinful division, which is a tendency also of the old nature of God's saints, is now instituted the unity meal of the covenant of grace. Here they all meet one another again, those who by life have been so far distanced from each other, and thereby felt no bond of a sense of brotherhood drawing anymore. Here they come together from the palace and the workers' quarters, from the country estate and the village hut. And they take the bread, the aristocrats with unsullied hand, and the hand that bears the raw scars of slave labor!

There they sit at one table and eat of the same *bread*, the served are those in society who have more than enough bread, and still more in addition to that bread and on that bread, and he also who has his moldy piece of bread at the cost of the most severe exertion.

There they drink from the one cup, not only that man whose table is lavished with fine drinks, but also that one whose scanty morsel of bread is moistened with his tears.

There they are united, man and woman, graying and youth, boss and worker, men great and small, professor and student, mistress and maid, the instructor who otherwise is set apart behind the pulpit and the listener who hears him from the pew.

There they are together, the soul who rejoices in her God for the benefits poured out upon her, and the distressed one who goes in black on account of oppression.

Together are the young wife, who a few days before wore her bride's dress and now lives in the springtime of wedding bliss, and the widow who just poured out tears upon the casket in which her treasure sank from her.

Here they find each other, those who may live in the certainty of being a child of God, and who there call out: my soul waits for the Lord!

> Both high and low before his majesty,
> All those that turn to dust, will bow the knee;
> And he whose strength cannot himself keep free
> From death and ruin.[7]

Is it a wonder that the Christian congregation in the heat of her first love felt need to extend this unity also in her sunset years of love, to the everyday life, and thus to anticipate the eternal fellowship at the wedding feast of the Lamb?

Those who look back on the early glory of the bride of Christ sense indeed some pain for the cooling off of the love and the decline in spirituality, but at the same time they thank their God that in the Lord's supper the entire, unique heritage of belonging together yet lives on, and that the king of the church continues to gather his diverse people in holy unity, and is preparing them for living in one and the same Father's house.

3. MANY GRAINS, ONE MEAL; MANY BERRIES, ONE WINE

Now comes to our attention that the form draws as a conclusion from Paul's words something other than one would naturally expect.

The apostle sees the symbol of unity in the one bread, of which all the guests gathered are partakers. This one bread is the figure of the one body of the church.

The logical reason that would follow is that, "as we all eat from one and the same bread and drink from this one cup, so shall we all for the sake of Christ, our beloved Savior, all together be one body, and show this not only with words but also in deed."

However, there follows a somewhat different conclusion from the established fact of unity. Our form draws this admonition from it:

---

7   Tr. *Genevan Psalter* 22, trans., W. W. J. VanOene.

"For as out of many grains one meal is ground, and one bread baked, and out of many berries being pressed together, one wine flows, and is mixed together; so shall we all...be altogether one body."

It doesn't take lengthy reasoning that our form here deduces something from the word of Paul that is not intended by the apostle. Paul did not mean the unity of the bread in the gathering of the existing parts, but the unity that precedes the *breaking* of the bread.

On the plate is bread that is broken into various pieces and is distributed, and in these many still is one bread. Paul did not have in mind the many grains that together make one bread but the many pieces that together form one bread. Every communicating believer receives one small piece. As now all the small pieces together are the one bread, so are all believers together the one body.

The image as intended and signified by Paul is more natural. It is evident and is conclusive in the ritual of the supper itself.

In contrast, the symbolic language of our form seeks to illustrate something else. Who in the receiving and the eating of the bread immediately thinks of the many grains from which it is prepared? The bread itself speaks nothing of this to us. Only intentional recollection brings to mind the preceding process of preparation.

Yet this is why this image is not faulty.

The bread is, as we have noted above, a symbol of the body of Christ not only regarding its choice composition and nourishing character, but also regarding what concerns its manner of preparation. The grain goes through a lengthy series of strenuous events before it is bread. It dies in the ground, it is reaped, threshed, crushed, baked, and in all of these moments we are reminded of what Jesus went through, before his body became food for us and his blood drink for us.

Well now, the symbolic inference that is permitted with respect to the real body of the Lord may also find a place in relation to the mystical body of Christ, the church. Also, the preparation of the bread presents to the congregation a lesson and instruction. It tells us of the strength of the small, and of effectiveness in the way of intimate connection.

How puny and insignificant is a single granule of grain of itself.

But what then happens with that granule?

Together with thousands and millions of other granules it is crushed under the heavy millstones and ground into one meal with the others. The granule is still in that meal, but in an entirely different form. It has become in such a way one with the other granules that it can no longer be distinguished on its own. It has dissolved in the mass, has become a part of the fellowship.

Even stronger this unity of togetherness becomes when the meal is kneaded and baked into one loaf. Now the single granule is entirely unrecognizable. And yet, it is still there. Now it is brought to its destiny. One granule alone cannot make for a loaf. In their combination with each other, they are precious nourishment for people. This teaches a Christian that he reaches his purpose only in the spiritual fellowship with his fellow believers. However, also that uniting must be so close that in a certain sense he abdicates his independence and desires to live only *in* the fellowship and *for* the fellowship.

This same thing can be also said for the wine.

Here also the way of preparation is rich in symbolism.

As long as it is in the cluster of the grapevine, the berry is independent, blooming in its own existence of comeliness. But then the berry is stripped from its small cluster, brought in a winepress in one heap, and there trod flat. And as they are pressed, there flows out of all those berries one wine and drink, and the countless little streams mingle themselves together so that you can no longer say, "This wine droplet came from this berry and that other droplet is from that cluster." Each berry's independent existence has been dispersed and sacrificed for the whole. There are no more berries but only wine that pearls in the cup.

We sense that with the symbolism we are also near the border of application, indeed, perhaps have already crossed it.

For in the bread the granule and in the wine the berry loses the independence of its own life, as the fellowship to which Christs gathers his own comes exactly to its right as ordained of God. That is why the metaphor that the formulary here applies must be allowed as accurate with respect to the point of comparison (the so-called *tertium comparationis*). This point of comparison is the entire surrender and devotion to the whole by which each little part reaches its potential in the whole. This, the many granules that are united unto the one bread and the many berries that are united unto the one wine teach us.

But all further comparison ceases, and there comes before our spirit the organic image of the *body*, which stands much closer to the reality. Actually, it is true that the bread is the image *of an image*. The image in the sacrament leads our thought to the image outside the sacrament: the body. And this body speaks to us very wonderful things concerning the congregation of Christ.

It testifies also to an earnest obligation.

First the form established the *fact* of unity. The Lord's supper states and assures us that we by the same Spirit are united among each other as members of one body in true brotherly love.

Then the form indicates the calling that flows from this fact: *so shall we all*, that is, must, through brotherly love be altogether one body.

Thus is also the idea of the communion of the saints.

In the catechism this communion is viewed first as the fact of communion with Christ and all his riches and gifts (and thus also with the members of Christ, wherein shine these gifts), but then also as an obligation, namely that everyone must know it to be his duty, readily and cheerfully to employ his gifts for the advantage and salvation of other members.

4. FOR OUR DEAR SAVIOR'S SAKE

This last important point is raised in our form and that indeed in a warm, mystical tone.

The members who are admonished to the practice of fellowship are those who *by a true faith are engrafted into Christ.*

This is genuine Reformed language that attaches itself to the symbol of the body. The members of the covenant have their fellowship with Christ thanks to God's sovereign and omnipotent love. They are one in Christ because they are elect in Christ and as the result of their election engrafted into him. They take part in the congregation of Christ not by their own choosing but by God's choosing, just as the members of the body are not of their own choosing but by a determining power outside them are grown together with the body.

The bond to Christ is that of faith, but this faith is working by *love*. With an abundance of words the form brings out that by the implantation of faith is also established the bond of love, and this love *of* Christ and *to* Christ is what must inspire the mutual love of the members. We all must through brotherly *love*, for Christ our *beloved* Savior's sake, who before has so exceedingly loved us, be altogether one body.

Thus, there must be a correlation in the love relationships.

You see, there is Christ, the king who gathers the church, who seeks her love. He thirsts for her love, he breathes in her love, and he cultivates her love.

How? Is not Christ the mediator who has no other purpose than to lead his people to the Father, and then to reunite Father and child in love?

Indeed, but the child lives with the Father forever *through* him. Christ does not save the sinner in order to let him go once he has rescued him. The bond of redemption between Jesus and his own is not mechanical, but organic. It is a living bond, a bond of love. Christ requires of his own not only faith in his *work,* but also in his *person,* and this faith expresses itself, unfolds itself in love. Here also is love the bond of perfection.

And this love carries a very intimate and special character.

This love exudes a pleasant, heavenly fragrance.

There was also a love-relationship between God and his people in paradise. Adam lived in accordance with the command: love God with all your heart and with all your strength. And God loved his creation-child so much!

But then, after the fall into sin, the fallen and hating children of man are recreated, and the prodigal son falls back into the arms of his forgiving and reconciling father. In this restored love is something special. The lost son of the parable loves his father differently than the elder son because the former prodigal has a deeper awareness of the heart of the father and has received more from him.

Note well, this love toward Christ, which by the operation of the Spirit awakens in the sinner's heart, shows an entirely unique stamp. It is a love as never experienced between creatures, and also as never before existed between God and the creature.

For we love Jesus Christ because he first loved us.

As the language of the form puts it, Christ *hath so exceedingly loved us.*

Christ brought us, embodied, personified to us then delivered to us, the eternal love of God, that already in the decree of redemption was at work before the foundation of the world. The Lord says to his people: I have loved you before the foundation of the world. And Paul is never weary of repeating in all kinds of expressions that God in Christ has predestinated us unto the adoption of children.

The entirely unconditional, sovereign, enchanting love of God proclaims Christ, displays Christ, *is* Christ.

Without the love of God, there would not be this mediator. For God so loved the world, that he gave his only begotten Son, that whosoever believeth in him should not perish, but have everlasting life.

Nevertheless, that same Christ who is the object of the love of God is also the subject of divine love.

He who was given by love also himself gives love.

For ye know the grace of our Lord Jesus Christ, that, though he was rich, yet for your sakes he became poor, that ye through his poverty might be rich. There is an indescribable, incomparable love in the total self-surrender of Christ.

Love glitters in the act of his birth in Bethlehem's stall.

His word breathes with love; love gleams in his eyes. Love is announced in the miracles of deliverance.

And this love reaches its zenith when he lays his body and soul upon the altar of the sacrifice.

Because Jesus, knowing that his hour was come that he should depart out of this world unto the Father, having loved his own who were in the world, he loved them unto the end (John 13:1).

Who has greater love than he who lays down his life for his friends?

Yes, Jesus has even more love, because he gave his life for his enemies.

For when we were yet without strength, in due time Jesus died for the *ungodly*. For scarcely for a righteous man will one die; yet peradventure for a good man some would even dare to die. But God commends his love toward us, in that, while we were yet sinners, Christ died for us (Rom. 5:6–8).

Truly, Christ loved us *to the uttermost.*

And this love must the congregation know, admire, thankfully extol. The Lord's supper is the ordinance that has for its purpose to render this love, to bring it near to the heart of the redeemed flock. As the form says earlier: "As often as ye eat of this bread and drink of this cup, you shall thereby, as by a sure remembrance and pledge, be admonished and assured of this *my hearty love and faithfulness* towards you."

The bridegroom *gives* love, but he also *requires* love.

Exclusively in the reciprocal love of his people does the king of the bride encounter the fullness of his glory.

And the bride also returns that love. Indeed, her love is often weak, dull, and sporadic, but the issue of her heart springs toward Jesus. She longs for him more than ten thousand and cries out: let him kiss me with the kisses of his mouth: for thy love is better than wine (Song of Sol. 1:2). Indeed, when a child of God by the Spirit is thereby determined (and not the least does this happen at the table upon which stand the signs of the bloody drama of his sacrifice of love), what Jesus wholly, freely, and without hesitation has endured and struggled through, out of pure mercy for a distantly lost and deeply depraved child of sin, when the soul enters into this, with what tears and sighs, what a shedding of blood and hellish agony it cost Jesus, in order to deliver her from the eternal wrath of God and to secure for her the spotless heavenly glory, indeed, then can at times and moments that delivered of the Lord cry out on occasion from the heart: I love because the Lord hears my voice! Then springs that love up as water from the fountain of life of the renewed heart, and the redeemed soul is safe in her love toward her God.

5. ONE THROUGH BROTHERLY LOVE

However—and here it now comes up especially in the context of our Lord's supper formulary—embracing the exceptional love of Christ inspires us not only to grateful love in return, but also arouses mutual love of the communion of the saints.

We shall, so the form explains the will of God, *for Christ's sake, our beloved Savior,* who hath so exceedingly loved us, be altogether one body, through brotherly love.

Let us try to grasp this idea with clarity and depth.

The idea is that *for Christ's sake,* we must love one another.

But why does the love of Christ obligate us to have love for one another?

You see, if we love Christ, and this love is genuine and alive, the necessity of showing this love automatically wells up in the heart to be evident in deed. And how shall we show him that love? Certainly, there is already an expression of love in the particular *affection* of gratitude that burns in the heart. There is a revelation of love in word, the prayer of adoration in which the soul pours out its content in the presence of the king.

Nonetheless, there trills also another necessity within the forgiven and blessed heart.

The necessity that moved Mary to break the vase of ointment upon the blessed head of her beloved Savior.

That prompted Magdalene to clasp his feet and to cry out to him, "Rabboni."

That inspired the pious female friends of the Lord to minister to him with their goods.

However, because he is no longer on earth, we can no longer show Jesus these acts of love that specifically apply to his person. For that reason, Jesus requires that love to him be transferred in practice to those he established as our fellow-redeemed neighbors in the organism of his body, the church. In particular, we naturally think here of the needy members of Jesus' body. When Mary anointed Jesus, the Lord did not reject that honor. To the contrary, he defended this spontaneous act of love by saying: for the poor always ye have with you; but me ye have not always. Therein lies the indication: soon bring your love to me upon my poor friends, until you shall be with me in the reunion of my kingdom; then again give me your love.

Still, this mutual love of the bride of Christ may not be limited to the poor members. It must embrace all brothers and sisters belonging to the same household. To every member of the congregation, to every covenant member at the Lord's supper table, a Christian shows *Jesus'* love. Not first of all for the lovely qualities, the attractive character of that brother (indeed, there is often so little that is lovely about God's children!), but because that brother is a member of *Christ.* This idea of love arouses us to love that brother whom Christ himself had so exceedingly loved even to the death of the cross. This is the inspiring idea: those whom the great, royal, and divine Jesus loved are therefore not too insignificant for you to love. There is thus no single member of Christ, though poor of spirit, though also disregarded by the world, where there is not something of the glory of Christ, there yet shines in him a faint ray of the king's glory.

Truly, Christ is glorious, and becomes increasingly more glorious through the unity of his people.

Where sin divides and hate destroys and disintegrates, there is the glory of Christ that he by his re-creation power reassembles the divided parts. That is his goal with the amazing, awakening work of redemption, that in him again is gathered together all things that are in heaven and that are on earth.

When the members of Christ's congregation are divided in jealousy and commotion, or even by indifference, so that no difference is perceived between her and the world, such does not honor Jesus. The world reviles God's name for this monkey business and makes fun of it: and now that is the church of that Christ!

But if, on the contrary, the bond draws, and the world sees how good and how pleasant it is when brothers dwell together, they behold the miracle that all, no matter how different in standing and disposition and gifts, are in one accord, indeed (like how this happened at the dawn of the New Testament days) that they have all things in common. Then the world must recognize, notwithstanding, the greatness of the master, for whose name's sake the bonds of love between these brothers are so tenderly weaved. Then arises the thought: it is like a single personality, if the love for one erases all borders, fills all cracks, and dispels all discord.

You see, then comes, as in the days of the apostolic congregation in Jerusalem, a fear upon every soul. So much love radiated, that they had favor with all the people (Acts 2:43, 47).

It is in the most compelling tone that Jesus awakens his disciples to this revelation of love. Hereby, so he said, shall I make it known that you are my disciples, if you love one another. This is my commandment, that you love one another as I have loved you (John 15:12).

And John, the disciple who apparently had the deepest understanding of this love command, resonates with the sweetest arrangements of this theme in his letters. He puts it radically (gets to the root) that brotherly love is a characteristic of the new life, saying: "We know that we have passed from death unto life, because we love the brethren. He that loveth not his brother abideth in death" (1 John 3:14).

Indeed, his entire letter makes a compelling case for the ordinance of love.

He places the commandment of love for the brothers *next to* the command of faith in Christ: "And this is his commandment, that we should believe on the name of his Son Jesus Christ, and love one another, as he gave us commandment" (1 John 3:23).

He borrows from the fact of the priceless love of God that obliges mutual love, from the fact of the critique of the hostile world that urges caution, from the fact of the spiritual unity in Christ that constantly calls to a higher level of commitment to others, repeatedly the admonition that runs as a recurring theme through all his word: little children, love one another!

And truly, John is not the only one who embroiders his song of praise and word of admonishment on this canvas.

How deeply Paul grips into the heart of the congregation when he says:

> Fulfil ye my joy, that ye be likeminded, having the same love, being of one accord, of one mind. Let nothing be done through strife or vainglory; but in lowliness of mind let each esteem other better than themselves. Look not every man on his own things, but every man also on the things of others. *Let this mind be in you, which was also in Christ Jesus.* (Phil. 2:2–5)

6. NOT ONLY IN WORDS, BUT ALSO IN DEED

Now yet follows in the form an addition with which to clearly sense the practical intent of our fathers. There stands, namely, that the unity of the mystical body, wherein we are all bound by brotherly love, we are to *show not only in word, but also in deed towards one another.*

Certainly, this idea is taken from John, who says: "My little children, let us not love in word, neither in tongue; but in deed and in truth" (1 John 3:18).

Especially in the area of love words are often cheap, indeed worthless, when they are not validated by deed.

Undoubtedly, words of love are not worthless *in and of themselves*.

Oh, love-filled words can be like raindrops in a thirsty land. The word of love can be like a sunbeam in a dark prison cell. How different, how much sunnier our harsh world would be if there would be more amiable words spoken. And also, how the garden of Jesus' church would give off a more pleasant fragrance if the disciples who bear his name were more filled with love in the language that they speak to each other. How much more joyful and devout our lives would be if at church gatherings and in the Christian press a more genuine tone of brotherhood would be heard, which reflects the royal expression: "Learn of me; for I am meek and lowly in heart."

After all, God himself also speaks to his people *with good words and comfortable words* (Zech. 1:13).

Nevertheless, good words have only relative value. Of themselves, they are no more than a vibration of air that passes by. A word has meaning insofar as it is an expression from the heart and leads to action. The everyday so-called chats among friends are worthless if they serve no other purpose than an aesthetic dimension of society. What a pitiful performance the "hero" delivers who is only courageous in words, but hits the road when the enemy rattles the sword. Horrible is the display of the "philanthropist" who jabbers about love for mankind and then hangs on to his wallet when a donation is requested. James was aware of this sort of do-gooders and was talking about them in his letter: "If a brother or sister be naked , and destitute of daily food, and one of you say unto them 'Depart in peace, be ye warmed and filled'; notwithstanding ye give them not those things which are needful to the body; what doth it profit?" (James 1:15–16).

No. True religion is not a matter of nice words, but love-filled deeds: "Pure religion and undefiled before God and the Father is this, to visit the fatherless and widows in their affliction, and to keep himself unspotted from the world" (James 1:27).

Note that this is the purpose of the Lord's supper form, as its concluding call to the congregation emphasizes: "and not only show this in word, but also in deed towards one another."

When the deed may be called the mature word, the fully developed fruit of the word, then there is much unripe religion. Precisely in the sphere of the Christian religion, where genuine Christian living requires heavy sacrifice, is the danger so great to be content with unripe fruit. There is in this territory so much "brotherly love," and a psalm-singing of "Behold, how good, how pleasant is the union, when brethren in the Lord have sweet communion,"[8] without life living up to the language.

That being said, there is nothing more slanderous to the character of Christian service to God than precisely this bifurcation between word and deed.

Among the heathen religions there is commonly a conviction that the divinity must be satisfied with words, endless formulas, and especially a formal sacrifice.

The Christian religion obligates the whole man, extending from the deep root to the extended contour of his life, to the living God.

Brotherly fellowship, which is foundational to Christianity, is a grand creation, an activating oneness of life whereby exist entirely new relationships, and the form of life is transformed. Confessors of Christ are united to an organism that has a *purpose* and bears fruit, such as those committed to socialism in a worldly sphere declare their solidarity toward one goal: a new society.

Constantly the Scriptures place the emphasis on that organic, i.e., living and working, character of the communion of the saints.

---

8   Tr. *Genevan Psalter* 133, trans. L. Bourgeois.

The unity is like that of a body wherein all the members work together for the same activity.

In Romans it is described in this manner:

> For as we have many members in one body, and all members have not the same office: So we being many, are one body in Christ, and every one members one of another. Having then gifts differing according to the grace that is given to us, whether prophecy, let us prophesy according to the proportion of faith; Or ministry, let us wait on our ministering: or he that teacheth, on teaching; Or he that exhorteth, on exhortation: he that giveth, let him do it with simplicity; he that ruleth, with diligence; he that sheweth mercy, with cheerfulness (12:4–8).

That is the *evidence* for brotherly love in *action* encouraged in the Lord's supper form.

Not a *deed* under the compulsion of feelings but from an absolute principle; not striving for the disintegration of the individual among the masses, but safe-guarding personhood for the salvation of the whole.

The apostle also expresses this in Ephesians 4:

> But speaking the truth in love, may grow up into him in all things, which is the head, even Christ: From whom the whole body fitly joined together and compacted by that which every joint supplieth, according to the effectual working in the measure of every part, maketh increase of the body unto the edifying of itself in love (4:15–16).

Especially in the classic passage in 1 Corinthians 12:12–18 is described the practical fellowship of God's people:

> For as the body is one, and hath many members, and all the members of that one body, being many, are one body: so

also is Christ. For by one Spirit are we all baptized into one body, whether we be Jews or Gentiles, whether we be bond or free; and have been all made to drink into one Spirit. For the body is not one member, but many. If the foot shall say, because I am not the hand, I am not of the body; is it therefore not of the body? And if the ear shall say, because I am not the eye, I am not of the body; is it therefore not of the body? If the whole body were an eye, where were the hearing? If the whole were hearing, where were the smelling? But now hath God set the members every one of them in the body, as it hath pleased him.

Finally, there is the powerfully expressed admonition flowing from the unforgettable song of praise to love in 1 Corinthians 13, where the gospel of the deed, the practice of brotherly love, is glorified.

There sounds the hymn of love not as that of a dreamer who idealizes it, but as that of an apostle who does his utmost to realize it: Christian love "suffereth long, and is kind; charity envieth not; charity vaunteth not itself, is not puffed up, doth not behave itself unseemly, seeketh not her own, is not easily provoked, thinketh no evil; beareth all things, believeth all things, hopeth all things, endureth all things."

This love never fails because it lives on in its fruit.

Indeed, especially here may the example of Christ inspire the congregation as they gather at the Lord's table.

The sacrament summons her; it depicts *the love of Christ.*

Love in words only?

No, love in *action.* Jesus *proved* his love for us, by serving, by helping, finally by giving up his life for his friends. If Jesus were only a prophet who had *spoken* to us the love of the Father, he would not be our Savior. By the high-priestly *love-deed* of self-sacrifice he became the surety for us in which is our salvation.

And not the least at the sacramental meal, in which are the signs of his bloody love-history, he speaks to his own, that we show this brotherly love toward one another not only in word, but also in deed.

7. ACTUALIZATION OF THE LOVE COMMAND

In our age especially there is in this part of our form something again relevant to note.

First, there is the viewpoint of contrast.

Certainly, in all times the fraternal unity of believers has been of decisive importance for the triumph of the kingdom of God. Nevertheless, many note a particular crisis today. Incredibly much of Christianity's strength has already diminished by the diversity of its confessors, but now, as the spirits of the age develop, as the awareness of the masses is increasingly aroused, and as emancipation is also penetrating the lowest levels of societal life, is this weakening influence increasingly observable.

In earlier times the word *church* still had a certain enchantment, at least a binding power for the people, and due to this power of custom people remained attached to the church and entrusted their children to her nurturing guidance. This has now been abandoned in huge numbers. From the so-called heavens of science the rain of unbelieving science has oozed unbeknownst upon the flock, and a spell has been cast upon the church. Eyes open all the more with the horrible schisms and endless variations in church life, so that in the midst of numerous slogans of sectarian streams, the question more strongly presses: what is truth? The smallest division between ecclesiastical brothers is spied upon with Argus eyes, every quarrel between ecclesiastical parties is taken up meticulously, and constantly the divisions of Christ-confessors are spread as a means of propaganda for unbelief. Impossible to tally are the numbers of those, due to the spectacle of spiteful quarrelling among "church-types," who have turned their backs on organized Christianity.

And are we exempt?

Are we responsible, responsible before God, to say that unity of thinking and feeling is once and for all impossible among those in this dispensation bearing the Christian name? Is not a foremost factor of the division confessing the failure regarding genuine, heartfelt brotherly love? Not schism itself, nor even the struggle of the divisions, will bring the greatest scandal to the reputation of Christians, but the lack of *love* on the part of the combatants; the sneaky jealousy, the entirely tainted bitterness, that the world instinctively senses, or worse, clearly sees.

As the demonstration of the example of unity in love of the first Christian congregation silenced the world, stifled slander, and generated triumph for the kingdom of God, so now the church is the cause that the name of God is enormously defamed, and in its wake the gospel is dismally arrested. This all the more as the revolutionary spirit sharpens the critical capacity of the masses and brings it into action. In the eyes of the world, there is such a flagrant contradiction between the high ideal of Christianity's fraternal concordance and the grim reality of ecclesiastical discordance and societal friction that even in the now cooled-down sense of the people, the church *must* lose in strength and beauty. The dreadful fact of the ongoing escalation of those leaving the church finds that the most significant reason is the un-churchlike disunity of the church itself.

But the stimulation in our form to immediate love must be recognized as actual in great measure not only because of the antithesis, but also because of the apparent relationship between church and world.

It appears that according as the glory of unity is extinguished within the borders of the church, outside the church in the territory of unbelief, the bond of unity gets stronger and more glorious. Is it not known that in the circle of the socialists solidarity is lauded as a basic principle? One of their most well-known leaders proclaims that the fellowship between party members should be so close and protected that thereto every sentiment, idea, and necessary asset must be sacrificed. He who loves father or mother, home or land, or any other thing more than the party is not worthy of the party. In fact, the camp of the unbelievers sometimes provides a show of such great and powerful togetherness that the communion of unbelievers appears to outshine the communion of the saints.

Thus, the world gives the church competition for the crown exactly in this her noblest possession, completely in harmony with the prophecy that the antichrist, who shall be revealed, draws his external glory from Christendom itself. According to the prophetic vision of Revelation 13, the beast that comes from out of the earth has two horns like the horns of the Lamb (thus likened to the Christ of God, the Lamb, who takes away the sin of the world) and seduces those who live upon the earth.

Just as the Christian religion, this socialist religion also proclaims a oneness, a brotherhood, that recognizes no national borders. In this new world order (that is how they speak of the humanism of socialism) there is no Jew nor Greek, no slave nor freeman, no male or female.

Precisely the poor and oppressed are comforted in the new solidarity and shackled to the fellowship with sturdy chains. The lie is that by great deeds of practical love he will be liberated from his pitiful situation.

Indeed, as Christian brothers gather at the same table, eating the same bread and drinking from the same cup, so desire the men of the new gospel to feed the entire mankind from one treasure chest that is held in common and drink from the same spring that wells up in the fellowship.

Naturally this idea is a delusion insofar as it intends for all mankind to capture a paradise. The repetitious arguments, already on the march to great fortune, allow no doubt regarding the destination.

But with all of that there comes with this new brotherhood an irresistible enchantment of countless numbers of hearts.

Measured with the external standard, the oneness and sense of brotherhood in the sphere of the new religion especially appears in the territory not less than in the territory of the old (and men mean obsolete) Christianity.

Many young mercenaries are already leaving the old path in order to do battle under the new banner.

Weighed in the balance, over the divided and crumbling Christianity is expressed the *mene, mene, tekel, upharsin.*

And for this—and what profit is there to deny it—the confessors of Christianity are themselves to blame for their deficiency in *practical* love.

Therefore, from the Lord's supper there emanates a call for renewal.

Here is still the tie that binds, entwined by Christ for his believers. Here is still the place where what is divided can again find each other. Here are all summoned together at the foot of the one cross, gathered before the throne of the same king.

May the Lord's supper again draw with old ties that bind, and kindle in the hearts something of the early enthusiasm regarding this ancient symbol. In this way, there is hope. This sacrament must be as a hub of grace from which is nourished again the unity of life.

And for this can also be serviceable the listening to the robust, devout language of the fathers, that in the tradition of the Lord's supper formulary lives on with us to this day.

8. THE "QUIETLY BURSTING PRAYER"

The didactic portion then concludes with these words: *Hereto assist us, the almighty, merciful God and Father of our Lord Jesus Christ through his Holy Spirit. Amen.* Also these words were borrowed from the Württemberg formulary. In that form they stand immediately following the portion that handles the brotherly love, and there are apparently intended as a prayer especially with an eye toward the exercise of fellowship with each other, to which the Lord's supper summons us.

In our form, this prayer is so placed that it appears as if the framers allude with it to the entire preceding form, and thus it will crown this entire initial section.

Indeed, this may be seen as a fortuitous encapsulation.

Differences can be posited regarding its character.

Van Houte, in his already-cited exposition in *The Formulary of Holy Communion*,[9] devotes to the meaning of this part of the sentence a rather heavy-handed observation, an example of the Reformed scholasticism of those days.

It is indeed interesting to hear him out for a moment.

After saying there is no single reason why the cited words apply only to the last portion and not also to the first, he poses the problem that calls for a solution, namely, whether we here have to do with a *quiet burst of prayer*, a *solemn pledge*, or indeed a *strong yearning and desire*.

If one seeks to comprehend these words as a quietly bursting desire, then the idea is that in order to respond to all of this the soul finds itself between a rock and hard place, seeing and noting that they so attend the Lord's supper with nothing less than divine grace and a strong faith necessary, in order in that way to exercise communion with a blessed God in Christ, and through him with all his people.

However, taking this thought as a solemn pledge that the soul makes, "before God, angels and men," gives these words to mean

> ...a clear awareness, which the soul has regarding her disposition, such as with confidence it can say that it seeks its salvation life and blessedness nowhere than only in Christ, and that now anew embraces and receives him as the bread of life, with the explanation that its exercise of communion exists only in the fellowship and union with him and all his people, indeed, that such constitutes its glory and joy, resting completely in him as its rod and staff.

---

9   Van Houte, 309ff.

That said, understanding the conclusion of this part as a *man*, "then it will express a wonderful picture, that the soul being persuaded of the truth, so as a proper participant of the supper shall use the signs according to the purpose of Christ, views the same not only as necessary, but also as desirable for its feeling."

In the end, it appears that the choice among these three conceptions of the author is not easy. He says that "as one considers it all, it comes down to that the soul is completely persuaded of the propriety and desirability for approaching the Lord's table in such a manner."

If he must decide, there is indeed a preference for a particular conception. While he allows others freely, "What choice they embrace from this statement," he himself finds it best, "as a solemn oath with sighing in order that afterwards, with faith strengthened in the Lord, we may be made fit that we may also confirm it with deeds."

This last opinion rests primarily upon this ground, that in the language of the form ostensibly the *form* of an oath is used, like the phrase, "So truly help me God Almighty." This pronouncement would then be a worthy answer to the promises that are sealed in the sacrament. In the Lord's supper, God pledges faithfulness to his people. Now it lies within the nature of the matter that also the blessed people pledge faithfulness to their God, promising "willingly to keep the laws of God's righteousness with a purpose of heart always to abide with the Lord."

The reader notes how behind apparently simple words a weighty problem might be sought (or must I say, created?).

Likely here is nothing other meant than (to speak in the language of Van Houte) a "quiet bursting prayer," that precisely in a formulary (think also of our marriage form) goes well.

Especially here in the last portion, where a task is held before the congregation that nearly transcends the limits of her spiritual ability, a task upon whose fulfillment the blooming of Christ's church and the honor of the Lord's name depends—especially here is a prayer in place: help us, merciful Lord!

The connecting particle *hereto* indicates that first of all attention must be paid to the immediately preceding admonishment to practical love.

However, there all further description is lacking. It is reasonable also to reflect on the part in which is considered how we are to observe the Lord's supper in remembrance of Jesus. The form paints for us this celebration of remembrance as a reflection on the suffering in its fullness, and thereafter as an exercise of fellowship with the living Christ.

Is it any wonder then that the congregation, faced with such a high spiritual task and sensing her weakness to climb to such a high level, utters the petition to God for help?

And what an austere but rich-in-meaning prayer!

The help of Christ's church from ancient times is in the name of the Lord, who made heaven and earth (Ps. 124).

The church of the new covenant may seek her help from this God who reveals himself even more richly, namely, *by the almighty, merciful God and Father of our Lord Jesus Christ through his Holy Spirit.*

And this her prayer is in the form of a *confession.*

A confession not only of unworthiness to take such an honored place at the table, but also of the impotency for such a relationship as behooves the bride of Christ.

Before the congregation proceeds to proclaim the death of her Lord, she lifts up her hands on high, fastens her eye toward the holiness, and confesses: I cannot, and I know not, for all this, help us, the triune God!

This is the language with which God's people may anticipate the blessing of the sacrament.

Chapter Seven

LIFT UP OUR HEARTS ON HIGH

1. TEXT AND INTRODUCTION TO THE PRAYER

In this chapter, we begin consideration of the ritual section of our form. Certainly, with regard to building up the faith-life of the church, nothing can compare with the meaning of the rich didactic portion that precedes, yet here come sentences of striking liturgical beauty, and the supper's light of Scripture also shines in this section, which we take up with thanksgiving.

Right now is not the place to interrupt the general flow of our explanation with an overview of the historical development of the Lord's supper ritual. That is why we determine first of all to recall the text of the form, that we distinguish three parts in the ritual portion.[1]

First, there is a preparatory portion (*preafatie*), in which we encounter the prayer and the call to genuine celebration of the Lord's supper.

Then we are led to the actual celebration of the supper (*communie*) by the declarations of the sacramental formulas and indication of what must happen during communion.

Finally, there is a conclusion in which is presented the admonition to thanksgiving and the thanksgiving itself.

This is the same structure, therefore, that we also come across in the form for baptism, except here it happens that the admonition to right usage of the sacrament precedes the sacramental discourse.

In the other forms of excommunication, installation of office

---

1 Cf. *supra*, I.7.

bearers, and the administration of marriage is missing the preparatory prayer.

Let us first give our attention to the prayer before the celebration of the supper, which is as follows:

> That we may obtain all this, let us humble ourselves before God, and with true faith implore his grace:

> O most merciful God and Father, we beseech thee, that thou wilt be pleased in this supper (in which we celebrate the glorious remembrance of the bitter death of thy beloved Son, Jesus Christ) to work in our hearts through the Holy Spirit, that we may more and more with true confidence, give ourselves up unto thy Son Jesus Christ, that our afflicted and contrite hearts, through the power of the Holy Spirit, may be nourished and refreshed with his true body and blood; yea, with him, true God and man, that only heavenly bread; and that we may no longer live in our sins, but he in us, and we in him, and thus truly be made partakers of the new and everlasting testament and covenant of grace. That we may not doubt but thou wilt forever be our gracious Father, nevermore imputing our sins unto us, and providing us with all things necessary, as well for the body as the soul, as thy beloved children and heirs.

> Grant us also thy grace, that we may take up our cross cheerfully, deny ourselves, confess our Savior, and in all tribulations, with uplifted heads expect our Lord Jesus Christ from heaven, where he will make our mortal bodies like unto his most glorious body, and take us unto him in eternity.

> Answer us, O God and merciful Father, through Jesus Christ, who taught us to pray:

> *Our Father who art in heaven,*
> *Hallowed be thy name.*

Thy kingdom come.
Thy will be done on earth, as it is in heaven.
Give us this day our daily bread;
And forgive us our debts, as we forgive our debtors.
And lead us not into temptation, but deliver us from
*   the evil one.*
For thine is the kingdom, and the power and the glory,
*   forever.*

Strengthen us also by this holy supper in the catholic undoubted Christian faith, whereof we make confession with mouth and heart, saying:

I believe in God, the Father, Almighty, Maker of heaven
and earth; and in Jesus Christ his only begotten Son
our Lord; who was conceived by the Holy Ghost, born
of the virgin Mary, suffered under Pontius Pilate, was
crucified, dead and buried, he descended into hell: the
third day he rose again from the dead, he ascended into
heaven, and sitteth at the right hand of God the Father
Almighty; from thence he shall come to judge the living
and the dead.

*   I believe in the Holy Ghost; I believe a holy catholic*
church; the communion of saints; the forgiveness of sins;
the resurrection of the body; and life everlasting. Amen.

We have already made reference to the fact that in this prayer we hear clearly what is found in the formulary of Calvin.[2]

Ens himself says that this prayer is an abbreviation of that from Geneva, and Mensinga admits that here strong Calvinistic phraseology is evident.[3]

The expressions that specifically are inspired by Calvin, and

---

2   *Supra,* I.5.
3   Mensinga, 260ff.

wherein mystical depth is unmistakable, are these: "That we, our afflicted and contrite hearts, through the power of the Holy Spirit, may be nourished and refreshed *with his true body and blood; yea, with him, true God and man, that only heavenly bread.*"

Also: *"That we may no longer live in our sins, but he in us, and we in him."*

And especially:

"And thus truly be made partakers of the new and everlasting testament and covenant of grace, that we may not doubt but thou wilt forever be our gracious Father, nevermore imputing our sins unto us, and providing us with all things necessary, as well for the body as the soul, as thy beloved children and heirs."

These last lines are from Calvin word-for-word. There is only one small difference.

In Calvin the above citation is split up into two independent parts. First, there is, *"and that we be made partakers of the new and everlasting testament and covenant of grace."* Hereafter is a period, and then follows as a new sentence: *"That we may not doubt but thou wilt forever be our gracious Father."*

In our form the sentence runs through so that the "not doubting" is identified as a fruit of the partaking of the covenant of grace. This sentence construction follows the original Palatinate form and serves for a smoother and more logical arrangement that is preferable to the above. In many old publications of our form, the phraseology of Geneva was followed. In the publication that we are using, the original text is restored.

2. THE SUMMONS TO PRAYER

The concise, heartfelt summons to prayer immediately gets our attention: "That we may obtain all this, let us humble ourselves before God, and with true faith implore his grace."

In the form for baptism, it strikes a distinctively different tone. It has: "That we therefore may administer this holy ordinance of God to his glory, to our comfort, and to the edification of his church, let us call upon his holy name."

If we would have to choose, we would undoubtedly give that of the baptism form preference above that of the Lord's supper form.

It sounds more to the heart of the Reformed Jerusalem when in the celebration of the sacraments the glory of God is prioritized. After all, also in the supper, in which we exercise the remembrance of our king, it is in the first and highest instance not about our comfort but his glory.

Thus, it would be better if there stood: "That we may administer this holy supper to God's glory, and to our comfort, let us humble ourselves before God in true faith and implore his grace."

Notwithstanding, the introduction that our form provides is indeed understandable. The congregation that is here speaking is the church under the cross that thirsts for the only comfort. It is the persecuted church that is like the hart that pants after the water brooks, that especially at the table seeks refreshment for the parched soul, because there the fountain of comfort wells up in abundance.

Does it now not make sense that Olevianus, who contributed to drawing up the little book of only comfort, took account in the Lord's supper form of this same thirst for comfort, and opens the prayer as a petition to "obtain all this" that God has promised in his covenant for the strengthening of his frail flock?

Truly, to pray may yet truly be to pray *requests*. It is not displeasing to the Father when his child seeks to *take possession* of what the Father himself has promised.

Perhaps the complaint could be levelled that often our prayer is not sufficiently, genuinely childlike praying and too little stresses the necessity for pleading that we truly may *receive* something.

And that in the form is not speaking the self-satisfying soul who concentrates only on its own anxieties, but indeed truly the Christian, who is aware of his position with God, is evident from the addition: *let us humble ourselves before God, and with true faith implore his grace.*

Here sounds not the tone of the one who is unsaved, who in the deepest sense is seeking himself, but the childlike tone of the redeemed who yearns for the glory of his Father.

To *humble* oneself before God, that is to say: If thou should come in judgment, Lord, who shall be able to stand?

Truly to humble oneself before God is to concur that eternal damnation is deserved, that is, has to do with God's right.

To humble oneself is to deny oneself and to glorify the excellence of God as the highest good.

When God's people pray with this spiritual disposition, it never asks too much and never in vain.

To call upon God for his grace with true faith is to plead upon the "right" to a child's inheritance, and to yearn for the preservation of fatherly favor that God has pledged to his heirs.

So, the introduction to the prayer is certainly God-glorifying.

3. THE PRAYER'S TRAIN OF THOUGHT

And the prayer itself is also purely in that tone. At first sight, it seems somewhat strange that within the prayer is included another prayer, and then at the end a confession, namely the Apostles' Creed. It does require a bit of effort to find this compilation tidy and fitting. It has something to do with whether this method of prayer is somewhat antiquated and no longer harmonizes with our spiritual taste.

Therefore, the obligation rests all the more upon us, as clearly as possible, to do justice to the purpose of the form, to enter authentically as much as possible into the spirit of the fathers, and perhaps that which still speaks too little to us will be spoken to our heart and from our heart.

So first then in this prayer is a straightforward petition pertaining to the Lord's supper celebration.

Requested is that the Holy Spirit would draw our hearts in the supper to greater surrender to the Lord Christ, so that communion with him is deepened and the mystical union is strengthened (he living in us, and we in him).

Further, that as a result of this more intimate fellowship, the covenant be advanced to us, i.e., that Christ the Mediator unite us more with the Father, and from the covenant cause to come our temporal and eternal covenantal possessions (providing with all things).

Also, that the supper cultivate the life of sanctification, by teaching us to take up our cross, to deny ourselves, and to confess our Savior.

And finally, that the supper place before the mind of the Christian the heavenly future, instilling in him a holy idealism, teaching him to expect Christ from heaven, "where he will make our mortal bodies like unto his most glorious body, and take us unto him in eternity."

To this warm, authentic petitioning prayer is then joined the Lord's prayer and the classic confession of the catholic, undoubted Christian faith.

4. THE COMMENCEMENT AND CLAIM OF THE PRAYER

As we attempt to comprehend the meaning of the particular words, we immediately stand speechless before the majestic opening of the prayer.

Sometimes at the beginning of the old prayers, something of an argumentative and reasoning nature occurs that we would prefer be omitted. So, for example, in the prayer of the baptism form, where in the opening the history of the flood and the Red Sea is entwined. In our estimation, we might think this as a kind of drag and as more a distraction than truly praying.

The prayer of our Lord's supper formulary is better from this perspective, but nevertheless, not entirely without fault.

So the framers could not let it go that after the word *supper,* immediately to allow to follow a certain description regarding the purpose and idea of the Lord's supper, namely, the words: "in which we celebrate the glorious remembrance of the bitter death of thy beloved Son, Jesus Christ."

Likewise, for this reason, the opening sentence indeed becomes rather long and too heavy for ordinary folks to suddenly absorb. Indeed, one might say that almost the entire prayer is woven into one sentence and therefore does not meet the requirement that the prayer before all things must be succinct and clear. Note how brief the petitions of the Lord's prayer. Such is a model.

In contrast with this lapse in its form, however, stands the warm abundance of its content. It is to the framers' credit that the prayer in a good sense of the word is given a genial character. There is immediately granted the mystical tone with the description of the supper. Not less than three times in the scope of that one parenthetical sentence an adjective gives powerful emphasis. They are: *glorious* remembrance, *bitter* death, and *beloved* Son. Here reasons not the retired theologian, but here prays the needy child of God.

And the formulary prayer carries on this same tone all the way to the end. Petitioned is that God might work in our *hearts* through his Spirit, and the *afflicted* and *contrite* hearts may be nourished with Jesus' body and blood. Indeed, the tone approaches childish naivete where the Father is asked to provide for his own as his "beloved children and heirs." In this place the form lets us hear its finest notes and is beautiful for its tenderness.

But more beautiful still is the prayer of the form with regard to its entire design and structure. If anywhere, then here would be the occasion to direct the prayer to the Lord Jesus. It is *his* thoughts that are celebrated here, *his* death that is proclaimed, *his* food and drink that are enjoyed. Indeed, is he not the host who invites his people to the meal?

Still, the prayer itself is not directed to the Savior, but to the *Father*. And that is to be our preference. Such is always the main idea of the Calvinist Reformation, that the work of redemption in its entire depth, length, and width involves the *Gloria Dei*. All that the mediator accomplishes has an eye for giving glory to the Father, to reunite the damaged creation with him. Jesus himself sees all things based on this principle and carries this out in the prayer that he teaches us so consistently that he does not use his own name even once.

See here how our fathers (as in all the formulary prayers they have left to us) also proceed from this standpoint in their prayers. From the *Father* it is asked that *he* work in our hearts through *his* Holy Spirit, that we may more and more with true confidence give ourselves up unto *his* Son Jesus Christ. Without exception, Christ is referred to in the third person, chiefly in his mediatorial relationship to the Father. And as the chief gift of grace it is asked that we not doubt *thou* wilt forever be our gracious Father.

In this method of prayer lies more than what many might superficially suppose.

This form of prayer issues forth from a supreme view of life that also sheds extensive light upon the supper.

In short, this view of life always involves the relation between creation and re-creation, nature and grace. Redemption is viewed as a restoration of the creation, so that both are anchored together, and the Lord God himself (speaking reverently) especially where it is possible unites his work of redemption with the work of creation and makes each serviceable to the other.

The bath water of baptism finds its foreshadowing and symbolism in a creation ordinance, namely that the water is designated for cleansing.

Even so, the symbolism of the Lord's supper receives its force from the institution of creation, that man lives by nourishment. The meal of the covenant finds its origin in the meals of regular living that are also ordained for man by God.

"A meal," says Dr. Kuyper in a beautiful development of this idea,

> ...is not something that stands beneath the dignity of the holy, but the meal *qua talis* (as such) is by God intended, by God designed, and by God himself furnished for mankind.

He created men in this way so that they *lose* strength and so must renew strength with food. He ordained it as such, that they would receive this renewal of strength by taking *nourishment*, wherein with his blessing that means for the renewal of strength was prayed for. He granted them even the capacity that they would not be *constantly* taking food, but have an appetite according to a certain timetable, or, if you will, the necessity for food would again be felt. And finally, hereby at the same time, it was he, who effected the appetite at the social, so that societal assembling or seating at a meal was born.[4]

Precisely in the pure, natural character of the mealtime lies thus the appropriateness for the symbolism of a higher, spiritual world. Just as God created *body* and *soul* related to each other and in connection with each other, so there is in every terrain a bond between material and spiritual things, in this case between the natural and spiritual mealtime. Thus, Jesus honored the institution of the Father and attached himself to it when in the passion night he ordered the supper.

It is true that the meal at which Jesus sat down that night was not your everyday meal. But the passover meal itself was indeed instituted in connection with the natural life. Especially in eastern life was felt the close bonds of blood in household and family. The mealtime was the point of union where this fellowship was exercised. There were even required (by princes as fathers of their tribe) enormous banquets to which the poor were invited so that the togetherness of the entire nation would be expressed.

From these mealtimes it is but one step to the religious feasts where the people with the priest, as a representative of God, were guests. On sacred terrain, the Lord granted to his Israel such religious mealtimes on a small scale in the meals that were connected

---

4   Kuyper, *E Voto*, III, 89.

to the sacrifices in the temple, but in an entirely unique and broadly national form in the passover meal, where the great exodus from Egypt's house of slavery was celebrated.

It is this meal that Christ in New Testament beauty transformed, granting us his holy supper. But then, therein appears also unmistakably that this supper—when reflecting upon the entire chain of foregoing types and shadows—stands in relation to the creation ordinance of the natural mealtime.

Therefore, in the deepest sense is the Father, who created all food and nourishment to all that lives, the host at the supper. Also here is the heavenly Father, who, knowing what his child needs, supplies the spiritual poverty from his abundant storehouse. From this Father also here are all things. And the bread with which he nourishes his children is wonder bread, living bread, that is from heaven, that is from the Father, that is bestowed upon us.

The congregation of God stands before this truth in earnest, thoughtful stillness. Especially for this point right thinking is necessary, that this amounts to a substantial criterium for a Calvinistic view of the supper.

God *the Father* is the one from whose direction the Lord's supper originates, first regarding the creation of the signs of the supper. The supper is unthinkable without bread and wine. Bread and wine are created things of God. And these creatures are so made by God that they foreshadow, typify, the nourishing body and the drenching blood of Christ. God, who all his works has known from eternity, anticipated Christ, as it were, with the creation of wheat grains and the grapevine. And in this creation, God is great and greatly to be praised. Jewish people understood this already at the passover meal when they said, as they were sharing the first cup, "Blessed is he who is the Creator of the fruit of the vine." And in the passing of the second cup was said, "Blessed is he who causes bread to spring forth from the earth."

This is the first idea regarding the divine Fatherhood that we must hold on to at the supper.

However, the second truth, which goes yet deeper, deserves no less attention.

Christ, who in the supper is the spiritual food for his people, is himself directly a gift of God. The thorough-going idea of Scripture is that God has *given* his only begotten Son. Jesus himself testifies that he is sent into the world by the Father and that it is his "meat" to do the will of his Father, to accomplish his work.

Therefore, he who draws near unto the Lord's supper does so with a view from the Christ of God on high, to the Father of lights, from whom comes down not only every good gift, but also this perfect gift.

And then also the institution of the supper itself directs us to the work of the Father. Indeed, it was Jesus personally who took the bread and the cup, and so ordained the supper, but Christ did this as mediator, fulfilling the will of the *Father.* Also in this Jesus was the official minister of God, who came to do God's good pleasure. And as Jesus instituted the supper applies here the prayer, "Father I have finished the work that thou gavest me to do" (John 17:4).[5]

Note that in this light the formulary prayer of our fathers is doubly beautiful. Nearly every word breathes this world-and-life view. And we might add at the same time that this Calvinism speaks no less out of the prayer of thanksgiving, where the Father is praised that he has bestowed upon us his only begotten Son unto a mediator and sacrifice for our sins, and where in so many words is said that *the Father*, through his beloved Son, has granted the institution and ordaining of the supper.

5. TO GIVE OURSELVES UP TO CHRIST

Following this perspective on the initial principle of the prayer, it is now our task to analyze its content proper.

As in the prayer in the baptism form, there is here a core idea around which the other petitions are organized.

---

5 Cf. Kuyper, *E Voto*, III, 137–39.

This central petition is "that we may more and more with true confidence, give ourselves up unto Jesus Christ." As a result of this giving-up (there always follows: *so that*) is asked that our contrite hearts may be nourished with the heavenly bread. And thereafter follows in the same breath prayer for the indwelling of Christ and partaking in the covenant of the Father with all his gracious benefits. The prayer in its conclusion for strength to take up the cross is more to be viewed as an addendum.

Before the congregation goes to take communion, they are thus asking first and foremost that they *give themselves up* more to Christ. Actually, it is this same idea for which the Heidelberg Catechism lays the foundation. The only comfort, which the Christian esteems, is nevertheless nothing other than that he is not his own but belongs to his precious Savior.

The character of sin is to want to be independent, to will to be an autocrat over against God. Their being independent is, as in the known poetic term *niet-zijn,* to will to be independent is hellish agony.

The great liberation and spiritual revolution that the Holy Spirit accomplishes in man exists herein, that man no longer desires to be autonomous, but a creation of God, a servant, a child of God, and this in the way that he is engrafted into Christ and more and more gives himself up to him.

A noteworthy harmony in this point with the form for baptism!

After all, the central idea in the prayer of the baptismal formulary is: "That thou wilt incorporate this your child by thy Holy Spirit into thy Son Jesus Christ."[6] This incorporation happens by secret regeneration. However, the Lord's supper speaks to the covenant member who affirms the covenant of the conscious and ongoing incorporation. This conscious incorporation is nothing other than what is here called more and more giving oneself up to Christ. So connects the

---

6   See my *The Reformed Baptism Form,* 210ff.

second sacrament to the first and completes the gracious work of this sacrament. If one compares both forms on this point, it is as if they were written by the same pen.

To give oneself up to Christ is to enter into his surety, to trust in his sacrifice. It is obedience to his urgent call: Come unto me, all ye who labor and are heavy laden, and I will give you rest. It is joining oneself to Jesus like sheep that follow the shepherd.

The Lord's supper is God's ordained means regarding this giving up of oneself. We nonetheless partake of this supper—speaking in the language of the form—unto the glorious remembrance of the bitter death of God's beloved Son. In a particular sense, the recollection of Jesus' bitter death is also bitter. The soul of God's child bows down as it ponders the sorrows of the king of sorrows. But as it arrives to tasting of the fruit of this suffering, then the remembrance of the atoning death is glorious for the soul, more glorious yet than the remembrance of the exodus from the Egyptian imprisonment for the passover-celebrating Jew.

Glorious remembrance, that is of the atonement for sin and victory over death! Unencumbered fact of grace and power! Everlasting miracle of radical redemption.

Note that at the Lord's supper, where we exercise remembrance of that salvation-granting death of Christ, is the place where we give up ourselves more and more to Christ. According to the measure that this recollection becomes clearer, and the more the signs speak to us of forgiveness accomplished, the more the soul can abandon itself unto its redeemer. If the eye looks away from Christ's atoning passion, then doubt covers up the life of the heart and smothers faith in its refuge-taking strength. Oh, that faltering struggle to go on the path of justification in one's own power! Oh, that toilsome seeking to satisfy God in the adornment of our own righteousness. Oh, that wandering around away from Jesus and his cross to find the way to the Father's house!

Take and eat, this is the body of Christ that is broken for you!

Take and drink, this cup is the New Testament in his blood, shed for you!

Let these signs move you to relinquish yourself and your delusions of righteousness, and more and more to give up yourself to Christ. To give up yourself to him is from weakness to become strong, it is profit in courage, in joy, in *living*.

The viewing itself of the sign does not bring the man to this self-sacrifice, striving as he does with his old nature. God must make him malleable. Therefore, the Christian *prays* to the Father, that he *by his Holy Spirit* will *work in* him to give himself up to Christ. By his almighty grace, God's Spirit must compel the stronghold of the obstinate sinner's heart to give up. He must compel the counter-resistant man to become strong, to overwhelm and take him captive to the obedience of Christ. He must also by sweet persuasion entice the fearful heart that was initially broken, enticing, presenting the glory and dearness of the Redeemer in such a manner that it learns to cry out to the living God, and soon to whisper in trust: you are my hiding place!

That is the task for which the divine Father sends the Holy Spirit to dwell in the hearts of believers at the Lord's table. And what a priceless "material" the Spirit has here to oblige the covenantal people to salvation-granting giving-up to Christ! How the broken bread and the purple wine call with the gospel voice: give yourself up to Jesus, rest at his feet, know yourself accepted at his heart!

Truly it is a rich prayer that the church here utters to the Father.

And indeed is her celebration of the Lord's supper a royal blessing, when the result is an intimate giving up of the child to the father, of the bride to the bridegroom!

6. CONTRITE HEARTS REFRESHED

However, we see that the central petition is more broadly expounded, and indeed in the words: *that our afflicted and contrite hearts, through the power of the Holy Spirit, may be nourished and refreshed with his true body and blood; yea, with him, true God and man, that only heavenly bread.*

The giving up to Christ that is first requested is what the fathers called an act of faith taking refuge. But this taking refuge is the root of our strength. He who goes to Christ is satisfied, comforted, and encouraged. A poor child of humanity never gives himself to Jesus without being enriched. *As he gives himself up the man will live, but also *according as he gives* himself shall he live. The deeper the soul immerses into the stream of life, the mightier he will live.

The form presents this enrichment (entirely in line with the Lord's supper idea) as nourishment and refreshment with the heavenly bread, Christ. This nourishment happens (and this idea is actually from Calvin) with the true body and blood, yea, with Christ, true God and man.

It was our fathers' intention, *also in their prayer*, to give up nothing of the mystical riches of the sacrament, and as it were to counter the complaint that our Lord's supper grants more meager treasure compared to the Romish mass.

The church requests no less than to receive Christ himself, with him to be bound to the oneness of life of the mystical body.

What this wants to say is understood most deeply when we pay attention to the offices of the Mediator that Christ bore *and bears,* his offices so that we should be partakers of his anointing. To be nourished with him is to say: to have communion with the treasures and gifts that come to us primarily from these offices, namely his prophetic wisdom, his priestly holiness, and his royal righteousness.

Everything that Christ is for us he is *through* his offices. The offices are like channels whereby the benefits flow to us in constantly diverse forms and fresh beauty. From the offices come to us primarily the forgiveness and the life, the most precious fruits of Jesus' atoning death.

These fruits come to us for the benefit of nourishment, not detached from Jesus, but so closely bound to the Savior that we can say (and the formulary also says it here) that we with his true body and blood, indeed, even stronger, with him, true God and man, are nourished and refreshed.

This refreshment happens in the *soul*, in all the organs and sources of the spiritual life, but primarily in the heart, or as it is said here, in "our afflicted and contrite hearts." There again is displayed our form's encouraging and comforting character. Also in the didactic portion we heard that sound, for example, where it is said that the judgment of exclusion was not for the purpose of discouraging the *contrite hearts* of believers. And here in the prayer is as a sigh from the depths, misery from the despondent disposition, climbing to the throne of grace.

How demonstrable here is God's hand extended to *the little ones*.

Indeed it must be put on the foreground that here the afflicted and contrite hearts concern not so much the so-called anxiety over the eternal state of salvation, one's justified relationship to God. Our fathers, neither in their confessional writings nor in their liturgy, were on this point weak or of little faith. They did not know that doubt with respect to the state of sonship that is observed today in our churches in some as a chronic symptom of illness. They were in their faith as the saints of Scripture, whom you do hear (think especially of the Psalms) lament over distress and alarm, agonies of hell, and the bands of death, but you do not hear whining "that they may yet receive assurance as to whether they have come from the darkness to the light."

Nevertheless, also the "troubled," provided it is for them true concern, may discover themselves in this message of the formulary, because their doubt regarding the state of salvation is a *disease* that God also wills to heal at the supper. Also, these spiritual wretches (the word they grant us), whose souls cannot stand the light, are invited, *admonished*, to be seated at the meal of the assurance of faith, and to pray beforehand that God may nourish and refresh their afflicted and contrite hearts with the heavenly bread, Christ.

7. HE IN US AND WE IN HIM

The prayer then moves ahead, gaining even more in warmth and power: *and that we may no longer live in our sins, but he in us, and we in him.* Here also is a result of the giving oneself up to trust Jesus fully.

Certainly, no longer living in our sins is also a *calling* and obligation of the covenant. In the baptism form, we are admonished and obliged to forsake the world and put to death our old nature. But this leaving the sphere of sin is also a gift of God and a reward of grace connected to trusting faith. In Scripture, sanctification is also always presented as two-sided: responsibility of faith and fruit of faith.

There indeed lies a sad indictment, a tragic, personal reprimand in the word: no longer live in our sins! Man has sunk so deeply that even a child of God must pray before going to the supper that he no longer in sin, *in his sins*, lives.

But what is now even more remarkable is the contrast with the triumph of grace. This still consists in the fact that Christ lives in us and, what is no less, that *we live in Christ.* First our heart, the center of life in which Christ resides with his salvation power, is being renewed, reformed, reenergized, so that "I live; yet not I, but Christ liveth in me: and the life which I now live in the flesh I live by the faith of the Son of God, who loved me, and gave himself for me" (Gal. 2:20).

But Christ is also the sphere in which we live, or rather, Christ is the source of strength from which we live. Certainly, our fathers had the image of a vine in mind when they penned these words. The tendril is *in* the vine so that it lives *from* the vine and bears fruit. After all, Jesus himself says: "Abide in me, and I in you. As the branch cannot bear fruit of itself, except it abide in the vine; no more can ye, except ye abide in me" (John 15:4).

At the Lord's supper the mystical union is strengthened, whereby the tendril draws life-sap from the vine and swells with fruit.

8. THAT WE NOT DOUBT THOU WILT BE OUR FATHER

But there is more requested. The prayer ascends higher. As a result of seeking the giving up to Christ, we also may *truly be made partakers of the new and everlasting testament of grace. That we may not doubt but thou wilt forever be our gracious Father, nevermore imputing our sins unto us, and providing us with all things necessary, as well for the body as the soul, as thy beloved children and heirs.*

In this way the form here again weaves in the covenantal idea, and what emerges is the view of life in which this language is grounded.

We know that the world-and-life view of the fathers was actually a covenantal view. All of their religious thinking came from that root, from this principle.

One cannot say that in the Lord's supper form the idea of the covenant is placed too prominently in the foreground. But whenever the matter of the covenant is brought up, one senses also that the covenantal idea is the backdrop of the entire form.

So, for example, in the didactic portion it is said that Jesus has instituted the supper "that we might firmly believe that we belong to this covenant of grace."

And here is clearly a summary of the already-identified benefits of salvation, as petitioned, that we be made partakers of the new and eternal testament and covenant of grace.

The content of the covenant is nothing other than *Christ*, but according to the form, it is more because Christ is the gift (at the same time mediator) of the covenant. When God established the covenant with Abraham, the fundamental promise of the covenant was *Christ.* And when the new and eternal testament (that which is the transformation of the old, shadowy covenant) is sealed by the shed blood of the cross, then the opening of that testament brings us *Christ.*

No, the doctrine of the covenant is not a dogmatic formulation that is *over against* the gospel; it is the strengthened and clear-cut formulation of the gospel itself. The covenant is the silver platter upon which the golden apples of the gospel are presented to the people of God. Exactly because our fathers were so covenantal in their conception of the truth, were they so thoroughly gospel centered.

Notice here what by the partaking of the covenant becomes the conscious possession of the Christian: that God is forever his gracious Father! Can it be more tender, more lovely, more evangelical? This is the great benefit that the covenant pours out in the child's heart: the complete certainty (the not-doubting) that God is *our Father.*

Pay attention that it is not to speak of the fact of his being Father. This is already a fact by virtue of the covenant. And of this baptism is already the seal. No, the benefit identified here is the sweet *assurance* of this fact, the joyfully assured faith: I am a child of God. To which end God granted the institution of the supper, that the last doubt regarding this salvation fact would be banished. The sacrament serves to make the Christian aware of his wealth, his salvation status, his future. Not to doubt the truth regarding child-status: that is joy, strength, and blessedness.

Because what in turn does such fatherhood contain? The form for baptism has already declared this:

> For when we are baptized in the name of the Father, God the Father witnesseth and sealeth unto us that he doth make an eternal covenant of grace with us, and adopts us for his children and heirs, and therefore will provide us with every good thing, and avert all evil or turn it to our profit.

According to this presentation is thus the establishment, the institution, of the covenant particularly an act of the Father. The covenant leads us to the Father, and the more we are partakers in the covenant, the more God is our Father. But this covenant itself is first come to us from the Father; it has its origin *from the Father.* Not that we through the covenant first come to God, but God first comes to us in the covenant. We are *given birth* in the covenant, and even before we have consciousness of the covenant, it is sealed unto us. But growing up in the covenant, the man himself by grace goes into action, more and more he lives in the covenant, he continues increasingly to be made more a *partaker* (as our form here expresses it) and seeks not the least covenantal communion with the Father at the meal of the covenant. Here he implores of the Father that which was already promised him in baptism, namely the blessings of the fatherhood of God.

Only—as we have already noted—it is not asked bluntly: "Be O God, forever our gracious Father," but *"may we not doubt but thou wilt forever be our gracious Father."* This is very purely perceived and expressed.

The petitioner establishes himself on the standpoint of the covenant, that God *is* his Father (this was sealed unto him in baptism), and he now requests at the Lord's supper that in this way his faith may be so strengthened, that he may possess the joyous, saving certainty of this fatherhood. So it is not here about the fact but the awareness of the fact, not about the being of the faith but the well-being of the faith.

And also note how the language of the congregation softens here.

Almost naively the praying church says of itself: *thy beloved children and heirs*, while the baptism form merely states, "adopt us as his children and heirs."

Furthermore, while the baptism form as benefit of the fatherhood only identifies providing us with every good thing, the Lord's supper form mentions first of all the forgiveness of sins. Here is this the most eminently esteemed in the fatherhood, that God "nevermore imput[es] our sins unto us," and then immediately comes the others: "providing us with all things necessary as well for the body as the soul."

Indeed, that is at the heart of Jerusalem. At the supper, the soul seeks the blessedness of remission of guilt. This testimony she desires to make *her* testimony: "Blessed is the man unto whom the LORD imputeth not iniquity, and in whose spirit there is no guile" (Ps. 32:2).

9. THAT WE MAY CHEERFULLY TAKE UP OUR CROSS

With this same intimate tone the prayer goes even further. There is yet a special grace requested from this treasure chest of the covenant of grace. The congregation prays:

> *Grant us also thy grace, that we may take up our cross cheerfully, deny ourselves, confess our Savior, and in all tribulations, with uplifted heads expect our Lord Jesus Christ from heaven, where he will make our mortal bodies like unto his most glorious body, and take us unto him in eternity.*

Here also resounds an echo of the baptismal form. In the prayer before the baptism it is asked that this child "may be raised with him in newness of life, that he may daily follow him *joyfully bearing his cross*."

And further one meets there with the same train of thought of cleaving to Jesus with the blessed prospect of leaving this life in order to appear before Jesus' throne of judgment without terror.

However, these ideas are also in the Lord's supper form and even more warmly articulated and summarized more tenderly.

Oh, it is not surprising that the church here at this meal, where the cross is pictured before her eyes, thinks of her own cross, and especially in those days when near to this passion meal the enemy is leering as the children of God are reckoned as sheep for the slaughter. Indeed, for here in the supper the congregation feels nearest to the sufferings of Christ, the presentation of Jesus suffering in his body that is on earth. Here, with the signs of the covenant the host apportions to each of his own also the cross.

And the "dear children and heirs" take up their cross, saying: "Grant us also thy grace, that we may cheerfully, taking up our cross, deny ourselves."

Note well here that the *action* of faith is petitioned. In the baptism form, it is only a matter of joyfully *bearing* the cross. Here the petition goes further, namely that God grant grace also *to take up* the cross. Thus, not only that God *lays it on*, but also that the Christian *takes it up*.

And if he has taken it up, then *bearing* it, through the all-conquering power of faith, by the quiet energy of a "cheerful" disposition.

Through the tears, laughing on his way, he follows Jesus with his cross on his back.

After Jesus, because without Jesus there would not be this cross. It is not a common cross of earthly cares that the entire world also bears. It is the cross that necessarily is the portion of everyone who walks in the steps of the great cross-bearer. For Jesus said: "If any man will come after me, let him deny himself, and take up his cross, and follow me" (Matt. 16:24).

It is moving that the church herself requests the power of grace for self-denial. Here speaks awareness of weakness in sinful egotism, but also deep-rooted trust that the Father, who lays claim to self-denying love, will pour love into the heart of the child and stir it up.

It is the beautiful triad of Christian virtues that the praying congregation here seeks: *self-denial*, *profession*, and *expectation*.

The first is the wonderful power of soul for abstinence, for "not-doing." The nature of man is to let himself go, to relax the bridle to the passions of the heart, with the *I* hoisted to the highest possible throne, and, if need be, denying all and everything including Jesus, requiring of everything for the purpose of total self-fulfillment.

Grace teaches a man to curb his passions, to place his "I" in the background, indeed, as necessary, even to suppress cravings that are good in and of themselves so that the things of the Lord not suffer loss and Jesus might reign more and more.

Listening to the sound of his old nature, man repudiates the Savior for himself; following the voice of the new life, he denies himself for Jesus.

And he is not released from this self-denial if he will be a true disciple. Jesus' advent, Jesus' presence, Jesus' word, Jesus' church creates a crisis, provokes enmity, tension, division, and constantly calls for a decision in the crisis: What about you? You cannot hang on to both. "He that loveth father or mother more than me is not worthy of me: and he that loveth son or daughter more than me is not worthy of me" (Matt. 10:37). "If any man come to me, and hate not his father, and mother, and wife, and children, and brethren, and sisters, yea, and his own life also, he cannot be my disciple" (Luke 14:26).

However, the negative act of self-denial comes with the positive act of *profession*. Actually, there is here an interaction between the two. On the one side, only those who deny themselves can make a profession. On the other, those who profess are thereby called to self-denial. According to the measure the profession is more vigorous, fiercer is the reaction of the world. The profession is therefore the proof of true love. However, he who does *not* profess, but denies, cuts the cord of true fellowship with Jesus because he does not love Jesus enough to deny himself for him. That is why Jesus says: "Whosoever therefore shall confess me before men, him will I confess also before my Father which is in heaven. But whosoever shall deny me before men, him will I also deny before my Father which is in heaven" (Matt. 10:32–33).

And *expectation* follows profession.

The profession of the church bears here on earth an antithetical character because the world denies the profession. This antithesis causes pain and is cause that the Christian increasingly knows himself as a stranger. In a world in which his Savior meets protest and enmity, the Christian does not feel at home. That is why he also asks that he "in all tribulations, with an uplifted head may expect his Lord Jesus Christ from heaven," and indeed so that Jesus will "make our mortal bodies like unto his most glorious body, and take us unto him in eternity."

Also here the train of thought and choice of words in the formulary is impeccable.

The congregation does not first petition from her valley of suffering to be taken to heaven. No, she first *expects her Savior from heaven.* Before the congregation goes *to heaven*, the Lord Jesus must come *from heaven.* He must be revealed as judge. He must shine as king overall in the eye of every creature.

In this petition the church longs first of all for the advancement not of her own glory, but the glory of Christ.

But the advent of Christ also brings inseparable blessedness for the congregation. Her blessedness will be that this her heavy, sin-tarnished flesh, which reflects enmity against God, puts on glory, and he then with that spiritual, heavenly body is taken by the bridegroom into eternity and becomes like the body of Jesus.

Note that he who has this expectation need not live here below as a pilgrim who has no hope. He may live with *uplifted* head expecting his Savior. This hope may soften all his misery. In the pitch darkness this star gently beckons him. For such a Savior need he never be ashamed. He may stride with a high-spirited pace through a world that disparages him. He walks as one who *apprehends* and *anticipates.* And at the Lord's table he receives the promise, enjoying the foretaste of that coming triumph. Here the Savior who is acquainted with his weakness, by means of the symbolic sitting at the supper, which represents and pledges the heavenly wedding, grants him the grace with an uplifted head in every sorrow to expect the Lord Jesus Christ from heaven.

Is not this true? The prayer for this grace is snatched from our heart, even though we are no longer burned at the stake. And the church of Christ, which, even though the ages change, passes through what is essentially the same struggle, prays the noble, courageous language of faith of this prayer of the form, from the heart, after the church of the martyrs.

10. WHO TAUGHT US TO PRAY

It can hardly be denied that after the uplifting language of this last petition the word *Amen* would not have sounded inappropriate. Rather it must be said that he himself who is praying must in a measure feel obliged *not* to conclude the prayer here and yet to continue on another note. We do perfectly understand that in the centuries of redactions differing from the official text, the next concluding portion might be abandoned and the prayer that precedes already be concluded with the word *Amen*. Inadvertently, you get the feeling that the portion of the prayer wherein the Lord's prayer and the Apostles' Creed are taken up form a sort of appendix, which does not seem to fit with the foregoing independent prayer, and that is why it can without damage be missed from the whole.

We do not deny that the prayer taken as a whole indeed appears in a sense to have an artificial character. Especially connecting the confession of faith may seem as something *contrived*. This creed (that we in and of itself would not want omitted from our form) could just as well be separated from the prayer and receive its place following it. Nevertheless, we have the revisors to thank that they took it up to restore this last portion to its rightful place.

Especially the Lord's prayer may indeed be incorporated into this prayer. We already pointed out how the Reformed view of the Lord's supper ascends to the Father, and in the fatherhood of God, as revealed in the covenant, reaches its zenith. That is precisely why the Reformed can sincerely pray the Lord's prayer at the Lord's supper. And in this Lord's prayer, prayed precisely at this point, he is guarded against a biased view of the supper that limits itself to a mere Jesus service and savior celebration. In this connection, Dr. Kuyper admonishes us with regard to the Lord's prayer:

> So as you approach the holy supper, discover not only the bread, that God the Father created, and the wine, that he caused to be made, and the holy *Lamb of God,* that he granted and sent you, but also a *Lord's supper* that is from God the Father as a sacrament, from whom comes all things.
>
> So you come to the holy supper in order to pray *Our father,* is it not? After all, whenever you come to the holy

supper it is to pray, *Our Father*. First in that holy circle and at that holy meal you sense fully what it says to pray: Hallowed be thy name, thy kingdom come, thy will be done! And likewise what it says, to pray for all temporal and spiritual needs. For then you suddenly see it, how at the supper you really first feel the deep sense of that "Our Father who art in heaven." That is why from days of old our church had the good practice to even pray the Lord's prayer twice at the Lord's supper. You can see it in our formulary. And it is nothing but spiritless pedantry that we usually omit that second Lord's prayer from the holy supper as if there were not enough time for God's people to pour out that glorious prayer from their soul. We seem to have ample time for extensive and lengthy follow-up meditations. But the Lord's prayer in which the adoration should culminate is omitted entirely formally for the sake of brevity.[7]

And then Dr. Kuyper adds the advice that the church honor more the fatherhood of God in the Lord's supper and seek to stress the abundance of being a child of God: "Experience teaches that this makes the administration of the Holy supper more natural and healthier, and more truly *God-glorifying*."

Nevertheless, concerning not only the one idea of the fatherhood of God that in the Lord's prayer is so strikingly emphasized, but also we may be thankful concerning the prayer itself, that it is inserted into our form. At the supper, the soul of God's child seeks the ultimate height, to reach the most intimate activity of faith, and that always presents Christ to his people in the Lord's prayer. The devout heart cannot ascend higher than this prayer (when sincerely prayed).[8]

---

7   Kuyper, *E Voto*, III, 139.

8   On this Dr. Kuyper says: "The Lord's Prayer follows, which is in the appropriate place here, as the soul in this spirit-charged context feels the need to express itself in the perfect prayer." *Our Worship*, tr. and ed. Harry Boonstra (Grand Rapids: Eerdmans, 2009), 285–86.

Our Father who art in heaven, so the congregation says, and thereby confesses on the basis of her childlike fear and reverence, deeply humbled before the heavenly majesty but also in meek expectation for the meeting of her need.

Hallowed be thy name! because where brighter than at this table does the God of great deeds shine in his omnipotence, wisdom, goodness, righteousness, mercy, and truth, to bless, to magnify, and to glorify, where God brings to remembrance his most exalted miracles?

Thy kingdom come! because here it is that God wills to teach his people more and more to submit themselves to him (in the previous prayer it said *to give up* ourselves to Jesus) and in this way to consummate his church.

Thy will be done on earth as it is heaven, because in this place God's people are drawn by the image of him whose food was to accomplish the will of the Father, and who at the drawing near of his cup prayed, "Not my will, but thine be done."

Give us this day our daily bread! because would the Father who bestows the living and heavenly bread deny the earthly bread; would he who did not spare his only Son not with him bestow all things?

And forgive us our debts as we also have forgiven our debtors, because here the devout one beholds that God has punished sins, *our* sins, in Jesus with the bitter and shameful death of the cross.

And lead us not into temptation but deliver us from the evil one! because the Lord's supper is the place, in communion with him who withstood all temptation and was victorious over Satan, to obtain spiritual strength "that we may not be overcome in this spiritual warfare, but constantly and strenuously may resist our foes, till at last we obtain a complete victory."

And finally: *For thine is the kingdom, and the power, and the glory, forever!* because here is preeminently the place, in view of the great deeds and great perfections of God, so that to be strengthened in the confidence that God wills to hear and to help us, and all that "thereby not we, but thy holy name may be be glorified forever."

Therefore, also concerning the content, the Lord's prayer is a genuine Lord's supper prayer.

Whereby then the conclusion follows, that in its entirety it is a ground in the service of all other prayers.

This is indicated in the way in which the Lord's prayer is firmly tied to the foregoing prayer.

"Answer us," it goes, "O God and merciful Father, *through Jesus Christ, who taught us to pray.*"

This formula contains not an aesthetic attempt to join the perfect prayer to the other prayers in a somewhat gracious manner. The ground for the plea of the prayer to the Father is *Jesus Christ* who said that whatsoever we ask of the Father in *Jesus' name* shall be given. In order to inspire us to pray without inhibition, and at the same time to enliven within us expectation that we will be heard, Jesus himself prompted us to pray this prayer. He gave it thereby to know: see, this you may ask in my name, and this shall the Father certainly give you. Seeing that the content of the Lord's prayer is all that we could desire for our spiritual and physical necessities, there lies in this prayer incalculable strength for pleading before the Father's throne. All that we could imagine to ask is as a kernel, or as summary, comprehended in the perfect prayer. Thus, when the congregation, as in the preceding formulary prayer, petitions the Father for great spiritual benefits—to be nourished and refreshed by the only heavenly bread, Christ, and to be provided for all things in body and soul, as dear children and heirs—then the Lord's prayer spreads out the evidence: see, Lord, we ask not too much and nothing inappropriate, because your Son, Jesus Christ, taught us how to pray: "Our Father, who art in heaven..."

11. TO STRENGTHEN THE CHRISTIAN FAITH

And then in the prayer comes the profession of faith. We have already made known our opinion that we sense that the intertwining of the Apostles' Creed might have something artificial about it. We are not used to such, and have difficulty with *praying* the Apostles' Creed, or at least for it to be presented as an actual part of the prayer.

Perhaps it would not be undesirable if these twelve articles were to be placed independently after the prayer, attached as an actual confession. Immediately following the prayer, the minister would then say: "Before we approach the table of the Lord, let us now confess our catholic, undoubted Christian faith."

Then the requirement would be met that the form bear not only an instructional but also a *confessional* character. This character tends not to be overdone in our forms. If the celebration of the sacrament truly answers to the goal of glorifying God, then that goal must not be left to the *feeling* of the congregation but also in so many words *be expressed*. The congregation must speak with mouth and heart of her faith, and let this confession resound as a *Te Deum*, a proclamation of the *excellencies* of him who has called us out of darkness into his marvelous light.

But now that it has pleased the framers to include this confession in the prayer itself, let us not overlook what is good in this deed.

The form takes up the creed quite fittingly in connection with the holy supper. The supper is instituted for the strengthening of *faith*. What faith? Note: "I believe in God the Father..."

Thus, the creed here indeed has a real form of a *prayer*. There is here actually something *petitioned* of God.

Indeed, one could note that the faith that seeks strengthening at the Lord's supper is especially faith in Jesus Christ, the bond of personal living communion with the beloved. We admit that it sounds somewhat odd at the supper requesting strengthening, and so on, for the faith of the holy catholic Christian church. That appears in a sense to hint of formalism. But remember also that our fathers in their life of faith always strived for the highest, the universal. Their faith is not a mood, an emotion, but a *faith perspective*. Their faith does not stop at Christ, but ascends from Christ to the triune God and embraces all his attributes and works. And this faith is not only an intellectual apprehension of a list of truths and facts, it is a giving up of the whole soul to the personal God. That is why the congregation says, I believe *in* God the Father, *in* Jesus Christ, and *in* the Holy Spirit.

The one praying does not think of this triune God in the abstract, not as the God who lives in unapproachable light, but as the God of revelation, the God of history, who makes great his wonders to his people and has displayed his excellencies for his people.

The congregation believes in God the Father, the Almighty *maker of heaven and earth.*

She believes in Jesus Christ, his only begotten Son, our Lord, *conceived by the Holy Spirit, born of the virgin Mary.*

She believes in the Holy Spirit, by whose power *the holy, catholic, Christian church* exists and upon which God grants the benefits of *the forgiveness of sin, the resurrection of the body, and life everlasting.*

The church treasures this confession and continues to love it as the concentration of her ideas of faith. From this mini-confession speak centuries of history. It is the deposit of a struggle for the holiest truths of the faith that brought the entire Christian church into upheaval. It is the apostolic foundation upon which the Christian church was built, preserved in the midst of the breakers. And even though church life has deteriorated due to division and schism, by depending upon this confession, all churches of a Christian confession remain one.

It is therefore a good idea to place this confession on the lips of the congregation at the moment that it more than ever appears as a confessing congregation. It is exhilarating to hear her speaking this language at the supper of her king, in the midst of a world that boasts at its forsaking of God. Therefore, we should, although also feeling something for an insertion of this creed in the prayer, have welcomed that the Apostles' Creed was included separately as a *confession*, and the congregation, not only by the mouth of the minister, but also herself actively expresses this confession.

This is how it was in the communion form of Zurich.

The *minister* began by saying, I believe in one God;

Then spoke *the men*: In the Father, the Almighty;

Women: and in Jesus Christ, his only begotten Son, our Lord;

Men: who was conceived by Holy Spirit;

Women: Born of the virgin Mary;

Men: suffered under Pontus Pilate, crucified, dead and buried;

Women: he descended into hell;

Men: the third day he rose again from the dead;

Women: he ascended into heaven;

Men: and sitteth at the Right hand of God, the Father almighty;

Women: from thence he shall come to judge the living and the dead;

Men: I believe in the Holy Spirit;

Women: the holy, catholic, Christian church, the communion of the saints;

Men: the forgiveness of sin;

Women: the resurrection of the body;

Men: and life everlasting;

Men and Women: Amen.[9]

Although this manner of expression alternatively by men and women brings something refreshing and compelling, we would nevertheless prefer a communal recitation of the creed by the entire congregation. And if even this form of confession may pose objections, the method that could be followed is in use in the German church, where the minister recites the confession and the congregation, which listens to it standing, would make heard their amen.

---

9 Hermann Adalbert Daniël, *Codex Liturgicus Ecclesiae Universae In Epitomen Redactus* (Lipsiae: T.O. Weigel, 1851), III, 151–52.

12. LIFT UP OUR HEARTS

Thus the prayer has been prayed, and the soul, which was raised to such a high deed of praying confession, relaxes. A brief moment is necessary to compose oneself in light of the continued instruction of the form. That is why the recommendation serves that after the prayer the minister assures sufficient pause for the quiet attention of the congregation to be assured. Some ministers have the practice to read the *Sursum Corda* that now follows at the table rather than in the pulpit, a practice against which indeed a weighty objection can be leveled. The objection is that by this one brings an arbitrary division into the form and also into the congregation, seeing that the minister at the table directs himself not strictly to the gathered congregation, but to the guests seated at the table.

After a moment of silence, the minister speaks forth from the pulpit:

> *That we may now be fed with the true heavenly bread, Christ Jesus, let us not cleave with our hearts unto the external bread and wine, but lift up our hearts on high in heaven, where Christ Jesus is our advocate, at the right hand of his heavenly Father, whither all the articles of our faith direct us; not doubting, but we shall as truly be fed and refreshed in our souls through the working of the Holy Ghost, with his body and blood, as we receive the holy bread and wine in remembrance of him.*

This arousing is a Reformed rendering of the ancient *Sursum Corda* (Lift up your hearts!), by which in the Roman ritual the congregation is brought into the proper state of mind.

We have already remarked that the language of this majestic introduction for the most part is purely Calvinistic.[10] With respect to these words the framer of our form followed that of Geneva:

---

10 *Supra*, I.5.

For this purpose, let us lift up our hearts and our spirits on high to heaven to where Jesus Christ is in the glory of his Father, and from where we await him onto our redemption. And let us not cling with our hearts to these earthly and corruptible elements which we see with our eyes and touch with our hands.[11]

Even more strongly it resembles the London liturgy:

And so that we may powerfully taste and enjoy the sweetness of the merits of Christ's death as we partake of the supper, *we should not cling to the outward exercise or to the elements of bread and wine. Instead, being exhorted by them, we must lift up our senses, heart, and mind into heaven, where alone Jesus Christ is according to the body*, a faithful Advocate for us, *being assured beyond all doubt that we are nourished much more certainly by the spiritual communion of Christ's body and blood unto eternal life* than our mortal bodies are daily maintained through food and drink, and [much more certainly] *than we enjoy bread and wine in the Lord's supper according to the institution of Christ.*[12]

Especially in the original it is evident that the purpose of this *Sursum Corda* is polemical. While the Genevan form as a whole bears a peaceful demonstrative, in this last portion the conflict with Rome and Luther comes forth so strongly that it is impossible not to think polemically when hearing this language.

"Let us," it says, "not cling with our hearts to these earthly and perishable elements, that we see with the eye and touch with the hand." And then further, "*to seek him as if he were contained there in the bread and the wine.*"

---

11 *Reformation Worship*, 328. Tr. "Let us not waste time with" as translated in *Reformation Worship* is here replaced with the traditional English translation, "let us not cling with our hearts."

12 Mensinga, 227–28.

And at the end: "Let us be fully satisfied then that we have the bread and the wine as signs and seals while we seek the spiritual food of which we are assured, there, where God promises that we shall find it."

In our form this polemic (or apologetic) seems to be pushed into the background and minimized so that only the admonishment remains not to cling to the external bread and wine for a direct reminder of the battle against Rome and Luther.

That this *Sursum Corda* sometimes remains somewhat strange to the congregation and has little hold on the mind rests not so much on this shrouded polemic as in the fact that it appears to demand too much of many listeners, after the exertion of listening to the extended instruction regarding the Lord's supper, including not too brief of a prayer, to now take in yet more instruction and admonishment. At least this writer has frequently noted this, that by the time you get to reading the *Sursum Corda*, a bit of unrest has come over the congregation that even with a preceding moment of silence and a solemn tone of voice was not to be overcome.

In our estimation the *Sursum Corda* would better accomplish its purpose if it were shortened by half its length.

We would seriously miss its complete absence.

A certain transition at this point from the instructional part and the prayer to the actual communion is indeed desirable.

And the idea that the congregation is here addressed is as fine as it is rich. The admonishment is as tender as it is appropriate.

Apart from all conflict with Rome it is indeed necessary for the soul to be reminded of her natural attachment to the material. It requires a sanctified effort, a spiritual adroitness to not cling to the external signs. The bodily senses speak so powerfully. Thus it is that the mind, which began to direct itself to the spiritual, at once again leaves off. We creatures of the dust sit so in our entire being as it were shackled in space and time.

That is why the gathering of the devout listen to the bold word of admonishment: *Lift up your hearts! Look on high!*

Let one say with David: Unto thee, O Lord, do I lift up my soul (Ps. 25:1).

Certainly, here on earth is the awesome work of the deliverance in principle accomplished. Here has stood Jesus' manger. Here was his cross planted. Here is borne the salvation banner, his church gathered, his kingdom built. But he himself the King is not here. He is with the Father, encircled by a multitude of the redeemed. There he is as the priestly advocate, preparing a place for us, as the sovereign one seated upon his royal throne, reigning in majesty.

Indeed, there are times when heaven descends to the church militant, it opens its prospects, it sends its showers of blessings and signs of comfort to us below, and it shall in time annex the earth as part of the great city of Jerusalem, but the center of the Christian life was taken above with Jesus' ascension. His home is there where one's Savior and Father live. The child belongs there where the father's house is.

That is why the exercise of his soul ascends to that kingdom that is above. And God gave wings to the soul so she can lift herself up, namely, the wings of *faith*. Such faith not only is a spiritual inspiration, a soul-momentum, but also a deep-seated knowledge of the truth of redemption, the faith according to the *content* of salvation.

This is what the form means when it says: "*whither all the articles of our Christian faith direct us.*" Thus in the preceding prayer is the Apostles' Creed especially inserted to facilitate the climb of the praying soul, because this creed speaks of the almighty Creator of heaven and earth, makes mention of the only begotten one, who following his humiliation is ascended into heaven and sits at the right hand of God the Father almighty, from whence he shall come to judge the living and the dead. Yes, this entire rich-in-content confession is as if it were fastened to the praying confessor to carry him up to the ivory palace where the Father, the Son, and the Holy Spirit take up their residence.

How obviously does this reminder of the Apostles' Creed cause to see that its insertion into the prayer was marked by genuine prudence, as from this point of view, continuity in the form is not much broken.

The admonishment not with the heart to cling to the external bread and wine thus proceeds from the supposition of a certain danger that is a threat in the Lord's supper. There is danger by the appearance of a meal that contains common, earthly nourishment to remain stuck on the material. In contrast, it must not be missed that in the appearance of this meal of the sacrament also can hide an element of inspiration. There is already on a superficial view of the meal something strange, something mystical that stirs the heart. The table is so white and quiet, it is so somber and small what here is offered to the guest. A haze of the spiritual rests over everything that happens here. A heavenly frame of mind prevails. So those who come not unprepared, but with a heart set at rest through self-examination, abandoning itself to the supper, receive an incitement to spiritual ascension even in seeing the meal.

The Lord's supper not only *requires* faith, but is also an *inspiration* to faith. This table, with what is on it, and by that which happens there—everything here cries out: Christ is on high, there is the wedding ceremony! Proclaim the death of the Lord *until he comes!*

This meager little piece of dry bread and this sip of wine that is presented to you says to you that you must not seek it here below, that you make yourself awfully poor if your heart clings to the bread and wine. You must not as Rome, and in part also Luther, seek Christ here in the signs, but with Calvin celebrate the Lord's supper soaring to heaven with the wings of faith. Christ comes to you with his Spirit so that by the power of that Spirit you should seek that which is above instead of that which is upon the earth.

If you have thoughtfully paid attention to this admonishment, then your heart is open for the genuine Lord's supper blessing. The form says: *That we may now be fed with the true heavenly bread, Christ Jesus,* let us not cleave with our hearts unto the external bread and wine. Here follows that the not cleaving to the external is a condition of being fed with the true heavenly bread.

Just then, as the soul relinquishes the temporary and detaches itself from the earthly, is the way made plain for the highway of the King. Then takes place the wonderful, the mutual, hidden union, uniting between the head and the members.

From here thus follows, that before the celebration of the supper there is not only a mood of passive expectation but truly also a spiritual *action* of the soul. There must be a *lifting up* from our side, if there is a true *descending* from God's side. Also here it is true: draw nigh unto God, and he will draw nigh to you.

In what now follows is also this, the Lord's obligation, revealed. The form continues: *not doubting, but we shall as truly be fed and refreshed in our souls through the working of the Holy Ghost, with his body and blood, as we receive the holy bread and wine in remembrance of him.*

God's requirement is here established: be not faithless, but believing. Doubt douses the Spirit's fire and cuts off the supply of the Lord's supper blessing. Doubt blinds the heavenly rays from shining through the window.

One would then ask—and rightly so—whether the supper could serve precisely to release the fragile soul from her doubting. Isn't here the order reversed when before the partaking is asked that which is granted by the Lord's supper?

Still, in the instructional portion it says that the *heavy* and *contrite* hearts of believers not be discouraged, but that we, even though *we have not perfect* faith, and have to strive daily *against the weakness of our faith*, nevertheless can be worthy participants of this heavenly food and drink.

Certainly, the form does not here contradict itself. It does not say that the soul that doubts may not go to this supper, but precisely at the moment of the summons to the table of the Lord, it encourages the heavy heart to let go of all doubt, and thus to be receptive to the Lord's supper blessing. Also here it is: he that hath, to him shall be given. According to the measure the sacrament is enjoyed in faith shall faith be enriched. You must not forget that the supper serves not only for strengthening the functional working of faith, but also by the working of faith to receive from Christ grace for grace, to become partaker in the riches of the covenant.

Indeed, far now from retraining the timid soul, the form encourages the fainthearted still not to doubt, but now, in this solemn moment of approaching [the supper], to receive the holy bread and drink in the full assurance of the promised grace.

Chapter Eight

THE DISTRIBUTION OF THE BREAD

1. THE SOLEMNITY OF THE FORMULARY

Now draws nigh the long-awaited and prepared-for moment, that the congregation sits down at the meal of her king. The actual celebration of the Lord's supper commences.

Certainly, what has happened so far, the reading of the form and entire foregoing service, makes up a part of the supper's celebration, but nevertheless the listening crowd has the feeling, as if now through a wide, high entrance they enter the bona fide, majestic, and mystical temple.

In the narthex, the soul is already tuned for adoration, and not only tuned as the strings of a harp, but also taught and instructed like a disciple who has listened at the feet of the teacher. The heart is now prepared and directs itself to God. The action from the side of the congregation begins. The believers desirous of salvation step (perhaps with hesitation) over the threshold to meet their God, to honor him in the celebration of the remembrance of Christ's atoning death, and in this celebration themselves to be spiritually strengthened and blessed.

How now shall the congregation perform such an extremely holy act in the right God-glorifying form?

So, we seize the opportunity to say something deeper and wider regarding the ritual of the celebration of the supper.

The form here itself provides us occasion in mentioning what the minister says *in the breaking and distributing the bread.*

335

Certainly, the form displays in this place a noteworthy, corresponding solemnity. The form does nothing else than provide the formula that is to be pronounced by the minister, with further indication of what will happen during the communion.

It could scarcely be simpler.

Truly here the form not only characterizes itself by solemnity in ritual instruction. In other formularies one finds the entire service outlined wherein the celebration of the supper takes place, not only the actual sacramental acts but everything that precedes. In the English liturgy, which in many respects is more finely nuanced than ours, one finds an example of this. Also, the form that was used in Zurich in 1525 provides more ritual. First there is an introduction in which the shameful and dangerous ceremonies are treated. Following that is a preface in which a few hints are provided for the proper celebration of the supper, for example, to which festive data this celebration is especially fitting; further that the men have to arrange themselves to the right and the women to the left; that "unleavened" bread and wine must be used; to avoid pomp, plates and goblets of wood must stand on the table, etc. And even further a service with various ceremonies is described that precedes the actual communion.[1]

That our form refrains itself from all such descriptions and limits itself to the necessities has good reason.

First of all, the Reformed church has a church order that deals with the most important provisions for the worship services, including that which is taken up regarding the Lord's supper. But the foremost reason is that in the Reformed church, in harmony with her character, much, indeed the greatest portion, of her worship is left to discretion (right of local usage). The Reformed only nail down in articles what is explicitly necessary for good order, and permit churches freedom in non-essentials.

This also pertains to the Lord's supper.

---

1   Daniël, *Codex Liturgicus*, 145ff.

One uniform regulation that prescribes every last ceremonial detail was not what the church wanted, and that is why all such requirements that would be restrictive are omitted from the form.

This can be proven from the acts of various synods.

The Synod of Dordt 1578 (art. 20): "In all non-essential things (regarding the Lord's supper) shall no churches be despised for making use of other ways of doing things."

Middelburg 1581 decided (art. 44): "Every church shall observe the Lord's supper in such a manner they judge to serve best for edification; understanding nevertheless, that the external ceremonies prescribed in God's word are not to be changed and all superstition must be avoided."

The Hague 1586 also made such a resolution and only added this restriction: "that after the conclusion of the sermon and the general prayers from the pulpit, the formulary for the supper, including its prayer, shall be read at the table."

The Synod of Dordt 1618–1619 determined literally the same as The Hague.

From these synodical decisions, it is crystal clear that not to be found in the ecclesiastical acts is a Lord's supper service regulated down to the fine details.

However, in general, through the centuries there has been a virtually uniform practice opened up and maintained in the churches, so that one almost would be able to speak of an unwritten law.

It is now our task also to discuss this unwritten law, besides permitting ourself the liberty to judge it as well according to personal insight.

2. THE CHARACTER OF THE REFORMED CELEBRATION OF THE LORD'S SUPPER

The Lord's supper celebration that is practiced in our churches clearly displays a kind that is unique. One could say that it most closely resembles the method that was birthed by the ancient Christian congregation.

The Scriptures do not provide a prescribed ordinance for the celebration of the Lord's supper, at least not in every detail, and neither in the apostolic church was there yet worked out a precisely defined rule, at least that has so far been discovered, so even in the early church emerged differences in the manner the Lord's supper was celebrated. However, there was nevertheless a basic form with a character that need not be doubted. The supper was, already at its institution and in the time following, celebrated in the use of both signs, bread and wine. These signs were officially distributed by the apostles, and soon by the pastors and teachers. The congregation received the sacrament as they sat around a table. In the case when believers were scattered the supper was indeed served in houses, but ordinarily the celebration was limited to the gathered congregation.

Gradually, there grew onto this sober solemnity a broadly expanded ceremonial that did not always harmonize with the original simplicity. There were special prayers pronounced, certain special gifts of money or goods brought by the congregation, a consecration or hallowing of the elements took place, and following communion was profession and thanksgiving.[2]

The church came squarely into conflict with the character of the supper's celebration when communion was entirely loosened from the ministry of the word, and an independent service for the Lord's supper was introduced in which the sacrificial theory triumphed. Before this service began, those who would not be partaking of the supper were "dismissed" with the words *missa concio,* i.e., the gathering dismissed (from which word *missa,* later the name *mis* originates).

Here is not the place to give consideration to the doctrine of the mass itself, which has been handled elsewhere, only to note that from the theory of the mass flows that the sacrament be implemented at

---

2 Biesterveld, *Het Gereformeerde Kerkboek,* 223.

least *daily*. In close connection with the doctrine of the sacrifice of the mass is the distinction between the clerics (spiritual ones) and the laity. Only the clergy could produce the miracle of the mass. What the priest did counted for the entire congregation. His administration of the sacrament contained power for him personally and all the people. There was thus related advantage (and without doubt this can also be proven) for the supper to be administered every day in the person of the priest. One communion a year could, if need be, suffice for the congregation itself.

The change that the Reformation effected existed primarily in a return to the simple, apostolic form. First was banished the extravagant pageantry and the luxurious ceremony under which Rome virtually buried the sacrament. But further came a change to the character of the Lord's supper celebration. The divorce between the clerics and laymen ceased. The congregation itself again extended her hand to the sacrament given her from God and desired personally to enjoy the heavenly food and drink.

However, there was not complete harmony among the Reformation leaders.

Luther not only held on yet to much of Rome's Lord's supper doctrine, but also to Rome's liturgy with respect to the supper. He kept the altar. Also, at first, he administered the sacrament in the Latin language. He maintained usage of the wafer, as well as a few ceremonies such as the lifting of the signs and making the sign of the cross.

To this moment, the Lutheran church, at least its state-approved churches, still hangs on to many rituals that remind one of Roman Catholic leftovers. Also, the English state church has a fuss of ceremony that maintains quite a distance from the apostolic form of the Lord's supper celebration. Also here is, though not an antithesis, indeed a noticeable distinction between clergy and laymen.

The Reformation in the Reformed churches was most decisive in these matters.

Without lapsing into the error of some Baptists who have abandoned all sacramental forms, the Reformed fathers threw overboard everything hinting of the impotent excesses and the priestly cult and returned the church back to the worship of the ancient church.

The main idea that was strongly preserved was that of the congregation as a gathering of believers. Indeed, in the Reformed church the administration of the sacrament was tied to the office so that it may appear that here does not take place merely a pious ceremony. The riches of the sacrament must come to expression in such a way that the minister as an *ambassador* of Christ distributes the signs of the covenant to the congregation. The gathered congregation must know that here blessings are poured out, miracles of grace are worked by Christ, the King.

However, in this same Lord's supper celebration there is no hint of priestly hierarchy or clerical privilege. At the Lord's supper are seated brothers and sisters from the same house. There is no greater or lesser. The minister, who first officially distributes, soon takes from the same loaf and drinks from the same cup as the seated guests.

That is why one can characterize the Reformed celebration of the Lord's supper as democratic.[3]

3. THE CYCLES OF THE LORD'S SUPPER CELEBRATION

In close connection with this particular character stands also the frequency (the number of celebrations) of the Lord's supper.

It appears that in the early Christian church just anointed with the Pentecost Spirit, the Lord's supper was celebrated in just about every gathering of the congregation. The heart beat with such turbulent urgency of love for the triumphant king that one felt continual need to proclaim the death of the Lord, thereby looking for his coming with heartfelt longing.

And also later, when the church had to buckle under the heavy

---

3 Kuyper, 461, etc.

yoke of persecution, the tormented flock of Christ knew no sweeter comfort than that resided in the Lord's table, that remembers not only the way of suffering of the surety, but also points to the impending victory of the bride of Christ. Even in Rome's catacombs, with smoking torches and under surveillance by spying eyes, Jesus' disciples refreshed themselves with the holy food and drink.

Rome's travesty facilitated a profound change.

On the one hand, the frequency of the Lord's supper celebration increased, then decreased. By restricting the *administration* of the sacrament mainly to the priest, there was *misadministration* every day; even in one day there would be repeated celebrations, as well as celebrations at special events.

But on the other hand, the *participation* of the supper became so seldom that one could speak of it as an exception. What else can you call a communion that took place in actuality only once a year around Easter?

From the beginning, the Reformed church designed another way.

They dared not latch on to a celebration of the supper in every congregational gathering as enjoyed by the apostolic church. Not without consequences does a church stretch beyond her spiritual capacity. The spiritual life does not allow itself to be coerced. It is a good that is given, a gracious good. A church to which believers came every Sunday to gather about the table of the Lord would of necessity lower the bar of the celebration of the supper. For many, the majority, to a degree it would become an exercise of habit so that there scarcely could be mention of a spiritual activity and spiritual blessing.

On the other hand, the Reformed church also was on guard for usage that was too sparse. Communion once a year estranges the congregation from the supper and by exaggerated trepidation and fear causes the blessing to go lost.

Therefore, it was quite generally decided to administer the supper four to six times a year. It was determined that before every Lord's supper celebration open preaching from the pulpit would take place, and also in intentional preaching the congregation would be prepared. This preaching would primarily intend to awaken the congregation to self-examination (from there the expression "preparatory sermons"). Usually this preparatory message was held on the Saturday before the day of the supper.

Also was the desirability expressed that there precede household visitations so that the members would be personally stirred to approach the table.

Finally, following the celebration, the congregation was required to assemble in a gathering for thanksgiving or application regarding that which had taken place.

It is certainly worth the effort here to bring to mind appropriate portions from the acts of the old synods. In the articles from the Assembly of Wezel 1568 (ch. 6, art. 6) we read: "We judge it highly useful, fourteen days prior to when the Lord's supper is to be observed, that it be publicly announced, so that especially members of the church can in the meantime prepare, and also that the elders can exercise their office in visitation of the districts in the right manner."

The Synod of Dordt 1578 (ch. 4, art. 16) determined:

> Prior to the administration of the sacrament, there shall be a sermon in which repentance, the self-examination of the person, his reconciliation with God and neighbor, and other such matters be dealt with. However, on the day of the sacrament, it is fitting to teach the people regarding the mystery of the sacrament, and to that end, to take up an appropriate text, unless the usual text can be appropriately suited. Nevertheless, the regular catechetical preaching shall proceed in the second service as usual.

Middelburg 1581 (art. 45) ordered that the Lord's supper, as much as possible, be observed every two months.

Dordt (1618–1619) established the same requirement and added that "it would be edifying, where opportunity allows, that the sacrament be observed on Good Friday, Pentecost Sunday, and Christmas" (art. 63).

By such stipulations, the celebration of the supper was recognized in the Reformed church as a special event, and the congregation sensed sufficiently the solemnity of this hour in order by it to be moved and edified inwardly, with the bi-monthly rhythm not so lengthy that there was a threat to be weaned from the supper.

Slowly, however, it was a common rule of thumb that the two-month cycle extended to three months. In outlying areas, the majority of Reformed churches observed the sacrament every three months. In some churches, the stretch extended even further. Indeed, in a few churches is the span so great that one might even speak of neglect or abandonment with respect to the supper.

The church in Amsterdam is one of the few churches that have restored in honor the practice of the forefathers, and so far as the experience of this writer extends, this institution is in every sense beneficial to the well-being of the congregation. It strikes us that the cycle of two months serves to be preferred above three months. First of all, the congregation experiences the supper more as an essential component of her spiritual life. The necessity and full meaning of the sacrament are expressed more strongly. The rhythm of the celebration is just often enough for it not to be diminished to a mere habit, but also not so infrequent that one is startled out of life's routine when the Lord's supper is announced.

Indeed, the congregation could not fare better if they would return to the ancient custom.

4. THE TABLE OF THE LORD

To proceed further in the details regarding the Reformed celebration of the supper, we must then first note that a unique essential of our worship is sitting down for a *meal*. The *table* is the focal point. Certainly, there are Reformed churches where the sacrament is administered to believers while they remain sitting in their respective places,[4] but the principle is nevertheless that it be a mealtime that displays similarity to what happens in our own homes.

Undoubtedly this form of celebration is the most scriptural because Jesus also sat with his disciples in the night when he instituted the sacrament, and the apostles also speak of the *table* of the Lord.

Truly, only when believers actually gather at the same table does it appear that *the congregation of the Lord* celebrates the supper, and this congregation is one people, one household. In the same way it would be in conflict with the character of a family if every member would eat separately; it also runs counter to the ordinance of ecclesiastical life if communion be commemorated without expression of the solidarity of the members. Over against the Lutheran practice (the participants follow each other in a line to the altar, where the minister distributes the signs one person at a time), the Reformed usage makes a much warmer, engaging impression. There is something indescribably compelling and uplifting as believers, frequently separated from each other by status, gift, and way of life, are now seen united around the same table, sitting close to each other like children from one home. Already mercy from this being together gives forth a sermon, a witness that we would not miss for anything. The table is an indispensable element in the Reformed celebration of the supper.

Moreover, it fits, from the influence of symmetry in everyday living, that the congregation *sit by each other* at the table.

In the ancient Reformed church, at first there lacked uniformity on this point. In some churches, people, in order to avoid disrespectful familiarity in the sacrament, did not dare to sit at the table. One feared that the meal would remind one too much of a meal at home.

---

4   In the north of our land there are churches in which only a small portion of the congregation gets to sit at the table and the rest of the guests are left to sit, albeit close behind, but in their places in the pew where the bread and wine is distributed to them. Certainly, this method is not recommended.

Indeed, it happened that out of deep respect for the sacrament one kneeled before the table to receive the signs of the covenant in this position.

Where the Reformed yet had the courage to seat himself at the table, this gave occasion for derision and defamation from the outsider. For example, in the Palatinate, it was said that the Reformed had degraded the supper to an ordinary meal, and at such meals spoons and forks were used to eat, one would toss bread to the dogs, and they toasted each other as if it were a festivity.[5]

Apparently, in order to take the edge off this slander, the elector forbade the use of the table, inserting himself heavy-handedly where the supper was still maintained. Only the dispersed believers in Frankenthal held on to the genuine method.

A decisive standpoint was not taken at the first ecclesiastical gatherings among the Dutch Reformed.

In the articles of Wezel (ch. 6, art. 15), "we intend that one can celebrate the Lord's supper just as well seated or standing."

The Synod of Emden (art. 21) determined: "Whether standing or sitting to receive the supper, we judge can go either way. Consequently, the congregations shall employ such manner that to them appears most fitting."

Dordt (1574) even gave the preference to standing (art. 76):

> The brothers judge that standing in the holding of the Lord's supper is the most fitting, but since the example of sitting is introduced into the church, we would hold that one cannot as yet desist from it without office. Nevertheless, in the meantime the people shall be taught that it is indifferent and after an appropriate time standing can place more decently.

The Synod of Dordt in 1578 made no decision, forbidding only the custom of kneeling at the supper to avoid superstition.

---

5   Barger, *Ons Kerkboek*, 225.

The Great Synod of Dordt was silent on this point.

It appears, however, that sitting at the table soon found its way into all the churches. And thus is the practice so ingrained that most do not know of any other practices that prevailed earlier.

The natural and healthy method has generally triumphed.

5. IS ONE TABLE POSSIBLE?

In line with this thought is also that the effort of the congregation must be directed toward a celebration of the supper where everyone is seated at *one* meal. In a home are occasional situations in which members eat at two or more "boards," but then this is still a separation of the family. And where the practice exists that the house-servants or the children eat separately, this practice is certainly not to be advanced as an example for the congregation of the Lord, where there is neither slave nor free.

In the springtime of the Christian church, believers undoubt-edly, as children of one Father, gathered together at the same table or at least (because soon their numbers increased) in the same celebration. We can be certain that the objective of the Reformed was also to restore this formal unity as much as possible. But the practice of life resisted the theory. The expanding flock of the Lord could no longer be gathered around one table. Churches built for the Roman worship service lent themselves with difficulty to the establishing of a table where hundreds could sit together at the same time. In the newly built churches, there was also soon a shortage of space. And so crept in the custom that a relatively short table was built in front of the pulpit to which the congregation came in various random groups.

Currently among our people, this divided Lord's supper celebration, even in the smallest villages, has become so usual that an attempt for change is no longer even imagined.

Nevertheless, such acquiescence is not to be praised. It is necessary that the congregation keep in view the shame and danger that hides in this form of Lord's supper administration and be continually mindful of improvement.

So there is first the objection that with the separation of the congregation into various groups there exists almost inevitably an undesirable division between men and women, between brothers who "amount to something" in the church and the ordinary people, between them who are certain in their faith and the fainthearted ones. Where according to Reformed principle also in the life of the church as much as possible the bond of the family is maintained, by the divided celebration of the supper members of the family are separated from each other. Men and women, parents and children, are not going together, but are classified and hardly see each other there. Hereby undoubtedly much of the blessing, specifically the binding-togetherness-power of the supper, is lost. Instead of cultivating as strongly as possible an outcome that we are all together one body, that we "by this same Spirit may also be united as members of one body in true brotherly love," this method of dividing rather promotes a classification that is in conflict with the character of the Christian church.

And another objection that we should not underestimate is that by the continual repetition of the same supper administration, the service is drawn out to weariness, and what is worse, the solemnity itself of its glorious and edifying working is lost. If a liturgical deed is repeated five, even ten times one after the other, it cannot but lose in power. Feeling begins to deaden. One longs for the end to come. And not the least, the administrator of the sacrament finds it difficult to remain fresh, that he not end up expressing the words of the sacrament in a mechanical routine. From one Lord's supper ceremony wherein everyone could experience one act with his whole heart would undoubtedly result a greater and more fervent spiritual influence.

Where it then finally ends up, naturally with numerous tables lined up behind each other, is that it is very difficult to prevent an inconvenient crowd or exhausting waiting. Usually our churches are not so huge and grandly constructed that one can escape interference from another. And also, where escape is unnecessary, yet remains the difficulty that supper participants will run into, for whom there is no place and they must go back to their pew or wait until the next table offers an opportunity. Especially those who have visited the administration of the supper in the large cities understand what difficult situations can happen in this regard.

Kuyper had it right in the following outburst on this manner of commemorating the Lord's supper:

> When the number of believers is still small, as in the first Christian congregation, then everyone still can be seated together at one meal. But when the number of believers to seat reaches in the hundreds, the matter becomes more difficult and becomes virtually undoable with hundreds to thousands to tens of thousands. What now has been substituted, namely, that successively again and again small groups of 80 or at the most 100 persons after each other would sit at the same table is naturally only a stop-gap measure out of necessity, but whereby much of the edification, captivation, and symbolism is lost. Only a *few* sit together then, and no longer the *entire* congregation. That ten, twelve-time tiring repetition of the same ceremony is always tiring and ends by weakening the solemn impression. And time limitations force a certain hastiness. One sits for no more than a couple minutes and then must again make room for the next ones. And without now taking into account the long waiting and much pressure that this way of doing it brings with it, is there thus in this manner of celebrating the supper always something that is left unsatisfied, and fails to reach the ideal of the entire flock of believers, without chasing or haste, quietly and serenely seated at one communal meal.[6]

---

6   Kuyper, *E Voto*, III:99.

In this same connection, Dr. Kuyper warns that with this divided manner of celebrating the supper, most of all one must watch out for a division of the members of the congregation, which would be in conflict with the character of the Christian church.

> The arrangement of tables for men and women, old and young, and especially for more or less substantial persons not only makes no sense, but must itself be repudiated. That a father and mother who come together with their son and daughter to the Lord's supper cannot be seated together, but must be separated as husband and wife, brother and sister, is in conflict with the basis for the Lord's supper. And that, as in most places, first is to make plenty of room for the gentlemen and ladies, in order afterwards to allow ordinary members of the congregation entrance, is a *worldly* phenomenon at the Lord's supper that may never be glossed over. Granted, the ideal can never be reached in our limited situations on earth, the matter yet remains that that basic idea of the sacrament of the Lord's supper should as much as possible be honored and preserved, and the basic idea is that the supper is before all things a *meal*, and at that meal the congregation sits down as they are in Christ, in whom there is neither man nor woman, rich nor poor.[7]

In his book on worship, Dr. Kuyper grants concession to the practice that he virtually renounces as the ideal communal celebration of the supper and will have the church buildings arranged so that the Lord's supper table stands prepared on a platform in view of the entire congregation.

> There are indeed experiments in the direction of a table around which 400 or 500 persons could gather at the same time, but such did not win the day. It made the church look

---

7   Kuyper, *E Voto,* III, 100.

rather odd. It was time-consuming. The service did not go smoothly. What the minister said could hardly be understood at the other end of the table. It was less than appealing to look into the backs of others. And also, by far and away, most churches did not lend themselves to it.[8]

That is why Dr. Kuyper's final judgment is: "Most likely, therefore, for now, we will stay with the time-honored custom of the past three and a half centuries... People are used to this and have settled for it."[9]

Although also according to our conviction the now already centuries-engrained custom since early times indeed cannot be changed, it nevertheless strikes us as advisable for the congregation to continue to point out the practical and principle objections against the present manner of the celebration of the supper. However much the other method may be hampered by difficulties, it remains the ideal that must be pursued. And that this ideal is more closely to be approximated than what is happening in the present usage, nonetheless need not earnestly be doubted. When the eyes are once opened to the objectionable in the now-customary form, one will easily overcome the practical objections that are brought against the ideal method, whenever any feast is celebrated, in much smaller localities than our churches with a hundred and more guests are gathered at one supper. In our large city churches, they could, *if they so desired*, without much difficulty, in the auditorium for example, set up a table in the length [of the place], a table that could accommodate the gathering of say two hundred guests. By such a table (that could perhaps best be in an oval shape) would already much be won. The entire administration would be finished with two or three table settings. And the appearance would certainly not be less edifying than it is now.

---

8   Kuyper, *Onze Eeredienst*, 471.
9   Kuyper, *Our Worship*, 270.

Certainly, the system that Dr. Kuyper in his *Our Worship* proposes, namely the Lord's supper table placed on the podium, is indeed appealing, also symbolically instructive, but by this method the danger of division shall be sooner intensified than lessened, seeing that a platform as a rule does not extend to the full width of the church, and thus there will be even less room than already at the present tables. Perhaps that is why this solution can be discovered, that the Lord's supper table on the podium remain only as a symbol, and that in addition, in the auditorium of the church, as large a table as possible can be built for actual use.

And as long as the old way of doing things continues, let one take measures that reduce problems to a minimum. Very appropriate is certainly the proposal of Dr. Kuyper to hand out numbers at the entry of the church so everyone can know to which table he has access. "If a table has no more than fifty places to sit, then not more than fifty cards should be available whereon is printed: *First table, second table, third table*, etc."[10] This manner offers at the same time the advantage that members of one family can go together to the same table, having arrived at the same time into the church building and having taken cards for the same table. In addition, Dr. Kuyper councils that to diminish tension and agitation, the guests on the one side, e.g., the right side, must allow for access, and on the other side must allow for return.

The last rule is in some churches already applied. In the church of Amsterdam, as well as others, this method has already been followed for quite some time with good results.

To further meet the objections that exist regarding a completely divided Lord's supper celebration, also the following serves as a recommendation.

In larger congregations with more than five tables, one shall clarify matters not before the sermon but at the beginning of the reading

---

10 Kuyper, *Onze Eeredienst*, 472.

of the form. We will soon come back to this but desire now to point out that there is no earnest objection in principle against this way of doing things, as the practical need wins the day.

Further it is desirable that instead of a (naturally usually the longer) address at the table should be reading from the Scripture of not more than a couple verses. The administration of the Lord's supper remains the main thing.

Also, it is good, to prevent too great an accumulation of people, that not only in the mornings but also in the evenings is offered the opportunity for participating in the Lord's supper. In places where there is more than one church building, the sacrament can be served on two consecutive Sundays in various churches.

Finally, the congregation should be admonished from the pulpit and in the bulletin as much as possible to come to the supper in an appropriate manner so that the genuine congregational character of the celebration results. Initially, due to the newness of the matter, this way of doing things awakens a measure of surprise, but before long shall the congregation understand and value this administration of the supper as the most biblical and wholesome.

6. THE PRECEDING SERVICE

Not a word is given in the formulary regarding how the service that precedes the Lord's supper should be arranged. The framers are apparently proceeding from the supposition that this service in form does not differ from a regular service, only somewhat briefer than usual. In other liturgies, e.g. that of the English, sometimes down to minutia are prescribed various ceremonies that must precede the administration of the sacrament. The Reformed felt no need for such. They viewed the sacrament as an addition to the administration of the word. A distinctive service of its own for the sacrament hardly fits in their framework.

Nevertheless it can be profitable that we examine this matter, also apart from a certain tradition, and pose the question which method best fulfills not merely the demand of the principle, but also that of the practical.

In general, the Reformed hold firmly to the principle that the sacrament contains no other content than that of the gospel. The word is primary, the sacrament secondary. Out of necessity, a Christian could do without the sacrament but not the word. And seeing that the sacrament mainly does nothing other than to grant better understanding of the promises of the gospel (according to the confession), it is according to good order that there is not a special service of the sacrament but that its administration be always paired with the administration of the word. And when these are joined together, it speaks for itself that it is logical for the word to go before the sacrament.

From ancient times then, this rule was also followed in the Reformed church. Even various synods have adopted specific regulations concerning this.

So decided the Synod of Dordt of 1574 (art. 74): "Before the holding of the supper, one shall also propose to expound in that principle of the church a suitable text, which services for the supper and explain the mysteries therein contained, unless the text, which is next in order can be fittingly adapted to this."

The Synod of 1578 determined (sec. 4, art. 16): "On the day of the Lord's supper itself, it shall be fitting to instruct the people regarding the sacrament, especially regarding the mystery of the supper, and to that end take up an appropriate text, unless the usual text can be appropriately directed to this."

Also it is known that Calvin preceded with a sermon that was related to the sacrament. For the same reason is the form made and intended by him.

We need not doubt for a moment that in general the preference is that the celebration of the supper follow the preaching of the gospel.

In practice, however, weighty objections arise.

According to church usage, the service in which the Lord's supper is celebrated is preceded by a special service, "wherein repentance, the self-examination, and reconciliation with God and one's neighbor" are handled. This is the so-called preparatory or examination sermon. Naturally, the Lord's supper itself is dealt with in the sermon so that it is indeed difficult to avoid repetition when on the day of the supper itself this sacrament is also at large. Even more, there is the danger of repetition and thereby exhausting the audience because also in the Lord's supper form the examination and mystery of the supper is handled. The form is a brief unfolding of the doctrine of Scripture regarding the celebration of the supper. So upon three consecutive occasions the same theme is discussed. Are not folks getting a bit here "too much of a good thing"?

But there is more.

In his *Our Worship*,[11] Dr. Kuyper correctly points out that one is truly in harmony with the principle (the ministry of the word before the ministry of the sacraments) when one does not, as up to now, suffice with a brief sermon that in reality is nothing other than a meditation. In order to shorten the service as much as possible, the minister usually makes the sermon that precedes as short as possible. He indeed selects a text, but then with reference more to this text speaks a brief warm chat than that he, as otherwise, serves the word. We agree with Dr. Kuyper that for a genuine administration of the word (under which we must still understand an exposition, doctrinal explanation, and application of the word) certainly almost an hour is necessary. Practically speaking, with multiple separate Lord's supper administrations, this is undoable as the service would certainly last three hours.

If, however, the minister limits himself to the "warm chat," there is in no way a preservation of the principle. One could better appeal directly to the form that is read beforehand, for in this is compliance

---

11 Kuyper, *Our Worship*, 279.

with the demand of the church, "teach the people the mystery of the supper," better than any minister of the word summarizes this.

To overcome these objections, Dr. Kuiper proposes to allow simply a reading of the form. After listing no less than four reasons why objection against preceding preaching exists (first, the service lasts too long; second, the form must be read too hurriedly; third, many put the short sermon above the administration of the supper; fourth, there is repetition), he says:

> For that reason it seems preferable not to combine the two services [i.e., of the word and the sacrament] but to limit the service to a brief introductory meditation, which is followed by a calm, quiet, well-intoned reading of the form. Following this, the people are invited immediately to the table. This makes for a shorter service that will proceed a lot more calmly and even with six or seven tables, will end within the normal time span. This improved method has been adopted by a number of churches and has not led to complaints; on the contrary, it seems to have been well received.[12]

We can confirm this from our own experience. In the church of Amsterdam, this way of celebrating the Lord's supper has been established for the last few years. Quite naturally were people here compelled to the practice. Imagine fourteen tables for the supper, with yet a preceding sermon to take place! But apart from the iron necessity that here pressured the elimination of the preceding sermon, they who organize this service testify that there is nothing unedifying or impoverished in it. Especially when some work is made regarding the reading of the formulary is this service precisely something appealing, something solemn. Now for once, it is not the minister engaged with the word, but the church with her tried-and-tested word that is the golden tongue. Now there is the serene idea

---

12 Kuyper, *Our Worship*, 280.

that everything is progressing in an orderly and timely manner. And because there is no sermon, from the beginning there is concentration on the sacrament.

Of course, this service requires a certain ecclesiastical-spiritual level of the congregation. There is sometimes with some little souls the idea as if the word from the formulary takes a back seat to the freely spoken word. In their eyes, a prayer from a form can never be a means of grace. And so, a sermon from a form rolls over their heads, coming across as a dry, mechanical word.

It is therefore necessary that the congregation also has a feel for the beauty and legitimacy of the worship service outside the preaching. And so if they are not getting there, they must be nurtured to it. They must mature and become more mature. They must not only be willing to be passive (as is mainly the case when the word is administered for them), but they must also be active (what is necessary for the rest of the worship service).

Without valuing the Amsterdam congregation to the detriment of another congregation, we can testify that in general we experienced the service with only the Lord's supper celebration as overall favorable, indeed valuable. One need not so much insist that this is how it must be, but for myself it felt that this service has much to recommend. The service without a sermon is rich enough to be edifying and blessed.

Naturally remains the question if also in services where there are only a few (say two or three) tables that this way deserves recommendation.

We answer that a truly good, purposeful sermon is never to be despised. Whenever we servants of the word were in charge of our task, in everything, a freely spoken word would indeed be in place at the supper meal. But experience teaches that in most sacred moments, the free word now and again detracts more than introduces. That is why in our opinion (while fully preserving the Reformed principle: the pulpit at the center!), the worship service must be developed, and the liturgy must be enriched and refined, more than has happened so far. In his already much-cited book, *Our Worship*, Dr. Kuyper accomplished thereto a great, more than one way, successful endeavor. Too strong a reaction against Rome has impoverished our ecclesiastical life more than it needs and ought to be.

Especially at the Lord's supper administration is there opportunity for the liturgy to be broadened and apportioned. Dr. Kuyper proposes a vision that we here gladly cite. After first having lauded and reproduced the English liturgy, Dr. Kuyper continues:

> Without intending to suggest that we should completely conform to the English example, we should acknowledge that we lack an important treasure in our worship service, and that the minister must supply this missing element. However, it is not an indifferent matter how that is done. The service must begin with a short prayer or *Votum*, which should be prescribed in the form. Then the law must be read, so that before approaching the supper one can humble oneself before God in penitence. A simple reading of the law is not sufficient, but it should be followed by a prayer for grace. Then the minister will read a portion of Scripture in which the promise of that grace in the name of God goes out to the congregation, with the congregation responding in song expressing its acceptance of that grace, followed by the believers' profession of their faith in the words of the Apostles' Creed. In this way the congregation will approach her God in the sanctuary. In God's house, she will be humbled by her guilt; in that humiliation her God speaks his grace to them; she would receive that grace with rejoicing and gratitude and declare it in her profession of faith. Thus the communion between God and his people comes to expression; this communion indeed must be present to fulfill the purpose of the Lord's supper.[13]

---

13 Kuyper, *Our Worship,* 283.

Undoubtedly, an expansion of the liturgy like this would make for an important advancement in the service. It is undeniable that the Lord's supper service as it is held now, when it is commemorated without a preceding sermon, would be indeed quite somber and requires an awakening of the spiritual life. Certainly, even in this somber form, as we have witnessed in our own experience, the service can be edifying. But whenever the celebration of the sacrament, without offense to the principle, can be lifted to a higher liturgical level, this may not be disregarded.

As long as the liturgical service is not improved, in small churches where the service concludes in one or two tables, a preceding sermon, as long as it moves along the lines of the Lord's supper celebration, would still be difficult to do without.

7. READING THE FORM

The reading of the form, when the sermon is omitted, so not following the introductory prayer and song, forms a supreme weighty element in the Lord's supper service. The form is a fitting and heartfelt styled liturgical component, containing moving passages, and therein it is perfectly calibrated to touch the heart of the congregation, but a first requirement is that it is read out loud with the correct intonation. Avoided must be the resounding roaring, as the rapid rattling off of the form. As a liturgical presentation it must be neither recited nor lectured. The minister must merely attempt in the simple reading of the document to speak from his *heart*. He must bring warmth, loftiness with the *tone*, and this is not as easy as may appear. Unless the minister possesses an innate gift, he cannot naturally fulfill this without earnest practice. For with all its beauty for which the form is noted, it has (from a liturgical point of view) difficult moments. For example, the passage in which the various grievous sins are listed is not easy to express. And similarly, even more difficult is that sterling section wherein the passion of Christ with its fruits is described. To do justice to this portion of the form, a restrained energy and sensitive intonation are necessary.

Further must be kept in mind that the formulary presents special requirements due to its fairly great length. If the form is not read at too great a tempo, reading it out loud requires not much less than a half-hour. Where most of the congregation has taken in the language of the form from childhood on, the liturgist must not take for granted the task to captivate the gathering for such a long time with such a well-known piece. This task requires his entire personality, the best of his ability.

Provided that these criteria are fulfilled, the reading of this emotional as well as intellectually rich piece results in an uncommonly edifying influence. It gives the congregation pure spiritual enjoyment and leads her into the proper Lord's supper frame of mind. It introduces a mystical affection into the congregation that engrosses the soul for a long time.

A question of a purely formal nature hereby is where the form should be read, from the pulpit or at the table? Tangentially, we have already indicated the first as preferable,[14] but here is the place to devote attention intentionally to this matter, which already has come up as a question.

It appears that in the church of the Reformation it was customary to read the form at the table. The Synod of Dordrecht of 1618–1619 (art. 62) stipulated that "after the conclusion of the sermon and the congregational prayer from the pulpit, the form for the Lord's supper, together with its prayer, shall be read at the table." This matter was not left to the freedom of the churches but was explicitly prescribed as a requirement of the church order.

However, the churches themselves did not adhere to this regulation. As a rule, the form is read from the pulpit. By exception it happens at the table, and then only to the extent that only the *Sursum Corda* that immediately precedes the communion, and moreover the prayer of thanksgiving, are read [at the table].

---

14 *Supra,* VII:11.

What is the cause for this?

Apparently, one is soon met with practical difficulties. In many church buildings, it is difficult for oneself to be understandable from any other place than the pulpit. Also, often the minister, when standing at floor level, is visible only to a small portion of the congregation, something that brings with it a disagreeable situation both for him and for the congregation. It came across oddly that the form was read at the table and that the first part of the service was led from the pulpit. Hereby came an inadvertent bifurcation in the liturgical movement. The impression is given that the first part counts for all and the other action only for the communicants.

Consistency would then also require that the entire Lord's supper service be performed from the table. The question, however, is which consistency is preferred, and we do not hesitate to choose that as much of a service as possible occur from the pulpit. For the most part, our churches are not set up so that one can allow himself any freedom in the area of acoustics. Also the fact must be reckoned with that a portion of the gathered congregation does not partake of the Lord's supper, namely the younger members who have not yet made profession of faith. By administrating the service from the table, one could well give the impression that it does not concern this portion of the congregation, and all who do not approach the table may as well leave. The abuse that now grievously prevails in many places, namely the failure to participate at the Lord's supper, would be promoted even more by this. Finally, the reading of the form at the table does not have the desired symbolic and liturgical effect because the Lord's supper celebration is divided. Thus, one must choose whether to read the form at a table that is entirely empty or to give the reading of the form a place at the first table. Naturally, the first is empty and senseless. It is an ice-cold display of the minister only to be seen reading before a large table where not one guest is seated. When the latter happens, one meets with the unfairness that the form was read at the table only for the first guests, and members following are excluded from this position of privilege (because that is what it is considered).

For these reasons, in our opinion, preference is given to the service from the pulpit, a preference that is even more pronounced when, as described above, the liturgy of the Lord's supper service is expanded.

It is not at all for these reasons that Dr. Kuyper in his book on worship pleads for the reading of the form from the pulpit. He says, among other things:[15]

> The formulary must be read while the minister is still in the pulpit. The place from where the introduction is given is also the place for the reading of the form. If, therefore, to the arrangement of a new church building is of that nature that the minister gives the introduction at the table, also the form goes out from the table. Nevertheless, if he begins, like we must in our old buildings, by climbing into the pulpit, and from there giving the introduction, then he must not leave the pulpit to read the rest of the form before the table. The introduction and the form are a unit. The matter is mainly this that the introduction and the form count for all who shall be seated, and certainly not only for the first table. Because now the minister reaches *all* only from the pulpit, so the reading of the form in its first four parts find place from the pulpit. Then everyone in the entire church build-ing is able to hear, follow, and join in. Everyone experiences directly that, for example, the fourth part, the faith prayer, is not only for the first table but for all the tables together.

And then further this positive assertion:

> Nothing other than the administration itself must and may take place at the table. This is the reason why the words of

---

15 Kuyper, *Onze Eeredienst*, 496ff.

the institution properly so-called are there also repeated at each table, but everything that precedes and follows the administration is directed to *everyone* who is present, who are partakers of the Lord's supper; and that broad crowd can only be reached for hearing from the pulpit. That is also why it is to be rejected that the minister remains at the table after the last table and from there offers the word of praise and prayer of thanksgiving. Also, those concern all who are present, who sat down, and, therefore, they need to be given from the pulpit.

It is our desire that this not-unimportant matter be established by the churches with a uniform regulation, and indeed in the sense of the sufficient grounds provided above.

8. THE HOLY FOOD AND DRINK

There stands the table before the eye of the congregation, yet still and empty, as if expecting the holy activity that shall occur. The table itself is expansive and firmly built, but yet impressive in its simplicity because it is covered with a white tablecloth. Preferably one takes this lovely and radiant cloth to enhance the external decorum. Some are of the opinion that Reformed worship requires not only solemnity, but specially paucity and complete absence of beauty. This conception is understandable (by way of reaction against Rome's excessive lavishness) but not to be approved. It is more Baptist than Reformed. The Reformed will allow the gifts of nature to serve the work of grace. John the Baptist indeed appeared in ragged pilgrim's garments, but Jesus walked in coat without seam and attended the wedding feast.

Thus, the Lord's supper may not be ostentatious, but for the rest may be arranged in as nice and respectable a manner as possible. From of old were mostly used pewter Lord's supper utensils. Dr. Schotel notes that the table (which was covered with a pure linen tablecloth) used to have "three pewter plates (dishes) setting on it, one larger with a common loaf of white bread cut in large slices beforehand and set between two other empty, also large, plates on both sides, and in a square surrounding the plates were four large cups."[16] Later, plates and cups of pure gold were used. Eventually, it became more common to use silver, or at least silver-plated metal. Only the poorer churches continued to use pewter utensils. Also here is the rule of thumb that the church, while avoiding extravagance at the table of the Lord, gave the best they could to King Jesus. Silver goes best with white linen and therefore is preferable. Dr. Kuyper maintains:

> If possible, it is advisable that the utensils be made of silver. Not that this is essential to a proper serving of the sacrament; an earthenware plate and a glass cup are just as useful. But in desire for reverence for the supper preference is given to silverware, and rightly so. The form of the administration must be and remain this, that it is Christ' table, that Christ serves his meal, and that thus the utensils of the holy supper also bear a royal character. Should the means be lacking to acquire silver utensils, one can use silver-plated utensils, or indeed an earthenware plate and a glass would suffice, as long as no one assumes a higher holiness in this kind of simplicity, as some of the Baptists in North America do. Silver utensils best satisfy and are most harmonious with the regal worth of him who gives us the sacrament.[17]

Usually, as long as the service has not yet begun, this supper tablesetting remains under a cover. If this is not particularly needed to preserve the bread and utensils from dust, one should preferably see the cover removed at the beginning, because the supper then speaks more to the congregation right from the beginning.

---

16 G. D. J. Schotel, *De Openb. Eeredeinst der Ned. Herv. Kerk, in de 16e, 17e en 18e eeuw* [*The Public Worship of the Dutch Reformed Church*] (Haarl.: Kruseman, 1870), 488.

17 Kuyper, *Our Worship*, 281–88; *Onze Eeredienst*, 488.

While the congregation is singing, the minister descends from the pulpit and goes to the table, followed by the other serving office-bearers. Usually these servers are two elders, who have oversight of the approaching communicants and therefore are seated at both ends of the table, and two deacons, who offer assistance with the service of the bread and cup. Among other things, the latter take care that when the bread plates reach the end of the table after the serving, they are brought back to the middle, and that the cups, after *first wiping the rims clean* (also this is Reformed!), are refilled and replaced upon the table. Provided that one not think that this service specially belongs to the office of deacons because Acts 6 speaks of table service (which has nothing to do with the Lord's supper), there is no objection that the deacons do this work. Preference probably requires that also this service be directed by the overseers of the congregation.

The first thing that the minister of the sacrament and his assistants must do is to prepare the plates and cups for usage. He himself takes the bread that is cut in long strips and breaks them into pieces.

Sometimes a question arises regarding the elements served at the holy meal. In the early days of the Reformation, in some churches unleavened bread, crackers, indeed even wafers were used. However, in general, bread became an established usage. The idea was that as much as possible the supper must reflect an essential meal. That is why it came to be that bread replaced the Catholic wafer, as bread serves in daily life as a means of nutrition. In a few churches, it was still insisted that this bread, following Jesus' Lord's supper, be unleavened. However, also on this point a common usage soon prevailed, namely, that of leavened bread. The opinion was right that Jesus, who took the available *unleavened* bread of the passover, did not intend to establish an example for the New Testament church.[18]

As a rule, one chooses this bread in its most noble form, namely white bread. Some early synods prescribed that the bread must be

---

18 Bjiesterveld, *Het gereformeerde kerkboek*, 245.

sliced into large pieces. A few ministers, however, took the entire loaf, which was unsliced, and broke it into pieces.[19] Currently, most generally in use are small, long strips that were sliced beforehand.

Usually the minister breaks some of the bread right before he pronounces the sacramental formula so that the dishes are supplied and the circulation of the plates can begin immediately when the guests are seated. This is not at all in the form. According to good order, the formula must first be pronounced before commencement with the breaking. As the times have dictated, for practical reasons, however, men have generally preferred the former. This is a recent evidence of how the celebration of the supper that is divided in many ways pressures to haste and therefore to informality.

The consistory must also see to it that the amount of bread is not measured miserly. An incident has been made known to us that in a large city congregation one of the elders came to the minister during the service begging, "Don't break it in such large pieces, or there won't be enough to go around." Toward the end there was still too little, and the shortage had to be supplied from the private pantry of the custodian.

Such situations cause distress when it could be easily prevented. There must be ample supply so that the minister is not forced by economy to break the pieces so small that the idea of a meal is entirely lost. The piece of bread must be large enough that the guest is aware he is eating something. One should also see to it that the bread is of good quality, baked thoroughly. In our everyday life, we never eat dry bread. When someone receives dry bread at the supper, which is clayish and under-baked, then it is difficult for the communicant to eat, and this does not stir edification. In general, the writer's experience in these matters has not been favorable. In many cases in the administration of the supper, he has had to set aside pieces of bread that were unsavory.

Also, with regard to the wine, God's word provides no particular

---

19 Schotel, 426ff.

ordinance. There have been controversies over whether Jesus used fermented wine or whether he would have used grape juice. The prohibitionists tend to choose the latter. Although Jesus may have also used unfermented wine, so we have no particular prescription for us there. The churches, and rightly so, have deemed that wine must be taken; that is used in daily life. Required of the sacrament is that as much as possible it reflects everyday life. Dr. Kuyper confirmed quite precisely the stipulation that the bread and wine should not occupy the attention, nor distract the mind in any respect.[20]

Naturally, the church is free to choose the type of wine. With an eye toward the weak and sensitive dispositions, recommended is to get a mild, sweet sort of wine. Generally, such wine is used in our churches. One even calls this *Lord's supper wine.*

For the rest, it must be mentioned that our fathers were never narrow when it came to these smaller formalities. When the signs were not present in the usual form, they did not hesitate even to use alternative materials, such as *water* in place of wine when necessary. In exceptional circumstances, for the sake of the weaker brethren, they substituted grape juice for wine. At the Synod of Kampen in 1620, the question was handled: "How one should deal with such persons who are of a nature so wholly to have an abhorrence of wine that that they cannot tolerate the slightest taste of it." This question was considered important enough to be considered at a national synod. This synod was not held, but the gathering already judged that "if poured-out grape juice is to be obtained, and the person can be helped with it, that such take place."[21]

9. THE APPROACHING PARTICIPANTS

During the congregational singing, the first guests come forward. For them who see in this approaching something more than a ceremony, it is indeed a soul-gripping moment. In our Reformed worship

20 Kuyper, *Onze Eeredienst,* 489.
21 Barger, *Ons Kerkboek,* 227–28.

services, the member of the congregation is usually scantly active. The minister of the word does almost everything, and the member listens, pays attention, receives. But now the congregational member himself goes into action. He rises from his seat and in front of everyone makes his way to the front, in order to approach the sacred meal. This standing and approaching is already an *act* of profession. It is a sacred manifestation before Christ the King. He who so publicly draws near thereby shows and testifies to his faith, that Jesus is the Lord, and that only in his sacrificial death is salvation.

It requires a measure of self-control and composure during this going-forward not to think about the people who see us, but about the glorious purpose for which we have come. The action of the Lord's supper participant may not be an impulsive moment, not a result of emotional pressure, but it must be an act of obedience to God's command, an act of his own person, of his *life.* Especially the guest at Jesus' table must be on guard that he not act for the sake of man, the crowd. There is a mysterious influence in the masses, and there is danger that people, also Christian people, be driven to an action by this silent power, that he does something not out of personal responsibility but *because others are doing it*, or to let others see that he is doing it. Indeed, with the gathering of God's people, there is something appealing and inspiring, especially as the Lord's supper works the mystical power of the communion of the saints. But in this communion is only place for us when first the plea of redemption and of the choice of faith is settled in our own person.

Thus, the approach of the Lord's supper participant requires a particular posture. Perhaps we could call this soul-posture *earnest-gladness.* Naturally, according to the disposition of a Christian is a tendency to display either the earnest or the joyful element of faith, but yet it is necessary that there be something of both in the heart. The table where the believer approaches is the holy remembrance meal of Jesus' bitter suffering—that is why the soul must be disposed to *earnestness.* However, this same table testifies to a complete atonement for all our sins and prophesies eternal joy at the wedding feast of the Lamb—that is why the soul, filled with hope and joyful, in a festive disposition, must seek the Lord of the supper.

In the Reformed church, there has not always been agreement with respect to the opinion as to which disposition of the soul is best. To judge according to our Lord's supper form, earnestness dominates over gladness. After all, more than once it speaks of contrite and afflicted hearts. Only after the supper in the thanksgiving is a clear, trumpet sound of joy in God.

It certainly pleads for the deep earnestness of our fathers, a comprehensive soberness, that they often ate and drank nothing at home before the supper, but came to the table of the Lord not having eaten or drunk anything at all. This is the main reason why, actually contrary to the character of the *evening meal* and *night meal*, this sacrament is, nevertheless, commemorated in the morning. It is intended, primarily with an eye on the weaker brethren, not to demand a fasting for the whole day. Motivation for this fasting was that "no earthly food may be tasted before the heavenly food."[22]

There was not unanimity with respect to perspectives on the character of the Lord's supper. There was one "party" that tended toward the somber conception. With these, the remembering of the death of Christ was predominant. On the day of the Lord's supper, the city or village appeared to have sunk into mourning. The communion participants arrived clothed in black, the men in formal garb and cape, the women with the black church hats over their heads. Even the church building mourned, as on these days the organ was not heard. Some even went so far "that days before they carried on as mournfully, approached the table frequently with a sad mood, gloomy countenance and trembling hand, as if they went in order to escape punishment from the heavenly judge rather than to receive grace and salvation from the God of their soul, and their atoning Father in Christ."[23]

---

22 Schotel, 422ff.
23 Ibid., 425.

Among the Cocceians, some tended to the opposite concep-tion. In distinction from the other church members, those who did not work the day before the Lord's supper but separated themselves for self-examination and preparation, these dedicated themselves to their ordinary business that day. They would have nothing of an earnest testing or reflection. For them it was merely about a passing impression of ceremony.

However, extremes like these were seldom. In general, it can be demonstrated "that our fathers were level-headed as a whole, well-grounded, regular and faithful participants of the body and blood of Christ." And with a joyful heart, and a face that was not puckered, as to a wedding feast, they approached without inhibition and in full assurance the reception of the pledges and overtures of love.[24]

It can also be testified of our current Lord's supper celebration that the extremes of somberness and visible superficiality are rare. There are those on whom you can clearly read a sadness, indeed, those who do not hold back the tears. And others act by their disposi-tion as if not much is going on within the inner chamber of the heart. But in general, there is an unexaggerated earnestness in the attitude of the Lord's supper guests, which is fitting at this ceremony. Perhaps we fall a bit short in displaying the pure joy that is connected with the full assurance of faith. In the quiet, powerful assurance of faith we are certainly in general behind our fathers.

There also may well be reason to complain that in our cele-bration of the supper there is too little attention given to external decorum. We do not prefer mourning attire as was formerly worn. But yet it must also be evident in our attire that one sits down at a *spiritual* meal, of high and holy earnestness. It does not provide a good feeling and gives offense to others when men as well as women arrive in the latest fashions, in clothes that draw attention. It is not at all uncommon that our young daughters approach Jesus' table in brightly colored blouses and ostentatious head coverings. Also, one

24 Ibid., 424ff.

sees that our young men come in an outfit in which they would not dare show up as a guest at a family meal.

The deficiency in decorum that in general provides our church reasons to complain is especially annoying at the Lord's supper. Precisely the Reformed, who recognize and confess the connection between the natural and the spiritual, must be an example in these matters, and their external appearance should reflect an inward beauty with which Christ has clothed his bride, the church.

Also, let there be a taking care that in the seeking of a seating place, the external form is not damaged. In earlier times there was an awkward stampede to the table, instigated by the foolish desire to sit as closely as possible to the minister, with the goal of receiving the bread and wine from his hand. One viewed this as a special spiritual privilege in which one could take pride.[25] The pressure to commandeer such a "place of honor" is certainly in our days no longer much perceived. Sometimes there is an urge and haste in the tight lines that evidence a shortage of tact and patience. Folks go forward before the returning guests have passed by in an orderly manner. Even with the method that we offered above, namely that the one side is used for approach and the other for return, there is still unedifying pressure in that some do not exhibit self-control in the waiting where it concerns the return to and the standing up from the seating in the chairs or pews. Within the tight limits of the chairs or rows of pews, one seeks to push by the other instead of momentarily waiting until the way is clear. So also here our people still have to learn some more discipline and courtesy.

10. BREAKING THE BREAD AND GIVING THE CUPS

Now, all the guests are seated. According to good custom, they have placed their special offering of thanksgiving in the plate designated for this (for privacy covered with a napkin covering) or in the offering box (even the poor themselves deposit a coin). They take a moment for silent

---

25 Schotel, 427ff.

prayer to lift up their soul to God. Now everyone is seated in anticipation of what will happen, and their eyes are focused on the administrator of the sacraments. He takes the bread, raises it up so that everyone can see, and breaks it while pronouncing the sacramental formula. He does this slowly and solemnly, so that it may be clearly evident that here an essential sacramental action is taking place. Rightly, the church has judged this breaking of the bread as necessary for the genuine celebration of the Lord's supper. The gospel writers explicitly recount that Jesus broke the bread, and also that the Lord thereby intended his body "that is broken for you." By the breaking of bread, the supper guests must be graphically reminded of the crucifixion of Christ.

At the Synod of Middelburg of 1581 was also determined that the bread shall be placed on the plate in slices, but that the breaking shall happen in the presence of the congregation.[26]

Customarily, the minister hands pieces from one strip of bread, which he breaks, to the nearby guests, namely those both on the right and left and to the two who are seated directly across from him.

Here also is symbolism.

By offering the bread through the minister, Christ exhibits the earnestness of the spiritual offering of his atonement riches, as the participant with outstretched hand receiving the bread exhibits the spiritual longing for salvation that the King has obtained for him. That is why, if no practical difficulties were to ensue, the recommendation would be that the minister present the sacramental signs personally to *each* guest, everyone in turn receiving it from the hand of the minister. In smaller circles this distribution is indeed possible

---

26 There was not complete agreement by the reformers regarding the breaking of the bread. Under the influence of Zwingli great value was attached to the breaking of the bread in the *German* Reformed churches. Luther wanted nothing to do with the breaking of the bread and Calvin did not commend it. The liturgy of Calvin, then, is also silent regarding the breaking of the bread. The bread was broken beforehand and as such set on the table. The example of the German Reformed church, however, eventually found a following in the French congregation, and from there the custom of the breaking also prevailed in the Dutch church.

and is also accomplished in practice. Also by the Lutheran method, where every communicant comes before the minister, this administration is possible. However, when the guests are seated at a table, the meal is in a sense extended and, as in the case of most of our churches, the aisles here and there narrow, it would not make for an edifying, at least not dignified, impression if the minister made the rounds with plate and cup.

So now the method is followed, that the minister fills two plates with pieces of bread and hands these to the nearest guests, so that each in turn takes thereof as the plate is then passed.

With the administration of the sacrament of the cups it would also be desirable that the congregation sees the minister himself doing the pouring of the wine. The sacramental action becomes richer when the guests see firsthand how the wine flows from the pitcher into the cup, and thereby are given a picture of the pouring out of Jesus' blood. In some churches exists the custom that the deacons who carry out the service set the continually filled cups on the table. Though it concerns an indifferent matter, this method is to be avoided as much as possible. At most, the deacons offer assistance at the pouring, for example, by repeatedly filling the cups for the greater portion so that it will suffice that the minister only pours out a little.

Usually, the number of cups involves four. The minister hands the cups to the four nearest participants, and the guests themselves pass them along.

In recent years, serious objection has been made against this drinking from the same cup by a number of people. Some postulate only the objection that there is something unpleasant and undesirable about drinking from a cup upon which another has set his lips, and this undesirability must be avoided at the Lord's supper so that the attention be distracted by nothing. Others also bring up the hygienic argument that by the contamination of the cup all the guests run in danger of an infection. From there folks have already proposed that each guest bring his own cup along to the supper so that any annoyance and contamination threat be avoided.

We recognize that a question as here stated is not unimportant. Satan also makes use of even the tiniest hindrance in order to hamper the mood of the Lord's supper participants and to rob them of the blessing. Therefore, it is no superfluous labor to examine this question for a moment.

The question could very easily be resolved if it could be determined that Jesus had specifically commanded the drinking from one cup. Some indeed suggest this on grounds of Jesus' words: "drink ye all of it." But that herein is implied a command to use one cup cannot be proved. In fact, one would already be violating such a command if two or more cups were set on the table. For then may more than one cup really not be used? As far as we know, no one has brought the command of the Lord in this sense into practice.

Hence, one can speak only of one ancient tradition regarding the passing of the cup that might still apply. Especially with the Eastern people existed this custom at feasts also of secular character, and also at Israel's sacred feasts, namely the passover, this custom of the people was practiced. The basis for the idea of making the rounds with the cup or goblet certainly rests in the desire for the symbolism of expressing intimate fellowship. Sitting at the same table and eating from the same plate are in themselves already a display of the idea of unity, but certainly the closest connection of one to another is when they set their mouths on the same cup from which also other guests drank. Here is the contact the most intimate. In life ordinarily such drinking from the same cup or glass occurs often for two lovers when they show each other how especially closely they are bound to each other.

Recognizing how this idea of unity also at the supper has led to the passing around of the cup, the church might think long and hard before they write off this intimate custom. They may well seriously ask themselves the question whether the removal of the common cup would not be seriously detrimental to the feeling of fellowship that is already growing cold in Christ's church.

On the other side, however, it must also be noted that a custom (provided it is not part of the explicit ordinances of God) also must be evaluated in terms of the spiritual level of the congregation. It can become necessary to let go of a praiseworthy institution because it is no longer harmonious with the spiritual life of the church. Initially, it was certainly a laudable custom of the church in every gathering, at least every Sunday, to celebrate the Lord's supper. However, when the momentum of the youthful faith and love calmed down, one has not dared to hold fast to this ideal celebration any longer but a use of the sacrament to six, even four, times a year.

Everyone esteems this as wisely confessed of the Lord's church.

So the question can also be raised as to whether a custom such as drinking from a common cup in our current situation may be required on the one hand in light of a weakening of a spiritual precision and on the other hand succumbing to a culture's precision.

Paying attention to the latter is also no small matter.

In God's order, the form of our life is changed. We live, eat, and carry out our lives differently than our fathers. If we imitated precisely the same customs, which were treasured in dignified company of former days, this would in some respects awaken annoyance. To name one example, we cannot imagine that two centuries ago a handkerchief was an unknown luxury even in polite circles.

It so happens that we, thanks to the development of the natural sciences, are better informed regarding the origin of contagions. Various sicknesses are sometimes transferred by slight contact, namely from what goes out of people's mouths. There are numerous examples that infections exist through the single, simple fact that the one drank from another's cup. In great measure, this knowledge has also spread among the people due to this: the warning goes around to be careful especially of such contact.

Now one could well say that at the Lord's supper this material idea must give way for the spiritual, and not the body but the soul should be the object of the concern. Nevertheless, a man is not only a spiritual being; he cannot alter himself. A rising fear can certainly be overcome, a rising feeling of distaste and irritability can be brought under control, but already the battle against such conflicting thoughts disturbs the soul's tranquility that is essential for the genuine enjoyment of the supper.

We find therefore the consideration whether to bring about a change in the form of the use of the chalice to be far from superfluous.

One can resolve the difficulty in one of two ways.

A special cup can be given to each participant. Naturally, this would not need be insurmountable or expensive to make.

But also the passing of the two or four cups could be continued, but with this proviso, that a couple serving brothers be at the end of the rows, and the cups pass on after their having cleaned the rims repeatedly with a cloth. Currently, in many churches this cleaning of the rim happens after each table service. Naturally, is there then only a relative difference than when the cleaning happens after each personal use? Undoubtedly, this entails some difficulty, and the congregation first must get used to this spectacle, but eventually everyone will find it very tactful and profitable.

However, we share an even better thought.

As long as the current manner of drinking from the cup is maintained, one takes every measure to prevent a complaint or offense. That is to attempt as much as possible for good hygiene. Brothers and sisters who suffer a contagious illness must either refrain from the supper or be seated at the last table in the last place in order not to put others in danger. One comes not with a pious slogan that God will always take care of us. A Reformed person knows that God protects us with means and punishes carelessness.

So long, however, as a change presented by us does not have the full sympathy of the congregation and would cause disharmony, or worse, then simply remain with the old way of doing things.

A change in the use of the cup should serve precisely to remove offense. As soon as it creates annoyance, a new method is to be condemned.

11. THE LORD'S SUPPER FORMULA

We now approach a very delicate point. The question that comes under examination is what the minister should say at the breaking and distribution of the bread and sharing the cup.

In the liturgy that we use (the Rutgers edition) is the following:

In breaking and distributing the bread, the minister shall say:

The bread which we break is the communion of the body of Christ. Take, eat, remember and believe, that the body of our Lord Jesus Christ was broken unto the complete remission of all our sins.

And when he gives the cup:

The cup of thanksgiving, for which we give thanks, is the communion of the blood of Christ. Take, drink ye all of it, remember *and believe that the precious blood of our Lord Jesus Christ was shed unto a complete remission of all our sins.*

There has in recent years been much commotion over the use of this formula. In the edition of the liturgy that has been used for a couple centuries in our church stand only the words that come from 1 Corinthians 10:16, namely, "The bread that we break is a communion of the body of Christ," and "The cup of thanksgiving, for which we give thanks, is a communion of the blood of Christ." The official, venerated text cites also the words that follow above: "Take, eat, etc." Now that the Rutgers men have taken up these words again in the text, some stand against this change. Some are opposed only out of reaction. They disapprove of everything that does not correspond to what they are used to. Others indeed recognize the right of the restoration of the old redaction, but yet are of the opinion that this edition that our sixteenth- and seventeenth-century fathers used is not recommended because it is human language. They mean that a formula that is used with the sacrament should come literally from the Scripture, as is the case with baptism. But this question thus in a sense takes on a different character. It is then not an historical but a liturgical question. Yet both of these hang closely together, so close that the one cannot be resolved without the other.

That is why Dr. Kuyper produced a good work in a rather lengthy composition in the *Heraut*[27] to shed some light on the question of the Lord's supper formula, and in this elucidation to give correction of the view of Mensinga,[28] among others, as one who for a long time has asserted it as the right view.

In an introductory article, Dr. Kuyper notes that regarding the baptism formula there is found virtually no difference in the Christian church, but indeed regarding the Lord's supper formula. The reason is that regarding the baptism formula there is only one account in Scripture, i.e., Matthew 28:19. Regarding that which Jesus spoke at the Lord's supper, we find no less than four accounts that all to some extent differ from each other.

Perhaps in the ancient congregation, one in general used no formula since in the Bible there is nowhere an expressed command to do this.

Later, men pronounced only the words: "The body of Christ. The blood of Christ, the cup of life," after which the congregation responded with, "Amen."

When the error of the sacrifice of the mass crept in with Rome, the administration of the sacrament was divided into two parts. There was first a sacramental offering whereby the bread would be changed into Christ's body, and after that there was a distribution of the sacrament to the believer. In harmony with this, they used two formulas: a consecration formula whereby the bread was consecrated for the

---

27 1090 (Nov. 13, 1898) and 1091 (Nov. 20, 1898).
28 Mensinga, *Over de Liturgische Schriften*, 263–68.

sacrifice, and a distribution formula that was pronounced with the dispensing of the signs. This last formula went like this: "The body of our Lord Jesus Christ preserve your soul unto eternal life, Amen." This formula, however, had no sacramental power. The emphasis fell on what happened with the pronouncement of the first formula, "for this is my body."

That Rome herein clearly handled this unbiblically and carelessly is clear in comparison with baptism. Baptism does not exist in two stages, first a consecration of the water and then the administration to the baptismal candidate. There is only one action. With the pronouncement of the baptismal formula, the water is "consecrated" at the same time as it is administered. So it should also be with the Lord's supper. At the same moment Christ spoke the words, "Take, eat, this is my body," he also distributed the bread, and similarly he did with the cup.

The Reformation brought change on this point, but there was no agreement.

Luther preserved the Roman practice in so far that he maintained the use of two formulas. With the actual sacramental formula he said: "This is my body." In the distribution of the sacrament, he pronounced: "The body (blood) of our Lord Jesus Christ preserve your soul unto eternal life."

Nevertheless, Luther did not mean that with the pronouncement of the first formula the great sacramental event took place. According to his conviction, the body and blood of Christ first became the property of the believer when he *ate* the bread and *drank* the wine. According to his principle, then, Luther did not have need for a preceding formula of consecration.

The reformer who most radically cleared away this Romish abuse was Zwingli. Actually, he discarded every sacramental formula. After all, for him, the Lord's supper was more an obligatory, symbolic activity. He always repeated Christ's words of the institution at the supper, but he did not believe any particular sacramental activity of

Christ in the supper. "For him, the Lord's supper was much more a clear representation than a sacrament."[29]

Calvin did not take a firm stand in the matter of using one particular Lord's supper formula. He judged that herein one must act in terms of local circumstances. As much as possible, he kept himself to the existing liturgies. So it is noteworthy to see that in the Genevan liturgy, a formula is completely absent, but it does appear in the Strassburg formulary: "Take, eat, this is the body of Jesus, that was given unto death for you." And with the cup: "This is the cup of the New Testament in Jesus' blood that was shed for you."

All said, Calvin brought clarity in two ways.

First, he tied the sacramental formula to the sacramental action. With the distribution of the signs there is no longer a sort of entreaty pronounced, that nevertheless is not really a sacramental formula (the body of Christ preserve you), but the actual sacramental words are heard at the moment of the distribution.

Further, we owe to Calvin that the Reformed sacramental formula itself is in good style. With the other reformers and also Rome, the formula was as much as possible a literal repetition of Jesus' own words. A literal repetition of what Jesus said is, however, inappropriate coming from the mouth of the minister. He may not and cannot say: "This is *my* body." He adds a paraphrase to it—"*The Lord said* this is my body"—then these words are not a sacramental formula but an historical recollection of what once happened.

That is why Calvin rightly judged that from the words of Jesus a formula must be *formed*, and therefore he said: "Take, eat, this is the body of Jesus that was given up unto death for you. This is the cup of the New Testament in the blood of Jesus that was shed for you."

Noteworthy and difficult to explain is the fact that Calvin did not take up this formula in the Genevan liturgy. And even less clear is the fact that the Reformed church in general did not take over the formula

---

29 Kuyper, *Heraut,* 1092.

from the Strassburg formulary, but chose for their formula the words of 1 Corinthians 10:16, which read: "The bread that we break is the communion with the body of Christ. The cup of thanksgiving for which we give thanks is the communion with the blood of Christ."

According to Mensinga, Melanchton is the father of this formula. Calvin derived it from a statement of Melanchton himself that he recommended the use of this formula to the prince of the Palatinate in order to put an end to disputes between Lutherans and the Reformed.

Dr. Kuyper notes, however, that the advice of Melanchton is dated 1559 and that the formula had appeared already earlier. Indeed, the advice of Melanchton would have contributed to this formula being in the liturgy of the Palatinate, and through this liturgy incorporated into the liturgy of the Dutch churches. However, the origin of the formula lies elsewhere and indeed very likely in the former congregation of Calvin in Strassburg.

To prove this thesis, Dr. Kuyper examines the liturgy of Polanus that in 1551 appeared in London. This liturgy is actually nothing other than a reproduction of how the liturgical service in the French congregation of Calvin in Strassburg was conducted. The Lord's supper liturgy of Calvin is there produced literally, except with this difference, that in the place of the sacramental formula of Calvin the words of Paul from 1 Corinthians 10:16 are taken up and indeed with this addition: *Take, eat, remember and believe, that the body of our Lord Jesus Christ was broken for you unto the forgiveness of your sins,* etc.

The intent of the supplement is apparent from the liturgy of à Lasco, who regarding this point said the following:

> Now, the minister of the word, as he sits at the middle of the table facing the people, takes the bread in his hands from the large plate and speaks with a clear voice in the sight and hearing of the congregation, the words of Paul: *The bread that we break is the communion of the body of Christ.*

And as soon as he has spoken these words, he breaks the bread into two small dishes until the bottom of it is covered with pieces of bread so that every guest may take a piece.

After he has distributed the pieces of bread to those who sit across from him and on both sides, he speaks thus with a clear voice: "*Take, eat, remember and believe, that body of our Lord Jesus Christ was given unto the death on the wood of the cross unto the forgiveness of all our sins.*"

Then the minister also takes a piece from the dish for himself and eats it.

Then the two dishes are passed by him in an orderly manner to both sides to the end of the table to the other seated brothers, so that each takes a piece from it for themselves and eats. When the minister notes that everyone seated has taken the bread, he takes the cup in hand and speaks thus with a clear voice: "*The cup of thanksgiving, with which we give thanks to God, is the communion of the blood of Christ.*"

Then he gives both cups to the brothers that sit on either side of him and thus speaks: "*Take, drink all from it, remember and believe that the blood of our Lord Jesus Christ was shed on the wood of the cross unto the forgiveness of all our sins.*"

The question as to how the Reformed church came to use a formula so composed, Dr. Kuyper answers by pointing to the custom of the breaking of bread that came from the German Reformed churches and was taken over by the French Reformed church at Strassburg. Calvin did not attach a formula, as we have already noted above, to the breaking of the bread. Thus, he attached a formula only to the distribution. So only the words "take, eat, the body of Jesus, etc." come into view. As soon, however, as the minister assumed the custom, before the breaking of the bread, the need was felt for a word that had relation to it. From this it happened that the words of 1 Corinthians 10:16 were connected to the already existing formula (of Calvin).

Later, on a weighty point, the formula of Calvin was expanded. That is, after the words *take, eat,* the words *remember and believe* were introduced.

It is the supposition of Dr. Kuyper that this insertion is thanks to the influence of Bucer, who in those days was the minister of the German Reformed church at Strassburg. Bucer had earnest objections to using only the words *take* and *eat,* because thereby could be misunderstanding. He himself used the formula: *Remember, believe,* and proclaim that Christ the Lord died for you.

The expanded formula that was introduced into our churches by à Lasco and Polanus was actually a combination of the formula of Calvin and the old Strassburg formula.

In the old Dutch liturgy drafted by à Lasco, this extended formula was in general use for a long time. Datheen, in his new liturgy, which was for the most part from the Palatinate, contrary to this common usage retained only the words of 1 Corinthians 10:16, and this was the origin that this point met with a bit of commotion and struggle. Already the assembly of Wezel dealt with the matter and decided (art. 5, 12): "The words at the Lord's supper, that are presented in the ecclesiastical regulations, we esteem with certitude[30] must be retained, because they are most in harmony both with the institution and with the clear prescription of Christ and finally with the declaration of Paul."

Dr. Kuyper deemed that here is intended not the short formula of Datheen, but the extended formula of à Lasco.

The Synod of Emden left it to the freedom of the churches whether to use the words of Christ or those of Paul.

At the following synods of 1574, 1578, and 1581, however, it was explicitly determined that the churches should employ the extended formula. In article 77 of the church order of 1574 is literally stated:

---

30 Thus is the Latin word *plane* (clearly, plainly) translated in the translation that Prof. Biesterveld and Kuyper provide in the ecclesiastical handbook.

It is decided that in the distribution of the bread of the supper the words of Paul in 1 Corinthians 10 be used, the bread that we break, etc., with the connective: take, eat, remember, and believe, that the body of Jesus Christ was broken unto the complete remission of all our sins. And in the distribution of the cups: The cup of thanksgiving, etc., take, drink, all of it, remember, and believe that the precious blood of Jesus Christ was shed unto the forgiveness of all our sins.

The Synod of 1619 was silent on this point.

Some concluded from this that the church had then returned to the short formula. This is incorrect, however. By remaining silent, the Synod of Dordrecht of 1618–1619 had recognized the expanded formula as the ecclesiastically valid form by the edition of the liturgy of 1611, in which the full formula of the supper appears, to indicate the authentic edition. In 1667, Voetius also mentions this formula as that which commonly is in force in the church. There need exist no doubt that the church in her glory years maintained the ancient Lord's supper formula, unabbreviated.

So much for the history.

Now that the historical witness has validated the expanded formula as the official, valid form, the question arises whether the churches do wisely to enter into it also at present, now that it was suppressed for nearly two centuries. How does our judgment sound, when we consider the formula now not historically but objectively critical?

We give the first word to Mensinga, who levels a serious objection against the old formula.[31] He pays homage to the peace-loving intentions of Melanchton, who, according to his opinion, is the cause the Pauline words have been introduced in place of those of Christ, but judges that the church must return to the "universal, ancient, worthy usage of the Christian church." Precisely by the changing of

---

31 Mensinga, 265ff.

the original words, the Lord's supper formula has become occasion to painful strife. Above all, the lawfulness and allowability of the liturgical use of Paul's words he notes is subject to very much doubt.

> If it cannot be absolutely proved that the words of the institution are binding, and that Savior has spoken them unto continuing formulaic use, so much the more certain is it proved that Paul at least has not given his word to that end and has written them in another sense with another intention. If Paul had intended to establish usage of a fixed formula, it appears that it would indeed to have been in the original words of the institution. And although it remains unprovable and uncertain whether such a Pauline or apostolic institution may be the institution of the sacred ceremony itself, the content and nature of the spoken words thereby by the Lord are such that everything praises the preservation of those very words, justifies the exchange of the one with the other.

Mensinga thus decidedly makes his choice for the ancient, catholic usage.

Upon first hearing his idea, there is indeed something to say, because it must be granted that the words of Paul in 1 Corinthians 10 are not prescribed as a formula for the churches.

However, we have already noted that the Lord's own words that he used at the institution also are not a prescribed formula in the sense that is clearly the case of the baptism formula. If one would nevertheless repeat the Lord's words of institution, they must thereby paraphrase or add an introduction because it does not go well that the minister says simply: "This is my body, etc." Precisely by such a paraphrase, however, the formula loses sacramental dignity.

We are most inclined to the point of view of the Reformed to recognize the formula at baptism as unchangeable, firmly established, and recognizing as legitimate only the baptism administered with the one true formula, but that there is some freedom regarding the formula of the Lord's supper. Among others, this is the position of Voetius. The question as to whether it is necessary that everywhere and for all time there is one established formula that must be used for the Lord's supper, he answers thus: "We deny this; it is sufficient when the main intention of the divine institution and promise with such words are presented to the listeners, that they thereby receive a plain and clear idea of the matter, and can receive then with a believing heart."[32]

Here is what it comes down to. The criterion for determination of the Lord's supper formula is contained in the question: Does the formula provide a plain and clear idea of the matter? According to this measure, certainly the formula taken from 1 Corinthians 10:16 is preferred. It emphasizes that the bread is a sign of the communion of the body of Christ, which is exactly the issue.

But what is the judgment then concerning the so-called appendage that, being lost for two centuries in the dust of forgetfulness, currently again in the churches has regained its ancient place?

Certainly, this appendage in one sense makes another impression than the preceding words. It does not sound so literally biblical as the first part of the formula. It has more of a human form.

Nevertheless, it is rightly noted[33] that this extension is actually nothing other "than an attempt to take up the original words of the institution of the Lord's supper formula, without slipping into the danger of strengthening Rome's teaching of transubstantiation." The words, "Take, eat, remember, and believe, that the body of our Lord Jesus Christ is broken," are (with a slight change) the same as the words of institution, as are shared with us by Paul in 1 Corinthians 11:24, "Take, eat, this is my body that is broken for you: do this unto remembrance of me."

The addition, "unto a complete forgiveness of all our sins," takes place in harmony with the words that Christ spoke with the passing

---

32 Gisbertus Voetius, *Politica Ecclesiastica*, II:IV:798.
33 Kuyper, *Heraut*, 1099.

of the cup, "This is my blood, which was shed for many, *unto the forgiveness of sins.*"

The extension is thus in order not only historically, but also biblically.

Nevertheless, the use of the entire formula has not found general sympathy in the practice. There are yet a number of churches where the appendix has been buried and forgotten. And those who attempt to dig it up from its grave are not always much appreciated for it.

Naturally, this antipathy in a great deal is attributed to dead conservatism. There is currently a large group of people who reject all changes because they esteem the old.

But there speaks in the objection of the same against this appendix an argument of feeling that cannot be entirely ignored.

The main objection (which we also share) against the full formula is the great length. Required for a sacramental formula is first of all that it be concise. It must not be exhausting, not detain one's attention for too long. It must immediately attach to the sacrament. Not the word, but the signs are what the matter is about. Experience teaches that a lengthy protracted formula, as now appears in our liturgy, tires the listener and also requires *too much* of the minister. Especially this is the case when the number of tables increases. There results then something monotonous in the Lord's supper administration that oppresses the whole. With a short formula, this monotony is not felt to be so strong, because not so much is demanded of the listener.

It is far from superfluous that the churches give special thought to this matter and by shortening of the formula seek to take away the objection that has been mentioned.

12. DURING THE PARTICIPATION

Now follows in the form of advice:

> *During the communion, there shall be uplifting singing or something read to serve the remembrance of the death of Christ such as from Isaiah 53 or John 13, 14, 15, 16, 17, 18, or the like.*

Naturally, here is not to speak of a law, but of advice. The ideal is certainly that only the sacrament speaks, and the communion, after the formula is pronounced, happens in complete silence. In some churches this has also been done from the start. There reigns a sacred silence. The presentation and reflection are everything.

But it appears that this ideal is difficult to reach. There is never *absolute* silence in a gathering of many people. There are yet noises, and even as slight as the noise is, it precisely detracts from the silence. Above all, it is difficult for men to focus their souls sufficiently in such a solemn, intense moment and to control their thoughts. That is why a few words during the communion, whether sung or spoken, work well.

In the German church is usually the singing of the song "O Lamb of God," translated from the Latin "Agnus Dei." This song was not sung by the communion participants but by a choir.

In the ancient church, they also sang Psalm 34, especially the applicable words (v. 9): "Taste and see that the Lord is good."

In the Dutch Reformed churches, the use of singing (by the congregation) and the reading of Scripture has soon come in vogue. However, this practice is considered as belonging to matters of the adiaphora.

The Assembly of Wezel determined that when the supper is being served, interspersed shall either Scripture be read or psalms sung.

The church order of Dordt in 1574 approved "that in all the churches in solidarity a few places from the Holy Scriptures shall be read while the supper is commemorated, and there shall be pauses, while the words of Paul in 1 Corinthians 10 are read."

The Acts of Synod of 1578 provides this advice: "It is determined that while the Lord's supper is being administered, shall be read some passages on the suffering of Christ from the prophets or the gospels, or a singing of a few psalms according to what each church 'considers appropriate.'"

In the eighteenth century the readings from Scripture were

replaced in most churches with so-called table-talks, a custom with which our church deviated from all Christian churches. Certainly, there were good intentions with these meditations, namely an increase in the edification of the Lord's supper administration, but it appears in practice that these little sermonettes more detracted the attention of the devout from the supper than strengthened it. It was with this as with baptism. Also here the warm chats supplementing the formulary were for increasing edification. However, in reality the ceremony suffered because there was more spoken about child-rearing and such things than about the sacrament. For many, the sermonette became the main thing and the sacrament secondary.

Also with respect to the Lord's supper celebration, the extemporaneous word of the minister has done more harm than good. Definitely there were ministers with special charisma who knew how to pull this off just right; nevertheless, in general the sermonette also here served more to detract from than to introduce. The people were seeking the blessing not from the sacrament but from the talk. People had celebrated a "glorious" Lord's supper when the minister had spoken "lovely." If the minister was less inspiring, then one had less "satisfaction." And naturally, in the large cities they flocked to the minister who provided splendid Lord's supper sermonettes, while the tables of the less-gifted brothers were almost empty.

In the churches of 1834, the sermonettes lasted for many years. The churches of 1886 immediately chose the patriarchal practice of the reading of Scripture. One might say that now the custom of the table-talk increasingly died out and the correct usage has prevailed. We are delighted by that. It is a sign that our people are beginning to have a purer feeling for the sacrament, becoming pedagogically more mature. Nevertheless, we do not judge the church where the table-talk is still held onto. It belongs to the adiaphora. And if a minister thinks that he "for the peace of Jerusalem" cannot yet break away from the table-talk, or even that his congregation is better blessed by the sermonette, no one can blame him for it.

All said, when it comes to the *reading* of Scripture at the table, the minister must not forget the high standards placed on him. Certainly, his work is not as difficult and demanding as for the minister who must do the table-talk. But to read a word from Scripture in such a way that the soul is truly edified is not everyone's gift. It requires refined sensitivities, delicate dictation, and a warm presentation.

And also, the choice of the Scripture passages to be read requires learned consideration. The formulary provides a good direction by identifying the passion passage Isaiah 53 and the last part of John's gospel. One especially should not neglect to put this next to the judicial dimensions of the gospel. Let the communicant hear after receiving the sacrament not only how certain is his salvation, but also how valuable his calling is. To that end, Scripture passages such as Romans 12, Colossians 3:12–17, 1 Thessalonians 5:14–23, 1 Timothy 6:11–16, and Titus 2:11–15, as well as portions from the letter of James and the first letter of John, may not be missed.

In some churches, as advised in the form, there is edifying singing during the communion, so conceived that people lift up the song while sitting at the table. There are no qualms about this, provided that this happens *after* one's participation. Usually psalms are sung while men go back and forth [to and from the table]. This appears to us the most practical way of doing it. In either case, one should not sing during the participation itself. "*Singing during the communion has objections. The eating of the bread and the drinking from the cup does not go well with singing.*"[34]

As far as we know, this practice mentioned in the form has not found general favor in our churches.

---

34 Kuyper, *Onze Eeredienst,* 501.

Chapter Nine

THE CONCLUSION OF THE SERVICE

1. THE CHARACTER AND MEANING OF THE THANKSGIVING

The sacred meal is finished: the last participants have left the table.
The minister climbs back into the pulpit and says:

> Beloved in the Lord, since the Lord hath now nourished our
> souls at his table, let us therefore jointly praise his holy name
> with thanksgiving, and everyone say in his heart, thus:

1. Bless the Lord, O my soul; and all that is within me, bless
   his holy name.
2. Bless the Lord, O my soul, and forget not all his benefits.
3. Who forgiveth all thine iniquities; who healeth all thy
   diseases.
4. Who redeemeth thy life from destruction; who crowneth
   thee with lovingkindness and tender mercies.

8. The Lord is merciful and gracious, slow to anger and plenteous in mercy.
9. He[1] will not always chide: neither will he keep his anger
   forever.
10. He hath not dealt with us after our sins, nor rewarded us
    according to our iniquities.
11. For as the heaven is high above the earth, so great is his
    mercy towards them that fear him.

---

1 This ninth verse that is found in the official text is absent in the generally circulated version, because it did not appear in the sixteenth-century edition.

12. As far as the east is from the west, so far hath he removed our transgressions from us. Like as a father pitieth his children, so the Lord pitieth them that fear him. (Psalm 103:1–4; 8–12)

Who hath not spared his own Son, but delivered him up for us all, and freely given us all things with him. Therefore God commendeth therewith his love towards us, in that while we were yet sinners, Christ died for us; much more then, being now justified in his blood, we shall be saved from wrath through him: for, if, when we were enemies, we were reconciled to God by the death of his Son; much more being reconciled, we shall be saved by his life. Therefore shall my mouth and heart show forth the praise of the Lord from this time forth for evermore. Amen.

O merciful God and Father, we thank thee with all our hearts, that thou hast of thy infinite mercy, given us thine only begotten Son, for a mediator and a sacrifice for our sins, and to be our food and drink unto life eternal, and that thou givest us a true faith, whereby we are made partakers of such great benefits. Thou hast also been pleased, that thy beloved Son Jesus Christ should institute and ordain the holy supper for the strengthening of that faith. Grant, we beseech thee, O faithful God and Father, that through the operation of thy Holy Spirit, the remembrance of our Lord Jesus Christ and the proclamation of his death may daily increase in us the upright faith, and in blessed fellowship with Christ, through Jesus Christ thy dear Son, in whose name we conclude our prayers, saying as he has taught us:

Our Father who art in heaven,
Hallowed be thy name;
Thy kingdom come;
Thy will be done in earth, as it is in heaven.

Give us this day our daily bread;
And forgive us our debts, as we forgive our debtors.
And lead us not into temptation, but deliver us from
the evil one.
For thine is the kingdom, and the power, and the
glory, forever. Amen.

First an observation regarding the place of the presentation.

Here and there is the custom that the minister reads the thanksgiving at the table. One pronounces the thanksgiving while the last participants are still seated at the table. Another allows the participants to return to their seats and then remains with just the serving elder and deacons.

It is necessary, in accordance with what we have already noted regarding this matter, that this form of handling is less proper. When the service was begun in the pulpit, it must also be concluded there. The congregation must feel that the administration of the supper does not count for a few but for everyone. The congregation is an *organic* whole. Belonging to her gathering are also members (e.g., the many non-professing baptized members) who do not participate in the supper. Also they must hear the formulary, the sacrament also concerns them, and especially the participants who previously sat at the table and have again taken their seats in the sanctuary. The thanksgiving is also spoken for them. They may not depart early. The logically proper place for the thanksgiving, therefore, is the pulpit.[2]

Perhaps the question can be raised as to whether the personal thanksgiving that the participants in silence do upon returning to their seats is not sufficient, and whether it is to be considered that with it there also must be held on the same day a special service of thanksgiving.

So why is there then a thanksgiving also in the form?

The answer makes sense.

---

2 Cf. Kuyper, 502ff.

The personal prayer that the participant is accustomed to offer at the table prior to the communion does not take the place of the communal prayer of the congregation that the minister prays on behalf of all from the form. In the gathering of God's people, the intimate, quiet prayer must never be held back, but never may it take place of the prayer of the worship service. For what other reason gathers the fellowship? And whatever the thanksgiving or contemplation after the supper in the first following service concerns, this cannot satisfy the feeling of joyful thanks welling up immediately after the service. There is a place for the immediate expression of praise. And the form provides here a good tone for it.

2. THE TWO PARTS OF THE THANKSGIVING

First is an expression of praise, a hymn of thanks in prose, and then a thanksgiving. The expression of praise is clearly distinguished from the prayer of thanksgiving with an *Amen.*

In the formulary of the Palatinate, from which this religious contemplation after the supper was also literally taken, the minister was given the choice to use either the expression of praise or the thanksgiving. Immediately after the first come the words, "*or in this way.*" And then followed the prayer.

Ens devotes special attention to this matter and says:

> With respect to the thanksgiving after the supper, in the Palatinate a distinction is made between two formulary prayers of which the one or the other can be used, similar to what occurs in our liturgy with two prayers for the sick and troubled persons. Because, after the conclusion of the first is: *Therefore shall my mouth and heart show forth the praise of the Lord from this time forth for evermore, Amen.* And then follows immediately, *or in this way*, that is, *or as such*—but in ours, both, for good reason, have been tied together.[3]

---

3   Ens, 224–25.

On this matter Ens cites Hoornbeek in his *Practical Theology*, who judges, namely, that they are two prayers. In the then-published editions the words were placed between the two: *And thus speaks each one with attentive hearts.* Naturally, Hoornbeek wanted to do away with these words, but indicates thereby at the same time that in our formulary the first part not be viewed as a prayer. With more right, Ens views the first part as an introduction to the thanksgiving. He says:

> That such appeals for thanksgiving prior to a following thanksgiving at solemn circumstances are often used, of this one sees an example of when the National Synod of Dordt in 1619 would adjourn in the 153rd session: there first happens a declaration of a similar nature as this in the Lord's supper, whereupon immediately follows the ceremonial thanksgiving of the entire gathering.[4]

This conception strikes us as quite reasonable.

Although it might have been the intention in the original formula of the Palatinate that this first part also serve as a thanksgiving, it is simpler and more natural that both (as they appear in our form) are combined to one unit. It is indeed much more striking and beautiful to prepare the heart for the prayer of thanksgiving by preceding baptism in the living waters of Scripture.

Indeed, is not the powerful, uplifting prose that here is taken from Scripture already a prayer?

Let us listen to this prepared song on the harp.

3. LET EVERYONE SAY IN HIS HEART

Beloved in the Lord, so says the minister with an intimate tone to the richly blessed people, *since the Lord hath now nourished our souls at his table, let us therefore jointly praise his holy name with thanksgiving, and everyone say in his heart.*

---

4   Ibid., Ens.

The congregation still has not reached the high point of view of the angels, who praise God for only the greatness of his attributes, apart from any benefits received. The heavenly hosts shout their *Glory to God* because they are full of God. But the church on earth needs an incentive by receiving a reminder regarding the blessings from her God. This is also true with respect to the Lord's supper: *Since* the Lord has nourished, let us now praise.

Nevertheless, it is not that the congregation only praises because she has received. Her thanksgiving is not a joy of self-interest. No, her adoration for God lives in the heart because the Spirit transforms the heart for this. The *principle* for her praise is the same as that of the angels of God. But the panorama of undeserved treasures, cast into her bosom, inspires her to a song of praise. She sees God's greatness in his *goodness*. And God's word itself tells her that she must praise. God requires thankfulness from his people. And this gratitude must express itself in praising his name.

Just listen how God's children lead us in this.

The form does not now itself arrange words into a song of praise but places on the lips of the congregation the language of the Holy Spirit.

The form braids two songs of praise into one. From the Old Testament, David's hymn in Psalm 103, and from the New Testament, it reads words of Paul together, who can write poetically in prose.

Let everyone say *in his heart thus.*

Especially when a child of God gives thanks with the words of another, it is necessary to stir up the thanks so that it comes from his heart. God receives the sacrifice of the lips only when it burns on the altar fire of the heart. Our God is a God who looks upon the *heart.*

Not the entire psalm is repeated by the formulary. Verses 3 and 7 are omitted, and further the portion following verse 13. Correctly, the framers intended that especially here, which requires a high action of the soul, in brevity is found strength. That is why they selected from the psalm those words by which God's name is *praised with thanksgiving.*

4. BLESS THE LORD, O MY SOUL

The first two verses express the theme of the song.

> *Bless the Lord, O my soul; and all that is within me, bless his holy name.*
> *Bless the Lord, O my soul, and forget not all his benefits.*

In typical Eastern form of speaking, the poet awakens his own soul to praise the Lord. He objectivizes himself for a moment and exhorts his own person. The soul is not a part of his personality like, for example, the heart or the intellect. The soul is the man himself viewed with respect to his sensory and spiritual life. Heart and intellect are functions of the soul. Yes, many are the known and yet unknown capacities of the soul. The psychological age in which we live turns up in this area increasingly more amazing things to light. It is as if the poetical seer, David, has surmised powers yet slumbering in the depth of his life of the soul and out of concern not to forget all these, he says: *and all that is within me,* praise his holy name!

In the recounting of the address to the soul is something noteworthy.

Therein lies a confession of weakness and lethargy in thanksgiving. The soul must be awakened from its deep slumber. Twice it must be called before it listens. And there is a gentle reproof in the words that it must hear in the arousal: *forget not all his benefits.*

There is a difference between receiving benefits unaware and forgetting benefits.

The first happens from moment to moment and is a natural consequence of our existence. A man is singularly dependent and *all* that he enjoys, every breath of his life that he takes, is a benefit from God. He cannot ever comprehend what God does for him.

But the second is designed to lay blame. When he receives a special benefit, and God's Spirit determines by the greatness of this treasure itself that he praise God for it, and then that benefit is quickly forgotten, this points to the sickness of the soul, a lack of love. Mostly is the *forgetting* not felt as guilt. One pleads forgetting exactly as an excuse. Experience teaches, however, that one does not forget that which truly interests him, that which is of great importance to him. If it concerns his own advantage or honor, a man does not easily forget. In the area of benefits, it is that he does forget the benefits that he receives, but not the benefits that he yet expects. Sin has made the human heart thoroughly self-seeking.

Bless the Lord, O my soul, and *forget* not all his benefits. Apply this also to the Lord's supper.

At the table, God granted numerous special treasures of grace. He granted an experience that his comforts are not insignificant. He poured out power for life and courage to die. He strengthened his inheritance when it became worn and weary.

But the soul tends to forget this. The impression of the God so near subsides. The awakened state fades. Despondency spreads its depressing wings out again. Impatience and doubt take over again. The desires of the flesh work stronger against the spirit. Indeed, sometimes barely a week has passed, and one could ask, is this now that Lord's supper participant who received so many benefits?

His soul has forgotten them.

And those who forget God's benefits forget *God*, who gave them.

There are thus reasons for the poetic admonition that the participant who has benefited from Jesus' table directs to himself: Forget not all his benefits.

Think once if someone highly important invited you to a banquet, how proud you would be. You would tell your children even years later that you had dined at the court. You would never forget it because you esteemed it such an honor, because you felt yourself so honored by it.

However, O my soul, especially do not forget all this benefit, that *the Lord* has nourished you at his table. Forget not that you were a guest of this King who filled your mouth with eternal good.

5. THE BENEFITS OF THE COVENANT

In order to get the soul into action for bringing praise to God, the poet names a few benefits. He lets them glide like pearls through his hand and casts the eye upon them with marvel. Then he raises the eye, moist with emotion, to the heavens and stammers: "Thank you, Father."

There is a fine symmetry in the enumeration of the benefits that the soul may not forget. Everything in the thanksgiving must also be worthy and occur with order.

The first the blessed singer names is the principal benefit of the pardon from guilt. But noteworthy is that here (as also in the following verse) not the benefit alone is named. He reaches much higher by naming *God* in connection with the benefit.

He doesn't say: Bless the Lord, *because* he forgives your iniquities. He says: Bless the Lord *who* forgives all your iniquities. He sees the greatness and praiseworthiness of God in the light that shines from this evidence of grace: forgiveness!

Oh how lovely already is the sound of this word. It is the pure organ pipes of the messenger of the gospel. It is the proclamation of good news. For the church of all ages, this word inspires awakening hope, renewing vigor, drying tears.

This is the sum of the preaching of salvation. The only, eternal, secure, God-glorifying way. This word already sufficiently provides the theme for the never-ending song of reconciliation. In endless shapes and forms shall the church triumphant praise her God as the God who forgives all her iniquities.

In order to accentuate the benefit as strongly as possible, the poet here uses the word *iniquities*. He sees sin as a violation of the irrevocable, holy law. Because sin is iniquity, it is from man's side irreparable, unforgivable from the earthly side.

But God forgives sin, even though it is iniquity.

Indeed, hear this, you benefited soul: he forgives *all* your iniquity. Also that which you have already forgotten, and that which on the last day would make you tremble if it would be recalled. Also the iniquity about which you are most worried, with which Satan attacks you the most, and which, although you detest it, you yet with the most difficulty can abandon.

God forgives you *everything*, completely, absolutely, forever.

Of this, this supper grants you again blessed assurance. That, Christ showed you again, fastened to the soul, whispered in your ear.

As you still see the table standing there, where you as with the rest of God's people receive the signs of the atonement, the proof of the surety, then you may, thinking of Jesus' death for you, rejoice: Who forgives all your iniquity!

But God does more.

When he *forgives*, the division between you and God is in principle removed. Then is God (said in reverence) no longer prevented from giving you *everything*. To *forgive* has fruit *to give*.

God grants you *life*. However, on account of your deeply sunken state, the benefit is first of all given you in a negative form. God takes away from you what impedes and consumes your life, namely, the disease.

He is the one who heals all your *diseases*.

Do not start spiritualizing this word. Do not view the sickness of the body as something unimportant, something impersonal. Sickness of the body stems from inner evil. Sickness is impossible without sin. This is the positive in the (apart from unsound mysticism) movement of the faith-healers, that the bodily condition is dependent upon spiritual action.

Not that every particular illness is the result of a particular sin. The finest children of God often endure the most serious infirmities. Even the saint Job endured festering sores. But indeed, in general, sickness is the result of our spiritual degeneration.

Above all, physical illness works against the spirit and also makes the spiritual woes worse. Israel's King Hezekiah peeped like a swallow and cooed like a dove when physical pain overwhelmed him, not due to the pain itself, but from the thought that he was cut off from his throne and work and descended near the gates of death.

Christ, knowing this suffering of life and woes of death of humanity, came into the world also to deliver him from this. Surely, he has also borne these sicknesses. And God, who forgives all your iniquities, wills also to heal all your sicknesses. In principle, regeneration heals not only the soul, but also the body, because he who is in Christ is a new creature. Old things are passed away. Behold, *all things* (thus also the body) are become new. A consequence of forgiveness is that soon the putrid body will be laid in the coffin as a seed of the spiritual body.

And also this is the Lord's supper, which before everything else assures you of the forgiveness of sins and prophesies eternal life for you, wherein no one laments: I am sick.

Although here in the first instance is the idea of physical illness, it would be unspeakably superfluous to think only of this suffering. When God says to Israel: I am the Lord, your Great Physician, no seasoned Bible reader would therein hear only a promise for the body. Israel was spiritually sick. The intellect, the will, the desires, the imagination, the entire life of the soul was sick. The finest capacities of the soul that was created in God's image function badly. They are out of harmony. They work against each other. What the man would, he does not do, and what he hates, he does.

Praise the Lord, O my soul, who healeth all thy diseases.

6. NO DESTRUCTION

But the wreath of benefits is woven still more broadly.

To the benefits that are sealed unto you in the sacrament and that you must not forget belongs also: *Who redeemeth thy life from destruction.*

With destruction, the Israelite meant the realm of the dead, Sheol, where the souls of the dead travel while the body is swallowed up by the earth. In general, *destruction* is the state of the dead, including the distresses of the soul that precede death.

From that destruction, God rescues his child. Initially, already at the acquittal, because he whose sins are forgiven descends into the grave, but not into perdition, not into eternal destruction. The destruction that pertains to him counts only for the tabernacle of the body. And that body God recovers once and for all from the pit of destruction. And the soul is completely liberated, because it is united with the body unto the complete glory of life.

7. THE CROWN OF LOVINGKINDNESS

Still further flows the river of grace.

Who crowneth thee with lovingkindness and tender mercies...

Now and then one says in everyday life, that someone who finishes his work thereby *crowns* his work. God also crowns his work, by giving to his child lovingkindness and tender mercies in full measure.

Certainly, forgiveness of iniquities, the healing of diseases, and redemption from destruction are in and of themselves cause for joy. But the jubilation first breaks forth when the crown comes. David was rightfully king immediately after his anointing. But he suffered a long and thorny path of life before he was crowned, then the sun of his life reached the zenith.

God *crowns* his child with *lovingkindness*, which is more than benevolence, because the word *lovingkindness* points to the goodness as being the *nature* and *essence* of God. It indicates thus the deep source and eternal permanence of the goodness of God.

And in the crown of lovingkindness glitters in soft splendor the pearls of the *tender mercies*. This word is in the plural in order to describe the fullness and the variety of the blessings of God.

Here already at the Lord's supper God grants tender mercies that quake the soul with joy. But the crown of tender mercies yet awaits.

In God's high dwelling place await the treasures to anticipate that the devout with Christ inherit. And at that inheritance, the Lord's supper brings the foreshadowing prophecy.

Here already says the redeemed: "Bless the Lord, O my soul; who crowns you with lovingkindness and tender mercies."

8. THE OMITTED VERSES

Noteworthy is that the form now takes a leap from the fourth to the eighth verse. In between are these verses in the Bible:

5. *Who satisfieth thy mouth with good things; so that thy youth is renewed like the eagle's.*
6. *The* LORD *executeth righteousness and judgment for all that are oppressed.*
7. *He made known his ways unto Moses, his acts unto the children of Israel.*

Why are these verses omitted?

Certainly not because they would be inappropriate for expressing the gratitude of the congregation, but indeed that it was desired to keep it as compact as possible. The most sensitive and powerful verses were selected in order to voice the highest gratitude.

The framers would have had the right to make the change, but then it yet remains strange that these words were left out, which most strikingly point to the supper: *Who satisfieth thy mouth with good things.* Where is this promise more richly fulfilled than at the Lord's table?

Also, the characteristic benefits of life renewal and life refreshment, which are fruits of the supper, could be well typified by the following words: *so that thy youth is renewed like the eagle's.*

Verses 6 and 7 are an historical reminder of what God did for Israel. God came to the aid of his oppressed people. The grace that he made known was on behalf of the covenant and the promise of *righteousness* and *judgment*.

And not only by the proclamation of the law, but also by the greatest deeds of redemption, *he made known his ways unto Moses, his acts unto the children of Israel.*

Which ways; which acts?

Listen, and let your soul praise him all the more with thanksgiving, at the reflection that he has wrought salvation no less for you.

9. THE LORD IS MERCIFUL

The Lord is merciful and gracious, slow to anger and plenteous in mercy.

The word *mercy* connects immediately to the end of the previously cited verse: "who crowneth thee with lovingkindness and *tender mercies*."

The poet, with a survey of the history of the chosen people, sees the heart of God: what he did for Israel over against the barbaric enemies with righteousness. In contrast with Amalek and Philistia, *right* was on Israel's side, because Israel had the promise. But from God's side it appeared that Israel was out of step. Because the people broke the covenant, Israel was faithless and rebellious. But even now, by still fulfilling his promises, God shows that he is not only righteous, but also merciful. Mercy triumphs over judgment.

Moses himself also had this godly heart that beats with divine mercy. He spoke, standing on the mountain, the words that the poet celebrates in this psalm: "*The* LORD, *the* LORD God, merciful and gracious, *longsuffering, and abundant in goodness and truth*" (Ex. 34:6).

There is reason for the New Testament church to take over this cry of jubilation, because they are *the inner-movements of the mercy* of our God with which the rising from on high has sought us.

At the Lord's supper are the symbols and pledges of this most tender mercy of God displayed and seen.

Here lives the remembrance of the most precious outpouring and God's supreme act of grace: the sending of the Son and the atoning death of the Son.

Here celebrates the mercy of God its victory by blessing the people of the covenant with the most exalted fruits of the sacrifice of redemption.

From the fullness of his soul, deeply moved, the poet continues to praise: *He will not always chide: neither will he keep his anger forever.*

Also here is an allusion to Israel's history perceptible. Constantly there was conflict between both participants in the covenant: God and his people. From Israel's side there was constant breakage. If God would have turned his people loose, there would be no dispute, only divorce. However, the Lord willed not to break the bond. He held tightly to his wandering people, and so the chiding, the *love-conflict,* that always ended in reconciliation. God does not let his people loose from his grip before they have confessed their guilt.

Thus, God will not *always* chide. The chiding is over as soon as the tears of repentance flow. He will not keep his anger forever. Immediately God lets his anger go when the guilt is recognized, because recognition of guilt is opening of the way of forgiveness.

He hath not dealt with us after our sins, nor rewarded us according to our iniquities.

Noteworthy is how the poet here changes his form of speaking.

First, he spoke to himself: Bless the Lord, O my soul! His language thus bore a purely personal character.

Along the way, his manner of speaking shifted, and he broke out into direct praise to God.

But now nearing the high point of his song of praise, the thought moves from strictly personal blessings, and he speaks out in the name of the *congregation*: he hath not dealt with *us* after *our* sins, nor rewarded *us* according to *our* iniquities. This same development from the personal to the general, one runs up against often in the psalms, especially evident in Psalm 22, where David climbs from the pain of purely personal suffering to the joy of the deliverance of the church, indeed the world.

Especially in this language the Lord's supper participant senses the life of his soul. The supper is always the place where Christ renews the tie of fellowship, and the believer, precisely in that fellowship, ascends to a higher level of life.

And what this singer throughout the ages testifies, out of his own experience of the soul in the name of the congregation, he also speaks for us, and it is also true for us: "He hath not dealt with us after our sins, nor rewarded us according to our iniquities."

Every supper, even this Lord's supper, where the Lord, despite the load of sins, stretches forth the hand of reconciliation and blessing, is the unspeakable evidence, the comforting signs of it.

10. THE IMMEASURABLE GOODNESS OF GOD

The idea of this incomparable forbearance and forgiveness of God causes the poet to reach a degree of reverence that borders on ecstasy, rapture.

He searches for an image with which to picture the goodness of God, some bar by which to measure it.

He finds the comparison only in the wonderful creation of God that proclaims the attributes of the same God. *For as the heaven is high above the earth, so great is his mercy towards them that fear him. As far as the east is from the west, so far hath he removed our transgressions from us.*Literally, the poet is saying with this comparison that the mercy of God is *incomparable.* He is expressing his inability to determine its greatness. The human spirit cannot fathom the distance of heaven from earth even by approximation. Already the clouds lift themselves above the tips of the highest mountain tops. Above the clouds in the sky is the dome of the stars. Indeed, science has been successful in measuring the distance of many stars. But even if one could record the enormous numbers on paper, the spirit cannot transpose them into its imagination.

But beyond the stars stretches yet an immeasurable expanse that expands beyond the limits of our ability to contemplate.

Is there not a heaven of the heavens that is kept from our view?

For as the heaven is high above the earth, so great is his mercy towards them that fear him.

So great means here *powerful, mighty.*

A height overwhelms more than a distance as wide as the earth. Thousands of miles to be seen on the earth's surface does not even awaken the emotion experienced when considering the thousands of miles upward. A steep mountain of a few hundred feet makes us dizzy. A steep-climbing aircraft amazes us. We feel so small and weak.

So is God's mercy great, *overwhelming*, towards them that fear him. It rises above and covers (and thus atones for) all our sins. It provides for all our needs. It confounds all our cares. It is always greater than our boldest thoughts dare imagine. Even where according to human calculations the goodness of God must be exhausted, it is still great over us.

Towards them that fear him.

Here for the first time is mentioned the ethical character of the people who revel in this goodness.

Not to stipulate a condition on our part that must first be fulfilled for us to participate in this mercy. No, the poet names the *instrument* through which this mercy is truly received: *fear.* Fear in the sense of deeply rooted reverence, holy timidity, spiritual affection regarding the greatness and holiness of God.

But also the connection between God's mercy and the fear of his people is insofar as God increasingly reveals himself more greatly to those who honor him in thought and life. God rewards and crowns with mercy his own work in the heart of his people.

Immeasurable is the height of God's goodness, but also the breadth.

As far as the east is from the west, so far hath he removed our transgressions from us.

In the tenth verse it says that God does not deal with us after our sins. It is left undecided whether the sins themselves then nevertheless remain. But now the poet is reaching back to the third verse, where it is said that God *forgives* sins. To forgive them, the Lord thus also takes the sins *away*. He removes them from us. He brings about a separation between us and our sins.

How far does this separation go?

As far as east is from west; that is, endless.

Never comes a man who is heading east to the point where he can say: here marks the end of the east. And the same goes for the border of the west.

God's liberated child never sees his transgressions again.

The Lord's supper has strengthened him anew in the faith that there is a radical and final separation between him and his guilt.

11. THE COMPASSIONATE FATHER

So having climbed the mountain peak of a grateful faith, the poet can find no better way to sum up all that he finds admirable and praiseworthy in God than this one expression: *Like as a father pitieth his children, so the Lord pitieth them that fear him.*

The idea regarding the benefit that God grants is not new in these words, but indeed the idea regarding God is. With the covenantal name LORD, the poet has already addressed his God. Also he provided a series of shining descriptions of the work of God. But with the one name that stands out in the new covenant, the name of Father, he has not yet called him.

In this name is the heart of the covenantal idea expressed, because Israel, with whom God entered into the covenant, thereby became God's son, as the Lord showed already to Moses: "And thou shalt say unto Pharaoh, Thus saith the LORD, Israel is my son, even my firstborn" (Ex. 4:22).

However, Israel in general did not deeply sense this relationship of son. The thought of their God was mostly still high and far away. They were yet driven by the spirit of bondage again to fear.

First in the new covenant does the fullness of the soul-enchanting light rise upon the name of father.

Christ displays to the church the Father's heart. He who was in the bosom of the Father declared him to us. And he sends us his Spirit, the Spirit of adoption to children, by which we call, "Abba, Father!"

See what great love the Father has lavished on us, that we should be called children of God!

12. HE SPARED NOT HIS OWN SON

Is it surprising that at this point the approach of the formulary is to leave the Old Testament and enter the better covenant? No matter how warmly and tenderly the devout of the old days explain their life of faith to us, especially in the intimacy of the Lord's supper meal, where the blood of the new testament is symbolized for us, the church needs also another language.

Now from the most beautiful pearls of the New Testament the framer weaves a crown to the glory of God.

> Who[5] hath not spared his own Son, but delivered him up for us all, and freely given us all things with him. Therefore God commendeth therewith his love towards us, in that while we were yet sinners, Christ died for us; much more then, being now justified in his blood, we shall be saved from wrath through him: for, if, when we were enemies, we were reconciled to God by the death of his Son; much more being reconciled, we shall be saved by his life. Therefore shall my mouth and heart show forth the praise of the Lord from this time forth for evermore. Amen.

Genuine New Testament timbre. In principle, it is not different from that which we heard with feeling in Psalm 103 and stammered in response, but in form, it is as different as the flower differs from the bud. Also, the devout of the old dispensation were not saved in

---

5   For earlier notes on these, cf. *Supra*, 1:7.

any other way than through our mediator, but what a different sound the gospel trumpet gives as a new day shines in full beauty.

The framer has taken the material for the New Testament thanksgiving from the letter to the Romans.

First he takes a word from Romans 8, an authentic Lord's supper sound: Who hath not spared his own Son, but delivered him up for us all.

With the negative, Paul makes the greatness of the positive deed of God come out all the more sharply. God *spared* not his *own* Son. There was every reason to spare him because this Son is the firstborn of the Father. The Father loved him with an eternal love. And the Son was in himself holy and innocent, wholly desirable, and lovely.

There was every reason to spare him because the sinner, in whose place Jesus stood, actually earned the punishment, and for Jesus this punishment was doubly heavy due to the absolute character of his innocence.

And the reasons that God could have spared his Son multiplied themselves when the pains increased, the Son himself asked whether or not it was possible the cup could pass by him, and the world scoffed around the cross that would save it.

And yet, God did not spare. Indeed, he spared his people, but not his Son. Isaac was taken from the altar, but the sacrificial lamb must die.

And would God, who provided this sacrifice for his people, now not with him give us all things?

So asks Paul. In the formulary, the question becomes a confirmation: *and freely given us all things with him.* This change was not in any sense necessary because precisely in the form of the question lies the power of the reason.

It is contrary to reason that God would withhold anything from us after he had granted this one.

Van Andel spoke very well here in his exposition of this letter:

It is impossible that he would withhold anything from us; because he would dishonor the Son if he, after delivering him, would deny us anything. Because he would dishonor the Son, if he, after having given him, withheld something from us, for by this he would declare that what he withheld to us is more precious than the Son. No one fears that he with that one would not grant everything. Everything for all, sounds out the motto of the gospel. Everything between the grace of justification and the grace of glorification is included, for the one to lead to the other, the enlightenment and the perseverance, the purification and the sanctification, the power and the victory, the resurrection and the acquittal. God shall grant everything or nothing, with willingness of the heart, the signs of his favor; that is the lovely sense of the words utilized by Paul. God will not withhold anything from us, which depriving would make the gift of his Son in vain. God shall constantly make grace the trailblazer of grace. God will never give himself rest before we are fully conformed to the image of the Son.[6]

13. GOD'S LOVE CONFIRMED

With a quotation from Romans 5 the praise advances. The words here cited from the Scriptures are slightly rearranged. They (vv. 8–10) say this:

Therefore God commendeth therewith his love towards us, in that while we were yet sinners, Christ died for us; much more then, being now justified in his blood, we shall be saved from wrath through him: for, if, when we were enemies, we were reconciled to God by the death of his Son; much more being reconciled, we shall be saved by his life.

---

6 J. Van Andel, *Paulus' brief aan de Romeinen: met de gemeente gelezen* (Kampen: J.H. Lok, 1904).

In our form, verses 8 and 9 are as such combined so that they form one sentence. In a sense, this hinders the reading. Better would be to start a new sentence: *Much more then, etc.* Truly, it were desirable to borrow the entire structure of the text simply from Scripture. Here, our Dordt Bible is perfect.

Regarding what the idea is regarding the cited words themselves, the choice could not have been better. This expression of praise provides the hope that is within us. It is extolling the assurance that the Lord has strengthened in the supper.

Paul follows the same theme in the passage. The apostle is seeking for his readers to make the certainty of salvation absolutely inviolable. First he mentions the peace with God that is the fruit of justification through faith. Then he gives assurance that this hope will not be ashamed, as the love of God is poured in our hearts by the Holy Spirit who has been given us. And then he gives the grounds upon which this hope rests. Really there is only one ground, namely that God alone has cause in himself, because Christ, when they were yet powerless, in his time died for the ungodly.

The great mistake of our life and the great cause for our doubting is that we seek to explain the love of God toward us from the object of the love that we are *ourselves*. We cannot comprehend that God loves *sinners*, and so we seek to make God's love comprehensible by uncovering something nice, something loveable in ourselves. The unconditionality, the omnipotence, the sovereignty of God's love is a riddle for us. We want to solve this riddle by attempting to construct a justification for God.

This is the ailment with which at times the most outstanding Christians struggle and hinder the blossoming of the Christian life. In this way we can never become absolutely certain of the state of our salvation. In this way there is always ground for uncertainty.

That is why we must know that from our side, the love of God is to be considered as groundless. It is, humanly speaking, unmotivated. It is never to be explained from its object. It is rooted in God alone. It was already there before we could arouse it or even know it. Therefore, that love is eternally steadfast.

God always confirms his love toward us that Christ died for us when we were yet sinners.

In the fact that Christ died for us, when there could not be the least mention that we could make ourselves worthy of that love, rests the *confirmation*, literal commendation, *recommendation*, of the love of God. He who pays attention to that marvelous fact that God loves *sinners*, so much so that Christ died for them, then need not, *may* no longer, doubt that love that must be adored.

Yet further is the ground of this trust displayed by a comparison.

"Much more then, being now justified by his blood, we shall be saved from wrath through him. For if, when we were enemies, we were reconciled to God by the death of his Son, much more, being reconciled, we shall be saved by his life."

The work of redemption by God can be distinguished in two stages or phases. First there is a justification by the death of Christ. Then there is a regeneration by the life of Christ.

In the work of justification, God had us over against himself as *enemies*. Though true that God has loved his own from eternity according to his sovereign good pleasure in Christ, in so far that sin lives within them and they bear Adam's guilt, they were enemies of God, and God their enemy. Although they really stood over against God as enemies, and there was in them every reason for them to be damned, nevertheless God justified them. They are justified by (literally *in*) his blood; they are reconciled to God by the death of his Son.

However, if this fact is now established, then is also inviolable, indeed (if here there may be mention of more or less certain) then is yet more certain the preservation from the coming wrath.

Even so, the justified stand in a wholly other relationship to God. He is no longer an enemy, but a child. If the Father would now be wrathful on him, the work of Christ would be forgotten. Above all, by virtue of the atonement, the redeemed child of God constitutes one body with Christ. Atoned by the death of Christ, he is now saved by (literally *in*) his life. Now, is the life of Christ surely not less powerful than his death? The risen Christ, who triumphed over the grave and world, is not less powerful unto redemption than the dying Christ on the wood of the cross.

Paul calls this second stage of redemption, namely, what happens as the result of justification, much stronger than justification itself. Naturally he intends this as seen from the human side. From God's side is every step of the way of redemption, every development in the redemption process, absolutely certain. It is all realization of the eternal, unchanging council of love. But viewed from our side, then is it more reasonable, more plausible, more faithworthy, and thus more certain that God now also completely saves the one once justified, that he justifies the man when he is yet an enemy.

The Lord's supper testifies to both of these phases in the work of redemption. By the signs it brings to mind the atonement by the death of Christ. It symbolizes the wonder of being justified; it evokes this wonder.

At the same time, the sacrament points above to the living Christ. It tells us that Christ himself has become for our souls a true food and drink unto eternal life and that he has obtained for us the life-giving Spirit, so that we by this Spirit (who in Christ as in the head, and in us as his members lives) would have true communion with him, and became partakers of all his benefits, eternal life, righteousness, and glory.

Thus, the supper proclaims that with absolute certainty the once accomplished work of salvation shall be completed. Internal and external strife, assaults of discouragement and doubt, collapse and falling back, pollution and failure, cannot nullify this work. The living Christ maintains and finishes what he put into motion with his death. All the power that has been given him by the Father he puts in service for his people. Throne and crown, heaven's glory and Father's favor come in Christ to this people for the good. The church then may anticipate (expect) the coming glorification. Lying in the midst of death, they may sing of life. Walking in the midst of the misery, they may celebrate the coming joy. Crawling through the valley of persecution, they can already breathe the gentle breeze of the mountains of God. Bearing her cross, she stretches her hand out to the crown.

Therefore shall my mouth and heart show forth the praise of the Lord from this time forth for evermore. Amen.

14. WE THANK THEE WITH ALL OUR HEART

This praise is immediately attached to the prayer of thanksgiving. We have already dealt with the connection between both, also from a historical perspective. Here is only the observation that a small introduction to the prayer would not be undesirable. It is true that such an introduction is absent with respect to the prayer of thanksgiving in our form for baptism, but in this place, an introduction is more necessary because the congregation would not so suddenly be able to shift from the praise to the thanksgiving. There needs to be a brief alert beforehand. What goes before is indeed also a profession before God, but the prayer is still something else of its own. It requires a special act of separation and a lifting up of the soul to God. It is a seeking the face of God, an approaching to his throne, a meeting with the Lord.

So then, now climbs the thanksgiving from the mouth of the minister, from the heart of the covenantal people who have been blessed:

O merciful God and Father, we thank thee with all our hearts, that thou hast of thy infinite mercy, given us thine only begotten Son, for a Mediator and a sacrifice for our sins, and to be our food and drink unto life eternal, and that thou givest us a true faith, whereby we are made partakers of such great benefits. Thou hast also been pleased, that thy beloved

Son Jesus Christ should institute and ordain the holy supper for the strengthening of that faith. Grant, we beseech thee, O faithful God and Father, that through the operation of thy Holy Spirit, the remembrance of our Lord Jesus Christ and the proclamation of his death may daily increase in us the upright faith, and blessed fellowship with Christ, through Jesus Christ thy dear Son, in whose name we conclude our prayers, saying as he has taught us:

Our Father who art in heaven,
Hallowed be thy name;
Thy kingdom come;
Thy will be done in earth, as it is in heaven.
Give us this day our daily bread;
And forgive us our debts, as we forgive our debtors.
And lead us not into temptation, but deliver us from the
    evil one.
For thine is the kingdom, and the power, and the glory,
    forever. Amen.

It is not our preference to explain this prayer down to the smallest details. It contains no expositional difficulties, and new ideas regarding the supper are not put forward.

Yet we want to endeavor to point out the train of thought in this prayer and offer remarks regarding the spiritual beauties.

It forms a worthy conclusion to this noble liturgical piece. It exemplifies the brevity of the form as well as the clarity, depth, and richness of ideas.

From believers in holy Scripture, the framers learned the difficult art of praying much with few words.

The official address is literally the same as that of the prayer that precedes the communion. Also here is the God of the supper addressed tenderly and in a childlike manner: "O merciful God and Father!"

In some circles of Reformed people (the writer speaks here from ministerial experience), it is taken somewhat ill of the minister if he in his prayer dares to use the Father name of God. One considers this as too presumptuously intimate. One intends that such may happen only in exceptional circumstances. It is judged that there must be a very special spiritual kind of need before people may address God in this manner.

But notice how our Reformed fathers preferentially, regularly, use this name in their formulary prayers. They accept with thanks the high privilege that they as the New Testament church have received from their king. They say amen to the voice of the Spirit of the adoption unto children, who cry: Abba, Father!

The prayer of thanksgiving itself consists of two parts. There is first gratitude for receiving grace and further prayer for continuing grace.

There is gratitude of all our hearts for the core of the Lord's supper blessing, namely, that God *hast of his infinite mercy, given us his only begotten Son, for a Mediator and a sacrifice for our sins.* That is justification. And then, that he has given us this mediator *to be our food and drink unto life eternal.* That is the making alive and sanctification.

Striking also is the theocentric (God at the center) character of the prayer. The congregation does not call on the Mediator himself; she ascends from the Mediator up to God, culminating in the highest fountain of all goods. They see Christ in the light of the divine mercy as an outpouring of the eternal, predestinating love. Christ himself has set the example for his people in this, by always and again speaking of the Father, who has sent him, for all whose work he accomplishes, and to whom he, following the redemptive suffering, returns in order in the house of the Father to prepare a place.

But that is why grace, which especially flows from Christ himself, is not forgotten. The Father grants us the Mediator as a sacrifice for our sins and for food and drink unto eternal life. However, the Son himself brings this priceless sacrifice, by the shedding of his blood.

He gives himself as food and drink by identifying himself with his people unto one body in the communion of the Holy Ghost and pouring out his Mediator's life in his people. What a child of God lives in the flesh, he lives by the faith of the Son of God, who loved him and gave himself for him.

Extremely special is the fact that in this prayer of thanksgiving is the general and all-encompassing benefit of the forgiveness of sins and eternal life, yet follows a prayer of thanks for the special benefit of faith: *and that thou givest us a true faith, whereby we are made partakers of such great benefits.*

Let us not let these noteworthy words get by us. They form one of the most priceless passages in our formulary. There lies within the expression the high estimation of this gift. Due to the antithesis with Rome, our fathers deeply felt the absolute necessity of this gift for a Christian. The gospel of the Reformation can always be summarized in these words: the just shall live by faith.

But most of all it deserves observation that our fathers *give thanks* for the possession of faith. One can only truly give thanks if one knows that he truly possesses the gift for which he gives thanks. One thanks not for a thing about which one doubts. How clear therefore was the consciousness of faith of the church when this formulary originated. Would we still dare to write such language in our liturgy?

Now it is true that faith as a rule is not the object but the *instrument* for giving thanks. There can be faith without that the believer himself is conscious of this spiritual function, even as a child sees with his little eyes without thinking about the seeing. But as a person matures and reflects upon life, then he makes these gifts his own. And when the Christian thanks his God for life and the possession of his senses, would he then not praise God for the gift of faith, to which he owes his eternal salvation as means?

Especially at the supper is this praise appropriate, because this institution serves to make faith stronger and to put it in the consciousness of the Christian more certainly.

In the prayer of thanksgiving at once follows then: *Thou hast also been pleased, that thy beloved Son Jesus Christ should institute and ordain the holy supper for the strengthening of that faith.*

15. WE BESEECH THEE, O FATHER!

And thereby connects now the prayer for blessing with the progress.

So is the child of God. The sound of thanks barely dies away on his lips, then he opens the mouth for making new desires known. His existence, also spiritually, is one of complete dependence. Indeed, the giving thanks reveals precisely his poverty. When he says, I believe, he adds, help mine unbelief.

So also here. First there is gratitude for this benefit. But now is the heart of the petition: please use this supper for *daily increase in us of upright faith.*

Repeated again is addressing God as *Father.* Now, however, not with the adjective *merciful,* but *faithful: We beseech Thee, O faithful God and Father!* Quite appropriately the congregation, now as it concerns the maintenance and extension of the received blessing, pleads upon the attribute of God's faithfulness. The believer himself is aware of his unfaithfulness. At the supper, in the nearness of the Lord, shall he have the earnest intention from now on, with his whole life, to show genuine gratitude with respect to God the Lord. But as soon as the Lord's supper table is cleared and the ordinary life again takes hold, so often Israel's blessedness appears as the morning dew. That is indeed why she pleads in advance for self-knowledge as the congregation already calls up for itself the faithfulness of her God. She fears, she *knows* that moments shall come in which she forgets her God, in which faith is inactive. And now she cries out: Grant, we beseech thee, O faithful God and Father, that through the operation of thy Holy Spirit, the remembrance of our Lord Jesus Christ and the proclamation of his death may daily increase in us the upright faith and blessed fellowship with Christ.

Also here the word choice is splendid, the line of thought pure and complete. There are few words, nevertheless nothing forgotten. The Lord's supper is *called the remembrance of our Lord Jesus Christ and the proclamation of his death.* The petition is that God will grant growth by the use of this sacrament, that is, will let increase the initial grace, so that there may be *a daily increase in us of the upright faith.*

In the form for baptism we hear the same note. The Holy Spirit assures us there not only of the washing away of sin, but also of *the daily renewing of our lives.* In our Lord's supper formulary, the daily development of faith is likewise attributed to the Holy Spirit because precedes: *through the operation of* thy Holy Spirit.

The need for an ongoing increase in the upright faith, that is the living faith, revealing itself as everyday fruit, is the mark of the healthy spiritual life. Indeed, experience teaches that the upward trajectory of the Christian's walk is interrupted with grievous difficulties. It stands fast that the moments of spiritual advancement as enjoyed at the supper are followed by times of decline, even collapse. But the believer's desire of the soul is the *daily increase* in the upright faith. Not only the day of the Lord's supper, but also the coming days of strife must bring him closer to God. Every day that he does not increase in the upright faith he views as a lost day, a day for which he is to blame before God.

That is why before he leaves this place for the life full of difficulties, where so much seeks to cut him off from his God, he turns his eye on high to his God, who granted his Son Jesus Christ as food and drink unto eternal life, and prays that this hour of blessed renewal be fruitful for every day of his life.

Yet the great moment of eternal reunion is not there. The Lord's supper evidences that there is yet a separation, that we walk by faith and not by sight. The redeemed are not yet with Jesus to whom they belong in body and soul, as purchased by his blood. But the salvation-rich sacrament is for him more than a prophecy that the glorious future of the Lord draws near; it is for him a pledge of God's faithfulness, that also in this life he is God's chosen, and by him shall be preserved as his beloved child and heir.

The supper guarantees him not only eternal union of life above with the royal bridegroom, but also the ongoing increase *in blessed fellowship with Christ* in the valley of death here below.

They go from strength to strength; each and every one of them will appear before God in Zion!

16. THE PRAYER JESUS TAUGHT US

Finally there is here yet the Lord's prayer for concluding the prayer.

In the form of Geneva, the Lord's prayer does not appear. In the Palatinate formulary, it is only in the preceding prayer. Our form lays it twice on the lips of the congregation.

For those who have tested this prayer in its spiritual beauty, this is certainly welcome. It provides rest to the heart that is filled with longings, which can be restored with such difficulty, to be able to pray in the Lord's own words wherein all our spiritual and physical needs are comprehended.

Safely goes the church, and assured is her future, when it calls upon the Father with the words that his beloved Son has himself taught her:

Our Father who art in heaven,
Hallowed be thy name.
Thy kingdom come.
Thy will be done on earth, as it is in heaven.
Give us this day our daily bread;
And forgive us our debts, as we forgive our debtors.
And lead us not into temptation, but deliver us from the
    evil one.
For thine is the kingdom, and the power and the glory,
    forever. Amen.

BIBLIOGRAPHY OF CITED WORKS

Acta Nationale Synode van Dordrecht 1618–1619. Houten: Den Hertog B.V., 1987.

Acta van de Nederlandsche Synoden der zestinede eeuw. Comp. F. L. Rugers. Dordrecht: J. P. Van den Tol, 1980.

Ames, William. *Conscience with the Power and Cases Thereof: Divided into V. Bookes.* London: Forgotten Books, 2018.

Barger, H. H. *Ons Kerkboek.* Groningen: J. B. Wolters, 1900.

Bavinck, Herman. *Reformed Dogmatics,* I–IV. Trans. John Vriend. Ed. John Bolt. Grand Rapids: Baker Academic, 2006.

Biesterveld, P. *Het Gereformeerde Kerkboek.* Kockengen: Het Traktaatgenootschap Filippus, 1903.

_____. *Het karakter der catechese.* Kampen: J. H. Kok, 1900.

Bogerman, Johannes, and Walaeus, Antonius, et al. *The Dordrecht Bible Commentary: Authorized by the*

Synod of Dort 1618–1619 According to the Th. Haak Translation 1657 Commissioned by the Westminster Assembly 1645. I–VI. Trans. Th. Haak, et al. Ed. H. David Schuringa. Otsego, MI: Nsmpress, 2019.

The Book of Common Prayer and Administration of the Sacraments. 1552, 1559.

Bouwman, H. *Gereformeerde kerkrecht: het recht der kerken in the practijk.* Kampen: Kok, 1934.

Calvin, John. *Commentaries on the Epistles of Paul to the Corinthians.* Trans. John Pringle. Grand Rapids: Christian Classics Ethereal Library.

_____. *Institutes of the Christian Religion.* Ed. John T. McNeill. Trans. Ford Lewis Battles. Philadelphia: The Westminster Press, 1960.

Christelijke Encyclopedie, III. Eds. F. W. Grosheide and G. P. Van Itterzon. Kampen: J. H. Kok, 1958.

Daniël, Hermann Adalbert. *Codex Liturgicus Ecclesiae Universae In Epitomen Redactus.* III. Lipsiae: T.O. Weigel, 1851.

Dathenus, Petrus. *De Psalmen Davids 1566.* Intro. N. Ijkel, J. N., van't Spijker, W. Houten: Den Hertog B.V., 1992.

Emminghaus, Johannes H. *The Eucharist, Essence, Form, Celebration.* Trans. Matthew J. O'Connell. Collegeville, Minn.: The Liturgical Press, 1978.

Ens, Johannes. *Kort Historisch Berigt van de Publieke Schriften: Rakende de Leer En Dienst Der Nederduitsche Kerken Van de Vereenigd Nederlanden.* Kampen: S. Van Velzen, Jr., 1861.

Gibson, Jonathan and Mark Earngey, eds., *Reformation Worship: Liturgies from the Past for the Present.* Greensboro, NC: New Growth Press, 2018.

Godet, Frédéric Louis. *Commentary on St. Paul's First Epistle to the Corinthians,* 2. Trans. A. Cusin. Edinburgh: T & T Clark, 1890.

Gooszen, M. A. *De Heidelbergsche catechismus en het boekje van de breking des broods, in het jaar 1563–64 bestreden en verdedigd.* Leiden: E. J. Brill, 1892.

Gunning, J. H. *Waarom niet toegetreden: het avondmaalsformulier onzer Gereformeerde Kerk voor bekommerde Christenen toegelicht.* Nijkerk: Uitgeverij Callenbach, 1913.

Hoornbeeck, Johannes. *Theologia practica.* Utrecht, 1666.

Koelman, Jacobus. *Het Ambt en de Pligten der Ouderlingen en Diakenen.* Ed. S. Van Velzen.'sGravenhage: J. Van Golverdinge, 1837.

Kuyper, Abraham. *Encyclopaedie der Heilige Godgeleerdheid,* III. Kampen: J. H. Kok, 1908.

_____. *E voto Dordraceno: toelichting op den Heidelergschen catechismus,* III. Amsterdam: Höverker & Wormser, 1904.

_____. *Honey from the Rock: Daily Devotions from Young Kuyper.* Trans. James A. Dejong. Bellingham, WA: Lexham Press, 2018.

_____. *Onze Eerdienst.* Kampen: J.H. Kok, 1911.

_____. *Our Worship.* Trans. and Ed. Harry Boonstra. Grand Rapids: Eerdmans, 2009.

Kuyper, H. H. *De authentieke tekst der liturgische geschriften gehandhaafd tegen M.A. Gooszen.* Amsterdam: Höveker & Wormser, 1901.

_____. *De Post-acta of Nahandelingen Van de Nationale Synode Van Dordrecht in 1618 en 1619: Een Historische Studie.* Amsterdam: Höveker & Wormser, 1899.

á Lasco, Johannes. *De korte onderzoeking des geloofs.* London, 1553.

Mensinga, J. A. M. *Verhandeling over de Liturgische Schriften der Nederlandsche Hervormded Kerk.* The Hague: Thierry en Mensing, 1851.

Ökolampadius, Johannes. *Form und gstalt wie der kinder tauff, Des herren Nachtmal, und der Krancken heymsuochung, jetz zuo Basel von etlichen Predicanten gehalten warden.* Basel, 1526.

Rutgers, F. L. *Acta van de Nederlandsche Synoden der zestiende eeuw.* Dordrecht: Uitgerverij J. P. van den Tol, 1980.

Schaff, Philip. *History of the Christian Church,* III. New York: Charles Scribner's Sons, 1899.

Schotel, G. D. J. *De Openb. Eeredeinst der Ned. Herv. Kerk, in de 16e, 17e en 18e eeuw.* I–VIII. Haarl.: Kruseman, 1870.

Statenvertaling met kanttekeningen. Van Ravesteyn: Uitgave van de weduwe van Paulus Aertsz, 1637, 1657.

Südhoff, Karl. *C. Olevianus und Z. Ursinus: Leben und ausgewählte Schriften.* Elberfeld: Verlag von R. L. Friderichs, 1857.

The Confessions and the Church Order of the Protestant Reformed Churches. Grandville, MI: Protestant Reformed Churches in America, 2005.

Van Andel, J. *Paulus' brief aan de Romeinen: met de gemeente gelezen.* Kampen: J.H. Kok, 1904.

Van Hout, Jacobus. *Het formulier des heilgen nagtmaals verklaard en praktikaal uitgebreid: Zooals hetzelve dient tot ontdekking van alle dezulken, die het H. Avondmall onwaardig gebruiken; en bijzonder ter bemoediging van swakke, gelijk ook to sterkte van meer gevorderder christenen; om door der Ledenmaten der kerk met vrugt aangehoord, en nageliezen te worden, opdat zij volgens het oogmerk van de Opstellers des Formuliers tot Troost des Heeren Nagtmaal mogten gebruiken. Voorgesteld in zeven afdeelingen. Na alvoorens eenige gemeene aanmerkingen tot voorbereidzelen gemaakt te hebben, zoo met opzicht op dit zin- en zaakrijk Formulier: als tot dat geen, dat de wijze van Voorbereidinge, Betragtinge en Nabetragtinge van elk waar Bondgenoot bij gelegenheid van de bedieninge des Avondsmaals betreft, door Jacobus van Houte, lidmaat der Hervormde gemeente te Valkenburg.* Leiden: Joh. Hasebroek en Zoon, 1761.

Voetius, Gisbertus. *Politica Ecclesiastica*, I–III. Amsterdam: Johannnem Janssonium á Waesberge, & Elizeum Weyerstraet, 1663.

Wielenga, B. *Ons Huwelijksformulier.* Kampen: J. H. Kok, 1913.

———. *The Reformed Baptism Form: A Commentary.* Trans. Annemie Godbehere. Ed. David J. Engelsma. Jenison, MI: Reformed Free Publishing Association, 2016.

The Reformed Baptism Form

A Commentary

B. Wielenga, translated by Annemie Godbehere,
edited by David J. Engelsma

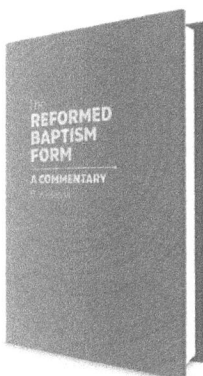

Brought into English for the first time is this commentary on the Reformed baptism form by Bastiaan Wielenga, a prominent minister of the word in the Reformed Churches in the Netherlands (GKN) in the early to mid 1900s. This commentary sets forth, defends, and applies the creedal Reformed faith concerning the covenant of grace—the foundation of baptism. This commentary will be especially helpful to Reformed churches, ministers, and other members in its explanation of the baptism form's authoritative treatment of covenant and election in relation to the baptism of infants. The faith of every believer concerning the sacrament of baptism will be expanded and enriched by the commentary.

448 pages, hardcover (ebook available)
Retail $39.95, Membership $25.97 USA • $27.96 International

—

rfpa.org
mail@rfpa.org
616-457-5970

REFORMED
FREE PUBLISHING
ASSOCIATION

The Church Order Commentary
A Brief Explanation of the Church Order
of the Christian Reformed Church

Idzerd Van Dellen, Martin Monsma

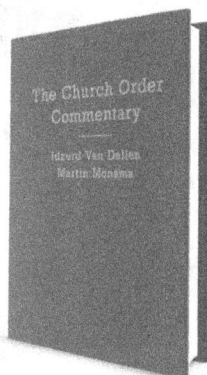

This revised third edition is the accepted standard for the interpretation and application of the Church Order of Dordrecht by Reformed and Presbyterian denominations.

This authoritative, time-tested commentary instructs us today on the need for a book of order for biblical consistency in church government.

464 pages, hardcover (ebook available)
Retail $19.95, Membership $12.97 USA and international

—

rfpa.org
mail@rfpa.org
616-457-5970

REFORMED
FREE PUBLISHING
ASSOCIATION

The Belgic Confession
A Commentary (Volumes 1 and 2)
David J. Engelsma

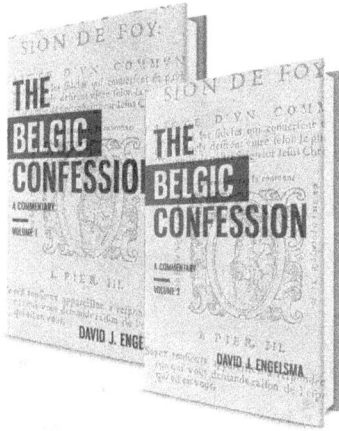

As a comprehensive commentary of the Belgic Confession, this work explains each article of the confession. While scholarly, it is written in a clear and simple style such that this work is suitable for anyone who desires to learn and appreciate more this important document of the Reformed tradition.

Volume 1: 368 pages, hardcover (ebook available)
Retail $31.95, Membership $20.77 USA, $22.36 international

Volume 2: 400 pages, hardcover (ebook available)
Retail: $34.95, Membership $22.72 USA, $24.46 international

—

rfrfpa.org
mail@rfpa.org
616-457-5970

REFORMED
FREE PUBLISHING
ASSOCIATION

Grace and Assurance
The Message of the Canons of Dordt
Martyn McGeown

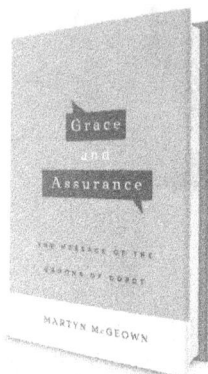

In 1618–19 the great Synod of Dordt met to counter the Arminian error that was threatening the peace and welfare of the Reformed churches in the Netherlands. The fruit of their deliberations was the Canons of Dordt, a creed which has defined the Calvinist, Reformed faith for centuries.

This accessible commentary on the Canons leads readers through the comforting message of the creed: being wholly saved by God's grace—not one's own merit—comes with the steadfast *assurance* of eternal and unchangeable election.

384 pages, hardcover (ebook available)
Retail $31.95, Membership $20.77 USA, $22.36 international

———

rfrfpa.org
mail@rfpa.org
616-457-5970

REFORMED
FREE PUBLISHING
ASSOCIATION

REFORMED
FREE PUBLISHING
ASSOCIATION

Our Mission

To glorify God by making accessible to the broadest possible audience material that testifies to the truth of Scripture as understood and developed in the Reformed tradition.

Reformed Free Publishing Association
1894 Georgetown Center Drive
Jenison, MI 49428-7137
Website: rfpa.org
E-mail: mail@rfpa.org
Phone: 616-457-5970